THE WASHIN CONFERENCE, 1921–22
Naval Rivalry, East Asian Stability and the Road to Pearl Harbor

Edited by

Erik Goldstein and John Maurer

FRANK CASS

First published in 1994 in Great Britain by
FRANK CASS & CO. LTD
Newbury House, 890–900 Eastern Avenue, Newbury Park, Ilford,
Essex IG2 7HH, UK

and in the United States of America by
FRANK CASS
c/o International Specialized Book Services Inc.
5602 N.E. Hassalo Street, Portland Oregon 97213

Copyright © 1994

British Library Cataloguing in Publication Data

Washington Conference, 1921–22:
Naval Rivalry, East Asian Stability and the
Road to Pearl Harbor. – (Diplomacy &
Statecraft Series, ISSN 0959–2296)
    I. Goldstein, Erik II. Maurer, John H.
    III. Series
    327.1
    ISBN 0–7146–4559–1 (cased) ISBN 0–7146–4136–7 (paper)

Library of Congress Cataloging-in-Publication Data

The Washington Conference, 1921–22 : naval rivalry, East Asian
    stability and the road to Pearl Harbor / edited by Erik Goldstein
    and John Maurer.
        p.   cm.
    "This group of studies first appeared in a special issue of
Diplomacy & statecraft, vol. 4, no. 3 (November 1993)" — T.p. verso.
    Includes bibliographical references and index.
        ISBN 0–7146–4559–1 (cased) ISBN 0–7146–4136–7 (paper)
    1. Conference on the Limitation of Armament (1921–1922 :
Washington, D.C.).   2. Disarmament.   3. Sea-power.   4. Pan-Pacific
Relations — History — 20th century.   I. Goldstein, Erik.   II. Maurer,
John H.
JX1974.5.W26   1994
327.1′74′09042 — dc20   93–35641
                                                                        CIP

This group of studies first appeared in a Special Issue of *Diplomacy &
Statecraft*, Vol. 4, No. 3 (November 1993) [The Washington Conference,
1921–22: Naval Rivalry, East Asian Stability, and the Road to Pearl Harbor].

Typeset by Florencetype Ltd, Kewstoke, Avon
Printed in Great Britain by Bookcraft (Bath) Ltd, Midsomer Norton

Contents

Foreword

ERNEST R. MAY

The Washington Conference on 1921–22 has often been a source for historical lessons. Through the 1920s, the conference served as an example of how bold risk-taking could advance disarmament. Charles Evans Hughes, the American Secretary of State, had opened the conference with a dramatic offer to stop building big-gun warships and even to scrap some, provided other naval powers would do likewise. The conference ended with agreements setting such limits. It also produced accords promising an end to longstanding rivalries in Asia. When later conferences yielded less, commentators chided the negotiators for not showing Hughes' courage.

In the 1930s and 1940s, different lessons were drawn. Military and naval officers had criticized the Washington treaties from the beginning. They maintained that force levels should be calibrated to potential threats, not set at fixed levels dictated by financial and domestic political concerns. Caught unawares by Hughes' proposal and its instant popularity, the admirals attending the Washington Conference had been powerless. (The chapters here by Michael Fry, William R. Braisted, and Sadao Asada illustrate wonderfully the illusions of the admirals when preparing for the conference.) In later negotiations, as detailed here by Braisted, Asada, Brian McKercher and Thomas Buckley, professional military and naval officers had greater say. That had something to do with the slow progress toward setting limits for other types of warships and weapons. Then, in the 1930s, when warship building resumed and conflicts over Asia revived, the naval officers' view of the Washington Conference gained adherents. Commentators now pointed to the Washington Conference as exemplifying wishful thinking.

The first serious history of the Washington Conference, Harold and Margaret Sprout's *Toward a New Order of Sea Power*, published in 1940, supported both positive and negative readings of the conference's lessons for the future. The Sprouts argued, on the one hand, that the conference had prevented a new arms race. They pointed out, on the other hand, that the conference had fostered illusory expectations. Too much had been left to hope alone. The democratic nations had been relatively slow to abandon hope. As a result, they had found themselves at a disadvantage. In effect, the Sprouts said that the Washington Conference pointed a double moral. The first was the virtue of risk-taking for the sake of peace, but the second was the need to nail down details, to police performance, and to depend as little as possible on simple good will.

In the early Cold War, the second of these lesson dominated. In debates over the Baruch Plan and other proposals for international control of nuclear weapons, sceptics cited the inter-war naval agreements as evidence of the need for tightly drawn enforcement provisions.

Later, as Cold War tensions lessened, the Washington Conference came again to be seen as teaching multiple lessons. The American and Soviet governments turned to arms limitation negotiation as a means of stemming 'overkill'. Drawing on historians' studies, the Oxford political scientist, Hedley Bull, urged that negotiators note how the naval limitations agreements had produced unanticipated consequences. Agreed limits on big-gun warships had stimulated work on alternative systems, particularly aircraft carriers and submarines. Bull argued that something similar could occur if the American and Soviet governments focused only on intercontinental-range nuclear weapons.[1]

At about the same time, several new histories appeared. They largely supplanted the earlier study by the Sprouts. Stephen Roskill and William Braisted dealt with the Washington Conference in the context of their histories respectively of the British and American navies. Sadao Asada dealt with it in the general context of US–Japanese relations. Thomas Buckley and Roger Dingman wrote about the conference itself. Each emphasized the extent to which domestic politics had shaped governmental policies.[2]

These new histories highlighted points particularly appropriate for the 1970s and 1980s. In that period, SALT negotiations foundered as a result of executive-legislative differences in the United States and sensitivities in the Soviet Politburo. There followed the election of Ronald Reagan, 'evil empire' rhetoric, the Strategic Defense Initiative, and new Soviet missile deployments, all seeming to portend a second Cold War. Then came Mikhail Gorbachev's *perestroika*, START, and eventually genuine *détente*. Drawing on studies such as those of Buckley and Dingman, political scientists cited the Washington Conference to warn against arms limitation agreements signed without clearly sustainable public support. They warned also against agreements that assumed a constraint like public opinion on the Soviet side.[3]

This volume begins a third wave of historical writing on the Washington Conference and its aftermath. In addition to bringing up to date the accounts in earlier histories, it places more fully on stage the governments of France, Italy, China, and the British Dominions. In addition, this volume tells the story of the Washington Conference from a vantage point beyond the Cold War.

Because of the prominence of arms control both during the inter-war years and during the Cold War, policy lessons taken from the Washington Conference have had to do mostly with that subject. In fact, of course, as is most apparent here in the chapters on the dominions, the continental powers, and China, the conference had a much larger agenda. It produced agreements promising stability and cooperation throughout the Pacific area.

In post-Cold War retrospect, the Washington Conference looms more clearly as one of several linked efforts to create a new international order. The comprehensive effort at Paris in 1919 had failed. It had provoked resentment or disappointment or both and had satisfied almost no one. Except for British Prime Minister David Lloyd George, the principals were all repudiated at home. (And Lloyd George clung to office by his fingernails.)

Dealing with problems piecemeal rather than with any thought-through formula, the successors of the Paris peacemakers developed regional arrangements. The Treaty of Riga of March 1921, ending a war between Russia and Poland, allowed the new, revolutionized Russia to isolate itself temporarily from the great power system in which Tsarist Russia had been an integral force. The Washington Conference stabilized relationships on the seas and in East Asia. The Lausanne treaties of July 1923 effectively isolated the former Ottoman Empire. Then, in October 1925, the Locarno treaties sought to transform the former great power system into a regional system in which, as French Foreign Minister Aristide Briand said, governments would no longer ask about a treaty: 'against whom?' Instead, they would ask: 'for what?'

These interlocking systems proved fragile. In one way or another, they all depended on the great storage battery of the North American economy. When that battery ran dry, the new order of the 1920s disintegrated. Its short life should not, however, diminish its interest or relevance. There are in the 1920s parallels with contemporaneous efforts to create regional systems and comprehensive regimes, such as those for the oceans and the environment. The fact that the earlier new order came to such a quick end is itself instructive, for it suggests the need to worry whether the current systems and regimes could withstand a shock comparable to that which ushered in the Great Depression.

Like those who convened in Washington in November 1921, we who live in the 1990s face a future more full of uncertainty than the futures faced by our immediate forebears. We have no clear sense of what will be the sides or stakes in the future. We are even in doubt whether future competition will be essentially international. The eminent political scientist, Samuel P. Huntington, argues that civilizations rather than nations will be the key competitors in the world to come.[4]

In these circumstances, it is surely worthwhile to look closely – as this volume does – at the specifics of past attempts to construct new systems of relationships crossing national and cultural boundaries. As the Sprouts' book stimulated thought during and after World War II and as works such as Asada's, Buckley's, and Dingman's stimulated thought during the era of SALT and START, so this volume ought to help the thinking of those who are trying to see their way into a post-Cold War world.

NOTES

1. Hedley Bull, 'Strategic Arms Limitation: The Precedent of the Washington and London Naval Treaties', in Morton Kaplan (ed.), *SALT: Problems and Prospects* (Morristown, NJ: General Learning Press, 1973).
2. Stephen Roskill, *Naval Policy between the Wars* Vol. 1: *The Period of Anglo-American Antagonism, 1919–1929* (London: Collins, 1968); Williams Reynolds Braisted, *The United States Navy in the Pacific, 1909–1922* (Austin, TX: University of Texas Press, 1971); Sadao Asada, 'Japan and the United States, 1915–1925' (Ph.D. dissertation, Yale University, 1962); Thomas Buckley, *The United States and the Washington Conference* (Knoxville, TN: University of Tennessee Press, 1970); Roger Dingman, *Power in the Pacific: The Origins of Naval Arms Limitation* (Chicago: University of Chicago Press, 1976). Though Asada's study has never appeared in English as a book, it was published on microfilm (Ann Arbor, MI: University Microfilms, 1966), and in this form it has been more widely read than many books.
3. See particularly Robert A. Hoover, *Arms Control; The Interwar Naval Limitation Agreements* (Denver, CO: Graduate School of International Studies, University of Denver, 1980); Steven Miller, 'Politics over Promise: Domestic Impediments to Arms Control', *International Security*, Vol. 8, No. 4 (Spring 1984), pp. 67–84; and Robert Gordon Kaufman, *Arms Control during the Pre-Nuclear Era: The United States and Naval Limitation between the Two World Wars* (New York: Columbia University Press, 1990). A more polemical work, stressing the risks of any arms control agreements, is Harlow A. Hyde, *Scraps of Paper: The Disarmament Treaties between the World Wars* (Lincoln, NB: Media Publications, 1988).
4. Samuel P. Huntington, 'The Clash of Civilization', *Foreign Affairs*, Vol. 72, No. 3 (Summer 1993), pp.22–49.

Introduction

The Washington Conference was one of the most celebrated diplomatic meetings between the two world wars. In late 1921, representatives of the world's leading powers met to establish a naval arms control regime and to bring stability to East Asia. Their deliberations took almost three months. At the time, the work of the delegates received almost general approval. The Washington Conference provided the basis for the great powers to cooperate in mutually limiting their navies and avoiding conflict in the Pacific. In reaching an arms control agreement, a looming arms race between Great Britain, Japan, and the United States in monster capital ships was averted. The delegates also reached agreement to promote cooperation in working out potentially disruptive security problems in the Far East. Britain and Japan, for example, agreed to drop their 20-year-old alliance and replace it with agreements that included the other major powers concerned with East Asia. At Washington, the negotiators appeared to achieve their most ambitious aims in reconciling the conflicting security aims of its participants.

Yet the agreements reached at Washington ultimately failed. Less than ten years after the conference, Japan's actions in Manchuria showed up the flimsiness of the agreements reached to construct a new order in Asia. By the mid-1930s, the naval arms control framework established at Washington no longer worked. As a result, the competition in monster warships resumed. When viewed from the perspective of the Second World War, the Washington Conference appears a futile exercise. Not only did it not produce a lasting settlement, the Washington Conference contributed to the failure of Britain and the United States to defend a liberal international order. Because of the arms control regime established at Washington, Britain and the United States did not rearm quickly enough in the 1930s. These two countries also failed to restrain Japan within the cooperative framework called for by the Four-Power and Nine-Power treaties.

Because of its significance, the Washington Conference has been the subject of many fine studies over the past 70 years. Evaluating the strategies of the various participants and the results of the conference nonetheless remains a difficult problem for study by historians and international relations specialists. First, five major naval powers were involved in arms control negotiations. Analysing multilateral arms control negotiations is a demanding research assignment, requiring an examination of the motivations of each participant. Several major studies already exist that deal with the decision making on naval arms control in Britain, Japan, and the United States. Italy and France, on the other hand, have received far less attention in studies dealing with the Washington Conference. The Washington Conference thus remains a valuable case study for analysing multilateral arms control. Second, the Washington Conference tackled the difficult issues of establishing an international order in East Asia that could withstand the conflicting security aims of the major powers. The ongoing revolutionary turmoil in China posed an especially difficult task. Japan's security rested ultimately not only on the naval balance achieved in arms control but by resolving Japanese claims on the mainland of Asia. In addition, study of the Washington Conference must include an examination of the Anglo-Japanese Alliance. Third, no study of the Washington Conference can afford to ignore an examination of the relationship between domestic politics, economic pressures, and foreign policy. Quite clearly, this is a daunting research agenda.

By putting together this collection of essays the editors have sought to overcome the inherent difficulties in providing a comprehensive treatment of the Washington Conference. Our goal is to provide in-depth coverage of the genesis of the Conference, its actual course, and its aftermath. An essay appears on each of the major participants at Washington. The objective throughout the issue has been to provide a genuine multinational perspective on the Washington Conference.

It is our hope that a fresh examination of the Washington Conference will also appear timely. The twin objectives of promoting international stability and mutual arms reductions in the aftermath of a great war are no strangers to today's decision-makers and policy analysts. With the end of the cold war, today's major powers are attempting to establish a new liberal world order and resolve the potentially explosive international rivalries in East Asia. The Washington Conference provides both a model and a cautionary tale on the limits of cooperation.

The Evolution of British Diplomatic Strategy for the Washington Conference

ERIK GOLDSTEIN

Introduction

The evolution of British diplomatic strategy leading to the Washington Conference is part of a continuum of British thinking on the position of the United Kingdom and its Empire stretching from the last months of the Great War through to the Second World War. For Britain 1919 marked the zenith of empire, the age of expansion was over and a period of consolidation had begun. The Paris peace settlement had established the framework of a post-war order which was generally congenial to Britain; Germany had been reduced to a manageable size for European equilibrium, France had been prevented from achieving western European hegemony, the League of Nations enshrined British principles without undue British commitments, and the richest colonial spoils had passed to Britain through the facility of League mandates. Many critical matters remained unresolved, however, and throughout 1920–21 British policy makers searched for ways to resolve these problems, and to resolve them in a way favourable to Britain, for although the Empire was at its height it faced terrifying vulnerabilities.

After the first flush of victory in 1918, when all had seemed possible, Britain began to confront a series of crises which had been obscured by the concentration of attention on the war effort. There were rising demands for independence as seen by revolts in Ireland and India, while the stretched nature of British military power was revealed by fighting in Egypt and Afghanistan – and that was only during the latter part of 1919. Britain's ability to remedy this over-extension of its existing capabilities was constrained by an economic position weakened by four years of war. This was already causing severe domestic labour unrest, which made it unlikely that any government would be able to allocate extra resources to imperial defence, particularly in the expensive category of naval supremacy, a supremacy under direct threat through the escalation of naval building being projected by the United States and Japan. The Japanese had just launched the world's largest battleship, the *Mutsu*, the United States was constructing seven battleships and six battle cruisers, and in an attempt to maintain its position Britain had four Hood class super-dreadnoughts under way. Japan and the United States were continuing to drift further apart in their relations, causing the potential for confrontation in the Pacific. In these circumstances Britain had to consider how to safeguard its regional security in areas of concern such as the Pacific, where it had to date relied on an alliance of convenience with Japan which was now due for renewal. All these concerns led Britain to a reassessment of its strategic position. As it became evident throughout late 1919 and 1920 that the Empire had now entered a period of consolidation, a debate ensued as to what Britain should do to respond to these problems, at the same time taking stock of its international position.

The catalyst for this reconsideration was the conjunction of three key events: the looming expiry of the Anglo-Japanese Alliance, a change of administration in the United States, and the convening of the first Imperial Conference since the end of the war. The latter event provided the forum for airing this debate, while simultaneously indicating the growing divergence of strategic view amidst the components of the Empire.

British Perceptions of World Order

As the paladins of the Empire gathered in London during June–July 1921 for the Imperial Conference they were in no doubt that they had done well in the war. The ebullient Billy Hughes of Australia exclaimed, 'We are like so many Alexanders. What other worlds have we to conquer?', while the more judicious Jan Smuts of South Africa observed that the British Empire 'emerged from the war quite the greatest Power in the world, and it is only unwisdom or unsound policy that could rob her of that great position'.[1] Such self-assurance was matched by a strong moral belief in the Empire's role, possibly inspired by the need to compete with the moral pronouncements of Wilson and Lenin. Lord Curzon, the Foreign Secretary, observed that

> The British Empire is a saving fact in a very distracted world. It is the most hopeful experiment in human organisation which the world has yet seen'.[2]

Britain, however, now needed a period of international quiescence in which to consolidate its position. Curzon defined the object for Britain to be 'to keep what we have obtained . . . not to seize anything else; to reconcile, not to defy; to pacify, not to conquer'.[3]

This was likely to be a difficult policy to follow in what was acknowledged to be a world still shuddering from the upheavals of war. Curzon noted that 'the whole world is still, although the war has ceased for two years, in a state of disturbance'.[4] Smuts commented that, 'The world is bankrupt and half mad, and it must come to a crisis again'.[5] He argued that imperial policy should be one of independence from Europe and of close cooperation with the United States. Curzon, however, was worried by this reflexive drift to 19th-century views. He saw all the problems of the global situation as interlocking and advised that 'A policy of splendid isolation is no longer possible, is not possible for a country like Britain, geographically situated as we are'.[6] Given the global nature of British concerns what was needed was to identify its prime threat, or at the very least the region of the world upon which it had to focus its attention. The debate, however, preferred to focus not on threat assessment but on the more congenial task of ally selection. For an empire under strain it was an indulgence not to think in terms of potential enemies, comforting itself instead with the fantasy that all states craved the possibility of an alliance with Britain.

The Anglo-Japanese Alliance

An issue which had to be resolved was the problem of whether or not to renew the Anglo-Japanese Alliance, first concluded in 1902, and renewed in 1905 and 1911, and now due to expire in 1921. It had served both partners well during its life, but now the interests of the partners were more obviously divergent than previously. It was clearly an unsympathetic alliance, with little sense of common purpose. The Foreign Office advised in February 1921, 'Japan aspires to the hegemony of the Far East . . .'.[7] There was also growing Anglo-Japanese economic competition. There was concern over Japanese envy of Britain's world-wide Empire, which invited comparison to Germany's pre-war jealousy which had caused so much friction. Curzon thought that if this were the case, and Japan was indeed an aggressive power,

> There can be no doubt that while the Anglo-Japanese Alliance has lasted, whether we continue it or not, it has enabled us to exercise a very powerful controlling influence on the sometimes dangerous ambitions of Japan.[8]

The growing divergence of Japan and the United States also made renewal a potential further cause of difficulty with the United States. The Foreign Office, however, advised maintaining the Anglo-Japanese Alliance while attempting good relations with the United States, at least until a tripartite agreement on the points of conflict had been reached between these three great Pacific powers.

On the second anniversary of the signing of the Treaty of Versailles the Imperial Conference began its discussions as to the future of the alliance with Japan. Both Balfour and Curzon warned of the danger of ending the alliance. Balfour delivered the Committee of Imperial Defence's (CID) view that renewal was required from a purely strategic point of view:

> we may turn a faithful friend into a very formidable enemy, and to turn a faithful friend into a formidable enemy at a moment when you find yourselves relatively unprepared to meet any attack from the former friend and the present enemy is the very worst policy you could possibly pursue from a strictly military point of view.[9]

This captures the tenor of the ensuing discussions, where unease with the Japanese alliance was balanced by worry over the impact of ending the arrangement. Japan, however, was not the only wartime ally to be causing concern to Britain.

Fear of France

Much of British diplomacy at the Paris Peace Conference had been aimed not at punishing the defeated central powers, but at assuring that France did not dominate western Europe.[10] The concurrent collapse of the carefully constructed Paris settlement and of President Wilson had led France to return to a policy of assuring its position through establishing regional hegemony. Britain throughout the post-First World War period was always keeping a weather eye on French intentions. Curzon in briefing the 1921 Imperial Conference noted,

> The Ministers present will see at once what her [France's] object is – with Lorraine, the Saar Valley and the Ruhr in her occupation, she becomes the mistress of Europe in respect of coal, iron and steel, and with those countries under her military command she would also become the military monarch.[11]

While he admitted that this was not necessarily the policy of the current government in Paris the idea was there, permeating French thinking. Smuts advised against having any ties with France: 'We have found it difficult to work with her under war conditions; we find it more difficult to work with her under peace conditions'.[12] He warned that French aims were significantly different from Britain's as France was busy creating its vision of Europe and that the result of this would be that 'we shall have a Continent under the leadership of France, which would be a very dangerous thing for this country'.[13] Curzon admitted that France was a problem, but that it was therefore better to be in a treaty relationship with it:

> We go about arm in arm with her, but with one of our hands on her collar, and if we relax that control I myself should be very much alarmed at the consequences that would ensue.[14]

It was the potential of difficulty with France which was one of the factors driving Britain to look to the United States. The General Staff in a briefing document on the question of disarmament voiced its concerns, with the assessment that France's aspiration was 'to become the dominating Continental Power in Europe'.[15] There was a real fear that the success of an arms reduction settlement evolved on the basis of Pacific problems would leave Britain weakened in Europe, particularly against France. The Cabinet noted the view in November 1921, in the wake of the opening of the conference, that

> so long as France maintained her powerful army in being, the state of Europe would remain unsettled and that it would be a most serious matter if as a result of the Washington Conference Great Britain was the only European power to be disarmed.[16]

This view, and the data supporting it, was considered important enough for Lloyd George to communicate it to Balfour, the head of the British delegation at Washington, who was informed of the CID's estimates that a French army could field when fully mobilized 100 divisions, if overseas forces were included, to which its east European allies could add a further 79 divisions. The Air Staff estimated that the French Air Force could drop daily 31 tons of bombs on London and south-east England. The French demand at the Washington Conference to be allowed a large submarine fleet particularly worried Britain as to French intentions. While not doubting current good relations, the CID viewed

> with apprehension the situation in which Great Britain may find herself in a few years hence with obsolete battleships and negligible military and air forces, with France in possession of large military air forces, and a fleet to which may be added up-to-date flotillas.[17]

The submarine issue deeply concerned Churchill, who observed that 'A French submarine fleet could only be built against *us*'.[18] There was a whimsical belief that the United States shared this distrust of France. Sir Auckland Geddes, the British Ambassador in Washington, reported 'the intense dislike of the French people felt by many ex-soldiers who served in France . . .'.[19] Such a shared common dislike could help provide the basis for an alliance, and it is clear that Britain continued to look with hope for any evidence that an alliance with Washington was possible.

The United States

Much as Britain wanted amity and cooperation with the United States in principle, in practice there were many obstacles. One consideration which underlay all these discussions were the financial difficulties between the two countries. The Wilson Administration in its last days had been adamant on repayment of the war debt. Geddes warned that the incoming administration would be no better and intended 'to prevent us from paying our debts by sending goods to America and they look for the opportunity to treat us as a vassal State so long as the debt remains unpaid'.[20] The Lloyd George Government hoped that good relations could be established with the new administration, and throughout the Washington Conference period it never forgot the need to try to ameliorate the debt question. Curzon reminded Churchill that the United States could always say that

> If you don't agree to leave off shipbuilding, i.e. to accept the second place and quit your objectionable association with Japan, will you please at least pay interest, and arrears of interest, on your debt.[21]

One of the many subtexts to British concerns at the conference was the need to persuade the Americans that it would be just as profitable to be friendly with Britain as to exact repayment. The Cabinet on the eve of the Washington Conference noted that 'the financial position between Great Britain and the United States (which though not part of the Agenda of the Conference) has an important bearing'.[22]

On East Asia the Foreign Office observed in February 1921 that, 'in spite of similarity of interests, a working agreement is of extreme difficulty. If we were able to count with certainty upon the active co-operation of the United States, the need for an alliance with Japan would not be apparent'.[23] The difficulty was that close cooperation with both Japan and the United States was made impossible because their interests were seen to clash at every point.[24] The Foreign Office summed up the conundrum facing Britain:

> Our future course lies between our ally with whom our interests conflict, and our friend who is united to us by race, tradition, community of interests and ideals. It will be difficult for us to steer a straight course, both parties will no doubt reproach us, as they have done in the past, for not giving them more whole-hearted support against the other, but this course as outlined must be steered, our interests demand it.[25]

British thinking clearly yearned to return to the age of Castlereagh. Lloyd George compared the situation to the unsettled state which followed the Napoleonic wars, and like his predecessors at that time there was an instinctive turning to the United States as a counter-weight. Having called the New World into existence to redress the balance of the old during the recent war, it had no desire to see it retreat again into its hemispheric fastness. Britain since 1900 had acknowledged its growing need for allies, but it remained suspicious of the continental powers. The United States was considered a much more suitable ally than any continental power, and many figures supported a move to smooth out existing difficulties with the United States in order to open the way for some form of common under-standing. The way for this seemed to be opening with the swearing in of a new administration in Washington in March 1921. Changes of administration always offer new opportunities and there is a discern-ible drive towards a *rapprochement* with the United States from early 1921 to the end of the Washington Conference, when it was assumed this had been achieved.[26]

Lloyd George in opening the Imperial Conference of 1921 observed to his fellow premiers that 'Friendly co-operation with the United States is for us a cardinal principle, dictated by what seems to us the proper nature of things, dictated by instinct quite as much as by reason and common sense'.[27] This view was seconded by Smuts who stated: 'To my mind it seems clear that the only path of safety for the British Empire is a path on which she can walk together with America'.[28] Unlike the Australian and New Zealand premiers who were concerned about good relations with Japan, or the Canadians who were concerned with their immediate neighbour, or the London Government which kept a wary eye on the European continent, Smuts was able to take a detached view of the situation of the Empire as a whole. As such his views carried unusual weight. He was clearly of the opinion that the direction Britain should look in was that of the United States. He hoped that, 'If we could get America once more to work with us, even if she were not in the League of Nations, it might alter the whole situation'.[29] His view was that Britain should stay independent of European entanglements and work for close cooperation with the United States. 'I am strongly for union with America and for coming to some general settlement with America as the basis for our foreign policy'.[30] There was therefore strong sentiment in favour of cooperation with the United States, the difficulty posed was how to get the United States involved.

United States Re-entry

Curzon observed that at the end of the Wilson administration, 'Official relations with the American Government almost ceased to exist, and for ten months we practically did no business with America at all'.[31] The United States had slowly withdrawn from the Allied councils, but there were indications that the new Harding Administration was interested in finding ways for the United States to participate in international councils, although the structures developed by Wilson were clearly impossible for domestic political reasons. The United Kingdom had grasped hold of what was interpreted to be a signal to this effect when Harding spoke of an Association of Nations.[32] These tantalizing indications showed that first of all Britain faced the necessity of puzzling out what the views of the incoming administration were. Anything probably seemed an improvement to the grating moralism of Wilson, and more pertinently his commitment to a large navy. Britain hoped that the new administration would not only be more effective through its control of Congress, a situation very reassuring to products of the parliamentary tradition, but also less committed to navalism.

The year 1921 began with a dispatch from Geddes reporting a newspaper article which was suspected of reporting Harding's views.

This article projected American naval power surpassing the Royal Navy within three years, and suggested the United States should wait until then to be able to negotiate from a position of strength.[33] These reports were reinforced by such evidence as a conversation between Lord Riddell and a prominent American journalist only a few days after Geddes' dispatch, in which Riddell was told that 'The Americans were justly entitled to desire a powerful navy and mercantile marine'.[34] Geddes followed his report with a dispatch expressing the view that, 'any formula that would preserve British naval supremacy will be rejected and we shall have to face results of an extensive American naval programme . . .',[35] and Geddes reinforced these views in a personal letter to the Prime Minister's secretary in which he stressed the influence of a strong anglophobe group in Harding's entourage, viewing their object as being, 'to transfer the centre of English speaking power to North America. . . . They regard England as crippled and this as their opportunity and they propose to grasp it – not in hatred but in fulfilment of their country's destiny'.[36] Sir William Tyrrell of the Foreign Office, with his experience of the United States and a generally acerbic view of the world, noted that Britain still had a chance to defuse the problem, as unless the Middle West was converted to navalism it would remain a paper fleet. Tyrrell at least perceived that the new administration would be facing similar pressures for financial cutbacks, and that Britain could take advantage of this.[37]

Reports as to the United States' intentions came in at frequent intervals from the Washington embassy. As the new administration finally settled in Geddes reported: 'View held by administration is stated to be that any international conference on this special question attracting as it would wide publicity would only breed suspicion and would be unlikely to achieve concrete results'.[38] The fear remained that the United States would not negotiate until it had built its navy, forcing Britain into an expensive naval race in order to maintain its one-power standard. Churchill even went so far as to tell the Japanese Ambassador that he considered Britain's 'most important object was to avoid a naval rivalry between Great Britain and the United States, but that, subject to that, I was a well-wisher of Japan',[39] while to his colleagues he observed: 'It would be a ghastly state of affairs if we were to drift into direct naval rivalry with the United States . . .'.[40]

The need to avoid this was clear to both the British Cabinet and the Imperial Conference.

Naval Rivalry

Of all the problems confronting Anglo-American relations none was more worrying to Britain than America's ambitious 1916 Naval Building programme, which had the clearly defined goal of creating a navy second to none. Tyrrell had observed to Edward House, in the last days of the Wilson Administration, 'We are hearing a great deal about the naval agitation in your country, and I cannot help being struck by the similarity of arguments being used in support of that policy with those that were trotted out by the Tirpitz crowd'.[41] Britain had undoubtedly heaved a sigh of relief when the German officers scuppered their fleet at Scapa Flow, thereby putting an end to a threat that had haunted Britain since 1899. The ghost of the pre-war naval arms race still haunted the Government. Lloyd George told the opening session of the Imperial Conference that 'sea power is necessarily the basis of the whole Empire's existence'.[42] In November 1918 the Royal Navy had indeed achieved a nearly equal tonnage and number of ships with all the remaining major fleets of the world combined. By 1921 it had reduced its strategic naval doctrine from that of a two-standard to a one-standard navy, but the threat to what was a seaborne empire connected only by tenuous nautical strands was there. Although Britain had laid down no new capital ships since 1916, the Cabinet in March 1921 reluctantly accepted the American challenge and authorized the appropriation of funds to begin four new giant battle cruisers.[43] The naval arms race with Germany had been bad enough, and now, as Billy Hughes noted, 'The appalling race for naval supremacy has already begun, although the fires of the Great War are not yet cold'.[44]

The CID warned in a paper on the eve of the Imperial Conference, 'The United States of America and Japan . . . already possess the second and third strongest navies in the world and undoubtedly will in the next few years, unless further construction is undertaken in the British Empire, become the first and second naval Powers in the world . . .'.[45] Any British naval building though would also require substantial infrastructural developments in Asia to adapt facilities to much larger capital ships and to store oil. One reason the CID advised a renewal of the Anglo-Japanese Alliance was to avoid dealing immediately with these eventual calls on the British purse.

Smuts was of the opinion that 'The most fateful mistake of all . . . would be a race of armaments against America'.[46] Churchill expressed a similar view as he 'considered our most important object was to avoid a naval rivalry between Great Britain and the United States, but that, subject to that, he was a well-wisher of Japan'.[47] Churchill indeed was one of those most concerned with the implications of a naval arms race with the United States, and he thought its avoidance should be a principal aim of British policy. He was frank in warning the Cabinet that if the United States chose 'to put up the money and persevere, [it would] have a good chance of becoming the strongest Naval Power in the world and thus obtaining the complete mastery of the Pacific'.[48] Any competition with the United States would involve Britain in ruinous expense. The advantages were clearly felt to lie with the United States, Churchill noting that, 'In all this business the United States have a great deal to give and a great deal more to withhold'.[49]

The Initiative

How to draw the United States back into the international conference circuit posed several problems. Geddes reported that a reliable source had informed him that the Harding Administration believed that any conference on disarmament would of course attract wide publicity and would therefore only breed suspicion without much likelihood of achieving concrete results.[50] Whatever the reliability of this report it was indicative of the widespread belief that in the aftermath of the Paris Peace Conference the United States had developed a severe case of conferencephobia. It had, however, shown an interest in naval arms reduction in the Borah Resolution, passed by the Senate as an amendment to the Navy Bill, which called for a 50 per cent reduction in naval building programmes by Britain, Japan, and the United States.[51] Hughes of Australia suggested to the Imperial Conference that some initiative should be taken to follow up the Senate resolution, an idea with which Curzon agreed. With the full support of the conference, who in the midst of trying to reach a decision on the

Anglo-Japanese Alliance were anxious to discover if the United States would really be open to negotiations, Curzon initiated discussions with the new American Ambassador to London, George Harvey.[52]

Harvey now emerged as one of those factors that so often frustrated the British when dealing with the United States. Harding's appointment of Harvey, a fellow newspaperman with no previous experience of diplomacy, was not a happy choice. He was wont to make pronouncements while the worse for drink, and his subordinates would subsequently labour to mend any damage he had done.[53] The policy makers in London were developing an unfortunate picture of American diplomacy; having first encountered Wilson, who seemed attached to making grandiose agreements he was then unable to implement, they now found themselves dealing with an egregious envoy who blithely acted without instructions.

Nonetheless the British desire to avoid further alienating the United States is seen from the fact that the same afternoon the conference had agreed to probing American attitudes, Curzon met with Harvey and informed him that the conference was discussing the alliance and that they were interested in United States views.[54] The United States Secretary of State, Charles Evans Hughes, had already expressed, informally, that 'he viewed the renewal of the Anglo-Japanese Treaty in any form with disquietude . . .' because of the effect it would have on United States opinion regarding Britain.[55] Curzon though was hoping for more detail and he now proceeded to encounter, to his bewilderment, the eccentricities of United States diplomatic representation. The Foreign Secretary assumed that the United States Ambassador would be in a position to give advice reflecting his own Government's views, if need be through the most guarded and subtle diplomatic signals. Harvey assured Curzon that there was a great gap between the vapourings of the American press and the views of the Administration. Harvey also indicated that the United States would be interested in a discussion with Britain and Japan on naval strength in the Pacific.

When Geddes learnt of this discussion he was horrified that Harvey had conveyed an impression so contrary to what Secretary of State Hughes was saying in Washington.[56] Nevertheless Curzon, with the support of the Imperial Conference and after consulting Japan and China, held another meeting with Harvey and informed him that the idea of a conference had been favourably received by the Imperial

Conference, and that they hoped the United States would summon it. Harvey was delighted, engaging immediately in a discussion of possible participants and venues.[57]

Geddes had meanwhile been hard at work in Washington to iron out the discrepancies emerging in London. In a meeting on 6 July with Secretary of State Hughes he learnt that Harvey had received no communication from his Government on their attitude to the Anglo-Japanese Alliance.[58] Hughes now drafted instructions to Harvey, on which he briefed Geddes, so that London would be informed by a second channel in case Harvey generated any more chaos. Geddes's report indicated that the United States would probably be willing to act on naval arms limitation if agreement could be reached on Pacific issues. United States interest in naval arms limitation and British concerns about East Asia thereby became linked in one conference. The Americans, as initially requested by Curzon, took the initiative in issuing the invitations to a conference to be held in Washington. What was intended originally as a conference of, in effect, the war-time five allied great powers plus China, grew once the proposed conference became public knowledge. The Dutch, Belgian, and Portuguese governments all clamoured to be allowed to attend. In all nine states would participate at Washington.[59]

The Abortive Preliminary Conference

The summer of 1921 proved something of a silly season for British diplomacy, as it became obsessed with the issue of the holding of a preliminary conference with the United States. The Government in its desire to escape from the albatross of the Anglo-Japanese Alliance welcomed the possibilities offered by a conference on Pacific questions. There was the logistical difficulty posed by the widening of what was originally intended as a tripartite discussion into a nine-power conference. The preliminary conference was intended to provide a way round this difficulty by providing the basis for more efficient talks. The aim was 'to arrive at a common understanding on the wider principles which should underlie the future Pacific policy of the three powers'.[60] More specifically, the Cabinet saw, 'the main object of the conversation would be to induce the United States of America to make a concession and to abandon her intention to build a great Navy . . .'.[61] Secretary of State Hughes rejected out of hand any preliminary meeting.

Harvey again seems to have been the source of the confusion, which during the summer of 1921 looked likely to poison Anglo-American relations. The idea of a preliminary conference had been raised with Harvey at Chequers on 10 July, when Lloyd George accepted the American invitation, and again on the following day. Lloyd George clearly believed the idea had been accepted as he referred to it in his statement to the House of Commons accepting Harding's invitation.[62] Harvey had even gone so far as to suggest possible venues, such as Bar Harbor, Maine.[63]

The source of the misunderstanding seems finally to have been clarified in a meeting between Geddes and Hughes in which they compared notes. Hughes observed: 'We are faced, then, with this position: that British Government believes that American Government has been committed by its ambassador in London to a course of action which American Government does not approve'.[64] Curzon was infuriated, and when he again met Harvey he noted, 'As His Excellency never leaves me a copy of his instructions, and apparently experiences great difficulty in giving me a summary of them afterwards, I made notes of the contents of his message as he delivered it.'[65] Harvey's relations with the Foreign Office never recovered and, as William Castle discovered the following year, Tyrrell in particular would 'have nothing to do with Harvey since the Conference misunderstanding', while another member of the Foreign Office later told him with some understatement that 'Harvey was intensely disliked, that people did not care for his speeches but that the real harm he did was in personal conversations with individuals'.[66]

Geddes reported that the view in America was that in proposing a preliminary conference the British were trying to 'hoodwink' them, and that Britain hoped to regain the kudos lost by Harding having initiated the conference.[67] Curzon recognized the futility of continuing to press for such a preliminary conference, and adopted instead the petulant attitude that the United States should be left to make all the arrangements.[68] This would have the advantage that if the conference failed it could then be blamed on American diplomatic incompetence. The United States was certainly aware of British irritation, as its Office of Naval Intelligence reported 'the great regret that the British feel over the fact that no preliminary conferences were held'.[69] This possible descent into Anglo-American acrimony in the lead-up to the conference began to be dispelled by a report from Geddes noting a change in the popular attitude in the United States to Britain throughout the summer of 1921.[70] Although Britain had wanted a preliminary conference with the United States in order to cement its transatlantic ties and to establish a common front in the negotiations, Britain avoided any similar arrangement with France, rejecting a similar French proposal for an Anglo-French preliminary conference.[71]

British Perceptions of the United States

The events leading up to the Washington Conference help to demonstrate that despite the shared experience of war and a common language, the United States remained a puzzling country to the British Government. The *Spectator* observed that 'The American nation has a dual personality. Americans are at once the most idealistic and the most practical people in the world. They vibrate between Emerson and Edison'.[72] Geddes, from the vantage point of Washington, felt compelled to remind London that the American mind was not a European one, and that the war had not had the same impact on American thinking as it had on the European psyche. Austen Chamberlain had already observed to the Cabinet that

> The American government and people are living in a different continent – I might say in a different world. It is useless and worse than useless to criticize their insularity, blindness and selfishness, and it is not compatible with our dignity to appear as suitors, pressing for a consideration which is not willingly given.[73]

Only Herbert Hoover among the new, Republican, Cabinet had any direct experience of Europe and the war, and he was probably the least well inclined toward Britain of that group. As a result, Geddes asserted, 'Their mental state is descended without abnormal break or interruption from the mental state of 1913'.[74] Geddes also lectured Lloyd George in person about the United States when opportunity arose, but after one such session Lord Riddell noted, 'I don't think he

[Lloyd George] really appreciates what modern America is'.[75] British officials had a tendency to see the Americans as simple and idealistic, as seen in Geddes's advice to Curzon,

> that vague generalization, the typical American, is a being compounded of contradictory traits. He can be ruthless, not too scrupulous in business and blatantly Chauvinistic but he is also a great idealist with a simple but sincere faith in the ultimate triumph of righteousness.[76]

Victor Wellesley reiterated these views in an important briefing survey for the delegation going to Washington with the observation that

> They profess to be animated by certain principles of an altruistic and self-denying character, but this lofty idealism is not entirely divorced from practical business instincts. In point of fact, their conduct is often erratic, inconsistent and bears the stamp of political inexperience.[77]

There were baffling differences in the British and American mentalities. The impact of this, undoubtedly compounded by the antics of Harvey and the residual frustrations of dealing with Wilson, led London to underestimate the ability of Washington to formulate and carry through coherent policies. When the idea of an arms control conference began to emerge Sir Eyre Crowe, the Permanent Under-Secretary at the Foreign Office, noted,

> No one has ever been able so far to suggest a practical scheme for general reduction of armaments which would be accepted as fair and safe by all parties. I should let the Americans raise the question and see what they propose. I doubt whether they have thought out any proposal at all.[78]

When the United States began to discuss the agenda of the coming conference Wellesley observed haughtily,

> The extraordinary nebulosity and ignorance displayed in these tentative proposals suggest such a complete lack of grasp of the situation on the part of the United States Government that nothing short of a regular course of education seems to offer the slightest chance of the matter being put on anything like a rational basis.[79]

Curzon remarked to Lord Hardinge of the outline American agenda that 'it is partly obscure and partly absurd . . .', and that 'there is too much fear that the whole thing will end in a fiasco'.[80]

Lloyd George did not expect much to come of the conference once his own offer to come over for a preliminary conference had been rejected. He told Lord Riddell that 'He thought the Washington Conference would open with a great blare of trumpets, that the papers would be full of reports for a week or so, and that then the proceedings would begin to lose interest'.[81] After the initial exultation of getting the Americans interested in a conference, the difficulties that followed persuaded London that in all likelihood nothing would come out of this American-hosted nine-power circus. This helps to explain the paucity of British planning for the conference, and Lloyd George's reluctance to attend and thus be publicly associated with failed expectations. That was a role he preferred to bestow upon a leading statesman selected from his Tory coalition partners. Indeed Curzon was thinking along similar lines, as he suggested to Lloyd George that as the conference was likely to fail it would be a good idea to add a member of the opposition to the delegation.[82] It is no wonder that with these assumptions about the conference the British delegation was caught flat-footed by Hughes's proposals at the opening session of the conference.

The British Empire Delegation

One of the issues confronting London was the mounting of its preparations for and representation at the conference. A month after the conference had been announced Crowe exclaimed in despair, 'Nobody, so far as I know, has any plans . . .'.[83] The anxiety at the Foreign Office must finally have focused attention on the problem, for immediately afterwards the Cabinet decided to refer the matter to the CID.[84] Who was to represent Britain also posed great difficulties, given the generally held views about its likely failure. It was agreed Britain needed to be represented by a political heavyweight. Almost comically the choice seems to have fallen on the most senior figure who was absent – Balfour, who was abroad. It was only on 27 September that a cable was sent to Balfour warning him of the impending task and asking when he might be returning.[85] Balfour

clearly was not very happy with the idea, as he responded on 29
September with the suggestion that Bonar Law be sent.[86] Bonar Law,
however, readily declined the honour, and the choice finally fell on
Balfour. This left little time for him to be actively involved in planning, though given Balfour's general lassitude this probably suited
him. All agreed, including Curzon and Crowe, that he was an excellent choice. A former First Lord of the Admiralty, Foreign Secretary,
and Prime Minister, as well as a long-serving member of the CID, he
had played a significant role in concluding the Anglo-Japanese
Alliance in 1902. All this gave him a breadth of knowledge on these
subjects that would be hard to equal. Perhaps it was hoped his
experience would compensate for lack of preparation. He left for the
conference on 2 November, sailing on the *Empress of France*, spending the journey, between bouts of seasickness, studying the available
documents.[87]

There was a school of thought that Lloyd George should attend.
Churchill argued for this, as in any tough bargaining it would be
better to be represented by the head of government.[88] As late as 16
October Lloyd George still thought of going to Washington, but this
can only have been half-heartedly.[89] Churchill also hoped to attend if
he could escape from the toils of the Irish negotiations.[90] He no doubt
would have much preferred to discuss battleships. Even as Balfour
sailed he had no idea if he would remain head of the delegation or if
Lloyd George would make a dramatic appearance. This possibility
evaporated with Hughes's show-stealing performance, and the subsequent reasonably smooth flow of the negotiations, which would
have made any such appearance an anti-climax.

Similar problems of coordination also troubled the organization of
the delegation. Lloyd George again decided to turn to Sir Maurice
Hankey of the Cabinet Secretariat to organize the delegation, in
preference to the Foreign Office, as he had done for the Paris Peace
Conference. This caused chagrin at the Foreign Office and Crowe
decided to insist on formal, written instructions. Hankey was con-
scious of the need to diffuse the rivalry and offered Crowe the same
arrangement as at Paris between himself and Lord Hardinge.[91]
Tyrrell was aghast at the idea of repeating such an unhappy experience.[92] Hankey attempted to make it clear that the Cabinet
Secretariat had, 'no duties in connection with political or technical

advice outside its sphere of activity . . .' and that the Foreign Office was to advise on 'all questions of a political and diplomatic character'.[93] The Foreign Office, the only department which could have provided the global analysis necessary, was nevertheless alienated and made no special effort to assist in the planning.

The Planning

Compared to the extensive preparatory operations undertaken for the 1919 Paris Peace Conference those for the Washington Conference were barely rudimentary. The CID, which had once played such an important role, did not meet between February 1915 and July 1920, when it was decided to devolve its functions to a CID Standing Defence Sub-Committee, under the chairmanship of Balfour. Despite the problems facing Britain this sub-committee did not meet until 2 May 1921, when the Imperial Conference was looming.[94] In response to the prodding of the Foreign Office the Cabinet asked the CID on 15 August to consider the situation, although its chairman, Balfour, was busy representing Britain at the League of Nations in Geneva from August through to October.[95] The CID finally received the necessary advisory memoranda from the Navy and Army on 5 October, less than a month before the delegation was due to sail.

The Naval Staff recognized the interlocking nature of the Pacific and arms limitations aspects of the conference. For the Pacific settlement they were concerned with safeguarding Britain's established position. It hoped that Japan would accept no naval base further south than Formosa, thereby keeping it at a comfortable distance from British interests in the Pacific and India. The Naval Staff were able to contemplate the loss of Wei-hai-Wei, but were adamant on the need to safeguard Hong Kong. On arms limitation they advised, in order to avoid world public opinion rounding on Britain in the event of failure, leaving the initiative entirely to the United States. Britain could always then guide the discussions into suitable channels. Not surprisingly they carped at the adoption of the one-power standard, pointing out that Britain required a greater navy because it was the only one requiring deployment in all oceans. A naval building holiday was opposed on the grounds that Britain had already had a self-imposed one for five years, and as a result was slipping behind even the one-power standard. Technical objections were found for arms limitation on the basis of limitation by size or tonnage. It was recommended therefore for reasons of simplicity that limitation be based on numbers of capital ships, which were defined as being 'any ship fit to lie in the main line of battle'. The minimum number of ships required was based on a calculation of Britain's security needs in European waters, the Pacific, and the Atlantic. European waters posed little difficulty as the German Navy was gone, and the French and Italian Navies now possessed only pre-Jutland ships and had no building programmes. The Pacific, though, was much more dangerous. Here Britain required a significant multiple against Japan, calculated on the basis of equality with Japan, plus a percentage necessary to assure victory, plus a percentage to compensate for operating so far from their main bases, plus a percentage to leave in European waters for security there. This would mean a 3:2 ratio over Japan. In the Atlantic Britain had already accepted the concept of equality with the United States. Not surprisingly the abolition of submarines was wholeheartedly supported. The Naval Staff provided five recommendations; that limitation be done on the basis of capital ships, that Britain and the United States have a margin over Japan of 3:2, that only post-Jutland ships be counted, that replacement be effected over 20 years, and that the abolition of submarines should be considered.[96]

The General Staff seemed mostly interested in preventing limitation being applied to the army, which they argued had already been reduced, and in a curious justification for its role it observed that, 'from the Continental point of view the British army is almost negligible, and can in no sense be considered a menace to the peace of the world'.[97] Otherwise they warned of French aspirations in Europe, and of Japan's desire to control the region stretching from the Bering Straits to the Straits of Malacca.

The CID did produce an overview memorandum on 24 October. It suggested the not very remarkable proposal that the aim of the British delegation at Washington 'is to achieve the largest possible reduction in expenditure on armaments'.[98] The fear was expressed that the United States might agree to a settlement, which would then be rejected by the Senate, indicating an on-going nervousness about the efficacy of American foreign policy. At the Prime Minister's request

Sir Joseph Stamp had prepared a memorandum on the economic aspects in consultation with the various ministries, the London School of Economics, and even the Royal Statistical Society. The President of the Board of Education, H.A.L. Fisher, had even been invited to meetings of the CID because of his interest in the economic aspects.

The Foreign Office produced a set of summary memoranda on various technical matters. These were accompanied by a very curious survey by Wellesley, which was more of a polemic on the East Asian situation. At its base, he argued, the problems in East Asia were racial.

> It is a fact which is apt to escape notice that, after centuries of undisputed sway, the first real break in the spell of white supremacy came with the triumph of Japan over Russia in 1904. The great war in Europe has greatly accentuated this effect by breaking up the solidarity of the white races, and has undoubtedly produced a profound impression throughout the world, together with an immense loss of white prestige. A great deal would be done to restore white solidarity by a policy of closer co-operation with the United States.[99]

It is not altogether clear how this was meant to assist Balfour and the delegation in their negotiations. All this seems to suggest a last minute flurry of activity, partly to satisfy those who wished to feel they were involved, though it is questionable how much impact this had.

Indeed very little was done to assist the delegation. What planning there was seems to have occurred during Balfour's uncomfortable six day transatlantic voyage, during which he took the opportunity to go through with Hankey the handful of advisory memoranda that had been produced as well as the relevant past diplomatic dispatches. Balfour needed to do this if only to find out what he was supposed to be doing at Washington, for remarkably he seems to have been sent without a negotiating brief. The Lloyd George Government was known for its lax procedures, but this does seem an extraordinary example of it. Balfour on arrival felt the need to cable London (presumably so something would exist on paper) with a statement of what he thought his task was. He stated that he had formed the impression from discussion in Cabinet before he had left that his mission was 'to secure the largest possible limitation of armaments consistent with the safety of the British Empire'.[100] As this involved Britain primarily with the United States and Japan it would necessitate settling outstanding issues in the Pacific and China. The first issue to resolve therefore was the Anglo-Japanese Alliance. Balfour indicated he intended to propose to Hughes a tripartite agreement, according to a formula which became the basis of the Four-Power Treaty (when it was broadened to include France). Balfour must have been aware of a Foreign Office memorandum on the idea of such a pact which made clear that by stripping the agreement of the military clauses which had been in the old Anglo-Japanese Alliance, the new agreement became 'merely a declaration of policy. . . .' and that it would 'therefore be of a somewhat anodyne nature'.[101] Likewise he drafted an agreement over China which closely resembles the final Nine-Power Treaty. Here he suggested that the relevant powers agree to maintain peace in East Asia, preserve the independence and integrity of China, and apply the principle of equal opportunity for the commerce and industry of all states in China (in effect recognizing the open-door policy).[102]

Both these proposals were put to Hughes on the eve of the conference opening, in a bid to reach the sort of advance understanding that had been hoped for in the ill-fated preliminary conference. Hughes received the offer politely, but refused to give anything away.[103] There was no reason for him to do so now that he had the British Empire offering to give way on key issues even before the conference had opened.

The Conference Opens

The Washington Conference was opened with great solemnity in November 1921. The significance cannot have been lost on the visiting delegates, particularly the British Empire delegation, that the opening session was delayed one day to allow for the 11 November dedication of the Tomb of the Unknown Soldier. Nothing could have provided a clearer reminder of America's participation and sacrifice in the Great War. The opening session was held in the Continental Hall of the Daughters of the American Revolution, reminding all the delegates that the United States had consciously separated itself from the Old World. The two events therefore symbolized both America's bond with the conference powers and its detachment.

The British Empire delegation arrived with the presumption that the United States would be unprepared. Nothing could have been further from the truth. If anything America suffered from chronic overpreparation, too much, not too little. Wilson's Inquiry for the Paris Peace Conference must have been one of the greatest academic enterprises of the century. For this conference not only had all the relevant departments provided reports, but a lay advisory committee had been formed to provide an extra input. Hughes, the recipient of all this advice, quietly evolved his own plans. As Theodore Roosevelt Jr, the Assistant Secretary of the Navy, noted in his diary, 'The plan is to spring everything, including our definite naval program on the opening day'.[104] The American scheme was mimeographed in person by Rear-Admiral Pratt, delivered by hand to the Secretary of State by Roosevelt and then locked in Hughes's safe.[105] Under such maximum security, leaks were almost impossible. British cryptanalytic capabilities, on which British diplomacy relied so heavily in this period, failed against such simple precautions.[106] After the debacles of the summer Hughes was certainly not going to entrust any communications as to his intentions to Harvey. Hughes indeed hinted to Balfour on the eve of the conference that he had something big to announce, but in European diplomatic circles such honesty was probably discredited. The British delegation for the opening session of the conference was more concerned with providing Balfour with envelopes, his preferred medium for note taking.[107] Hughes's dramatic opening speech at the conference must have surprised the British delegation. Given their oft-expressed disdain for open diplomacy, its application must have come as a shock. Roosevelt noted in his diary the reactions of the British delegation.

> Lord Lee, the First Lord of the British Admiralty turned the several colors of the rainbow, and behaved as if he were sitting on hot coals. He threw notes to Beatty who was sitting on the far left. He half rose and whispered to Balfour. Beatty, after the first step, sat with eyes fixed on the ceiling. Admiral Chatfield, on his left turned red and then white, and sat immovable.

Balfour did not in any way show his trend of thought, whether he was either surprised or excited.[108]

Perhaps the difficulty that now faced Britain at Washington was that Balfour, when faced with a public forum, instinctively treated the situation as a simulacrum of Westminster. When judged against that measure he performed outstandingly. Yet in retrospect many historians have concluded that Britain's performance at Washington was poor. Without entering into this debate it is perhaps worth noting that Britain's effectiveness at Washington was undermined from the start by poor preparation and coordination in London, a divided view within the British Empire, and the instinctive response by Balfour of seeing the conference as a parliamentary challenge because of its public dimension rather than as an international negotiation. Nevertheless Britain emerged from Washington with most of its immediate aims achieved, and Balfour was rewarded for his services with the Garter.

Conclusion

Governments rarely think in terms of long-term objectives, but rather of short-term victories. In this sense Britain won at Washington, and simultaneously some troublesome issues which had been evaded in Paris in 1919 were resolved. The fact that 20 years later Britain went to war with Japan is less significant than many have argued. This could have happened regardless of Washington; the Anglo-Japanese Alliance was not holy writ. Rather its significance lies in the slow, but obvious drift of London into the orbit of Washington. The founding fathers of the United States had initially only desired greater influence in London, and in 1921 at Washington this was achieved, when London deferred to its former colony, which had now firmly seized the initiative.

The Washington Conference was a continuation of the process begun at Paris in 1919, which inaugurated the attempt to frame a post-war order on the scale of that achieved at Vienna a century before. In a series of conferences stretching from Paris in 1919 to Locarno in 1925 Britain attempted to address the problems caused by the upheavals of the First World War. Paris had dealt with European affairs, but the British Empire was global and the future balance of power in the Pacific was also a matter of concern. Linked to the future of the Pacific system was the issue of comparative naval strength. After the destruction of German naval power in the war only the Royal Navy, the United States, and Japan possessed navies with significant power. All were Pacific Basin states. As such the questions of naval power and the Pacific balance of power became inextricably linked.

Britain had now entered a period of imperial consolidation after decades of expansion. While Britain is often identified with the balance of power as an underlying notion of its foreign policy, it was a doctrine which was applied only in the most limited sense, usually to western Europe. In the wider world Britain preferred either hege- mony or to be part of a dominating partnership. The Anglo-Japanese Alliance of 1902 had provided Britain with a powerful maritime and regional ally in the face of Russian and German threats. In 1921 with Germany defeated and Russia ravaged by war and civil war these threats had passed. In the Pacific there were only two possible allies or adversaries, the United States and Japan. Britain was faced with the uncomfortable task of deciding which offered the best security for assuring the future of British power in the region. Japan had been a useful ally for two decades, but America was clearly the coming thing. Britain could renew its Japanese alliance, but with a feeling that the links with Japan were tenuous, or it could shift to the United States, notoriously erratic after its rejection of the Wilsonian commitments of Paris, but a power nonetheless with which Britain enjoyed unusual cultural links and connections. The matter was complicated for Britain by the bifurcated nature of the Dominions' response to the issue. During the First World War the Imperial Government in London had been forced to allow the self-governing Dominions a greater status in the formulation of policy. As a result Lloyd George was forced to confront an unwieldy grouping of Dominion premiers with varied views based on differing geographical perspectives on security issues.

A purely Pacific Basin analysis of Britain's position might have led to the conclusion that the reality of the Japanese alliance was better than anything the Americans could offer. A global analysis, however, indicated other concerns, and in redressing these only the United

States could be brought into the scales. The decision to approach the United States with the idea of a conference to resolve some of the matters of common concern was meant to begin a process of reintroducing the United States into the global equation. The reaction in London to the opening phase of the conference betrays some of the lurking anxieties. In a Cabinet meeting held on 22 November, discussing the third plenary session of the conference, the conclusion reached was that 'So long as France maintained her powerful army in being, the state of Europe would remain unsettled and that it would be a most serious matter if as a result of the Washington Conference Great Britain was the only power to be disarmed'.[109] In historiographical retrospect the conference is seen as having been concerned about East Asia and the Pacific, but in the minds of the participants the geographical remit was global. Britain's acquiescence in the American plan, while potentially weakening it in the Pacific, had evolved out of a global appraisal which fixed the primary threat as lying in Europe. The best method of insuring against this threat was to establish a close connection with the United States. This would take time, with a slow building of confidence and the removal of causes of friction. The Washington Conference was more than a meeting on naval arms control and the Pacific balance of power. It was the first instalment of an insurance policy, a policy on which Britain would from time to time pay premiums in the ensuing years, and which was to prove itself to be a sound investment when a Second World War erupted.

University of Birmingham

NOTES

1. Imperial Conference, 2nd meeting, 21 June 1921. Minutes of the Conference are in RG25/2279/file S/6/1, National Archives of Canada, Ottawa (hereinafter cited as NAC). Minutes of the Imperial Conference are also in CAB 32/2, and Notes of Informal Talks in CAB 32/4, Cabinet Papers, Public Record Office, Kew, London.
2. Imperial Conference, 1st Meeting, 20 June 1921.
3. Imperial Conference, 4th Meeting, 22 June 1921.
4. Ibid.
5. Imperial Conference, 6th Meeting, 24 June 1921.
6. Imperial Conference, 4th Meeting.

7. NAC RG 25/3414/file f1–1921/3, CID 122-C(a).
8. Imperial Conference, 4th meeting, 22 June 1921.
9. Imperial Conference, 8th meeting, 28 June 1921.
10. See Erik Goldstein, *Winning the Peace: British Diplomatic Strategy, Peace Planning, and the Paris Peace Conference, 1916–1920* (Oxford, 1991), pp. 229–41.
11. Imperial Conference, 4th Meeting.
12. Imperial Conference, 6th Meeting.
13. Ibid.
14. Imperial Conference, 4th Meeting.
15. CAB 4/7/CID 276-B, 'General Staff Note on Disarmament', 5 Oct. 1921.
16. CAB 23/27/C88(21) conclusion 5, 22 Nov. 1921.
17. FO 371/5623/A8711/18/45, Lloyd George to Balfour, 23 Nov. 1921. Foreign Office Papers, Public Record Office, Kew, London.
18. 9 Dec. 1921, Martin Gilbert, *Winston S. Churchill, 1874–1965*, Vol. 4, Companion Vol. 3 (London, 1977) (hereinafter cited as Churchill Companion volume 4:3).
19. FO 371/5619/A7148/18/45, Geddes to Curzon, 21 Sept. 1921 Also in *Documents on British Foreign Policy, 1919–1939*, First Series, Vol. XV (London, 1967) (hereinafter cited as DBFP). Document 381. See also NAC, RG25/F-1/916/file 14.
20. Geddes to Kerr, 3 Jan. 1921. Lloyd George Papers F60/4/11, House of Lords Record Office, London.
21. Churchill Companion Vol. 4:3, Curzon to Churchill, 29 Sept. 1921.
22. CAB 23/27/77(21) conclusion 5, 7 Oct. 1921.
23. NAC RG25/3414/f1–1921/3. 'Anglo-Japanese Alliance', 10 March 1921. This portion was a reprint of a Foreign Office memorandum of 28 February. Also listed as CID 122-C.
24. Ibid. [E-1].
25. NAC/RG25/3414/f1–1921/3.
26. Birn makes the point that Britain hoped to replace old Pax Britannica of 19th with an Anglo-Saxon policy, which '. . . had particular appeal to Conservatives, who saw it as an attractive alternative to entanglement in Europe.' Donald S. Birn, 'The Washington Naval Conference of 1921–22 in Anglo-French Relations' in Daniel M. Masterson (ed.), *Naval History: The Sixth Symposium of the U.S. Naval Academy* (Wilmington, Delaware, 1987).
27. Imperial Conference, 1st Meeting.
28. Imperial Conference, 2nd Meeting.
29. Imperial Conference, 6th meeting.
30. Ibid.
31. Imperial Conference, 5th Meeting, 22 June 1921.
32. FO 371/5624/A8854/18/45. There were apparently rumours that the United States invitation to the conference was part of a Republican plan to create such an association to replace Wilson's League. See Birn, 'The Washington Naval Conference of 1921–22 in Anglo-French Relations'; Balfour Papers, file 49749, British Library, London. These rumours circulated as late as the eve of the conference See Lodge Diary, 3 Nov. 1921, Massachusetts Historical Society. Harding did definitely pronounce against United States membership in the League of Nations on 12 April 1921.
33. FO 371/5616/A18/18/45, Geddes to Foreign Office, 2 Jan. 1921.
34. Lord Riddell, *Lord Riddell's Intimate Diary of the Peace Conference and After, 1918–1934* (London, 1933), 28 Jan. 1921.
35. FO 371/5616/A19/18/45, telegram from Geddes, 2 Jan. 1921.
36. Geddes to Kerr, 3 Jan. 1921, Lloyd George Papers F/60/4/11.
37. FO 371/5616/A19/18/45, Minute by Tyrrell, 4 Jan. 1921.
38. FO 371/5617/A3715/18/45, telegram from Geddes, 16 May 1921.

39. Churchill, 'The Anglo-Japanese Alliance', Churchill Papers 22/6, 17 June 1921, Churchill College Archive Centre, Cambridge. Also in Churchill Companion Vol. 4:3.
40. CAB 23/25, 30 May 1921. Also in Churchill Companion volume 4:3.
41. Tyrrell to House, 27 Jan. 1921. House Papers I/111a/3869, Sterling Library, Yale University.
42. 1st Meeting of the Imperial Conference.
43. 139 HC Deb 5s 1766ff (17 March 1921). See J. Kenneth McDonald, 'The Washington Conference and the Naval Balance of Power, 1921–22' in John B. Hattendorf and Robert S. Jordan (eds.), Maritime Strategy and the Balance of Power: Britain and America in the Twentieth Century (New York, 1989).
44. 2nd Meeting of the Imperial Conference.
45. NAC/RG25/3414/f1–1921/3. 'Strategic Situation in the Event of the Anglo-Japanese Alliance being Determined', 17 June 1921. Also listed as CID 144-C.
46. Imperial Conference, 2nd meeting.
47. 17 June 1921. Cited in Churchill Companion volume 4:3. Made in the context of conversation with Baron Hayashi of Japan.
48. 23 July 1921. Churchill Companion Vol. 4:3.
49. Ibid.
50. FO 371/5617/A3715/18/45, telegram from Geddes, 16 May 1921.
51. See Thomas Buckley, The United States and the Washington Conference, 1921–1922 (Knoxville, 1970), pp. 11–19. Also FO 371/5616/A918/18/45, Craigie (Washington) to Curzon, 28 Jan. 1921. Dayer has noted that, 'Ironically, the Anglophobic senator little suspected that, in launching an enormous campaign for disarmament, he actually was helping British strategy'. Roberta Allbert Dayer, 'The British War Debts to the United States and the Anglo-Japanese Alliance, 1920–1923', Pacific Historical Review 45:4 (Nov. 1976): 569–95.
52. Imperial Conference, 8th Meeting.
53. Castle Diary, 15 Feb. 1922. It should be noted that the London embassy was not a dynamic operation during Harvey's incumbency. Castle noted on an inspection tour that 'Oliver Harriman . . . is a nice dullard – so dull that to spend an hour with him is agony. Thurston is lacking in training and savoir faire. LeClercq is good, but very young. Boylston Beal is not a secretary and is careful never to put himself forward or overstep his position. Goold is a nice farmer. The situation is appalling. . . . We should have our best men in London and, instead, we have second or third-rate men . . .'. 9 Oct. 1922, Castle Diary, Hoover Presidential Library, West Branch, Iowa.
54. DBFP 313, Curzon to Geddes, 29 June 1921, reporting meeting of 28 June.
55. DBFP 308, Geddes to Curzon, 24 June 1921 (received 25 June).
56. DBFP 317, Geddes to Curzon No. 453, 2 July 1921 (received 3 July). There are small variances between original text and corrected version in DBFP.
57. DBFP 330, Curzon to Geddes, 9 July 1921. Harvey's version of this conversation is in Foreign Relations of the United States, 1921 (Washington, 1936), Vol. I., pp 19–21 (hereinafter cited as FRUS).
58. DBFP 323, Geddes to Curzon, 6 July 1921. See also DBFP 326, Geddes to Curzon, 7 July 1921, and DBFP 329, Geddes to Curzon, 8 July 1921.
59. The Soviet Russian government also wished to be invited, but as it was unrecognized by any other state, its request was refused. Sun Yat-sen's Canton government also made an unsuccessful bid to attend in addition to the internationally recognized Peking government.
60. FO 371/5617/A5489/18/45, Curzon to Geddes, 27 July 1921.
61. CAB 23/39, Conference of Ministers, 25 July 1921.
62. DBFP 343. Curzon to Geddes, 29 July 1921. 144 H.C. Deb.5s, 11 July 1921. Lloyd

George also reiterated this view to the Imperial Conference, 21st Meeting, 11 July 1921.
63. DBFP 342, Geddes to Curzon, 28 July 1921. Harvey's telegram to Hughes suggesting Bar Harbor as a possible venue is in FRUS 1921, Vol. 1, pp. 46–7.
64. DBFP 345, Geddes to Curzon, 30 July 1921.
65. FO 371/5618/A5607/18/45, 30 July 1921.
66. Castle Diary 2 Oct. 1922 and 27 April 1923. His informant for the second statement was Craigie.
67. DBFP 347, Geddes to Curzon, 31 July 1921. Also in FO 371/5617/A5552/18/45.
68. DBFP 349, Curzon to Geddes, 1 Aug. 1921. Also in FO 371/5618/A5606.
69. From X, a report issued by US Navy, Office of Naval Intelligence, file no. 101–100, 29 Sept. 1921. Theodore Roosevelt Jr, Papers, Library of Congress.
70. DBFP 384. Curzon to Geddes, 25 Sept. 1921.
71. Hardinge to Curzon, 16 Sept. 1921. Hardinge of Penshurst Papers 44, University Library, Cambridge.
72. 'The Washington Conference', The Spectator, 19 Nov. 1921, pp. 657–8.
73. CAB 23/23/C59/20, 3 Nov. 1920.
74. FO 371/5617/A5553/18/45, Geddes to Curzon, 31 July 1921.
75. Riddell, Diary, 26 Jan. 1921.
76. FO 371/5619/A7148/18/45, Geddes to Curzon, 21 Sept. 1921. Also in DBFP 381, and NAC RG25 F-1/Vol. 916/file 14.
77. DBFP 404, Wellesley, 'General Survey of Political Situation in Pacific and Far East with reference to the Forthcoming Washington Conference', 20 Oct. 1921.
78. FO 371/5617/A3715/18/45, Minute by Crowe, 17 May 1921.
79. FO 371/5618/A6675/18/45, minute by V. Wellesley, 16 Sept. 1921.
80. Curzon to Hardinge, 20 Sept. 1921. Hardinge Papers 44.
81. 30 Oct. 1921. Riddell Diary, p. 330.
82. Curzon to Lloyd George. Lloyd George Papers F/13/2/50.
83. FO 371/5618/A5907/18/45, minute by Crowe, 12 Aug. 1921.
84. CAB 23/26/C. 67 (21) 3, Cabinet meeting, 15 Aug. 1921.
85. FO 371/5619/A7066/18/45.
86. Lloyd George Papers F25/2/22.
87. DBFP 415, Balfour to Lloyd George, 11 Nov. 1921; DBFP 416, Memorandum by Hankey of Balfour's interview with Hughes, 11 Nov. 1921.
88. 29 Sept. 1921, Churchill Companion Vol. 4:3. The Cabinet as late as 7 Oct. 1921 supported Lloyd George attending the conference, CAB 23/27/77(21) conclusion 5.
89. Riddell, Diary, 16 Oct. 1921. According to Riddell's diary by 3 November the Prime Minister had begun to think it was unlikely he would get to Washington.
90. Churchill to Governor-General of Canada. NAC, Borden Papers, Vol. 294, reel C4448, pp. 172672–3.
91. FO 371/5621/A7797/18/45, Hankey to Crowe, 17 Oct. 1921.
92. FO 371/5620/A7797/18/45, minute by Tyrrell, 17 Oct. 1921.
93. FO 371/5621/A7702/18/45, 'Provisional Organisation of the British Empire Delegation', 19 Oct. 1921.
94. Max Egremont, Balfour: A Life of Arthur James Balfour (London, 1980), p. 317. Ruddock Mackay, Balfour: Intellectual Statesman (Oxford, 1985), p. 329.
95. CAB 23/26/C67(21) Conclusion 3, Cabinet Meeting, 15 Aug. 1921. The options considered were either a special committee or the CID.
96. CAB 4/7/CID 277-B, Memorandum by the Naval Staff, 5 Oct. 1921.
97. CAB 4/7/CID 276-B, 'General Staff Note on Disarmament', 5 Oct. 1921
98. CAB 4/7/CID 280-B. 'Memorandum by Standing Sub-Committee', 24 Oct. 1921.
99. DBFP 404.

100. DBFP 415, Balfour to Lloyd George, 11 Nov. 1921. This is the day after his arrival in Washington from Quebec, where he had landed.
101. DBFP 405. Foreign Office Memorandum respecting a Tripartite Agreement, 22 Oct. 1921.
102. DBFP 415 and 416.
103. DBFP 416; FRUS 1922, Vol. I, pp. 1–2. The British continued to push for a private meeting with the Americans in the hope of reaching an understanding as late as the morning of the opening of the conference. 13 Nov. 1921, Theodore Roosevelt Jr Diary. Library of Congress, Washington DC.
104. 10 Nov. 1921. Roosevelt Diary.
105. See J. Kenneth McDonald; Roosevelt Diary, 10 Nov. 1921; and Henry Cabot Lodge Diary, 9 Nov. 1921.
106. FO 371/5620/A7296/18/45. Note on security of communications, 11 Oct. 1921, shows Britain's own concerns about the need for secure methods of communication.
107. Riddell, *Diary*, 12 Nov. 1921.
108. Roosevelt, *Diary*, 12 Nov. 1921.
109. CAB 23/27/88(21) conclusion 5, 22 Nov. 1921.

The Politics of Naval Arms Limitation in Britain in the 1920s

B.J.C. McKERCHER

I

The 1920s was a decade when arms limitation and disarmament conferences became an integral part of international politics. For the British governments of this period, such conferences involved the necessity of restricting the size and strength of the Royal Navy – the Royal Army and the Royal Air Force were increasingly negligible quantities *vis-à-vis* the air and land forces of the other great powers. Interestingly, the policies of naval arms limitation in Britain in these ten years or so were shaped almost exclusively by the vagaries of domestic politics.[1] This is not to say that consideration of such policies ignored Britain's wider international interests. It did not. There was a recognition that an intimate connection existed between the power of the Royal Navy and Britain's external strength – the efficacy of its foreign policy, trade protection, and the effort needed to ensure imperial defence[2] – but naval arms limitation was a question dominated by domestic political considerations. This had two dimensions. In the first place, except during the war period of 1914–18, there existed a continual debate, often vituperative, about the nature of arms limitation policies, their creation, and their pursuit. Focusing in the Cabinet and amongst the civil service experts, this debate remained essentially hidden given the importance of sea power to Britain's position as a power of the first rank. Increasingly, however, because of the carnage brought about by the Great War, another element emerged in this crucial debate: politicians in Parliament and individuals representing national organizations interested in disarmament and 'open diplomacy' who sought massive cuts in arms expenditures.[3] After 1918, with victory in the supposed 'war to end all wars', why spend heavily on armaments? The efforts of this extragovernmental element on occasion brought the hidden debate out into public, thereby subjecting the politicians and civil servants to the pressures of public opinion.

The other dimension involved a second debate about the employment of sea power to protect Britain's national interests as an island nation with a vast overseas Empire. As much as the sailors and their political masters at the Admiralty might disagree, the Royal Navy was not a power unto itself; rather, it constituted an adjunct of the nation's external policies. In wartime, it served as the weapon used to attack the enemy, defend the Empire, and maintain the security of vital maritime routes allowing the import of food and raw materials and the export of industrialized goods. In peacetime, it underpinned British diplomacy. Moreover, in both war and peace, the Royal Navy consumed a large slice of government expenditure. There was little to quarrel with in this during wartime or in other moments of lesser crisis, but peacetime was different. Then, given the parsimony of the Treasury, the Admiralty had to compete with other spending ministries, mainly those concerned with administering domestic social policies, in persuading successive chancellors of the exchequer to support increased naval expenditures. Hence the fiscal priorities of government, crucial to electoral survival because they represented an easy target for opposition barbs, touched the Royal Navy and its fighting capacity. In peacetime, notably in the 1920s, cutting arms expenditures in order to pump more money into domestic social programmes – and not coincidentally obviating opposition attacks – represented an easy option for governments seeking to enforce a balanced budget and avoid increased taxation. This second dimension suffused the first: determining Britain's role in the world and how and what national interests should be defended, but doing so within strictures imposed by domestic fiscal and electoral considerations.

In this way a connection existed between sea power, on one hand, and foreign policy, imperial defence, and Britain's international economic survival, on the other. However, personified by the Royal Navy, sea power could not be divorced from either political manoeuvring in the Cabinet or interdepartmental rivalry, nor could it be separated from the concerns of the British public as represented in Parliament by the opposition parties and by extra-parliamentary organizations with an interest in disarmament and ancillary issues. Added to this, the Admiralty was just one of a number of important ministries in Whitehall that had to compete for money to fulfil its mandate. The Admiralty had to justify its needs to those who controlled the collection and disbursement of public funds, as well as the general public, who had to be convinced that Royal Navy potency could not be diminished without the international position of the country being imperilled in an economic, diplomatic, and naval sense. How successive British governments in the 1920s coped with naval arms limitation, how the Admiralty saw it best to fulfil its role, and how the parliamentarians and extra-parliamentary groups and individuals sought to shape policy underscores the overwhelming importance of domestic politics in the arms limitation question in Britain in this period. The unfolding of this story shows much about the way in which domestic politics imposed itself on the fighting capacity of Great Britain. And as important as this is, it has an additional benefit in shearing away a mythology that encrusts the history of British arms limitation policies during the first decade after the Great War.

This mythology surfaced first amongst contemporary left-wing critics of the predominantly Conservative governments that controlled British foreign and defence policy between 1918 and 1929, and it has been perpetuated since by historians who share the political proclivities of those critics.[4] Its essential point is that the Conservative ministries of the 1920s, particularly Stanley Baldwin's second government, which held office from November 1924 to June 1929, had little desire to limit arms, the supposed *sine qua non* for international peace and security, because they were imbued with a war spirit. Thus, these ministries did not participate honestly in the various efforts at arms limitation between the naval conferences at Washington in

1921–22 and London in 1930, and, at the same time, they ignored the very real desire of the general population in Britain to disarm. In the words of the most recent historian who advances this thesis to explain the evolution of British disarmament policy in the 1920s, 'Britain's policy was one of procrastination verging on duplicity'.[5] Such a simplistic view, a derivative of a purely polemical approach to this question, belies the complexity of the policy-making debate inside and outside Downing Street and Whitehall, a debate tied intimately to the survival of Britain as a power of the first rank.

II

In the dozen years after the First World War, British naval policy underwent a fundamental change. Three milestones mark the road to change. In 1920–21, in an effort to pare down government expenditure, the 'two-power standard' was abandoned in favour of a 'one-power standard'.[6] Then, at the Washington Conference, which lasted from November 1921 to February 1922, Britain conceded formal naval parity with the United States, the next greatest naval power, in capital ships – those over 10,000 tons, like battleships – and aircraft carriers. Finally, at the London naval conference in 1930, Anglo-American naval parity was extended to those vessels under 10,000 tons: submarines, destroyers, and, most important, cruisers. This change in British naval policy resulted from domestic political considerations. In the first place, the country emerged from the war under extreme financial pressure. To arm itself during the fighting and, in addition, help pay for its allies' war effort, the British Government had raised taxes, floated loans on the American money market, and forced the liquidation of a substantial portion of British overseas holdings.[7] Hence, the British had a sizeable debt to pay and the very difficult task of collecting from their former allies. Adding to this financial difficulty was the fact that prewar trading patterns had been disrupted, and this weakened trade. In the second place, something in the order of two million British soldiers were demobilized within a year or so of the end of the war, sending up the rate of unemployment at the very moment when the economy constricted because of lack of demand.[8] Already weakened by a total war for four years, the British economy would have to undergo a shift from wartime to peacetime production. This would take time, and the new Government would have to respond with social spending to help the new army of unemployed.

Suffusing all of this was a feeling within the country that 'the war to end all wars' had been fought. Why should the Government spend money on arms, even naval arms? The German Navy lay at the bottom of Scapa Flow, thus the main threat to British naval preeminence was no longer there. Coupled with this was the emergence of a vocal and organized dissent over the methods and means by which the British and other great powers pursued external policies. Even as the war began in 1914, a ginger group called the Union for Democratic Contol was arguing that the war was the result of secret diplomacy and a reliance by the Government on armed strength to support its foreign policy.[9] Verdun, the Somme, Paschendaele, and the other major battles of the war seemed only to confirm these beliefs as hundreds of thousands of young British soldiers perished in the mud of Flanders. As well, the terror of unrestricted submarine attack on shipping on the high seas, like that on the *Lusitania* in 1915, added to the revulsion against war. By 1918 the British people, including many political leaders on both the government and opposition benches, were tired of war.[10]

In the postwar period, and throughout the 1920s, very powerful domestic non-governmental organizations dedicated themselves to forcing successive British governments to reduce arms expenditures.[11] Many of the groups looked to the new League of Nations as the means to enforce international peace and security. Britain no longer had to defend its own national interests and preserve international peace unilaterally. Neither did the French, the Poles, the Italians, or anyone else. They could rely on 'collective security'. Therefore, states could reduce arms because, in moments of crisis, they could unite and still have more collective military and naval power than a transgressor of peace. In Britain, groups like the League of Nations Union, the remnants of the Union for Democratic Control, and other 'troublemakers' were successful in convincing a large segment of the British public that a significant reduction of arms was the order of the day. These issues – national financial strain, substantial unemployment, and the rise of national organizations that dissented from the traditional methods of foreign policy and armed support for this policy

– converged after 1918 in the humus of British politics. Successive British governments had therefore to contend with these domestic pressures in formulating and carrying out diplomatic and naval policies.

However, this was not just a matter of having 'troublemakers' amongst public opinion and within political minorities. In the pre-1914 period, following the formation of the Liberal Government in December 1905 – a Government which in various forms lasted until December 1916 – a sizeable number of dissenters suddenly found themselves in a position of influence on the Government backbenches and amongst junior positions in the Cabinet. These men, clustering around the radical Liberal, David Lloyd George, the President of the Board of Trade in the new Government and one of the most vocal and effective critics of the established course of foreign and defence policy within the country, were suddenly in a position to influence policy in a meaningful way. Until this time, the bipartisan nature of British foreign policy had rarely been subjected to sustained criticism from within the Government caucus that could deflect it in a telling way from its accepted course. As even William Gladstone, the Liberal Party leader and a staunch critic of the Conservative foreign policy in the late 1870s, told his Foreign Secretary soon after they took office in 1880, 'sensible of the expediency of maintaining as far as might be a continuity in Foreign Policy, we sought for a ground of action which might be possible for both political parties'.[12] However, the rise to positions of influence by Lloyd George and others like him 25 years later changed this. Rising to national prominence during the catharsis of the Boer War, when Lloyd George even travelled to Birmingham, the political satrap of Joseph Chamberlain, the Colonial Secretary, to attack publicly the foreign and imperial policies of the Conservative Government of the day, the criticisms of these men did not subside in the interim between the end of the South African war and the advent of the Liberal Party to national office. Although their criticisms after 1905 were eventually blunted by the perceived German threat to British interests in the years leading to the July crisis of 1914 – and, after April 1908, Lloyd George's position as leader of the radical wing of the Liberal Party was enhanced when he became Chancellor of the Exchequer – this element of having dissenting opinions within the Government did not abate.

After the armistice of 1918, this new era in making foreign and defence policy was marked by dissent becoming a partisan political issue. The great Liberal Party had broken up during the war. With the help of the conservative Unionist Party in December 1916, Lloyd George had overthrown the Liberal Prime Minister, Herbert Asquith, in an attempt to inject vitality into Britain's apparently stumbling war effort in the wake of the Somme. This was successful in that the British prosecution of the war became more efficient,[13] but anti-Lloyd George Liberals left the Government to sit in opposition. A few even joined the Labour Party, then steadily capturing the left in the British political spectrum. This proved to be significant in that the Labour Party adopted the dissenting views on foreign and naval policy in the postwar period completely and almost without question. By 1918, and, indeed, throughout the 1920s, it was the Labour Party which held itself to be the political expression of a new approach to the conduct of British external policy. Showing typical social democratic self-righteousness, Labour Party leaders and their supporters attacked the foreign and naval policies of their political adversaries on the right and in the middle as misguided or malevolent – or both.[14] Once the Unionist Party had shorn itself of Lloyd George and his little band of loyal Liberals in 1922, and re-adopted its old name, the Conservative Party, the domestic battle-lines over shaping British foreign and naval policy were drawn clearly.

The difficulty for British diplomatists and sailors in the 1920s was that the traditional goals of British external policy – preserving the general European balance of power and defending the Empire – had not changed. However, with financial problems, the emergence of strong dissent over diplomacy and arms procurement, and the Labour Party replacing the Liberals on the left, the domestic situation had changed. The problem for the predominantly Conservative governments of the period 1918 to 1929 – and Lloyd George's Liberal–Unionist coalition, which lasted until October 1922, can be considered 'conservative' since the Unionists had two-thirds of the Government's seats in the Commons – was to juggle Britain's external requirements with its domestic reality. By 1919 Britain was overextended in the world. Revolutions in 1917 and 1918 had toppled the monarchical regimes in Germany, Austria-Hungary, and Russia, introducing economic, political, and social instability into European affairs, along with the bacillus of bolshevism. Added to this was the French bacillus. Blinded by victory into pursuing perhaps the most vengeful policies towards a defeated enemy since Tamerlane at Aleppo and Damascus, France threatened to disrupt the balance of power to the detriment of British interests. British diplomatists had to work hard to preserve some equilibrium between France and Germany, strengthening the latter without unduly antagonizing the former.[15]

Most important of all, the United States was beginning to challenge Britain as the only truly global power. The United States had clearly emerged from the war as the leading financial power in the world. Although the American Senate rejected the Treaty of Versailles in 1919 and, in doing so, isolated their country from the political affairs of Europe and the wider world, a wide range of American leaders, especially within the Republican Party, which captured the Presidency and both houses of Congress in the 1920 elections, determined to involve the United States economically wherever possible around the globe.[16] This involved collecting war debts owed Americans by their former allies, protecting established markets as well as those won from the British during the war, and seeking new ones in other places in the world. The basis of this American economic involvement in the world was to be a strong navy.[17] It was the rise of American navalism in the 1920s, and the British response to it, conditioned by domestic political considerations, that produced the fundamental change in British naval policy by the time of the London naval conference in 1930 – formal naval parity with another power.

The crucial change in British naval policy occurred through a series of events between mid-1927 and early 1930, that is, from the abortive Coolidge conference of 1927 to the successful London naval conference of 1930. Earlier in the decade, in 1920, the Admiralty's admission that 'the utmost we can hope for in the near future is to possess a fleet as large as that of any other single power'[18] was not made public. There was no need to state this to the world and take the chance that potential enemies might exploit the situation to the Royal Navy's disadvantage. Throughout 1921 the financial situation in the country did not improve, as levels of unemployment remained high and problems in British industry militated against a quick economic recovery from the war. Lloyd George's coalition Government recognized that some sort of retrenchment had to be implemented to alleviate the situation and divert more money to help the economically disadvantaged and revitalize industry.[19] When the chance to effect economies in arms spending suddenly presented itself in late 1921 with the American-sponsored Washington Conference, Lloyd George's Government participated willingly.[20] At Washington, the principal naval powers – Britain, the United States, Japan, France, and Italy – agreed to limit the size and numbers of their capital ships within a tonnage ratio of, respectively, 5:5:3:1.75:1.75.[21] The delegates attempted to restrict cruisers as well, but this failed for a variety of reasons. All the Washington treaty did was to limit cruisers to a 10,000 ton maximum, with guns not exceeding eight inches.

Limiting capital ships at Washington meant in essence limiting the battle fleets of the powers. The financial savings from this, especially for Britain, benefited successive governments in the 1920s.[22] But it was over cruisers that Anglo-American antagonism developed in the 1920s, and it was over the cruiser question that the crucial naval arms limitation debate was conducted in Britain, a debate involving the Cabinet, civil service advisers in the Admiralty, Foreign Office, and Treasury, the Labour Party, and various extra-parliamentary organizations. Cruisers were at once the chief naval weapon for attacking and for defending maritime lines of communication. During the war, the British had used the Royal Navy's cruisers to blockade successfully the central powers.[23] American trade with the central powers had suffered, as had the *amour-propre* of the United States as a great power, in the period until April 1917, when the Americans joined the Allied coalition. In the post-Washington Conference period, the Americans indicated that they were prepared to build a cruiser fleet to enforce their brand of 'the freedom of the seas' against any future application of British blockade.[24] The American assumption was that somehow the United States would always thereafter be neutral. The British were more realistic. As the leading maritime member of the League of Nations, Britain might at some time have to help enforce economic sanctions at sea against any League-defined transgressor of peace. More importantly, should they in future be involved in a war, the British would also need cruisers to protect seaborne lifelines both into the home islands and out to the Empire and foreign markets; by the same token, as had happened between 1914 and 1918, cruisers would also be necessary to blockade the enemy. Therefore, British foreign and naval policies had to respond to this American naval challenge. Given relative United States economic strength after 1918, American navalism was far more dangerous to Britain than that which suffused German foreign policy before 1914.

In November 1924 a Conservative Government under Sir Stanley Baldwin came to power. It was this ministry, lasting until June 1929, which resolved the intra-governmental debate over cruisers; when its Labour successor took office and then formalized complete Anglo-American naval parity at London in 1930, Labour followed a blueprint laid out by the successful resolution of the domestic debate during Baldwin's Government. The protagonists in this debate were many and varied, but six men were crucial to its conduct. Sir William Bridgeman, the First Lord of the Admiralty, and Sir Maurice Hankey, the Secretary to both the Cabinet and the Committee of Imperial Defence, advocated the navalist point of view. J. Ramsay MacDonald, the leader of the Labour Party and of the official opposition until 1929 and the Prime Minister thereafter, was the focus of left-wing dissent. He was joined at a crucial moment by Robert, Viscount Cecil of Chelwood, a renegade Tory who not only resigned from Baldwin's Cabinet in protest over the failure of the Coolidge conference in August 1927 but was throughout a leading light in the powerful extra-parliamentary League of Nations Union. Sir Austen Chamberlain, Baldwin's Foreign Secretary, had the moderate voice. Hovering above the fray was Sir Winston Churchill, the Chancellor of the Exchequer, who, in an unceasing attempt to achieve political kudos and thereby capture the premiership, was extending the dark hand of the Treasury into every facet of Government expenditure.

The American President, Calvin Coolidge, called for a new naval conference in the summer of 1927 to extend the Washington treaty ratios for capital ships to lesser craft: submarines, destroyers, cruisers, and auxiliary vessels such as mine-sweepers.[25] Although Coolidge's ostensible reason for calling the conference was to reduce arms spending by his Administration, he needed some major foreign policy coup to ensure the electoral success of the Republican Party for the scheduled 1928 presidential-congressional elections; in the November 1926 mid-term elections, the Republicans had suffered at the polls and had had their Senate majority almost wiped out. Baldwin's Government agreed to attend the conference, as did the Japanese. However, the French and Italians refused to participate because of mutual mistrust and suspicion over naval power in the Mediterranean. At Geneva, where the conference met, the three powers agreed on limiting destroyers, submarines, and auxiliary vessels.[26] Just as at Washington six years before, cruisers proved to be the sticking point. The British said they needed 70 cruisers – about 500,000 tons in aggregate – whilst the Americans claimed they needed 50 cruisers – about 400,000 tons in aggregate.[27] The central point of dispute was whether parity in cruisers should be at a figure convenient to Britain or to the United States. Cecil and Bridgeman represented Britain at Geneva and, when the conference broke up over an inability by the two home governments to compromise, Cecil left the Government, blaming his colleagues for the failure to reach an agreement.[28]

Cecil's resignation precipitated a vituperative domestic debate in Britain over naval arms limitation and, simultaneously, worsened Anglo-American relations.[29] Americans interpreted his resignation as proof that their policies had been correct at Geneva and hence, until the preparations for the 1930 London naval conference began two years later, Anglo-American relations were subjected to great strain. However, it was within Britain that the crucial debate about British naval limitation policy occurred, a debate which touched on the foreign and defence policies which those in power were executing to defend Britain's external position. The navalists led by Bridgeman and Hankey were adamant that 70 cruisers represented the minimum necessary to protect sea routes and blockade the enemy in time of war. The Admiralty Plans Division had come to this conclusion prior to the Coolidge conference, and this served as the basis of British proposals.[30] Bridgeman made public statements in November 1927 indicating that Britain remained unopposed to the United States building a cruiser fleet equal to that of Britain – this at the same time when, under pressure from Churchill to effect retrenchment, he announced that Britain would build just one of three projected cruisers in that year's building programme.[31] Nonetheless, the Baldwin Government had no intention of formalizing such an arrangement, since unforeseen events might necessitate increased cruiser construction and Britain did not want its hands tied.

This enraged the Labour Party, especially MacDonald, who put Anglo-American accord above all else, but he was also in the midst of preparing the Labour Party for the next general election, which might come in late 1928 or early 1929. By taking a firm line against the Conservatives over the need for good relations between Britain and the United States, as well as for reductions in arms spending, the savings from which could be redirected towards improving the social and economic conditions of the country, Labour's electoral appeal would be decidedly enhanced. Accordingly, in early November 1927, MacDonald introduced a motion of censure in the Commons which deplored:

> the lack of preparation by the Government and the military character of the British delegation which seriously contributed to the failure of the recent naval conference at Geneva, the slow progress made by the League of Nations Preparatory Commission [another arms limitation effort then trying to affect universal limitation] . . . and the refusal of the Government to accept the principle of arbitration and promote a scheme of international security guaranteed by the League of Nations.[32]

Outside Parliament, MacDonald charged Baldwin's Government with conducting the British case at Geneva with 'war methods rather than peace methods'.[33] These kinds of attack continued for almost two years, until the general election of May 1929, allowing MacDonald and the Labour Party to carve for themselves a position within the domestic political milieu in which they seemed to hold a fundamentally different view of foreign and defence policy from that held by the Conservatives.

MacDonald and his party were aided in their efforts by Cecil. Cecil was a prominent member of the League of Nations Union; indeed, he had taken a pivotal role as a member of the British delegation at the Paris Peace Conference in 1919 to help create the League.[34] Established to promote the League ideal in Britain, the Union was ostensibly non-partisan, but its leaders gradually became critics of the Baldwin Government's foreign policy after 1924 because Chamberlain and other ministers did not see the international organization as a diplomatic panacea for meeting every international crisis. Moreover, when Baldwin formed his ministry in November 1924, Chamberlain had bested Cecil in an intra-Cabinet dispute over control of British League policy – before this, the Foreign Secretary did not always determine this critical element of post-1919 external policy, which caused Britain to speak at times with two contradictory diplomatic voices.[35] When Cecil resigned from the Cabinet, the Union, especially Gilbert Murray, its chairman and Cecil's friend, took a partisan stance against the Conservatives. This angered Chamberlain, then seeking a way to keep Anglo-American relations running smoothly externally whilst, within the country, finding a compromise between the navalists and the 'troublemakers'.[36] Although the Union did not become an overt ally of the Labour Party in the 1929 election, its position on a range of foreign and naval policy issues touching British official attitudes towards the League put it squarely in the dissenters' camp.

However, it was Cecil who served to unite extra-parliamentary opposition to Conservative foreign and naval policy. From his seat in the Lords, he spoke out continuously against his former colleagues about the high cost of naval spending, as well as on a variety of domestic issues including the need for a variety of reformist social and political policies.[37] By the autumn of 1928, Cecil was attacking the Baldwin ministry for pursuing arms limitation and not disarmament.[38] At the same time, Philip Noel Baker, a friend and acolyte of Cecil, and an advocate of complete and universal disarmament, was also advising MacDonald on matters of foreign and defence policy.[39] Whilst MacDonald avoided the stridency of Cecil and Noel Baker in his public pronouncements – he dared not attack the hallowed institution of the Royal Navy – he laid great stress on the need for Anglo-American harmony; if this meant reducing British cruiser strength to appease the Americans, then it was worth the price.[40] By early 1929, just before the election campaign got under way, the dissenters had established a firm position over the cruiser question, and they had the Labour Party on their side.

During this whole process, Churchill tried to pursue policies at the Treasury to enhance his chances of succeeding Baldwin as leader of the Conservative Party. When he became Chancellor of the Exchequer in 1924, he had commented privately about the necessity of not endangering domestic programmes by building 'silly little

cruisers'[41] – a fascinating opinion from a man who had served as First
Lord of the Admiralty from 1911 to 1915. His purpose was to avoid
giving the 'socialists' an opportunity to attack the domestic record of
the Conservative Government, but in 1927, during the Coolidge
conference, Churchill had shown that he was as adamant as
Bridgeman and the navalists in maintaining British maritime supremacy, this despite the fact that he had almost broken the Cabinet in
1925 by seeking to limit cruiser construction in his first budget.[42] In
fact, in the summer of 1927, Churchill appeared as a dedicated
hardliner who showed definite anti-American tendencies. He argued
that the Americans were out to secure naval supremacy on the cheap
by forcing Britain to accept cruiser parity at a low level. So, to
preserve the Royal Navy's preeminence, this had to be resisted at all
costs. He emphasized this to the Cabinet in late July:

> No doubt it is quite right in the interests of peace to go on
> talking about war with the United States being 'unthinkable'.
> Everyone knows that this is not true. However foolish and
> disastrous such a war would be, it is in fact, the only basis upon
> which the Naval discussions at Geneva are proceeding. . . .
> Evidently on the basis of American Naval superiority speciously
> disguised as parity immense dangers overhang the future of the
> world.[43]

In the final phase of the conference, Churchill played a key role in
the Cabinets that forced Bridgeman and Cecil to take the hardest line
possible against the Americans.[44] His purpose was to enhance his
prestige both in the Cabinet and amongst the Conservative Party
generally, something not lost on Cecil, who, when he resigned, laid
the blame for the failure of the conference on Churchill.[45] However,
despite this vocal defence of Royal Navy paramountcy, Churchill
again went on to enforce Treasury parsimony in naval spending after
the summer of 1927. This led to his success in November in having
just one of the three projected cruisers built. In this way, Churchill
had come to advocate two paradoxical policies simultaneously: the
need for British maritime supremacy and a practical expression of
naval arms retrenchment by the Government. As the general election
loomed in late 1928 and early 1929, Churchill did all possible to

dampen public talk about naval expenditures by the Government.[46] In essence, although he did not wish it, Churchill had become an ally of the Labour Party in the run-up to the 1929 election because of his erratic tendencies.

It was in this context that Chamberlain sought to maintain a workable Anglo-American relationship whilst cooling the domestic debate over arms limitation. Unlike British navalists, Chamberlain and the Foreign Office reckoned that if the United States decided to build a fleet equal to or exceeding that of Britain, it alone of the great powers had the economic resources and industrial capacity to do so.[47] If the United States decided to build because of a perceived British threat, then Britain would be forced to build as well to maintain the 'one-power standard'. Chamberlain and his advisers based their arguments on the damage an Anglo-American naval race could do to Britain's external position – concerned with foreign policy, the Foreign Office was less inclined to weigh heavily domestic repercussions when fashioning diplomatic strategies; nonetheless, the ability of Britain to shift enough resources into a major building programme, coupled with the political price to be paid domestically, had a prominent place in Foreign Office arguments brought before the Cabinet. Accordingly, the Foreign Office accepted that Britain had a need for a minimum number of cruisers to protect its maritime lines of communication and support the nation's foreign policy. If people like Cecil and Noel Baker and their fellow travellers in the Labour Party had their way, Britain's naval strength would be diminished and the Royal Navy's ability to underscore foreign policy with strength hampered. Britain would slip from the rank of great powers, the Empire would certainly begin to disintegrate, and the domestic implications of this would be too much to contemplate. Such a decline would not happen overnight, but allowing the Royal Navy to be overtaken in strength by the naval forces of another power would certainly be the first step by Britain down the slippery slope to second or third rank status.

Therefore, Chamberlain and the Foreign Office suggested that the Baldwin Government consider some sort of agreement with the Americans over the twisted questions of maritime belligerent rights and the freedom of the seas. This, after all, was the nub of the cruiser debate. Chamberlain did not say that Britain should surrender its traditional rights of blockade, which had worked with spectacular success during the war; he only said that they should be investigated.[48] By March 1929, two months before the general election, Chamberlain had overcome the opposition of naval hardliners in the Cabinet, including the mercurial Churchill, to investigate this possibility with the Americans.[49] The key to such an investigation would be a visit by a high level British official to the United States after the election. Both Baldwin and Chamberlain considered the matter of such a visit in the twilight of the Conservative Government, and both were prepared to travel to the United States.[50] The essential point in this was to prevent a naval arms race between Britain and the United States, something which, for Chamberlain, could have an unfavourable impact on Britain both externally and internally.

However, the Labour Party won the election. MacDonald took personal control of Anglo-American relations and moved to resolve the naval question himself. In doing this, he followed essentially the blueprint that had been devised by Chamberlain.[51] MacDonald travelled to the United States in October 1929, meeting there with the new President, Herbert Hoover. They decided that an agreement on maritime belligerent rights and the freedom of the seas was unnecessary. Now, just as much as the British, the Americans did not want their hands tied over blockade in the future, nor did they want an expensive naval arms race. The crucial point here is that MacDonald could not conduct his policies in late 1929 and early 1930 in a political vacuum. He had restricted himself domestically by the position he had taken when appealing for votes in the two difficult years after the Coolidge conference. He had to balance Britain's external requirements with the domestic political support he received from his party, dissenters like Cecil, and groups like the League of Nations Union.

Of course, Labour did not have a fundamentally different external policy once it took office in 1929. The practicability of a 'social democratic' diplomacy proved to be a mirage when MacDonald and his senior colleagues actually held responsibility for protecting Britain's external interests, interests which were permanent and fixed: maintaining the balance of power in Europe, conducting imperial defence, and planning to protect seaborne trade in the event of some international crisis. In democratic countries like Britain, an opposition party must articulate policies which castigate those of the Government and show simultaneously a more enlightened approach to problem solving. This held for the foreign and defence policy pronouncements of MacDonald and the Labour Party issued between August 1927 and May 1929 – although their enlightenment is debatable. In the end foreign policy issues did not much influence the 1929 general election;[52] still, they probably added to the electoral appeal of Labour. That Labour ideas had to be modified after May 1929 showed the need of politicians when in opposition to appeal for votes and, once entrenched in office, make changes to proposed policy so that it could conform to the real situation.[53] Put more cynically, it showed the necessity of promising anything to gain power and, when in office, deviating from those promises when it was expedient to do so by appealing to the reality of practical politics.

Despite what some partisan Labour historians contend,[54] MacDonald's advent to power did not provide for a new diplomacy. MacDonald received and accepted with little question the same advice, from the same Foreign Office and diplomatic advisers at Downing Street, that had been tendered to Baldwin and Chamberlain – from Sir Robert Vansittart, the head of the Foreign Office American Department from 1924 to 1928 and afterwards the Principal Private Secretary in the Prime Minister's Office, and Sir Robert Craigie, Vansittart's successor in the American Department.[55] When he travelled to the United States to meet Hoover in the autumn of 1929, Vansittart and Craigie accompanied him – the same men who had advised his Conservative predecessors in formulating and executing the policy he had attacked after the failure of the Coolidge conference.[56] Significantly, full-blown navalists like Hankey and troublemakers like Cecil, the latter of whom had even been given a place at the Foreign Office after June 1929 to help make League policy as a reward for turning on his Conservative colleagues, remained at London. Had Baldwin or Chamberlain gone to meet Hoover, they certainly would have taken Vansittart and Craigie. Once in the United States, MacDonald made soothing speeches to obviate the hard feelings which had grown up amongst Americans during the last year or so of the Coolidge Administration.[57] Without doubt, Baldwin or Chamberlain would have done the same, the more so as the Foreign Office saw in the months prior to the 1929 general election that Hoover's taking of the White House the previous autumn had altered profoundly the mood of domestic American politics towards Britain and its naval policies.[58]

What was important in MacDonald's policies of naval arms limitation after May 1929 centred on the new Prime Minister's constituency within Britain. He genuflected to a certain degree to those supporting him both inside and outside Parliament. This meant an effort to secure formal naval parity as a means of resolving the cruiser controversy. It did not only constitute good politics, but was fundamental to inhabiting the ideological niche which Labour had carved for itself to the left of the Conservatives. Here arose the basic difference in the naval arms limitation policies of the two principal parties within Britain, differences which derived from domestic political considerations. If Baldwin and Chamberlain had approached the Americans, they, too, would have had to keep a wary eye on their domestic support, but where MacDonald and Labour were prepared to formalize Anglo-American naval parity as a means of effecting naval arms limitation – even if this meant doing so at a figure below the 70 cruiser level – Baldwin, Chamberlain, and the Conservatives would have bargained harder. They would have had to avoid antagonizing Bridgeman, Churchill, and those like them – the stance taken at the Coolidge conference and in the two years following had shown this. As a consequence, the goal of limiting naval arms did not divide the parties. Division stemmed from how this was to be arranged and, in turn, this arose almost entirely from the sorts of domestic support underpinning the two parties. The primacy of domestic political considerations was the telling factor.

Therefore, at the London naval conference Britain formalized complete naval parity with the Americans in a treaty.[59] MacDonald managed to secure 50,000 cruiser tons more than were allotted to the United States, an advantage of about eight vessels for the Royal Navy, but the number of cruisers allowed Britain was pegged at 50, 20 less than that sought by the Baldwin Government at Geneva in 1927. In the event that war broke out, there would now be restraints on the conduct of British naval operations, the basis of British global power, which had never before existed. A new age was dawning in British diplomatic and naval history, and it was the result of the growing strength of the dissenting view about foreign policy, this as a function of domestic political manoeuvring which had begun in a major way after the end of the Great War.

III

The story of how British politicians in the 1920s coped with naval arms limitation shows much about how domestic politics imposes itself on the fighting capacity of a nation. In the first place, it is easy when attempting to score political points at home to attack foreign and defence policy. This is especially so when the dissenters are not responsible for those policies. Indeed, for ambitious politicians on the make, especially those warming opposition benches, sniping at the men responsible for policy is easy. But it is also interesting to see that once the dissenters were in power and responsible for guiding the nation, they sought to be prudent and as cognizant of Britain's need for naval strength as the men they replaced. MacDonald after June 1929 shows this clearly.

The difficulty in suddenly turning from 'troublemaking' to managing the country's external affairs was that the attacks on those in power were designed to achieve domestic political advantage. Domestic groups who supported the dissent expected there to be some change in policy once the critics were in office. Cecil, Noel Baker, and others like them expected this after Labour's success in 1929; so, too, did the bulk of the Labour Party. To protect his position in both the country and the party, the focus of which was really the domestic reconstruction of Britain, limitations were put on MacDonald's handling of the negotiations with the Americans. He might follow Chamberlain's blueprint, but his domestic support restrained his bargaining power. The result was that Royal Navy cruiser strength was established at a level below 70 cruisers by the London naval treaty. The diplomatic impact of this was a relative weakening of Britain's bargaining power in international affairs. The threat of naval intervention in support of foreign policy, even in support of the League of Nations, was reduced significantly by the formal admission of the 'one-power standard'.[60] By 1930 Britain's fighting capacity had been affected by domestic political considerations, which restrained to a degree Britain's ability to go to war successfully to defend its national interests.

Lastly, there emerged amongst the dissenters, especially in the 1930s, the idea that those who desired substantial naval strength to maintain British interests abroad were somehow blinkered warmongers. This resulted from the change in attitude towards foreign policy and national armed strength that emerged out of the Great War. Cecil and others like him felt that weapons caused war, and that national defence had to be sublimated to a certain extent to the League. British naval arms limitation policy arose from within Britain, and it was the increasing ability of the dissenters to influence voters, and capture the foreign policy-making apparatus of the Labour Party, that affected the implementation of stronger foreign and naval policies. Moderate men like Chamberlain might seek a middle road; ambitious men like Churchill might waver from one extreme to the other; but it remains a fact that in the 1920s the vagaries of domestic politics in Britain largely shaped British naval arms limitation policy. For better or worse, they affected the fighting capacity of the nation.

Royal Military College of Canada

NOTES

I would like to thank the Social Sciences and Humanities Research Council of Canada, as well as the Academic Research programme of the Department of National Defence, Ottawa, for their assistance in the preparation of this paper.

1. It is not my intention to get involved in the *Innen-* versus *Aussenpolitik* debate now under way in the study of twentieth century British foreign policy. It seems clear that instead of policy being determined largely by universal unchanging internal or external factors, it is influenced at times by one or the other and, sometimes, by both. For two recent and contradictory views, cf. J. Joll, *The Origins of the First World War* (London, 1984); and K.M. Wilson, *The Policy of the Entente: Essays in the Determinants of British Foreign Policy, 1904–1914* (Cambridge, 1985).

2. For instance, cf. memorandum on 'Admiralty Policy. Replies to criticisms', Oct. 1906, Admiralty, CAB [Cabinet Archives, Public Record Office, Kew] 37/84/80; and memorandum [BR 39] on 'Belligerent Rights at Sea', 3 Aug. 1928, Admiralty, CAB 16/79.

3. This is not to say that such opinions held by politicians and others did not exist prior to 1914. See M. Ceadl, *Pacifism in Britain 1914–1945: The Defining of a Faith* (Oxford, 1980), 18–30; and N.W. Summerton, 'Dissenting Attitudes to Foreign Relations, Peace, and War, 1840–1890', *Journal of Ecclesiastical History*, 28(1977), 151–78.

4. For example, D. Carlton, *MacDonald versus Henderson. The Foreign Policy of the Second Labour Government* (London, 1970); 15–32; P.J. Noel Baker, *Disarmament*

    and the Coolidge Conference (London, 1927); A. Ponsonby, 'Disarmament by Example' (with discussion), *Journal of the Royal Institute of International Affairs*, 7(1928); pp. 225–40; and D. Richardson, *The Evolution of British Disarmament Policy in the 1920s* (London and New York, 1989).

  5. Richardson, *British Disarmament Policy* p. v.

  6. See J.R. Ferris, 'The Symbol and the Substance of Sea Power: Great Britain, the United States, and the One Power Standard, 1919–1921', in B.J.C. McKercher (ed.), *Anglo-American Relations in the 1920s: the struggle for supremacy* (London, 1990), pp. 55–80; and S. Roskill, *Naval Policy Between the Wars*, Vol.I: *The Period of Anglo-American Antagonism, 1919–1929* (London, 1968), pp. 218–19, 230–1.

  7. The work done by Kathleen Burk on Anglo-American economic relations during the First World War shows this; see her 'The Diplomacy of Finance: British Financial Missions to the United States, 1914–1918', *Historical Journal*, 22(1979), 405–16; 'The Mobilization of Anglo-American Finance During World War I', in N.F. Dreisziger (ed), *Mobilization for Total War* (Waterloo, Ontario, 1981), pp. 23–42; and *Britain, America and the Sinews of War, 1914–1918* (London, 1985). As Dr Burk's work deals with economic diplomacy and is not concerned with the wider questions of British economic policies and their integration with strategy and supply, something like K.E. Neilson, *Strategy and Supply. The Anglo-Russian Alliance 1914–1917* (London, 1984) should be examined as counterpoint.

  8. On the problems faced by the British government, led by David Lloyd George at this time, see Lord Beaverbrook, *The Decline and Fall of Lloyd George* (London, 1963); P.B. Johnson, *Land Fit for Heroes: The Planning of British Reconstruction, 1916–1919* (London, 1968); and K.O. Morgan, *Consensus and Disunity: The Lloyd George Coalition Government, 1918–1922* (London, 1979).

  9. E.D. Morel, the guiding light of the UDC, put it plainly in a pamphlet published within weeks of the war's outbreak: 'Potentates, diplomatists, and militarists made this war. They should not be allowed to rearrange unchecked and uncontrolled the terms of peace and to decide alone the conditions which will follow it': in Union for Democratic Control Pamphlet No.1 (E.D. Morel), *The Morrow of the War* (London, undated but September 1914), p. 14. Also see Pamphlet No. 3 (Bertrand Russell), *War – The Offspring of Fear* (London, undated); and Pamphlet No.4 (H.N. Brailsford), *The Origins of the Great War* (London, undated); and Pamphlet No. 14 (author unknown), *The Balance of Power* (London, undated). Cf. C.A. Cline, *E.D. Morel, 1873–1924. The Strategies of Protest* (Belfast, 1980); H. Swanwick, *Builders of Peace* (London, 1924); and M. Swartz, *The Union for Democratic Control in British Politics During the First World War* (Oxford, 1971). Of course, pre-1914 pressures had existed outside of Parliament and within which were critical of arms spending and secret diplomacy, but they were never really effective in influencing the course of policy.

10. For one telling example, see Churchill (minister of Munitions) memorandum for the Cabinet, 19 Nov. 1918, in M. Gilbert, *Winston S. Churchill*, Vol. IV: Part 1: *Documents, January 1917 – June 1919* (London, 1977), pp. 417–21.

11. Ceadl, *Pacifism in Britain* pp. 31–86.

12. 'Memorandum of conversation with Granville', 23 Sept. 1880, quoted in A. Ramm (ed), *The Political Correspondence of Mr. Gladstone and Lord Granville 1876–86*, Vol.I (Oxford, 1962), p. 181.

13. On Lloyd George becoming prime minister, see P. Lowe, 'The Rise to the Premiership, 1914–1916', in A.J.P. Taylor, *Lloyd George: Twelve Essays* (London, 1971), pp. 95–131; and P. Rowland, *Lloyd George* (London, 1975), pp. 350–77. On more effective war effort, see J. Ehrman, 'Lloyd George and Churchill as War Ministers', *Transactions of the Royal Historical Society*, 5th Series, 11(1961); K.O. Morgan, 'Lloyd George's Premiership: A Study in Prime Ministerial Government', *Historical*

Journal, 13(1970), pp. 130–57; and J. Turner, 'Cabinets, Committees, and Secretariats: the Higher Direction of the War', in K.M. Burk (ed), *War and the State: the transformation of the British Government 1914–1919* (London, 1982); pp. 57–83.

14. For example, A. Henderson, *Labour and Foreign Affairs* (London, 1922); J.R. MacDonald, *The Foreign Policy of the Labour Party* (London, 1923); A. Ponsonby, *Now is the Time: An Appeal for Peace* (London, 1925); and Swanwick, *Builders of Peace*, especially the 'Forward' 7–18, written by Morel, who became a Labour MP.

15. See G. Bertram-Libal, *Aspekte der britischen Deutschlandpolitik, 1919–1922* (Göppingen, 1972); A. Cassels, 'Repairing the *Entente Cordiale* and the New Diplomacy', *Historical Journal*, 23(1980), pp. 133–53; S.E. Fritz, 'La Politique de la Ruhr and Lloyd Georgian Conference Diplomacy: The Tragedy of Anglo-French Relations, 1919–1923', *Proceedings of the Annual Meeting of the Western Society for French History*, 3(1975), pp. 566–82; S. Marks, 'Menage à Trois: The Negotiations for an Anglo-French-Belgian Alliance in 1922', *International History Review*, 4(1982), pp. 524–52; A. Orde, *Great Britain and International Security, 1920–1926* (London, 1977); and K. von Zwehl, *Die Deutschlandpolitik Englands von 1922 bis 1924 unter besonderer Berücksichtigung der Reparationen und Sanktionen* (Augsburg, 1974).

16. Cf. J. Brandes, *Herbert Hoover and Economic Diplomacy: Department of Commerce Policy, 1921–1928* (Pittsburgh, 1962); F.C. Costigliola, 'Anglo-American Financial Rivalry in the 1920s', *Journal of Economic History*, 37 (1977), pp. 911–34; E.W. Hawley, 'Herbert Hoover, the Commerce Department Secretariat, and the Vision of an 'Associated State', 1921–1928, *Journal of American History* 61(1974–1975), pp. 116–40; M.J. Hogan, *Informal Entente: the private structure of cooperation in Anglo-American economic diplomacy 1918–1928* (Columbia, MO, 1977); and C.P. Parrini, *Heir to Empire: United States Economic Diplomacy, 1916–1923* (Pittsburgh, 1969).

17. W.H. Bickel, *Die Anglo-Amerikanische Beziehungen 1927–1930 im Licht der Flottenfrage* (Zurich, 1970); M.G. Fry, *Illusions of Security: North Atlantic Diplomacy, 1918–1922* (Toronto, 1972); and S.W. Roskill, *Naval Policy Between the Wars*. Vol.I: *The Period of Anglo-American Antagonism 1919–1929* (London, 1968).

18. Roskill, *Naval Policy*, I, p. 21.

19. J. Campbell, *Lloyd George. The Goat in the Wilderness 1922–1931* (London, 1977), pp. 12–27; and Johnson, *Land Fit For Heroes*.

20. Roskill, *Naval Policy*, I, pp. 300–306. This should be read in conjunction with the brilliant, if iconoclastic, J.R. Ferris, *Men, Money and Diplomacy: The Evolution of British Strategic Policy, 1919–26* (Ithaca, NY, 1989), pp. 1–52, 92–110.

21. US Department of State, 'Conference on the Limitation of Armament, Washington, November 12, 1921 – February 6, 1922' (Washington, 1922); and Cmd.2029: 'Treaty Between the British Empire, France, Italy, Japan, and the USA for the Limitation of Naval Armaments (the Washington Treaty)'.

22. This can easily be seen in the white papers on naval spending tabled in the House of Commons between 1920 and 1929: Cmd.619, 1581, 1582, 1603, 1818, 2071, 2366, 2595, 2816, 3052, and 3283. Overall British defence expenditures, of which the Royal Navy consumed more than one-half, are telling: (by year in £millions) 1919, 692; 1920, 292: 1921, 189; 1922, 111; 1923, 105; 1924, 114; 1925, 119; 1926, 116; 1927, 117; 1928, 113; 1929, 113; and 1930, 110. These figures are from the table on 'Government Expenditure and Tariffs' in D. Butler and A. Sloman, *British Political Facts 1900–1975*, 4th edition (London, 1975), pp. 314–15. It is significant that Richardson, *British Disarmament Policy*, fails to look at the reduced spending in the 1920s.

23. A.C. Bell, *A History of the Blockade of Germany* (London, 1937); and M.C. Siney, *The Allied Blockade of Germany* (Ann Arbor, 1955).

24. This is discussed fully in B.J.C. McKercher, *The Second Baldwin Government and the United States, 1924–1929: Attitudes and Diplomacy* (Cambridge, 1984).
25. See Kellogg (US Secretary of State) telegram to Herrick (US Ambassador, Paris) (*mutatis mutandis* to London, Rome, and Tokyo), in US State Department, *Papers Relating to the Foreign Relations of the United States, 1927*, Vol. I (Washington, 1942), pp. 1–5.
26. On the Coolidge conference, with varying interpretations, see C. Hall, *Britain, America, and Arms Control, 1921–37* (London, 1987); McKercher, *Baldwin Government*, pp. 53–76; Richardson, *Disarmament Policy*, pp. 119–39; and Roskill, *Naval Policy*, 1, pp. 498–516.
27. The British and American proposals were outlined in the speeches given by the heads of delegation at the first plenary session of the conference on 20 June 1927; these proposals are summarized in A.J. Toynbee, *Survey of International Affairs 1927* (London, 1929), pp. 45–7. They were then modified in the subsequent negotiations: see the sources cited in note 26, above.
28. CAB 21/297 contains all of the papers relating to Cecil's resignation. For Cecil's letter to Baldwin, and the Prime Minister's reply, see *The Times*, 30 Aug. 1927. Cf. Cecil of Chelwood, *A Great Experiment* (London, 1941), pp. 187–90; and K. Middlemas and J. Barnes, *Baldwin. A Biography* (London, 1969), pp. 371–2. Importantly, Cecil's antipathy towards his colleagues was only partly formed by their disagreements about arms limitation policy; Cecil also disagreed strongly with them over trade union policy, House of Lords and poor law reform, and extension of the women's franchise; see Cecil to Irwin (Viceroy of India), 27 Oct. and 4 Nov. 1926, 2 March, 7 June and 29 Sept. 1927, all in Cecil Papers [British Library, London] Add MSS 51084; Cecil to Salisbury (his brother), 8 April and 31 July 1927, ibid. 51086: and Cecil to Baldwin, Baldwin Papers (the University Library, Cambridge), Vol. 130.
29. McKercher, *Baldwin Government*, pp. 79–80. Also interesting is Craigie (Foreign Office American Department) 'Memorandum . . . respecting the Effect on Public Opinion in the United States of Lord Robert Cecil's resignation from the Government', 11 Oct. 1927, FO (Foreign Office Archives, Public Record Office, Kew). 371/12035/6019/93. This memorandum was circulated to the Cabinet; see CP 244(27), CAB 24/188.
30. Egerton (director of plans, Admiralty) memorandum, 17 Feb 1927, ADM (Admiralty Archives, Public Record Office, Kew) 116/3371/02773; and Egerton, 'Memorandum on cruiser limitation', 17 March 1927, ADM 116/3371/02807.
31. Bridgeman statement of 16 Nov. 1927 in *Parliamentary Debates. Commons*, Series 5, Vol. 210, Col.1013. Also see Churchill to Bridgeman, 27 Oct. 1927, and Bridgeman to Churchill, 28 Oct. 1927, both Bridgeman Papers (Churchill College, Cambridge), BGMN 1.
32. This motion and the debate upon it can be found in *Parliamentary Debates. Commons*, 5th Series, Vol. 210, Cols. 2089–2198.
33. McKercher, *Baldwin Government*, p. 38.
34. Cecil's prominent part can be traced in G.W. Egerton, *Great Britain and the Creation of the League of Nations: Strategy, Politics, and International Organization, 1914–1919* (London, 1979), passim.
35. This incident is analysed in B.J.C. McKercher, 'Austen Chamberlain's Control of British Foreign Policy, 1924–1929', *International History Review*, 6(1984), pp. 575–6.
36. See Murray to Chamberlain, 6 and 13 Jan. 1928, and Chamberlain to Murray, 11 and 28 Jan. 1928, all Chamberlain MSS FO 800/262; and D. Wilson, *Gilbert Murray, O.M., 1866–1957* (Oxford, 1987). Cf. Chamberlain's very positive views on the utility of the League in his 'Rectoral Address at Glasgow University' [1927], in A. Chamberlain, *Peace In Our Time; Addresses on Europe and the Empire* (London,

1928); and Gilbert Murray, *The Ordeal of this Generation. The War, the League, and the Future* (London, 1929).

37. See note 28, above.

38. For instance, see his attack on the disarmament record of the second Baldwin Government in early November 1928 in *Parliamentary Debates. Lords*, Vol. 72, Cols. 84–91.

39. For instance, Noel Baker to MacDonald, 1 and 8 Nov. 1928, both MacDonald Papers (Public Record Office, Kew) PRO 30/69/5/39.

40. See MacDonald's speech of 13 Nov. 1928, in *Parliamentary Debates. Commons*, Series 5, Vol. 222, Cols. 755–64.

41. He actually told Tom Jones, Baldwin's Private Secretary: 'Of course I shall have to give some relief to the taxpayers to balance the measures of reform. If trade improves I can do that, but we cannot have a lot of silly little cruisers, which would be of no use anyway.' Quoted in diary entry, 28 Nov. 1924. Jones, in K. Middlemas (ed.), *Thomas Jones. Whitehall Diary*, Vol. I: *1916–1925* (London, 1969), p. 307.

42. See Roskill, *Naval Policy*, I, pp. 145–449, which shows parallels between Churchill's actions in the mid-1920s and those of Lloyd George, as Chancellor of the Exchequer, from 1908 to 1914. In this light, see Churchill memoranda, 29 Jan. and 7 Feb. 1925, CP 39(25) and CP 71(25), and Admiralty memorandum, 5 Feb. 1925, CP 67(25), all CAB 24/171.

43. Churchill memorandum, 20 July 1927, in Gilbert, *Churchill*, Vol. V, Pt. I: *Documents. The Exchequer Years 1922–1929*, pp. 1030–35.

44. See Cabinet Conclusion 43(27)1, and Appendices, CAB 23/55.

45. Cecil to Irwin, 29 Sept. 1927, Cecil Papers Add MSS 51084.

46. For instance, see his statement to the Cabinet, 7 Feb. 1929, and Churchill to Bridgeman, 13 Feb. 1929, both in Gilbert, *Churchill*, V, Pt. 1, *Documents*, pp. 1422–4.

47. Craigie memorandum, 12 Nov. 1928, which was circulated to the Cabinet as CP 344(28), CAB 24/198.

48. Chamberlain memorandum, 26 Oct. 1927, with enclosures, CP 258(27), CAB 24/189.

49. B.J.C. McKercher, 'Belligerent Rights in 1927–1929: Foreign Policy Versus Naval Policy in the Second Baldwin Government', *Historical Journal*, 29(1986), pp. 963–74.

50. On Baldwin indicating that he might go, see diary entry, 1 Nov. 1928, Jones, in Middlemas, *Whitehall Diary*, Vol. II, p. 155; and on Chamberlain, see Chamberlain minute, 13 Feb. 1929, FO 371/13541/1040/279.

51. See McKercher, *Second Baldwin Government*, pp. 176–93; and B.J.C. McKercher, 'From Enmity to Cooperation: the second Baldwin government and the improvement of Anglo-American relations, November 1928–June 1929', *Albion*, 24 (1992), pp. 64–87.

52. See P. Williamson, 'Safety First: Baldwin, the Conservative Party, and the 1929 General Election', *Historical Journal*, 25(1982), pp. 385–409.

53. British defence expenditures for the period of the Labour government are telling; (by year in £millions) 1930, 110; 1931, 107; 1932, 103. For the essentially conservative National Government which followed and lasted until the 1935 general election, and had to contend with the rise of Nazi Germany on the continent, the figures are: 1933, 107; 1934, 113; 1935, 136. From the table on 'Government Expenditure and Tariffs', in Butler and Sloman, *British Political Facts*, pp. 314–15.

54. For instance, Carlton, *MacDonald Versus Henderson*, and Richardson, *British Disarmament Policy*.

55. For example, Craigie memoranda on the 'Question of an Agreement with the United States in regard to Maritime Belligerent Rights', the 'Question of the conclusion of an Anglo-American Arbitration Treaty', and '. . . the Naval Disarmament Question', all 10 June 1929, all MacDonald Papers PRO 30/69/1/267.

56. See McKercher, *Baldwin Government*. pp. 23–5.

57. D. Marquand, *Ramsay MacDonald* (London, 1977), p. 508. Cf. the US *Congressional Record*, Vol. 71, Pt. 4, pp. 427–5.

58. For example, Craigie memorandum, 27 March 1929, with Craigie minute, 8 April 1929, FO 371/13511/2334/12; and Howard (British Ambassador, Washington) to Chamberlain, 12 April 1929, FO 371/13511/2799/12. On Howard getting the maximum publicity for MacDonald on his journey to the United States, which he had also planned for Baldwin, see B.J.C. McKercher, *Esme Howard. A Diplomatic Biography* (Cambridge, 1989), pp. 340–49 passim.

59. Roskill, *Naval Policy*, Vol. II: *The Period of Reluctant Rearmament, 1930–1939* (London, 1977), pp. 37–70. Also see Cmd. 3485: *Memorandum of the Position of HM Government at the London Naval Conference 1930*: and Cmd. 3556: *International Treaty for the Limitation of Naval Armaments (April 1930)*.

60. Relative British weakness after 1930 can be judged by the nature of the policies pursued by London during the Manchurian crisis of 1931–33; see C. Thorne, *The Limits of Foreign Policy: The West, the League and the Far Eastern Crisis of 1931–1933* (London, 1972).

The Pacific Dominions and the Washington Conference, 1921–22

MICHAEL GRAHAM FRY

Security policy has four faces – arms, money, diplomacy and politics. Policy communities consider, unavoidably and in relative terms, each of these factors:

1. weapons systems built, under construction and planned for each branch of the armed forces, construction facilities and the supply of skilled labour, base facilities, and technological change which determines obsolescence;
2. financial constraints as a reflection of economic performance, in the light of alternative claims on budgetary resources;
3. alliances and alignments, bilateral and multilateral, under, for example, League of Nations auspices or outside such frameworks, in being and contemplable, ranging over political and strategic issues, that is over cooperation and arms limitation, and invoking a puzzle that rests less on simplistic calculations about joining or opposing actual or potential threats to the balance of power and more on central paradoxes – that is, that current allies are actual or potential enemies and that aligning with the friends of one's enemies may be as sound a way to undermine hostility and dissolve vulnerability as joining the enemies of one's enemies; and
4. the inescapable need to legitimate policy, to explain and justify the

course of action being taken as leaders explore the politics of decision in pursuit of the 'stay in office' imperative.

Policy communities consider these factors and the relationships between them as they weigh the merits of defensive and offensive strategic doctrines, calculate trends in the strategic balance, toward and away from relative inferiority, judge the credibility of deterrents, the probability of war and the temptation of preemption, identify enemies by intentions and capabilities, and estimate the proportions, imminence, location and circumstances of and in which a threat might have to be faced when deterrence fails, and, ultimately, the extent and nature of risk, of policy failure and political disgrace. Members of policy communities attempt to reduce this complexity to one of its essences – the relationship of resources to commitments and of capabilities to goals.

The Context: March 1917 to August 1921

The period from March 1917 to August 1921 ended as it began, with inconclusive deliberations at an imperial conference in London that were part of an intermittent, hesitant and unresolved debate about imperial security. The documentary trail of that debate is well marked.[1] It took place after 1918 in the midst of physical and psychological demobilization in Britain and the Dominions. Every considered report, each forthcoming meeting, all the recommendations had been an excuse for inaction and delay; Canada, for example, avoided committing itself to a long-term naval defence policy in the face of British indecision.

Australian, Canadian and New Zealand leaders, Billy Hughes, Sir Robert Borden (and Arthur Meighen, his politically doomed successor from July 1920) and William Massey, were both direct participants in and distant observers of what had and had not been accomplished by the Lloyd George Government in its attempts to furnish an adequate measure of security for the Asia-Pacific region since 1918. The Dominion leaders, however devoted to the Empire, were not of one mind on several vital issues; quite the reverse, in fact. By August 1921, they were not, for their various reasons, especially reassured. Certain aspects of the debate had been satisfying, to some degree, if not uniformly so; other features of the debate had been deeply disturbing. Canada, for example, defined security in terms of Atlanticism, of a *pax Anglo-Americana*. Despite idle talk of Canada as a 'Belgium' or a hostage, its leaders were unmoved, justifiably, by the predicament that would emerge from that most improbable of occurrences, an Anglo-American war. Indeed, Anglo-American accord was seen as the only credible basis for a regime of arms limitation. Australia and New Zealand could not define security exclusively in that way; they were more exposed and felt more vulnerable. Yet all three Dominions consumed the security provided by others, producing for themselves only those increments of security that polities and finance permitted, and commitment and status demanded.

The varying degrees of comfort felt by the Dominion prime ministers came from several developments. First, they had taken on the role they preferred, or could settle for, in the formulation of imperial security policies, evading less attractive positions. As economic and security policies had evolved alongside institutional growth and constitutional development, members of the British Cabinet had emerged as the most influential, engaged and informed members of an imperial policy community, that was, however, distinctly less hierarchical.[2] The trend had gone so far that Borden and Meighen could claim a decisive voice in imperial issues involving the United States, and suggest that Canada was neither automatically nor necessarily bound by commitments entered into by Britain. However, influence brought commitment and put an end to egregious free-riding; it also made the Dominion premiers in part responsible for the indecision, for the mixed record.

Second, they appreciated Lloyd George's financial difficulties and political predicament – his problems were, after all, their own writ large. But because of these post-war difficulties, the Empire's centrality to the British scheme of things, its meaning in terms of status, prestige, power and resources to Britain, was never in question. The Empire was the measure of Britain's global standing. The Lloyd George Government was wedded to the preservation of necessary sea power and to the provision of imperial security; those commitments were not oratorical. The Dominions were emerging as autonomous, modest but strategically significant allies, proto-regional small powers, which could make contributions to the common good as well as to their own security.

Third, despite Lloyd George's European, Russian, Near Eastern, Irish and domestic agendas, the Asia-Pacific region had gained a certain salience. Indeed, it had an unenviable identity born of simmering tension and discernible threat, of incipient instability and predictable conflict. The regional security concerns of Australia and New Zealand were valid. The Empire was strategically vulnerable and could not be underinsured in the Pacific. Whether or not it had been underinsured in the First World War was a mildly controversial issue, relating naval capability to the wisdom of relying on Japan. Whether Britain could, by a combination of naval preparedness and diplomatic manoeuvre, meet its global responsibilities and obligations, in the face of economic and political constraints, remained to be seen. Choices would have to be made, but the Dominion prime ministers were sure that there would be no British abdication, diplomatic or naval, from Asia-Pacific. The Pacific, and the approaches to it, like home waters and the Mediterranean, were included in the designation of vital seas and oceans. The Empire's interests in Asia-Pacific were clearly defined and most decidedly central – to protect trade routes and communication lines, to remove any threat of aggression against Australia and New Zealand and their island territories, and to South-East Asia and India, and to ensure that China's economic development and political modernization would take place free of external domination if not penetration, so that British interests in China were safeguarded. The Dominion leaders were equally sure, though Borden, the Atlanticist, arrived at the conclusion by different routes than Hughes and Massey, that the Empire could not find security in the League of Nations.

The fourth consideration was bound up with a paradox. The Empire's naval rivals (and one could argue that in 1918 a naval race was already in progress) and its principal competitors in Asia – Japan and the United States – were also its ally and associate. Whether there was something to be gained from a war between Japan and the United States was not at all clear, but the Dominion prime ministers, Borden far less than Hughes and Massey, were comforted by the decision, or the unavoidable tendency, to treat both Japan and the United States as 'normal powers'. That meant that they would be judged principally by their record and current behaviour, and less out of an excess of either nostalgia or idealistic sentiment. Two consequences flowed from this realism – a consensus that Japan was a formidable and immediate threat to Asia-Pacific security; and an assumption that the United States was almost as improbable an ally as it was an initiator of an Anglo-American war.[3] This last assumption led to a further conclusion – Australia and New Zealand, unlike Canada, could not consume the security provided by the United States. From Britain's vantage point, rumours and hints of the Pacific dominions turning to the United States for protection could be judged for what they were.

Finally, the Dominion prime ministers, each in his way, were satisfied with the racial dimensions of the predicament, gathering in both political reassurance and psychological bolstering. The Empire was held up for all to see as a bridge between the races, as a promising, even remarkable, experiment in racial cooperation. At the same time, Atlanticists exchanged 'kith and kin' phrases, and Japan's international racial aspirations had been checked. Dominion discri-minatory immigration and tariff policies were left untouched, if not unchallenged, wrapped in claims to sovereignty and axioms about non-interference in the domestic affairs of any state. The racism of Australian officials was particularly virulent; the Japanese were 'too many, too clever and too yellow'.[4] But this official racism was not allowed to undermine the Australian–New Zealand case for the perpetuation of the Anglo-Japanese Alliance beyond 1921. Indeed, the Japanese threat to Australia and New Zealand made the alliance mandatory.

Yet much was left unanswered definitively. All participants in the imperial conference of 1921 had agreed that the Anglo-Japanese Alliance could not continue in its current form and could not be replaced by an alliance with the United States. They recognized, furthermore, that a tripartite arrangement, an exchange of notes or a declaration of common purpose, but not a triple alliance, was the preferable, indeed, ideal outcome.[5] But was the preferable attainable? The signs were mixed, from both Tokyo and Washington. And would a tripartite arrangement once negotiated be ratified, or would it be hostage to United States politics? Only Meighen seemed confident. Lloyd George, under pressure from Hughes, confirmed on 27 July, therefore, that if a tripartite arrangement could not be negotiated, the alliance, modified principally to accommodate obligations under the League of Nations and eliminating any reference to India, would remain in force until either ally gave one year's notice of termination. The alliance would not be terminated without cause, thereby avoiding further damage to Anglo-Japanese relations and the appearance of racism, of a closing of the ranks of the white races against Japan. Indeed, Japan would not be constrained in China merely to satisfy the United States. Meighen and Smuts had not triumphed; the security interests of Australia and New Zealand had not been discounted. The Washington Conference would demonstrate whether the United States would join in a tripartite pact.

Strategic questions also remained unsolved, some of them as fundamental as the size and composition of the Royal Navy relative to the Japanese and US fleets, in the light of technological change (the Jellicoe reports,[6] and the value of the capital ship in the face of the submarine and air power). Its deployment rested on the provision of base facilities and fuel reserves. The United States, with its 1916 and 1918 naval programmes and Wilson's stubborn refusal to concede naval supremacy to Britain, was by far the greater source of complexity and uncertainty; Japanese naval plans seemed predictable by comparison, and threatening, but political and financial constraints might yet intervene and dampen down or end the naval race.

On the assumption that Britain could neither, in a heady moment of Atlanticism, ignore the United States in setting its naval policy, nor, on Admiralty advice, achieve security through naval construction, confronting the United States with the current reality and potential of British sea power, the question became what judicious mixture of naval construction and diplomacy would eliminate, or substantially reduce, the threats to British maritime security and prestige.

What of the Pacific? Beyond the assumption that the Empire would not face a joint United States–Japanese challenge, little was determined. The technical expertise of the Admiralty was never challenged, but strategic wisdom did not necessarily coincide with political and financial realities when the effectiveness of Dominion contributions to general security, to burden-sharing, was at issue. The Admiralty preferred a unified, integrated imperial naval service, a single imperial fleet, dispersed in peace, concentrated in war, but under unified control and command in peace and war, enjoying the freedom of manoeuvre that an elaborate system of bases and oil storage facilities provided. The governing concepts were unity of strategic direction, mobility, conformity, coordination and interchangeability, applied appropriately to construction, training, materiel, intelligence and administration. Dominion navies would reach peak levels of efficiency in this strategic arrangement; the Empire would achieve security if the imperial fleet controlled the vital seas. This vision seemed preferable to the development of separate Dominion navies under local control in peacetime, meeting local needs and hoping to be able to unite promptly and efficiently in the event of war. Compromise lay in the Dominions constructing their own naval forces, preferably concentrating on light cruisers and submarines, developing their own construction and repair facilities, training their own personnel, and accepting surplus British ships in the form of integrated fleet units. Dominion naval forces would cooperate and coordinate with their British counterparts as fully as possible in peacetime, helping, for example, to police trade routes and communications lines. In time of war they would come under imperial control and direction.

The British Government and the Dominions had, of necessity, examined the relationship between naval policy and diplomacy, between providing security for the Pacific and perpetuating the Anglo-Japanese Alliance. Such reasoning took them back to the United States. Somewhere between Atlanticist dogma and Hughes's charge that the United States was both an irresponsible and a militarist power, and a threat to the Empire on both counts, lay grounds for pragmatism. US official and public opposition to the alliance was unrelenting, and would help determine whether the United States judged the one-power standard, Britain's declaratory naval policy, to be a provocative warning or a conciliatory gesture. Meighen argued that the alliance would continue to serve as an excuse and a reason for US naval construction, undermining prospects for an arms control agreement and for avoiding a naval race. Termination of the alliance, on the other hand, would lead to a naval arms limitation agreement. Meighen, therefore, dismissed as unsound the suggestion that Britain could force a naval agreement out of the United States as the price of terminating the alliance.

Japan, because of its record, most recently in the war, was both controversial and inscrutable. The Standing Defence Sub-Committee concluded in May 1921, as had the Admiralty in February 1920, that the loss of the alliance made naval preparedness unavoidable, and that lack of naval power made the alliance mandatory. So the threads of relationships were spun out – Britain could neither deter nor coerce Japan without being able to project naval power into the Pacific, and that predicament made an alliance with Japan all the more desirable; to maintain the alliance and to recreate British naval power in the Pacific would be provocative to the United States; to have neither would be to abdicate to the United States. As arms and diplomacy went hand-in-hand, where could a solution be found? Ideally, in avoiding a provocative choice between Japan and the United States while negotiating an arms limitation agreement that spelled security for the Pacific.

Such reasoning led to the Singapore strategy, proposed by the Lloyd George Government and agreed on at the Imperial Conference in 1921. There would be no new imperial Pacific fleet. The main British fleet would cruise home and Mediterranean waters. A start would be made to remedying the obsolescence of Britain's capital ships fleet. It would be dispatched to the Pacific at short notice in times of crisis or war. It would operate in the Pacific from a modern, fortified naval base, the costs of construction of which would, Britain hoped, be shared by the Dominions. Oil fuel reserves would be stored *en route* to Singapore, until fleet tankers were built. Britain would thus be able to deter or counter any threat in the Pacific and provide for the security of Australia and New Zealand. Here at least was a decision, but one that did little to alter strategic realities in the near future. Unanswered questions remained – how quickly could the Singapore naval base be built, and made invulnerable; was the strategy sound if it rested on the absence of a European naval rival; what if that rival joined Japan to challenge the Empire; what impact on Japanese and United States policy would the Singapore strategy have; did it provide a credible deterrent; and, if the deterrent failed, could the fleet operating from Singapore defeat the Japanese fleet, at an acceptable level of cost, or at all?

Thus, by August 1921, little had been settled to the satisfaction of the Pacific Dominions. The future of the Anglo-Japanese Alliance remained uncertain; whether there would be security in Asia-Pacific was unclear, and the problems associated with the emancipation of China had scarcely been addressed. Imperial security was still to be attained in a world Jan Smuts of South Africa saw as near bankrupt, financially, politically and morally, and quite mad. What lay ahead? An omnibus conference in Washington on naval arms limitation, Pacific security and China, and perhaps more[7] – without prior exploratory conversations à trois, let alone a preliminary conference. The Lloyd George Government had failed to establish an order of priority that would have given precedence to diplomacy, settling the future of the Anglo-Japanese Alliance before turning to naval issues. Charles Evans Hughes, the US Secretary of State, wanted to seize the moment on arms limitation. Yet the omens were not especially promising, despite the expectations of Auckland Geddes, the British Ambassador in Washington. All the issues that had undermined Anglo-American accord since 1919 – debts, Ireland, mandates, commercial rivalry, international cable systems – remained unresolved, and the summer of 1921 had secreted more irritants than balm. The Anglo-American relationship suffered from erratic diplomatic representation. Geddes blamed George Harvey, his counterpart in London, for the confusion and distrust. Harvey blamed Lloyd George, and Lord Curzon, the Foreign Secretary, was visibly upset at Hughes. There had been an unseemly scrambling for effect and initiative on both sides of the Atlantic, which did not augur well. At the same time, a certain distance had emerged in Anglo-Japanese relations, and a new dimension of doubt followed the assassination of the Japanese Prime Minister just four days before the conference opened. The Washington Conference was thus wrapped in uncertainty and unpredictability, while public expectations about the prospects for disarmament had risen markedly. The delegations faced formidable challenges.

Preparations for the Washington Conference, August–November 1921

On 13 August 1921 the United States formally invited Britain, but not the Dominions, to attend the Washington Conference. Britain accepted on 19 August and informed the Dominions on 12

September.[8] Dominion preparations, such as they were, followed, in anticipation of participating in the British Empire delegation. This aroused only Smuts, who pressed for separate invitations to the Dominions in October, despite the fact that South Africa had no discernible naval policy and declined to participate in the conference. No other Dominion leader thought it either appropriate to interject constitutional questions into the preparations for the conference or wise to challenge the United States over status, thus damaging the atmosphere at the eleventh hour. Lloyd George finessed Smuts as he finessed the problem. He agreed with Smuts in principle, but Dominion participation in the British Empire delegation would result in separate Dominion signatures on every agreement reached. All the Dominion representatives would have to sign in order for the Empire delegation to be committed to any agreement, and any Dominion representative could reserve assent on behalf of his government. Arthur Balfour, the chief British delegate, would sign for South Africa, as Milner had in the treaty of St Germaine. These arrangements would be explained to the Americans during the conference 'at some convenient moment'. Lloyd George concluded that Dominion status would not be injured by, in effect, ignoring the issue. Massey and Hughes agreed. The essential consideration was that the Empire should speak with one voice, 'with no uncertain sound'. Dissension within imperial ranks would be fatal. Lloyd George should not capitulate to Smuts.[9]

It seemed reasonable to assume that an Empire delegation not led by the British Prime Minister could not be manned by Dominion premiers, but Lloyd George pressed Massey and Hughes to attend. If they did not, he wondered whether one delegate might represent both Australia and New Zealand, 'as your standpoints are identical'. Lloyd George had in mind Lord Novar, experienced in Australian affairs and understanding the United States. Massey should consult Hughes. Hughes agreed that identical interests suggested a single representative, who, by Cabinet decision, must be an Australian Cabinet Minister. Massey reported that he could not attend, that Hughes would not accept Lord Novar, and that each Dominion would send its own representative.[10]

The identification of the British Empire delegation as the unit of action, and its organization, emphasized one of the realities of the situation. Its political leaders were Balfour, Lord Lee of Fareham, the First Lord of the Admiralty, and Geddes. Its technical experts were Admirals Beatty and Chatfield, Lord Cavan and Air Vice-Marshal J.P.A. Higgins, along with Foreign Office and Board of Trade officials. Sir Maurice Hankey headed the secretariat.[11] British politicians, officials and technical experts, armed with their memoranda, dominated the delegation. It could hardly have been otherwise. Time was short and preparations even in London were hurried. Balfour was absent in Geneva, Curzon was overburdened, and the flow of information from London was initially thin and never impressive.[12] The Dominion representatives and their meagre staffs looked to their British colleagues for leadership, albeit in a searching and at times even critical way. It would be wrong to assume, however, that mere membership of the Empire delegation banished the Dominion delegates to the remote periphery of the Conference.

Massey sent Sir John Salmond, a distinguished constitutional lawyer, a former Solicitor-General and by then a judge of the Supreme Court. Salmond had little or no expertise in foreign or defence policy; the New Zealand archives contain no evidence of Salmond's formal briefing. He was to have an advisory role in the Empire delegation, presenting assertively the views of the New Zealand Government on matters pertaining to New Zealand. Massey seemed to assume that Salmond would not, therefore, participate in the conference proper.[13] E.O. Mousley, in London and known to Edward Grigg, Lloyd George's secretary, would serve as Salmond's secretary and publicity officer.[14]

Hughes chose Senator George F. Pearce, Minister for Home and Territories, former Defence Minister, and a student of Asia-Pacific affairs.[15] Pearce and Hughes were advised on Asia-Pacific affairs by E.L. Piesse, former Director of Military Intelligence, Director and sole incumbent of the Pacific Branch of the Prime Minister's Department from 1919 (renamed the Foreign Section (Pacific) in 1921), there being no Department of External Affairs as such. He was Australia's Japan expert. While not especially virulent, Piesse and those who reported to him saw conflict in racial terms, and identified imperialist, expansionist Japan, seeking to divide Britain from the United States, as the urgent threat to Australian security. Japan, sprung loose by arms limitation in the Pacific and by the relinquishing of British and

American offensive naval forces and bases, would pursue interests, including the domination of China, that threatened those of the white races.[16] But Piesse advocated the renewal of the Anglo-Japanese Alliance. G.S. Knowles, as legal adviser, accompanied Piesse, but Pearce took no arms expert to the conference.

Loring C. Christie, legal affairs adviser in the Department of External Affairs, had provided the link of intellectual unity in Canadian policy, as Meighen replaced Borden in July 1920. He was the principal architect of Canada's assault on the Anglo-Japanese Alliance. Christie coordinated the Canadian preparations for the Washington Conference, liaised with Hankey, and then accompanied Borden to Washington. He was well connected in London, had earned Hankey's confidence, and, Mousley's claims notwithstanding, was likely to be the senior Dominion member of the secretariat to the Empire delegation.[17] Christie, in fact, took over from Hankey late in January 1922. Meighen, on the hustings, locked in a futile election battle with MacKenzie King, his Liberal opponent, was not in Ottawa often enough to play a role in the preparations for the conference. Early in October, he named Borden as Canada's delegate. King, as the newly elected Prime Minister, asked Borden to stay on in January 1922 – a sound decision, but not one that was free of irritation on both sides.[18]

Christie was guarded about the conference's prospects, but, like Borden, he sensed its broader significance. It would be another step toward settling disputes by open, multilateral diplomacy rather than secret arrangements. Geddes was wrong to assume that the conference was merely an artifact of American domestic politics. The Harding Administration's substantive concerns were shared by several senators. The conference could bring a new round of Anglo-American cooperation; the leadership provided by the Empire delegation could ensure its success.[19] Canadian preparations must be, therefore, as thorough as time permitted and as discrete as Canadian interests demanded.

Christie brought Borden up to date immediately. The Immigration Department was working on Asiatic immigration to Canada, he had prepared a study of the legal issues associated with the civil rights of Asiatics in Canada, and T.C.T. O'Hara, Deputy Minister of the Department of Trade and Commerce, was drafting a memorandum

on trade matters relating to China, Japan and Siberia. Memoranda
were required from the Canadian Manufacturing Association to
assist O'Hara, from the Royal Finance Corporation on loans to
China, from the Bankers Association on Chinese finances, and from
the naval, military and air services on matters of disarmament, even
though Christie did not expect significant progress toward military
disarmament, and air power was not specifically on the agenda. The
emphasis in these preparations on economic and social issues was
predictable, given Canada's concerns in and with East Asia.[20]

The limitation of naval armaments, and all armaments for that
matter, was, however, an issue of driving concern to Christie and
Borden. They were convinced that the Canadian position on imperial
defence, articulated since 1918, was sound. A centrally directed naval
policy for the Empire and formulae to determine cost sharing were
inappropriate. Each Dominion must determine its own naval policy
while keeping in mind broader, imperial needs and consulting volun-
tarily and freely on imperial policy. No greater burdens or responsibilities were desirable. The aim, Christie suggested, was not to create an
imperial fighting machine in an effort to impose the Empire's will on
other states. Force was neither the basis of nor the reason for the
Empire's existence. Peace, not provocation, was its goal. The Empire
should be neither a centralized political unit nor a formidable concentration of power. There would then be no reason or temptation to
abuse power, and no incentive for other states to seek to destroy the
Empire. This was, Christie insisted, a defensive not a pacifist philosophy, one seeking to preserve the Empire's integrity. For, after all, the
Empire provided the greatest contribution to peace, and stood as the
examplar of civilized behaviour.[21]

Of the three memoranda from the naval staff, the one from the
Intelligence Branch was most troubling.[22] It depicted US naval policy
as a titanic struggle between public opinion and Congress on the one
hand, seeking substantially to reduce expenditure on naval and merchant marine construction, and, on the other, an administration bent
on completing the 1916 naval programme and achieving supremacy
at sea. The Washington Conference was designed, therefore, to recast
American opinion and secure public and congressional support for
the construction of the largest navy in the world. The United States
could then be 'a law unto herself'. The paper was, of course, seriously

flawed. Canadian officials clearly had no knowledge of US preparations for the conference with respect to naval arms limitation.

While the bureaucracy dutifully produced the requested memoranda, Christie turned to the other principal concern, the Anglo-Japanese Alliance.[23] The Canadian position had not altered. Political issues took precedence over arms limitation. There could be no naval disarmament until the future of the alliance was determined, and the matter was urgent. Unless Britain brought them together, there could be a war 'as early as next year' between Japan and the United States. Britain had three options:

1. to retain the alliance so as to restrain Japan;
2. to declare its neutrality and impartiality between Japan and the United States, ending the alliance and supporting China (but that option might make war more likely because of Japan's aggressive intentions); and
3. as Britain could not support Japan in a war against the United States, and as some parts of the Empire could not remain neutral in such a war, it would be wise to inform Japan that if it provoked war the English-speaking nations would stand together. As Japan would not risk war if it felt that Britain would support the United States, as Japan's hawks would be discouraged from aggression, this seemed the most desirable course of action for Britain to pursue.

In Canada, the Japanese population of British Columbia was so unpopular that British Columbia, its public attitudes mirroring those of California, would not expect Canada to be neutral in a war against Japan. Everything pointed, therefore, including the Irish situation, to the need for Anglo-American cooperation. At the Washington Conference the Empire delegation needed to work quietly, help resolve the troubled Japan–United States relationship, and leave public 'successes' to the naive and inexperienced Americans. An inclusive, multilateral agreement or understanding should and could be substituted for the Anglo-Japanese Alliance. Indeed, it was vital to arrive at such an agreement if a war embroiling all the Pacific powers, including China and France, was to be averted. Christie concluded the assessment by emphasizing that, while Canada was free to follow its own policy on the alliance, it was vital to arrive at and maintain a united imperial posture. There must be no hint to the press of any divisions within the Empire delegation on the future of the Anglo-Japanese Alliance.

The Washington Conference, 12 November 1921 to 6 February 1922

The Future of the Anglo-Japanese Alliance: The Four-Power Treaty

Lloyd George, in a decision duly reported to the Dominions, instructed Curzon after the imperial conference to ensure that there was close consultation and cooperation with Japan on all Far Eastern questions, and that the future of the Anglo-Japanese Alliance would be handled exclusively in *à trois* negotiation with Japan and the United States. He continued to assume that they must settle political questions relating to China and the Pacific before entering into naval arms limitation negotiations. Curzon, Secretary of State Hughes and the Japanese Foreign Ministry agreed to seek a tripartite agreement in informal negotiations outside but parallel to the main conference. Should these negotiations fail, Britain would retain a modified alliance with Japan.[24]

Balfour left England without an official draft document and with considerable personal latitude. Reclining in bed, taking refuge from seasickness, and closeted with Hankey and Foreign Office officials Sir John Jordan and Miles Lampson, Balfour concluded that two treaties were required. A triple agreement would replace the alliance and provide for the preservation of peace and the maintenance of the territorial status quo in and bordering on the Pacific. The other treaty would be devoted exclusively to China. Articles one and three of Balfour's draft treaty were gestures to the United States, in effect replacing the Anglo-Japanese Alliance with a tripartite, consultative pact to respect territorial rights and preserve the peace. Article two, providing for the perpetuation of the essence of the Anglo-Japanese Alliance through defensive military cooperation, was a gesture to Japan. It was, therefore, an astute compromise between established policy and new circumstances, reflective of the will of the recent imperial conference and especially of Australian and New Zealand interests, while forwarding Canada's Atlanticist concerns. It included the United States but did not ask it to undertake binding military obligations. It terminated their alliance but did not rebuff Japan. It left unfettered the option of recreating a defensive front against a Russo-German threat.[25]

Balfour's challenge lay first in securing the agreement of the Empire delegation and then in convincing Hughes and Baron Kato, the chief Japanese delegate. The former task turned out to be not at all formidable; the latter became wrapped in layers of uncertainty. At the Empire delegation dinner on 10 November Balfour, in great form and playing his hand skilfully, according to Hankey, secured Dominion support for 'this ingenious draft', his proposed tripartite agreement. Borden depicted the issue as the critical test of Anglo-American cooperation and of the avoidance of a war between the United States and Japan. He was 'the same as ever but in a most reasonable frame of mind', according to Hankey. Borden assured Salmond and Pearce that he was seeking a US guarantee in some form, to replace the alliance, that would satisfy Australia and New Zealand. Salmond, described by Hankey as 'garrulous', was, apparently, satisfied. Pearce, wrongly and prematurely judged by Hankey to be 'a light-weight', was willing to let Balfour proceed. He was, he assured Hughes, stressing the Australian viewpoint – reason, not force, must rule the international system, financial prudence was obligatory, and economic development must be vigorously pursued. There were grounds for optimism. The Harding Administration, anxious for political reasons to see the conference succeed, recognized that some arrangement involving the United States and acceptable to Britain and the Dominions had to be put in place if the Anglo-Japanese Alliance were to end.[26]

The initiative lay with Balfour. Armed with Dominion support, if not a formal consensus, he launched the negotiations in a meeting with Secretary of State Hughes the following evening, 11 November. Balfour brought a draft four-power agreement (including France), drawn up by Hughes, to a much neglected Empire delegation on 7 December.[27] He made no apology for the absence of formal consultation on the negotiations, and no protest was heard from any of the senior Dominion delegates, all being present. Borden was perhaps distracted by the dismal news of Meighen's election defeat.

Balfour claimed excessive credit for Hughes's draft, which owed more to an amended Japanese proposal than to his own original formula. After noting the non-applicability to China and the omission of Italy, the Empire delegation turned to the meaning of 'insular possessions and dominions'. Balfour emphasized the narrow geographical scope of the arrangement – Japan, Australia, New Zealand and the mandate islands north and south of the equator were included; the west coasts of Canada and the United States, China and Korea were excluded. He saw inclusion as beneficial to Australia and New Zealand. He also emphasized that the agreement was a treaty requiring ratification by the US Senate. Should the Senate reject the treaty, the Anglo-Japanese Alliance would remain in force. Against that, the Senate, anxious to kill the alliance, would have every incentive to ratify the Four-Power Treaty. Balfour assured his Dominion colleagues that the treaty was no more than an agreement to respect each others' rights. Its final approval depended on Japan and the United States reaching a settlement on Yap and agreeing to extend their commercial treaty to Japan's island mandates. He knew, moreover, that the treaty narrowed the differences between Australia and Canada.

Pearce was concerned to protect Australian trade and shipping with the Pacific islands and immigration laws. Salmond sought clarification on China's status, but, apart from suggesting certain textual amendments and ensuring that minor disagreements between the signatories would not require a full-blown conference to achieve a settlement, the Dominion representatives acquiesced. They undertook to consult their governments promptly. Pearce reported Australian approval on 9 December; Borden had Meighen's initial agreement by 10 December; Salmond, embarrassed by the absence of a cipher and forced to use the Australian cipher, waited until 12 December for authorization to sign the treaty.[28] Pearce recommended the treaty to Hughes in part on the grounds that it would help bring agreement on other Asian questions. Borden, noting that agreement was based on a draft which the British Government approved, which Australia, New Zealand and the US Senate should endorse, but which might founder in Tokyo, felt that Canadian interests were being served – the four powers would settle their disputes peacefully. He emphasized to Meighen that the treaty was not a military alliance, imposed no 'warlike obligations', and relied on conference diplomacy, with public opinion being able to assert its pacifying influence, to settle disputes. The treaty applied only to the islands of the Pacific, so as to satisfy the US Congress, but Borden felt that its scope would eventually be expanded to cover all Pacific territories. Borden concluded his recommendation by assuring Meighen that 'It is entirely in line with the proposal and purposes advocated by you at last summer's Conference'.

Borden was correct to point to possible complications emanating from Tokyo – a demand that Japan's main islands be excluded from the scope of the treaty, and a proposal that a conference should convene to settle a dispute only if both signatory disputants agreed to the step. Both were defeated, but all agreed that domestic issues were beyond the scope of the treaty, an understanding warmly welcomed by Pearce and Prime Minister Hughes. Secretary of State Hughes's insistence, however, that United States acceptance of the treaty did not jeopardize its rights and interests in the Pacific island mandates proved briefly contentious. Hughes of Australia acquiesced in Balfour's management of that challenge and waited on subsequent negotiations to confirm Australia's rights and policies. On 10 December the Empire Delegation accepted the Four-Power Treaty, which was signed on 13 December.[29]

Piesse welcomed the treaty.[30] Japan had recognized the White Australia policy and abandoned its reservation on the New Guinea mandate. There should be peace for ten years. If Japan had abandoned its aggressive intentions against Australia, then defence spending could be significantly reduced. Australia, 'in our future progress as a white country', would benefit also from United States support and friendship, if it avoided contentious trade policies. Indeed, relations should be improved all round, enhancing the security of Britain's Pacific and Asian possessions. In the same way, the United States had increased the security of the Philippines, Honolulu and its other Pacific islands. The Harding Administration was making amends for the mischief done to world peace by the United States since 1919. Japan, Piesse felt, benefited by securing recognition of her mandate for the north Pacific islands. Japan could reduce its defence expenditures as its fear of the United States diminished. Piesse saw the inclusion of Japan proper in the treaty as an advantage, adding to Japan's security, but he would not be surprised if that status were seen as an insult and Japan insisted on an amendment excluding its main islands. Although such a change would leave Australia and New Zealand with an inferior status, Piesse nevertheless argued that the Four-Power Treaty was a bargain of great value for both Dominions. Status, prestige and *amour propre* were not the issue; a Japanese amendment, excluding its homeland, should be accepted to preserve the treaty. Pearce agreed, forecasting correctly that the amendment would assist ratification by the US Senate. Piesse's prediction proved well founded. Japan's main islands were ultimately excluded.[31]

Salmond also reported Japan's objection to the inclusion of its main islands, while the US mainland was excluded, but did not feel that New Zealand's interests were affected by the amendment. The treaty was welcomed in the United States, and the degree of harmony it reflected was far more important than its terms.[32] Mousley described the treaty as general and pleasing everyone. Clarifications were required, Shantung and Japan's evacuation from Siberia might threaten ratification, but at least the United States had made a first and necessary step toward international cooperation.[33] Borden, predictably, also saw the value of the Four-Power Treaty more in its promise than in its specific terms. It might be, given the termination of the Anglo-Japanese Alliance, a major step forward in the history of the Empire's relations with the United States; its spirit might extend and embrace other issues and areas. The Four-Power Treaty could serve as a catalyst, educating public opinion, reversing the dismal transatlantic trends of recent years, bringing about greater United States involvement in international affairs, and producing an irresistible wave of moral leadership from the English-speaking peoples. Borden was concerned, therefore, understandably, lest the Senate reject the treaty. Christie actually described the treaty as perhaps the most significant achievement of the conference, but judged it to be vulnerable to US senatorial concerns about China.[34]

The Future of China: The Nine-Power Treaty

The Empire delegation, following Balfour's lead, began with the assumption that a treaty separate from the one replacing the Anglo-Japanese Alliance was required for China. The Dominion delegates had, in effect, been excluded from the negotiations leading to the Four-Power Treaty, but subcommittees of the Committee on Pacific and Far Eastern Affairs were required to address the complex issues relating to China – tariffs, taxation, cotton exports, leased territories and extraterritoriality, the open door, post offices, war lords, foreign troops, police and railway guards, arms trafficking and the Chinese Eastern Railway. The future of Japan's position in Shantung and Manchuria, Japan's lingering presence in Siberia, Britain's rights in Hong Kong and Wei-hai-wei, and French leases in China added to the complexity. There was ample work here for the Dominion delegations, alongside the British experts, and unavoidably, ample need for guidance from and reports to the Empire delegation. That process began on 19 November and continued regularly until 31 January 1922.

Borden was thrust into these issues and spared Meighen and then King few of the details. Borden also agreed to serve on the subcommittee on China's tariffs and revenues – more engrossing detail being despatched to Ottawa.[35] Salmond had no role in these matters. He lamented the public brawl between China and Japan, but drew comfort from the fact that publicity relieved him of the need to report in detail to Massey. Mousley confined his reports to noting the dimensions of the problem.[36] Pearce reported frequently enough, but briefly, on things Chinese. He was initially optimistic because he detected a distinct change of heart from the Japanese. Fearing a financial and trade boycott by the United States, and wishing to avoid further alienating their Asian neighbours and becoming isolated, the Japanese realized that their policies toward China and Asia must change. Pearce ended on an optimistic note: outstanding issues such as the Chinese Eastern Railway and even Siberia should not prove difficult to settle. But in the intervening weeks realities and membership on the subcommittee on extra-territorial rights (which Pearce described as *the* most important Asian issue for Britain) had their sobering effect. China's disarray made policies difficult to craft; the Japanese were at best evasive on Siberia; Shantung was a critical but thorny issue; the Nine-Power Treaty on China must wait on the Five-Power Naval Treaty; and while the United States was anxious to deal with the 'Twenty One Demands' and Siberia, the British delegation was decidedly less enthusiastic.[37]

One way or another, the issues were resolved or finessed, and the Nine-Power Treaty on China was crafted. It appeared, among other things, to guarantee both the integrity of China and the open door, and to provide much-needed revenues for China's recovery. Pearce concluded that China should serve as less of a source of international rivalry in the future, thus eliminating one of the reasons for naval competition in the Pacific.

The Future of Arms Limitation: The Five-Power Treaty

Naval security lay at the core of the agenda of the Empire delegation. Secretary of State Hughes launched dramatic naval arms limitation proposals, involving a ten-year construction holiday for capital ships, at the Plenary Session on 12 November. The next evening the Empire delegation endorsed Beatty's counter in a way that cut across Borden's preferences and rekindled his profound suspicion of experts. Borden, in pursuit of the Atlanticist agenda, wanted the powers to create and the United States to join an international tribunal which would arbitrate crises and prevent them from escalating into war. The Anglo-Saxon powers would be its core and its inspiration; public opinion would exercise its pacifistic influence. What hope was there for such innovation, Borden asked, if the British naval experts, who reversed reality and assumed that the nation lived for the Navy, were allowed to wreck Hughes's proposals? Surely the strong wine of professionalism needed diluting with the inspired common sense of the civilian viewpoint.

Borden promptly prepared, therefore, and secured Pearce's support for, a memorandum to outmanoeuvre the naval staff.[38] He proposed that the Empire delegation accept the Hughes plan in spirit and principle and improve on it in two ways. The ten-year naval holiday proposal was both courageous and popular, and had been made by a nation with the financial and material resources 'to outstrip the British Empire in any competition for command of the seas'. Schemes to launch programmes of gradual capital ship replacement, so as to maintain bloated, expensive and wasteful armaments plants and husband skilled labour, 'will be met with stern disapproval from the democracies of the British Empire and from the people of the United States'. To improve on Hughes's 'temporary expedient', to achieve a greatly extended and even permanent halt to capital ship construction, Borden advocated the convening of a further disarmament conference in three or five years, so that the naval holiday could continue for a further ten or 20 year period. Borden simply could not imagine that after that length of time the powers would resume the naval race. He then floated his international arbitration tribunal scheme. It was pointless, he argued, to reduce armaments but not attempt to banish war; and it was vital to involve the United States in international affairs and fill the vacuum created by its absence from the League of Nations.

Buoyed temporarily by Harding's careless oratory, Borden pursued his international arbitration scheme through mid-December, only to see it die of indifference. Hughes was sympathetic but sceptical, and preoccupied with the central business of the conference. The Foreign Office section of the Empire delegation judged the proposal super-fluous, in a response Borden found 'hardly relevant'. Balfour, not anxious to duplicate League procedures, was at best evasive. The single debate on the proposal in the Empire delegation, on 17 December, merely sharpened the differences between Borden and Balfour. Balfour carried the day; Borden acknowledged defeat. The Empire delegation did not expect Balfour to initiate discussions to create a new international organization.[39]

Encouraged by influencing Balfour's choice of words in respond-ing, on 15 November, to Hughes's naval arms limitation proposals – 'declare that you accept the American proposals in spirit and in principle'[40] – Borden pursued his defence of the ten-year naval holi-day in capital ship construction. Initially, aided by Pearce and with Lloyd George's support, he carried the argument. The holiday was a sound proposal that had 'touched the imagination of all the democra-cies'. Borden conceded that the review of the results of the Washington Conference conducted after five years might point to the wisdom of a sharply restricted programme of capital ship construc-tion. Modest, regular replacement construction programmes of, for example, two or three ships every three years, after the holiday, appealed to Pearce, as they did to Lloyd George. If, as Beatty claimed, the holiday was impractical, then the United States must concede the point, Pearce insisted. The United States, not the Empire, must walk away from the moral high ground. Salmond, described by Borden as being as talkative as Massey or Ward, inexperienced and full of impractical ideas, worried, quite unnecessarily, lest rogue powers build parts of ships during the holiday so as to assemble them rapidly after the holiday expired. Beatty's counter to Borden was part of an assertion that Hughes's naval proposals in total benefited the United States and threatened the security of the Empire. The Royal Navy had already gone through a five-year holiday. Hughes's holiday was poorly conceived, not well thought out, impractical, and riddled with technical difficulties. US naval experts would be forced to propose amendments. On 17 November, however, the Empire delegation accepted the holiday and Borden's proposal for a quinquennial conference to review progress.

However, that decision left unanswered the complex problem of the future of armaments plants. Borden wanted as many as possible of them closed down, but if plants were not maintained, if skilled labour was not husbanded, and as the holiday prevented the construction of ships for other states, how could the powers, the naval experts asked, begin even a programme of very limited capital ship replacement after the holiday? Also, such replacement programmes, as Lloyd George conceded, provided the only justification for subsidies in the order of £6 million a year to maintain Britain's naval construction capacity. The issue embraced, in other words, politics and economics as well as strategy. Borden countered that plants could be reopened or recreated if the quinquennial review conference pointed to that course of action. Then there was the question of government control of those plants maintained during the holiday. Hughes favoured government control; Borden doubted whether US opinion would endorse such a measure. Beatty, armed with indiscretions from the US delegation, put a sinister interpretation on Hughes's preference – the US Navy would strengthen, modernize and even reconstruct the capital ships retained. Borden felt able to report to Ottawa, however, on 16 November, that the Empire delegation agreed that it would be incongruous to scrap capital ships and yet retain construction facilities, but that governments should take over the plants retained.[41]

Borden's stand against Beatty had earned him a reprimand from Ottawa which Meighen did not rescind until early December.[42] By that time, the Empire delegation, in Borden's absence, had begun to swing back to Beatty's position on the holiday, despite Lloyd George's continued support and an endorsement from the Board of

Trade. Borden reported to Meighen on 8 December that the naval experts were finding altogether too much sustenance in their attempt to reduce or even eliminate the holiday.[43] Pearce and Salmond, in fact, had deserted him in the face of Chatfield's appeal for the Empire delegation to endorse Beatty's plan for the gradual replacement of obsolescent capital ships during the ten-year period. The holiday, Chatfield insisted, would arbitrarily limit one class of weapons, paralyse the naval construction capacity of the Empire, injure the fleet because of its vulnerability to air and submarine power, and, inefficient as it was, result in financial, plant and skilled labour losses. Pearce agreed. The holiday should apply to construction calculated to disturb the ten-year equilibrium provided by the capital ship tonnage ratios, but not to replacement construction aimed at creating that equilibrium. The fact that Britain and Japan each had only one post-Jutland capital ship spelled parity, not a 40 per cent margin of superiority for Britain. Britain had ten battleships, each mounting eight 15-inch guns; Japan had four battleships with a total of 48 14-inch guns. The advantage lay with Japan, and would move even further in its favour. Prime Minister Hughes, alarmed at this prospect, had instructed Pearce to follow Beatty's lead.[44]

Borden responded in characteristic fashion. To reverse their position would bring public disfavour. As the United States could outbuild Britain in a naval race, the holiday benefited the Empire. It was a wise step financially, which, reinforcing the Four-Power Treaty, would promote peace. They must remain committed to the holiday, therefore, to the extent that it was consistent with imperial security. Any risk involved was worth taking. Salmond's reasoning must have surprised his colleagues. Chatfield's arguments were not convincing; the capital ship was not vital to imperial security and, indeed, its obsolescence contributed to British strength because of Britain's large mercantile marine. But Pearce's analysis of the Anglo-Japanese naval balance was entirely convincing; striking power was the issue, not numerical totals. The holiday, Salmond asserted, had in fact no logical connection to arms reduction, and should be abandoned in favour of Lee's gradual replacement construction programme.

Geddes and Lee completed the assault. Geddes, less sanguine than Borden about the value of the Four-Power Treaty, acknowledged, along with Lee, the value of stopping the US and Japanese capital ship building programmes and the scrapping of America's post-Jutland capital ships. But, Geddes argued, British naval power must be projected into the Pacific, to help, for example, implement the Four-Power Treaty. Lee trivialized the holiday as an error and a last-minute contrivance; they must help the US delegation to evade or dispense with it.

Borden, privately, faced his isolation amidst colleagues willing to defy Lloyd George. The fault, of course, lay with the experts – narrow, self-serving and able to measure security only in terms of weapons. Chatfield, 'whom I personally like, indulged in some loose and foolish talk as to his willingness to fight the United States with an inferior fleet', oblivious to the fact that an Anglo-American war would be the equivalent of 'the destruction of a civilization already reeling under the impact of the late war'.[45] Borden wrote to Balfour and then, feeling ill, took to his bed. The Empire delegation, in his absence the next day, confirmed its preference for amending the holiday, a decision which pointed to the retention of a great number of arms plants.[46] Gradual replacement of capital ships would be undertaken, an infinitely more satisfactory solution than a holiday followed by an outburst of construction, from plants presumably largely recreated after the ten-year hiatus. The naval experts had insisted earlier that the holiday, involving the loss of plants, would make the resumption of construction well-nigh impossible; it was not a time, clearly, for close attention to the logic of argument. In any case, the Five-Power Treaty genuflected to the holiday.

The proposed reduction of capital ship fleets and the establishment of quantitative ratios limiting the aggregate tonnage of the British, United States and Japanese capital ship fleets were not initially controversial. They seemed even-handed strategically and wise financially, and reduced the temptation to risk war as a way to avoid losing an arms race. At Beatty's insistence, despite Salmond's eminently sensible point that to involve other states would increase transaction costs, the Empire delegation, on 17 November, agreed that a naval treaty must embrace France and Italy. The Japanese quest to retain the *Mutsu* ran up against US determination to preserve the tonnage ratios for capital ships, but that contretemps was a blessing to some in the Empire delegation because it led to the decision to allow Britain, and the United States, to build two new super capital ships.[47] It created an opportunity, however, for France to claim parity with Japan in capital ships, a claim that was highly disturbing in itself, and which concerned the Empire delegation all the more because of its tactical relationship to the unresolved question of submarines and anti-submarine craft.

The contretemps over the *Matsu* and the capital ship tonnage ratios was arresting also because it spawned the Japanese demand for an agreement prohibiting the further fortification of naval bases and thus the construction of new fortified bases in the Pacific. Japan saw Hong Kong, Hawaii, Guam and the Philippine bases as a threat to its security; every other Pacific power feared the development of Japanese naval bases in the Pescadores, Bonins and Luchus and at Formosa. Pearce, at the Empire delegation meeting on 2 December, put his finger unerringly on the central consideration for the Pacific dominions – Singapore must be excluded from any such agreement.[48] Balfour agreed, assuring Pearce that Singapore was never raised in his discussions with Hughes and Kato and that 'he preferred to leave it alone'. That was wise, and ultimately efficacious, but Japan's demand was met neither easily nor rapidly. One reason was Pearce's faulty assumption that Australia, New Zealand and their island possessions were excluded from any agreement while all other Pacific islands were included, amid an unnecessary and confusing debate over the status of mandated islands.

On 9 January 1922 the Empire delegation reviewed the draft naval treaty.[49] Borden reported to Ottawa that nothing of particular interest to Canada was discussed. Pearce, however, took issue with article 19, the fortifications status quo article, for it appeared to restrict Australia's right to construct naval bases in the islands to its north, such as New Guinea. Nothing could have been more revealing of the differing concerns and preferences of Australia and Canada. Pearce wanted the area included in the treaty to contain only the islands north of the equator, excluding islands under Australian administration. Japan wanted the status quo maintained in all insular possessions except Australia and New Zealand proper. The Jellicoe report, he reminded them, had specifically pointed to the need for such facilities, for Sydney could not serve as the base from which to conduct a war against Japan. Pearce regretted the misunderstanding – he had assumed that the islands to the north were excluded from the fortifications freeze because Australia itself was exempt. He had, therefore, felt it necessary to consult his government. Balfour reminded Pearce of the policy assumptions underlying the Singapore strategy, but took up the Australian demand with Hughes and Kato, somewhat reluctantly, according to Pearce.

Balfour reported, on 11 January, that he had argued that as the islands off Canada's and California's coasts were excluded so those islands administered by Australia and New Zealand should be exempt. The British map, attempting to plot the area in the Pacific included in the fortifications status quo, had as its southern line the equator. Kato had balked at this, and referred the matter to Tokyo. Pearce settled for Hankey's formula – excluding 'unmandated islands south of the equator under the administration of Australia and New Zealand' – but turned to the threat from Japan posed by aircraft carriers. Under the proposed treaty, Britain would have five and Japan three carriers, but only one British carrier would be stationed in the Pacific. Thus, in the event of war, Japan would enjoy a three to one margin of superiority. Chatfield took him back to the Singapore strategy; in the event of war with Japan, three carriers would proceed to the Pacific. Pearce was not finished – why not use the Cannes conference to reduce France's submarine fleet so that Japan would follow suit? Lee countered; further cuts in submarine fleets would force Britain to limit its cruiser construction, thus reducing, not enhancing, the security of the Empire.[50] The stalemate on the fortifications freeze persisted. The US delegation, according to Pearce, wavered, and was prepared to include the islands of the south Pacific lest the issue wreck the naval treaty. He had, he reported to Hughes, held firm. Further negotiations produced an agreement by 25 January. On 31 January, at its last meeting, the Empire delegation reviewed the final draft of the naval treaty, which included an acceptable version of article 19 on Pacific fortifications.[51]

Pearce and Salmond, rather more than Borden, understandably, found convincing Beatty's case that the Empire required an increment of cruisers and destroyers beyond those operating with the main battle fleet. The case rested on the need to protect imperial trade routes and lines of communication, and on the vulnerability of a widely dispersed fleet; but more than that, Beatty and Lee argued that further American and Japanese building of cruisers and destroyers, as permitted under article 18 of Hughes's proposals, spelled obsolescence and inferiority for the Royal Navy in those categories. The naval holiday should be applied to those vessels. Borden found the case argumentative and provocative, further evidence, in fact, that the experts could not face the reality that the United States could outbuild the Empire and achieve naval supremacy. Pearce agreed with Beatty. The holiday would restrict only capital ship construction by Japan and the United States, while, in effect, because of the current size of the Royal Navy, restricting Britain's construction of all classes of ships. Japanese and US construction of cruisers, destroyers and submarines would render British ships in those categories obsolescent, and the Empire, with its dispersed naval resources, vulnerable. Salmond's questions fed Beatty's reasoning. On 17 November, the Empire delegation agreed that the holiday must apply to all categories of ships and submarines.[52]

Beatty, initially, had been less than clear on how to respond to Hughes's proposals to limit submarine fleets, because Britain's opportunity to construct new submarines within the proposed limits was decidedly constrained in comparison with those of the United States and Japan. The issue again was looming obsolescence, that is, qualitative inferiority, a gloomy prospect, made more threatening by Beatty's assurances that non-signatories, and Germany, would be free to build both submarines and military aircraft. Pearce proposed scrapping and outlawing offensive submarines, and limiting total submarine tonnage, while permitting only the construction of defensive submarines with local operating radius. Japan, he warned, was building submarines with a radius of action, without refuelling, of up to 10,000 miles – that is, to Sydney and back. Beatty and Lee were sceptical of Pearce's claims, but Pearce reported on 18 November that the Empire delegation had swung round to his view. The United States, prompted by public opinion, would support his proposal; the Japanese remained inscrutable.[53] In all this, the Empire delegation found further reason to include France and Italy in the naval treaty and submarines in the holiday, while preferring the abolition of submarines from all naval arsenals. That goal invited a confrontation with France.

Aristide Briand's superb statement on French security on 21 November, and Balfour's moving response, erupted into a confrontation over proposals to limit land armaments, which Borden and Hughes attempted to diffuse.[54] Ultimately, the French delegation blocked all attempts to limit land armaments, but beyond that, Lloyd George had set Balfour a formidable challenge in the naval realm. He must persuade the French to accept an inferior battle fleet so that Britain could more comfortably accept parity with the United States, to agree that France did not need submarines because of the impossibility of an Anglo-French war, and to reduce its air force so as to increase British security. Some hope lay, Borden and Balfour agreed, in securing Hughes's support for the abolition of the submarines.[55] Should that strategy fail, then security would have to come from anti-submarine capability – cruisers (limited by number, not total tonnage, and with a maximum individual size of 10,000 tons) and destroyers. There again, as Pearce pointed out, US support would be critical. And the future of air power was not irrelevant to this and other issues.

If cruisers and destroyers were to be limited, then the case for the abolition of the submarine seemed compelling, though the prospect of war against a non-signatory with a powerful submarine fleet was reason to pause. Pearce felt that his distinction between offensive and defensive submarines, banning the former and permitting the latter, might be the answer. Moreover, should the Empire delegation accept restrictions on the development of British air power, restrictions that other states could evade? Pearce supported Higgins; states could develop dual purpose commercial aircraft with bombing capabilities ('bomb droppers'), thus leaving Britain, unable to counter with military aircraft, hostage to a European enemy. However, Chatfield had a different perspective: the development of military aircraft would threaten the capital ship – another reason to rescue it from the holiday.[56] The conference did not place limits on the development of air power, while looking to rules of warfare to govern its use.

The predictable confrontation with France came in the week before Christmas. French pretensions over capital ship ratios were sufficiently contentious; if the French delegation sought concessions from Hughes on submarines, indicting Britain for robbing France first of its capital ships and now of its submarine fleet, it would wreck the conference. The Empire delegation, deliberating on 19 and 20 December, was free of illusions, as Borden, Pearce and Salmond united tactically but not substantively in opposition to Lee and Geddes.[57] Japan, Italy and the small states would support France. While Hughes seemed to prefer abolition, his naval experts argued that submarines were the only defensive weapons available to small states with long coastlines. Three alternative courses of action, therefore, existed: seek abolition of the submarine and accept limitations on anti-submarine craft; restrict submarine fleets and seek freedom of action in anti-submarine craft; or live without restrictions in either category. Tactically, the issue was how to handle Hughes, who, for party political reasons, wanted to use quiet diplomacy to seek abolition of the submarine.

Lee and Geddes, convinced that US opinion supported abolition, and citing Lloyd George's preference, proposed a campaign of public diplomacy. The tactic, they acknowledged, would fail, but Hughes would then seek to limit submarine fleets to 40,000 tons and to adopt rules to inhibit their use in wartime, thus confining the submarine to essentially defensive purposes. Balfour, armed with the invincible weapon of 'moral grandeur', having sought abolition, could then insist on freedom to construct anti-submarine vessels. Hughes would be outmanoeuvred and compliant. Borden, Pearce and Salmond, for their various reasons, thought otherwise. Borden expected American opinion to support Hughes, and preferred quiet diplomacy in the pursuit of unselfish but unspecified goals. Pearce and Salmond agreed, but looked to quiet diplomacy to achieve what Geddes and Lee preferred. Balfour's policy was sufficiently philosophical for the pompous Lee to dissent, and for Borden to record that he had lost the argument. In the course of private negotiations that would be made public, and recognizing the futility of holding out for abolition, Balfour would enlist Hughes's support for limiting submarine construction and for freeing the construction of anti-submarine craft from any limits, sure that resolutions and rules of warfare had no deterrent value and that submarines would be used offensively in war. Mousley, at least, saw this ultimately successful strategy as a victory for the Empire engineered by Balfour, and gave due credit to Pearce and Salmond for providing the lead on the submarine issue.[58] The French had been forestalled. But Pearce continued to fret over the size of the Japanese submarine fleet.

That left a clutch of secondary issues for resolution – rules and laws

of warfare; the production and use of poisonous gases;[59] the termination of the naval treaty in the event of war between the signatories or
with non-signatory powers; defining what was an aircraft carrier;[60]
naval construction by non-signatories and by signatories off-shore
and for third parties; the arming of merchant vessels; the Root
resolutions governing submarine warfare; and the rules for the scrapping of capital ships. Borden and Pearce had a hand in some of these
issues, in, for example, the scrutiny of the Root resolutions, with
Pearce decidedly sceptical about the value of seeking to regulate the
conduct of war. Salmond found in them a *raison d'être*. Still on
occasions wearing his 'bewildered air', and seemingly at times unable
quite to follow the debate in the Empire delegation, according to
Borden, he demonstrated his value as an able lawyer in the various
drafting processes, for, for example, the termination of the naval
treaty in the event of war, and the rules on submarine warfare and the
production and use of poisonous gases.[61] He earned, finally, the
admiration of the condescending Borden, and his efforts provoked
Mousley to report, generously, that, in the midst of issues that were
'logical' rather than technical or political, Salmond's 'logical mind
and extraordinary faculty of weighing arguments and to eliminate
considerations that conflict with imperative policies, is invaluable just
now'.[62]

Salmond, moreover, found a cause – preserving the moral value of
the naval treaty against all threats. Capital ships to be scrapped
should be sunk in an orchestrated, simultaneous act of liberation.
Hughes should not be allowed to redirect doomed capital ships to
commercial and other purposes; scrapping should be prompt, not
slothful. To do otherwise, Salmond insisted, would be to inflict
psychological damage and convince the public that the naval treaty
was mere 'political humbug'.[63] In these ways, Salmond made his
contribution to the Five-Power Treaty which went to the conference
on 1 February 1922.

The Significance of the Washington Conference

An irritated Borden spent the last days of January and the first part of
February clarifying, with Christie's help, for a preoccupied, ill-
informed and confused Prime Minister, what had transpired.[64] The

Four-Power Treaty, which was *not* the naval treaty, followed Meighen's policy toward the Anglo-Japanese Alliance. The Five-Power Treaty, the naval treaty, restricted the navies of the Empire, including Dominion navies, in various quantitative and qualitative ways, but the treaty imposed no specific obligations on Canada, other than to conform to the limitations imposed. Borden might have added that Canada had, in effect, relinquished the right to construct what it had no intention of constructing. Furthermore, he reported, the Empire delegation had made no effort to discuss the irrelevant – the Dominion role in imperial defence. All treaties would require ratification by the Canadian Parliament; Canada had a free hand in every respect.

Borden's official report on the Conference was informative but routine. His more profound assessment came from his personal agenda. He had pursued Atlanticism by way of Asia-Pacific problems, looked to disarmament to provide security, and saw in conference diplomacy and international organizations the mechanisms of order and stability. In the final analysis, Borden had convinced himself that the future of world peace and justice lay in the minds of an enlightened, educated and pacifistic public opinion. He was, in a word, an idealist, an Atlanticist, and an internationalist. The concrete results, therefore, of the Washington Conference he judged to be limited, but they were all that could be reasonably expected. More importantly, the conference had removed layers of international misunderstanding, and as it spread its educational influence further progress would be made. The US delegation had purposefully cultivated the Empire delegation, and the two had worked in close harmony. Even Henry Cabot Lodge had abandoned his antagonism. Their cooperation, however, had been all too apparent, and had irritated other delegations; it must be made more subtle in the future. Problems persisted – and while US foreign policy remained closely tied to domestic politics, there would be no dependable US cooperation in international affairs.[65] In retrospect, Borden judged the Washington Conference, with some justification, to be Balfour's triumph; he could not claim it as his own. Borden had left faint marks on the Nine-Power Treaty and had been suitably prominent in the Empire delegation. But his advocacy of more far-reaching goals had been futile. Indeed, his own government had chastised him for defying the naval experts and for putting the unity of the Empire delegation at risk. Balfour subsequently, however, was generous enough in his praise of Borden's contribution.[66]

Salmond, learning the ropes from Borden and Pearce, according to a patronizing Borden,[67] saw the significance of the conference in terms of imperial policy-making. The Dominions had a central role in the management of the international affairs of the Empire, which now operated as a single, undivided entity. Exclusive British control was gone. The Empire delegation, after full consultation and free discussion, had reached unanimity on every issue, resulting in a unified imperial policy.[68] The contrast with the situation prevailing at the League was marked. This was not an unjustified claim. Balfour, assisted by his political colleagues and Hankey, and guided by British officials and experts, had conducted the negotiations, but the Empire delegation, receiving reports and privy to Balfour's exchanges with Curzon and Lloyd George, had ample opportunity to influence the course of events, except with regard to the Four-Power Treaty.

Salmond thoroughly approved of the Five-Power Treaty, which he judged to have far-reaching consequences. It would put an end to 'the present insensate and ruinous competition in the building of post-Jutland ships', and '. . . relieve England of an intolerable financial burden while preserving her relative strength substantially unimpaired'. The capital ship tonnage ratios were sound. The absence of restrictions placed on anti-submarine craft, and the limiting of the size of cruisers to 10,000 tons and their guns to eight inches, was beneficial. The scrapping of the cruisers *Australia* and *New Zealand* was not a threat to security.[69]

Salmond, wisely and fairly, made no claim to any special role and influence. Indeed, he had been anxious to get off to England by the end of December, delegating Geddes to sign for New Zealand, but he had stayed on to the end, increasingly satisfied with his contribution within the Empire delegation and with what the delegation, led by Balfour, was accomplishing. Even Borden came to appreciate his drafting skills and legal touch, which, in the final analysis, was Salmond's contribution.

Pearce joined in the applause for the accomplishments of the Washington Conference, articulated by Billy Hughes and others.[70] The Four-Power Treaty, necessarily replacing the Anglo-Japanese

Alliance and relying on moral force not military obligations, would help underwrite peace in the Pacific for the next ten years. Domestic issues such as immigration were not affected; US rights in mandated islands would be the subject of separate negotiations. The Five-Power Treaty, despite its flaws (the absence of restrictions on land armaments and military air power, and permitting submarine construction[71]) nonetheless halted the naval race in offensive weapons. It codified Britain's acceptance of the one-power standard, limited the US and Japanese capital ship fleets, made a substantial contribution to arms limitation, recognized political and financial realities, boosted confidence, enhanced security and contributed to peace. Britain could build anti-submarine craft without restriction. The agreement to freeze fortifications in the Pacific was especially gratifying. Pearce, steeped in the reasoning of the Jellicoe report, took personal credit for ensuring that it did not apply to Australia and its island territories, except the mandates. Japan could not build a naval base that could be used to launch aggression against Australia. Japan, moreover, comforted by the Four- and Five-Power Treaties, and reassured because of the fortifications agreement, originally a Japanese proposal which removed the threat of US naval base construction in the Pacific, was likely to be more accommodating. Pearce concluded that Japan 'does not harbour any designs on Australia'. Consuming the security provided by these treaties, the Singapore strategy and the British Navy, Australia could reduce its naval forces, slash its defence budget, preserve its white heritage and concentrate on economic growth.[72]

The Nine-Power Treaty, Pearce felt, would help China recover economically and politically. It would also remove China as an issue in great power competition, through the agency of positive and self-denying ordinances – including relinquishing extra-territorial rights, Pearce's specific charge. The Nine-Power Treaty would, therefore, reinforce the accomplishments of the Four- and Five-Power Treaties. Peace in Asia-Pacific for the foreseeable future seemed assured, but China must act in ways that helped its own cause; if not, the Nine-Power Treaty's impact would be limited. The future of Siberia, of concern to Canada and Australia, moreover, remained indeterminate.

All in all, Pearce felt that the Empire delegation had functioned well and decided on policy, unless overruled by Lloyd George. The Empire had, over the submarine issue, assumed the moral leadership of the conference, but not at the cost of damaging the rapport between Balfour and Hughes. Pearce, more than Borden or Salmond, had left his mark on the Empire delegation and the conference as a whole. He had more credibility than either of them on naval and Asia-Pacific affairs, and more helpful support from his own government. He had focused admirably on the issues of concern to Australia, and had helped accomplish all that could be expected to enhance Australia's security.[73]

However, the future was wrapped in uncertainty and unpredictability. The Singapore naval base was excluded from the freeze on fortifications, but when would construction start, and would it deter Japan from aggression, or even invite a preemptive strike? Perhaps the naval ratios and the freeze on fortifications actually benefited Japan. If they did, how would the United States respond to Japanese opportunism? Treaties negotiated required ratification, and why were the United States and Japan so slow in following Britain's lead in scrapping capital ships? What strategic balance would result from the continued construction of submarines and anti-submarine craft, and from the development of air power? Europe's Far East remained Australia's 'Far North'. Australians were European by race and interest, Pearce argued, but geographically Australia was 'Asiatic'. China and Japan were more salient than Belgium and Holland. War in Asia-Pacific, not Europe, was Australia's principal concern, and would moral force suffice to deter it? And what of the primordial racial conflict? Through such reasoning, sobering realities infiltrated the guarded optimism, the carefully constructed phrases on improved relations and the diminished likelihood of war, and the decline in Australia of public comment critical of Japan.[74] Within a year Australian optimism had begun to evaporate as politicians listened to military and naval warnings that arms limitation did not lead to security.

When Pearce supported Beatty's attempt to defeat the naval holiday, he assured his colleagues that Australia would continue to contribute to imperial defence as it had since 1910. Salmond stood with Pearce, but could make no commitment about New Zealand's contribution. New Zealand naval expenditures would not exceed £250,000. An apologetic Borden, according to Pearce, had admitted that Canada would not increase its contribution to imperial defence.

Canada planned to be rid of its fleet unit and reduce naval expenditures to below $4 million. Predictably, the Admiralty returned to the
issue of burden-sharing almost immediately after the Washington
Conference.[75]

The Admiralty agreed that a Pacific war was unlikely in the next
ten years, but warned against gambling with the security of the
Empire. The strategic position in the western Pacific had been adversely affected because of the freeze on fortifications. Hong Kong
was inadequate and vulnerable; the United States, relinquishing the
right to build naval bases west of Hawaii, could not deter or counter
Japan. That left the Empire as 'the sole Power to counter, with Naval
Forces, any aggressive tendencies on the part of Japan'. It necessitated
making '. . . preparations for a possible rapid concentration of the
main fleet in the East', and the construction, by the Dominions, of
submarines and light cruisers. That reasoning took the Admiralty
back to its policy set out for the Imperial Conference in 1921. The
Empire would be secure only if it had adequate naval forces capable
of offensive action and controlling maritime communications, and
able to operate freely from adequate fuelling and base facilities. Local
defence measures, separate navies, were 'entirely illusory'; unity and
cooperation were the only paths to security. The ideal remained a
unified imperial navy, with the Dominions providing ships and men.
Short of that, there must be burden-sharing, for Britain could not
fund the fleet and the bases unaided. The Dominions, unwilling to
make cash contributions, must maintain 'a healthy nucleus of a sea-
going squadron' which could be expanded later, provide oil-fuel
supplies where relevant, and help build the Singapore naval base,
secure and fortified. The development of the Singapore base would
take many years even with substantial Dominion contributions; it
was a matter, therefore, of great urgency.

The Admiralty expected Australia and New Zealand to act on all
three recommendations – the sea-going squadron, oil-fuel reserves,
and helping with the Singapore base. It was, frankly, disappointed at
Canada's decision to abolish its sea-going squadron. This meant that
Canada was making no real contribution to imperial defence, unless
it provided, along with South Africa, oil-fuel facilities. Canada, unlike
India, was not expected to contribute to the development of the
Singapore base.

These assessments of the Washington Conference, from Ottawa, Wellington, Canberra and then London, were judicious in that they balanced accomplishment against uncertainty and unpredictability. There was no excessive wishful thinking, no rampant idealism. Tensions were reduced and Anglo-American relations improved, but the Anglo-Japanese Alliance was forfeited, leaving much of the future to Japanese policy choice. The financial and political benefits of the naval treaty were to be gathered in promptly, and the Empire was no less secure in the immediate term, but the future was less certain. That was because both Japanese and US policies were unpredictable, and because the Singapore strategy was flawed. The Empire might face two, even three, global predators. Canada was ostensibly now more secure than Australia and New Zealand, but, as the Admiralty insisted, 'The fate of any or of all the Dominions may be settled one way or the other thousands of miles from their coasts'. As was always the case, defence and foreign policy, conducted in a political and financial setting, and in the context of policy decisions made in other capitals, would determine what security the Empire as a whole would enjoy.

University of Southern California

NOTES

1. These documents, from the British, Australian, Canadian and New Zealand archives, have been used by several scholars – Michael Fry, 'Anglo-American–Canadian relations, with special reference to Naval and Far Eastern issues, 1918–1922' (unpublished Ph.D. dissertation, University of London 1963); idem, *Illusions of Security: North Atlantic Diplomacy, 1918–1922* (Toronto: University of Toronto Press, 1972); J.M. McCarthy, *Australia and Imperial Defense, 1918–1939: A Study in Air and Sea Power* (St Lucia: University of Queensland Press, 1976); D.W. McIntyre, *The Rise and Fall of the Singapore Naval Base, 1919–1942* (London: Macmillan, 1979); idem, *New Zealand Prepares for War: Defense Policy 1919–1939* (Christchurch: University of Canterbury Press, 1988); I.C. MacGibbon, *Blue Water Rationale. The Naval Defense of New Zealand, 1914–1942* (Wellington: Historical Publications Branch, Department of Internal Affairs, 1981); and Ian Hamill, *The Strategic Illusion: The Singapore Strategy and the Defense of Australia and New Zealand* (Singapore: Singapore University Press, 1981).
2. The path to this changed status, reflected in praxis rather than law, was strewn with a host of preferences and schemes, none more curious than that in 1915 involving the

premier of British Columbia, Borden, Percival A. Witherby, posing as an agent of the New Zealand Government, and Massey (McBride to Borden, 18 Aug., Witherby to Borden, 30 Aug., Borden to Witherby, 10 Sept. and Borden to Massey, 10 Sept. 1915, Borden papers, OC 187A).

3. Jellicoe's report to the Canadian Government described war with the United States as 'almost inconceivable'. Jellicoe told Admiral Kingsmill, the ranking officer of the Canadian Navy, that he was under orders at Jutland to bring the capital ships back intact because, among other considerations, it was possible that Britain might have to defend itself in the future against the United States (interview with the late Rear-Admiral Walter Hose). But Jellicoe, in his report, unequivocally identified Japan as the enemy. Three addenda – an Australian intelligence report on Japan's dubious behaviour in certain occupied Pacific islands, a report on the Japanese threat to the Dutch East Indies, and a commentary on Japan's unreliability as an ally in the recent war and the influence of an extremist, pro-German element in Japan's policy formulating process – illustrated the identification.

4. W.J. Hudson, *Australia and the League of Nations* (Sydney: Sydney University Press, 1980), p. 12.

5. A variation on this speculation had Britain concluding a defensive alliance with Japan covering China and East Asia, and joining in a tripartite agreement on the Pacific which would provide for the security of Australia and New Zealand.

6. Jellicoe, in his reports to the Australian and New Zealand governments, proposed the creation of an imperial Pacific fleet, with the capital ship as its core, operating under unified command in peace and war. The fleet would give the Empire preeminent naval power in the Pacific, providing an impressive deterrent and ensuring victory should the deterrent fail. It would operate from several bases, including Singapore. Costs would be shared, based on population and the value of overseas trade, with Britain contributing 75 per cent of the cost. New Zealand would pay five per cent and Australia 20 per cent.

7. Siberia, military disarmament, war debts and Panama Canal tolls might get on to the agenda.

8. Colonial Office to Governor General, 12 Sept. 1921, Governors General papers (New Zealand), 9 May 1926.

9. Smuts to Meighen, 19 Oct., and Lloyd George to Meighen, 3 and 21 Oct., Borden papers (Ottawa) Vol. 283, reel C-4439 and Vol. 292, reel C-4448; Lloyd George to Massey, 3 Oct., and Massey to Lloyd George, 25 Oct., Governors General papers (New Zealand), 9/5/26; and Hughes to Lloyd George, 25 Oct. 1921, Australian archives (Canberra) A6661/1, 137OA. See also J.C. Vinson, 'The Problem of Australian Representation at the Washington Conference for the Limitation of Naval Armament', *The Australian Journal of Politics and History*, 3 and 4 Nov. 1957–Nov. 1958, pp. 155–64.

10. Lloyd George to Massey, 3 Oct., and Massey to Lloyd George, 7 Oct. 1921, Governors General papers (New Zealand), G/5/26; and Hughes to Massey, 4 Oct. 1921, Australian Archives, A6006/1. Pearce felt that Massey had pressed the Colonial Office for separate New Zealand representation, following Australia's decision, being unwilling to place New Zealand's affairs in Australian hands (Pearce to Hughes, 18 and 29 Oct. 1921, ibid., A4603).

11. Massey to Lloyd George, 12 Oct., and Lloyd George to Massey, 18 Oct., 1921, Governors General papers (New Zealand), 9 May 1926.

12. Hankey to Christie, 20 and 28 Oct., and Christie to Hankey, 1 Nov. 1921, Christie papers (Ottawa), Vol. 13, file 5 and Vol. 3, file 1; and Hankey to Christie, 25 Oct. 1921, Department of External Affairs files (Ottawa), (hereafter DEA) RG25F1, Vol. 915, file 7. See also Miles Lampson to Christie, 18 Sept. 1921, Christie papers, Vol. 3, file 7. Hankey sent the 25 Foreign Office papers to Christie, with a paper on the

organization of the Empire Delegation, but not the summary CID memorandum, which did not make 'very formidable reading'. Christie would get a copy in Washington. There is no similar evidence in the Australian and New Zealand files.

13. R. Shuker, 'New Zealand Naval Defense Policy and the Washington Conference, 1921–1922' (Wellington, Victoria University, Honors Research Paper 1909), pp. 23–5. Massey, the Navy and External Affairs departments, and even Jellicoe, the Governor General, may well have been involved in unrecorded briefings of Salmond. On Jellicoe's role generally, see I.C. MacGibbon, 'The Constitutional Implications of Lord Jellicoe's Influence on New Zealand Naval Policy, 1919–1930' *The New Zealand Journal of History*, 6, 1 April 1972, pp. 57–80. Salmond was a prolific author on legal subjects, but there are no Salmond papers and no biography of him. Hardly any of Massey's papers have survived.

14. Massey to Governor General, 11 Oct., Governor General to Colonial Office, 12 Oct., and Massey to Lloyd George, 12 Oct. 1921, Governors General papers (New Zealand), 9 May 1926. Mousley, with his Cambridge degree and legal training, was competent but opinionated and pretentious, confident that he was the best qualified of the four Dominion secretaries on Hankey's team. Mousley to Massey, 13 Nov. 1921, Prime Minister's papers (New Zealand), PM series 9, 4.

15. Pearce's selection, despite Labor's ridiculing of the prospect of a militarist attending a disarmament conference, has even been described as 'an inspired choice' (Paul Twomey, 'Small Power Security through Great Power Arms Control? – Australian Perceptions of Disarmament 1919–1933', *War and Society* 8, 1 (May 1990), pp. 71–99). See also Robert Thornton, 'The Semblance of Security: Australia and the Washington Conference, 1921–22', *The Australian Outlook* 32, 1 (1977), pp. 65–83.

16. Piesse memoranda, 22 March, 12 May, and 26 June 1920, Piesse papers, series 5, folder 1; Capt. W.H. Thring (RAN liaison officer at the Admiralty) memorandum, 14 Sept. 1921, Piesse papers, MS 882/5/271–4, and idem, Sept. 1921, ibid., MS 882/5/275–6. Piesse did not expect Japan to challenge either Australia's immigration policy or the New Guinea mandate, while raising again the issue of racial equality. He felt that Japan would neither probe into the Pacific Islands south of the equator nor fortify its mandatory islands north of the equator.

17. Christie to Hankey, 29 April 1921, Christie papers, Vol. 3, file 1.

18. Lloyd George to Meighen, 5 Oct. 1921, Borden papers, Vol. 292, reel C-4448; Borden to King, 26 and 27 Dec. 1921, King to Borden, 2 Jan. and Borden to King, 4 Jan. 1922; ibid., Vol., 283, reel C-4439; and Borden to Sir George Foster, 5 Jan. 1922; ibid., Vol. 269, reel C-4431. King instructed Borden to consult him on all unclear questions, and not to act on them until he received instructions.

19. Christie minute, on Geddes to Curzon, 21 Sept. 1921, DEA files, Vol. 916, file 14, and Christie to Newton Rowell, 28 Oct. 1921, Christie papers, Vol. 3, file 1.

20. Christie to Borden, 6 Oct. 1921, Borden papers, Vol. 292, reel C-4448. Borden responded promptly to ensure the flow of memoranda, adding a request to the Department of Agriculture for a paper on trade issues (Borden to O'Hara, 11 Oct, and Borden to Lougheed [acting Prime Minister], 11 Oct. 1921; ibid., Vol. 283, reel C-4439).

21. Christie memorandum, Naval Defense, n.d., 1921, Christie papers, Vol. 20, file 66, and Christie to Borden, 7 Sept. 1921, Borden papers, Vol. 266, reel C-4429.

22. Naval Service Department to Christie, 29 Oct., Intelligence Branch memorandum, n.d., and Naval Service Department memorandum, 28 Oct. 1921, DEA files, Vol. 916, file 17. The report to Christie summarized the state of the Canadian Navy. The memorandum of 28 Oct. compared the size and construction programmes of the British, Japanese and US navies.

23. Department of Trade and Commerce memoranda, e.g. 31 Oct. 1921, papers by the

Manufacturers Association, the Bankers Association and the Agricultural Department, ibid., Vol. 916, file 18; Department of Militia and Defense to Christie, 20 Oct. 1921, ibid., Vol. 920, file 43. (This included a report on the minuscule volunteer Canadian Air Force.) Also unsigned memoranda, 22 Sept. 1921, DEA memorandum, 29 Oct., and Christie note, n.d., ibid., Vol. 916, file 16.

24. Colonial Secretary to Governors General, 30 Oct. 1921, Lloyd George papers, F/10/1/ 5; and Fry, *Illusions of Security*, pp. 154–63.

25. Fry, *Illusions of Security*, pp. 164–65.

26. Hankey to Lloyd George, 11 Nov. 1921, Lloyd George papers, F/62/1/1; and Balfour to Lloyd George, 11 Nov. 1921. *Documents on British Foreign Policy* (hereafter DBFP), edited by R. Butler and J.P.T. Bury, 1st series, Vol. XIV, No. 415, pp. 466–70; Borden diary, 7, 9 and 10 Nov. 1921, Borden papers, Vol. 294, reel C-4449, and Pearce to Hughes, 11 Nov. 1921, Australian archives, A4603. No minutes were taken at the dinner.

27. Fry, *Illusions of Security*, pp. 165–71; British Empire Delegation, 7 Dec. 1921, Cab. 30/A1, and Australian archives, Pearce papers, A4719/14 (hereafter BED); and Borden diary, 7 Dec. 1921, Borden papers, Vol. 294, C-4449. Borden, lamenting press mischief on alleged differences within the Empire Delegation on the Anglo-Japanese alliance, attributed the problem to Salmond's inexperience (Borden diary, 24 Nov. 1921, ibid.; and Borden to Meighen, 24 Nov. 1921, ibid., Vol. 119, reel C-4345). This incident came on top of Salmond's initial indiscretion on the Dominion status question – not a very auspicious beginning.

28. BED, 9 Dec. 1921; Pearce to Hughes, 8 Dec. and Hughes to Pearce, 9 Dec. 1921, Australian archives, A4603; Hughes to Massey, 9 and 10 Dec., Jellicoe to Massey, 10 Dec., Jellicoe to Governor General of Australia, 12 Dec., and Massey to Salmond, 12 Dec. 1921, PM series, 9.4 and Governors General papers (New Zealand), G/5/26; Borden to Meighen, 8 and 10 Dec., and Meighen to Borden, 10 and 12 Dec. 1921, Borden papers, Vol. 119, reel C-4345. Meighen reported that the draft treaty had not yet reached him, 'but if Friday *New York Times* correctly indicates substance thereof you are authorized to sign on behalf of Canada.'

29. BED, 9 and 10 Dec. 1921; Pearce to Hughes, 8, 10, and 13 Dec., Hughes to Pearce, 12 and 17 Dec. 1921, and Hughes to Massey, 13 Dec. 1921, Australian archives, A4603. Balfour countered the Japanese demand for exclusion in part on the grounds of not differentiating between Japan's status and that of Australia and New Zealand.

30. Piesse memorandum, 27 Dec. 1921, Piesse papers, series 7, folder 2.

31. Pearce to Hughes, 29 Dec. 1921, Australian archives, A4603.

32. Salmond to Massey, 4 Jan. 1922, External Affairs Department, EAI, Acc W2619, 111/4/6 and PM series 9.4.

33. Mousley to Massey, 27 Dec. 1921, PM series 9/3.

34. Borden to Meighen, 8 Dec., and Borden to H. Wong, 30 Dec. 1921, Fry, *Illusions of Security*, pp. 177–78; Borden to Rowell, 15 Dec. 1921, and Borden to Sir George Foster, 5 Jan. 1922, Borden papers, Vol. 283, reel C-4439 and Vol. 269, reel C-4431; and Christie to Wrong, 21 Jan. 1922, ibid., Vol. 119., reel C-4346.

35. Borden to Lougheed, 19 and 21 Nov., Borden to Meighen, 22 Nov. and 12, 13, 14, 16, 19, 21, and 27 Dec. 1921, and Borden to King, 2, 6, 19, 21, 22, 23, and 25 Jan. 1922 and 1 Feb. 1922, ibid., Vol. 118, reel C-4345; Vol. 119, reel C-4346; Vol. 283, reel C-4438; and Vol. 292, reel C-4448.

36. Mousley to Massey, 27 Dec. 1921, PM series 9.3, and Salmond to Massey, 4 Jan. 1922, PM series 9.4. Mousley assured Massey that he was keeping a detailed record to compensate for the belated establishment of a cipher and for the way letters became outdated as they crawled home to Wellington.

37. Pearce to Hughes, 18 Nov. 1921 and 19 Jan. 1922, Hughes papers, series 16, II, 1,

folders 30 and 31; and Pearce to Hughes, 17, and 22 Nov. 1921, Australian archives, A4603.

38. Borden memorandum, 'American Proposal for the Limitation of Armaments', 14 Nov., and Pearce note, 14 Nov. 1921, Cab. 30/1.B.

39. Fry, *Illusions of Security*, pp. 178–86 and Christie note, 17 Dec. 1921, DEA files, Vol. 920, file 43. Beyond Pearce, Borden found little or no support. Hankey may well have encouraged Borden so as to put the matter to rest (Borden to Lougheed, 15 Nov. 1921, Borden papers, Vol. 119, reel C04345).

40. Ibid.; Pearce to Hughes, 14 and 15 Nov. 1921, Australian archives, A.4603, and Pearce note, 14 Nov. 1921, Borden papers, Vol. 292, C-4448.

41. BED, 15, 16, and 17 Nov. 1921, and Borden diary, 15, 16 and 17 Nov. 1921, Borden papers, Vol. 294, reel C-4449; Lloyd George to Borden and Borden to Lougheed, 16 and 17 Nov. 1921, ibid., Vol. 119, reel C-4345.

42. Lougheed to Borden, 18 and 23 Nov., and Borden to Lougheed, 14 and 28 Nov. 1921, Borden papers, Vol. 119, reel C-4345 and Vol. 283, reel C-4439; and Borden to Meighen, 3 Dec., and Meighen to Borden, 6 and 24 Dec. 1921, ibid.

43. Borden to Meighen, 9 Dec., ibid., and BED, 9 Dec., 1921.

44. Pearce to Hughes, 5 Dec., and Hughes to Pearce, 9 Dec. 1921, Australian archives, A4719/14, and A4603; and Pearce to Hughes, 18 Nov. 1921, Hughes papers, series 16, II, 1, folder 30. Pearce had already begun to voice concern about Japan's freedom to construct anti-submarine craft and submarines.

45. Borden diary, 9 Dec. 1921, Borden papers, Vol. 294, reel C-4449.

46. BED, 10 Dec. 1921.

47. Mousley to Massey, 27 Dec., PM series 9.3; and Pearce to Hughes, 2 Dec. 1921, Australian archives, A4603.

48. BED, 2 Dec., and Pearce to Hughes, 5 and 15 Dec. 1921 and 3 and 8 Jan. 1922, Australian archives, A4603.

49. BED, 9 Jan. 1922, and Pearce to Hughes, 10 Jan. 1922, Australian archives, A4603; and Borden to King, 10 Jan. 1922, Borden papers, Vol. 119, reel C-4346.

50. BED, 11 Jan., and Borden to King, 16 Jan., Borden papers, Vol. 294, reel C-4449 and Pearce to Hughes, 11 Jan. 1922, Australian Archives, A4603. Borden and Pearce reported that Hawaii was to be excluded, along with the islands off the coasts of Canada, Australia and New Zealand.

51. BED, 31 Jan., and Pearce to Hughes, 19, 23 and 25 Jan. 1922, Hughes papers, series 16, II, 1, folder 31, and Australian archives, A4603.

52. BED, 15, 16 and 17 Nov., and Pearce to Hughes, 14, 15 and 17 Nov. 1921, Australian archives, A4603, and Pearce to Hughes, 18 Nov. 1921, Hughes papers, series 16, II, 1, folder 30.

53. Ibid.

54. BED, 25 Nov.; Borden to Lougheed, 18, 19 and 20 Nov., and Borden to Meighen, 22, 23 and 24 Nov. 1921, Borden papers, Vol. 119, reel C-4345; and Borden diary, 18, 19, 21, 22, 23, 24, and 25 Nov. 1921, ibid., Vol. 294, reel C-4449. Borden could see how limiting land armaments could increase French security. He tried to convince Hughes that adoption of the international arbitration tribunal scheme would help resolve the dispute by diminishing French fears.

55. Borden to Balfour, 26 Nov., and Balfour to Borden, 29 Nov. 1921, ibid., Vol. 119, reel C-4345.

56. BED, 28 Nov., and 1 and 2 Dec.; Borden to Meighen, 12 Dec., Borden papers, Vol. 119, reel C-4345; and Pearce to Hughes, 2 Dec. 1921, Australian archives, A4603.

57. BED, 19 and 20 Dec. 1921.

58. Mousley to Massey, 27 Dec. 1921, PM series 9.3.

59. Balfour, primed by Lord Cavan to focus on the submarine issue, worked to derail the

subcommittee's work. Geddes provided the tactics – avoid angering an expectant public and let Hughes, recognizing the futility of it all, quietly drop the issue (BED, 1 and 2 Dec. 1921). Pearce supported Balfour and Geddes, and pointed to the peacetime commercial value of gas-producing plants; Borden did not, and threatened public dissent.

60. Pearce worried lest states build large cruisers under the guise of aircraft carriers; Chatfield assured him that any such ploy would be flagrant and detectable.
61. BED, 28 Dec. 1921 and 2, 4 and 6 Jan. 1922; Borden to Meighen, 21 and 27 Dec. 1921, and Borden to King, 2, 6 and 10 Jan. 1922, Borden papers, Vol. 119, reel C-4346, and Borden diary, 22, 28 and 30 Dec. 1921 and 3, 6, and 7 Jan. 1922, ibid., Vol. 294, reel C-4449.
62. Mousley to Massey, 27 Dec. 1921, PM series 9.3.
63. BED, 19, 20 and 28 Dec. 1921 and 2, 4, 6, 11, 13 and 31 Jan. 1922. Salmond joined Balfour in opposing Hughes's Annex B on exemptions from the scrapping of capital ships. He worked on the subcommittee on the retention of plants that would build new ships and modernize the capital ships being retained. See also Borden to King, 16 Jan. 1922, Borden papers, vol. 294, reel C-4449.
64. King to Borden, 25, 27 and 28 Jan. and 1, 2, and 3 Feb., and Borden to King, 27, 28 and 31 Jan. and 1, 2 and 4 Feb. 1922, King papers, Vol. 62, reel C-1948, and Borden papers, Vol. 294, reel C-4449; and Christie memorandum, n.d., DEA files, F1, Vol. 916, file 19.
65. Borden to Duke of Devonshire, 2 March 1922, Borden papers, Vol. 271, reel C-4432.
66. Borden to Hankey, 23 Jan. 1932, ibid.; and Grigg to Christie, 17 Feb. 1922, Christie papers, Vol. 13, file 8.
67. Borden to Smuts, 19 Jan. 1923, Borden papers, Vol. 266, reel C-4429.
68. Salmond to Massey, 29 July 1922, and Salmond notes, n.d., EA1, W2619, 111/4/8.
69. Salmond to Massey, 4 and 8 Jan. 1922, PM series 9.4.
70. Official report of the Australian delegate, 1 June 1922; various statements, 1922, Pearce papers, part III, MS1927, 3 and 17 86/1; five memoranda, n.d., ibid., CP 285/2/1; and Pearce to Hughes, 1 June 1922, Hughes papers, series 16, folder 31.
71. It is difficult to believe that either Hughes or Pearce placed great value on rules restricting the use of submarines and poisonous gases in warfare. They approved of retaining the right to produce poisonous gases as a deterrent and as a hedge against the risk of an enemy resorting to their use in war.
72. Defense Department to Hughes, 7 April 1922, Hughes papers, series 19, folder 5. Pearce had assured the Defense Department that there was no possibility of war in the Pacific for ten years. In the 1921–22 fiscal year the Australian Navy had cost £3,099,938. The estimate for 1922–23 could be set at £2,563,025. The overall defence budget would fall from £6,357,938 to £4,557,755. Australia would undertake no new naval construction; its small navy, like those of Canada and New Zealand, would become even more modest.
73. Hankey's initial disparaging comments about Pearce should be dismissed. The role of Mark Sheldon, the Australian High Commissioner in the United States, which Pearce applauded, remains to be examined. Piesse doubtless gave careful advice to Pearce, but there is no evidence on which to base an assessment of his role. He felt himself initially under-employed (Piesse to P.E. Deans, 30 Nov. 1921, Australian archives, A4063.
74. Piesse to Deans, n.d., Piesse papers, series 7, folder 1. Piesse was still concerned, however, about the continued growth of Japanese naval power, and, naturally, Japanese intelligence activities continued to come under scrutiny (Churchill to Governor General, 7 Feb. 1923, Hughes papers, series 16, folder 32).
75. Admiralty memorandum, n.d. (Feb. 1922 and to the CID on 28 July 1922), Navy Department files (New Zealand) N/10/76.

The Evolution of the United States Navy's Strategic Assessments in the Pacific, 1919–31

WILLIAM R. BRAISTED

The 12 years from the close of the First World War to the Manchurian Incident, 1919–1931, witnessed the emergence of what might be called the Washington Conference system of naval power. This was essentially a system in which Britain, the United States and Japan shared dominion over the high seas. Through these years, American naval officers, with considerable input from their army opposite numbers, worked on a range of plans for war against Orange (Japan) and, to a lesser extent, against Red (Britain), based on estimates, war games, fleet problems, and other exercises that reveal how the war planners tested their assumptions and why they modified their thinking.

For more than a decade before the First World War American naval strategists had been primarily concerned with the emergence of two rising naval powers, Germany and Japan, as potential threats to the security of the United States in the Atlantic and in the Pacific respectively. Whereas American naval men had been uncertain before 1919 whether Germany or Japan was the more likely enemy, they agreed that Germany was the more dangerous of the two, and that the Atlantic was by far the more important of the two oceans. The Navy, therefore, concentrated its most powerful forces in the Atlantic, notwithstanding that Britain's Royal Navy kept the German High Seas Fleet confined to its European ports. The Navy's Black Plans for war against Germany were designed to prevent intrusion by the German fleet into the western hemisphere. Its Orange Plans for war against Japan called for the projection of American sea power to the western Pacific for defence of the Philippines, and ultimately the defeat of Japan. For American naval men, the defeat of Germany in the First World War eliminated the German naval threat, but it also released the British Navy for operations in waters outside Europe. Whereas Japan was already fixed in American naval estimates as a possible enemy, there loomed in the minds of some naval men after 1919 the fear that Britain, no longer diverted by Germany, might turn against the United States as she saw her markets lost to Americans. Throughout the period 1919–1931, the Navy stationed important segments of its fleets in both the Atlantic and the Pacific, available for concentration by means of the recently opened Panama Canal.

The problem facing American war planners when they contemplated an Orange campaign was largely logistic – how to support the superior American battle fleet as it moved 7,000 miles across the Pacific to the Philippines. In 1919, American logistic support in a campaign against Japan was secure as far west as Pearl Harbor. Beyond the Hawaiian Islands, the fleet's course remained in doubt because the Navy had never been able to secure adequate funding for a main overseas base in the western Pacific, either at Guam or in the Philippines. The logistic outlook for the Navy after 1919 was otherwise significantly improved by the opening of the Panama Canal, by the progressive conversion of the fleet from coal to oil burning ships, and by the spectacular expansion of the American merchant marine. By no means least important was the transfer of Germany's islands in the north Pacific to Japan as an unfortified mandate of the League of Nations, which opened a path of potential way-stations for the American fleet during a movement across the Pacific.[1]

Estimates prepared by the secretary of the Navy's senior advisers on the General Board and by war planners in the Office of Naval Operations in 1919–20 reflected abiding suspicion of both Britain and Japan, then still joined in the Anglo-Japanese Alliance. In a draft building programme in 1919, the General Board estimated that Britain would not hesitate to enlist the support of Japan in war against the United States should Britain's maritime supremacy be threatened by an expanding American merchant marine. The board doubted whether the United States could afford to remain diplomatically isolated in light of 'the traditional and dominating policies of Great Britain and Japan'.[2] While the more moderate War Plans Division expected unpleasantness with Britain arising from 'commercial, financial, and shipping rivalry', it held relations with Japan to be 'considerably more acute' than those with Britain. The planners in Operations estimated in the spring of 1920 that American capital ships – built, building, or authorized – were sufficient to assure the United States of superiority in battle forces over Britain and Japan for some years. Their building recommendations called for rapid expansion of the inadequate bases in the Pacific, and ship construction in categories (cruisers and aircraft) in which the Navy was then deficient.[3] Admiral Robert E. Coontz, the Chief of Naval Operations, declared in February 1920 that the United States required a three-to-two naval superiority over Japan to compensate for inadequate bases in the Pacific, while a three-to-two inferiority would enable it to deny an enemy (Britain) use of its bases in the western Atlantic.[4]

These estimates from Operations were clearly based on the Navy's needs as exposed by studies in the new War Plans Division of war situations involving Britain (Red) and Japan (Orange). Perhaps the most significant product of the division's early labours was a new War Portfolio, completed in March 1920, that included a Pacific Strategic War Plan (Orange), a Combined Atlantic and Pacific Strategic War Plan (Red–Orange), and a Basic Readiness Plan.[5] As explained by the brilliant young planner, Commander Holloway H. Frost, it was then considered improbable that Red (Britain) would assist Orange (Japan) should war break out between Orange and Blue (the United States). On the other hand, should the United States become involved in war with Britain, it seemed 'practically certain that Orange would immediately declare war on Blue . . . either in alliance with Red or as an entirely separate operation in its own interests'.[6]

American war planners in 1919–20 and for years thereafter viewed the strategic situation in the Pacific and in the Atlantic as essentially similar, but with the United States cast in opposite roles. Whereas in a war against an equal or superior British fleet, Blue (American) naval forces would be marshalled in the western Atlantic to prevent Britain from deploying her fleet to win control of the sea from her western Atlantic bases, the United States would strive in an Orange campaign to force the submission of Japan by moving the superior Blue fleet to the western Pacific, ultimately to blockade Japan in her own home waters. War against a Red–Orange (Anglo-Japanese) coalition actually posed less serious problems for the American planners than did an Orange campaign, at least in its initial phases. Blue would concentrate its major units in the Atlantic to meet Red's advance, and would retain only sufficient force in the Pacific to prevent Orange from winning control of the eastern Pacific. The American planners predicted that Orange would surrender once she was cut off from communication with the outside world. It was expected, on the other hand, that Red would mount an invasion through Crimson (Canada) should she win control of the western Atlantic.[7] The war planners' immediate concern after the First World War, however, was their Orange Plan, in which they conceived a three-phased war: first, to defend American positions in the eastern Pacific while the fleet assembled in Hawaii; second, to advance to the mid-Pacific to capture the Japanese-held Marshalls and Carolines; and, finally, to win control of waters around Japan, preparatory to a blockade of the Japanese home islands. They then believed that Guam and the Philippines would both fall long before the arrival of the fleet in the western Pacific.[8]

Having learned from bitter controversy with the Army over the Navy's Philippine base plans that the Army's acceptance of the Navy's Pacific strategy was essential, the naval war planners in 1920 won from the reorganized Joint Army and Navy Board adoption of the Navy's objective to bridge the Pacific with bases. Apart from the Hawaiian Islands, the board stressed the importance of building up Guam as a main overseas fortified base. With such a base at Guam secure in American hands, the board held that American forces in the Philippines could deter an attack on those islands. It further recommended that, until completion of the fortified Guam base, the Army and the Navy hold to the joint mission in the Philippines assigned to them in 1916: 'To defend Manila and Manila Bay'.[9] Again on prompting from the Navy, the Joint Army and Navy Board in July 1920 adopted an order of priority for the development of Pacific bases: a fleet operating base in Hawaii, subsidiary bases at Guam and Cavite (in the Philippines), a fleet operating base at Guam, and lesser operating bases in California at San Diego and San Pedro.[10] By establishing a separate Pacific Fleet including half its battleships, the Navy in 1919 imposed unprecedented need for expansion of its Pacific coast yards.

The Washington Conference on the Limitation of Naval Armaments, 1921–1922, was important in providing a structure for the three-power naval system that had been evolving since 1919. Asked by the State Department for a plan for naval limitation, the General Board declared that the United States required a fleet equal to the British and double the Japanese to meet its rivals respectively in the Atlantic and in the Pacific. Should the Anglo-Japanese Alliance continue, however, the General Board wanted a fleet equal to the combined fleets of Britain and Japan, since it conceived that the alliance could only be directed against the United States. Ever mindful of logistics, the board wanted to acquire the French Pacific islands in order to open a southern route to the Philippines, and it warned against any proposal to neutralize or to allow fortification of Japan's mandated Pacific islands that might deny them to the United States. Based on Secretary of State Charles Evans Hughes' 'stop now' proposal, however, the Five-Power Naval Treaty of 1922 established limits on capital ships and aircraft carriers in the British, American, and Japanese navies in a ration of 5.5.3 respectively, with total tonnage levels set at about half those first recommended by the General Board. For American naval men, however, the really stunning provision in the naval treaty was the famous Article XIX, in which the United States undertook to halt further naval base construction and new fortifications west of a line from the Aleutians, to Hawaii, to Panama. While American naval planners came eventually to defend the 5.5.3 ratio as a goal to be achieved, they laboured until the Second World War to overcome the handicap imposed by Article XIX to successful American naval operations in the western Pacific. Naval men might welcome the end of the Anglo-Japanese Alliance, but the promise by Britain, the United States, Japan, and France in the Four-Power Treaty to support the status quo in the Pacific failed to banish from American Army and Navy thought the possibility of war against an Anglo-Japanese (Red–Orange) coalition.[11]

The Five-Power Naval Treaty of 1922 provided a base upon which American war planners could build their plans and estimates through the 1920s. Typical of the annual estimates from the Navy's War Plans Division is that for 1924, which, like others of the period, still pointed to Britain and Japan as the two nations then capable of disputing control of the sea with the United States. While there were sources of friction that might lead to war with either or both rivals, the War Plans Division still judged relations with Japan 'more acute' than those with Britain. It seemed only possible that Britain might join Japan in war against the United States, but should the United States be involved in war against Britain, the War Plans Division 'expected' Japan to join Britain. The division, therefore, gave highest priority to preparing the Navy 'to support national policies against Japan' and second priority to readiness for war against the British Empire or an Anglo-Japanese coalition.

The War Plans Division supported a distribution of the United States Fleet to facilitate its quick concentration against Japan in the Hawaiian Islands or against Britain in the New York–Narragansett Bay area. The best disposition to ensure a rapid concentration at Hawaii was to keep the entire fleet in the Pacific. Since the Pacific yards were inadequate to support so large a force, and since it was important to keep the east coast shore facilities efficient, the War Plans Division favoured the scheme, already adopted by the Navy Department the previous year, whereby the most powerful segment of the United States Fleet, including its 12 mightiest, oil-burning battleships, was concentrated in the Pacific as the Battle Fleet. A weaker segment known as the Scouting Fleet, of six older battleships and numerous lighter craft, was assigned to the Atlantic. This arrangement underlined the vital importance of the Panama Canal, through which the sub-fleets passed each year to join in one ocean or the other for battle practice.[12]

The naval planners moved promptly to replace the pre-conference War Portfolios with a new set of plans that were in line with the Five-Power Naval Treaty. The new plans were initially divided into two volumes: Volume One, a Basic Readiness Plan (WPL-8) that established the standards of readiness or preparedness toward which the

Navy should strive during peace, and Volume II, a volume of colour plans, the first of which would be a new Basic War Plan Orange (WPL-9) for war against Japan. The Basic Readiness Plan established a point in time, Zero-Day, the day for beginning operations. It assumed that the Navy Department would issue preliminary orders 40 days before the hypothetical Zero-Day in an Orange war and 70 days before Zero-Day in a Red–Orange war. Given the 40-day alert, the plan called for the concentration at Hawaii ten days after Zero-Day of an expeditionary force 50 per cent superior to the Japanese naval strength and 50,000 army troops. In a war against the British Empire, the Navy was expected to assemble in the New York–Narragansett region by Zero-Day a force equal in strength to the active British fleet. The plan also provided for naval building to achieve equality with the British Navy, including 40 10,000 ton eight-inch gun cruisers and aircraft carriers to the level permitted by the treaty. The section on shore establishments accorded highest priority to naval base development in the Pacific: the Hawaiian Islands, Guam (for maintenance only), Manila Bay (for maintenance only), San Francisco Bay, and Puget Sound. An ingenious secret Appendix F, adopted later in the year, outlined a mobile base project, including floating dry-docks and other facilities sufficient to provide for one main outlying base and one outlying support base. The mobile base material was presumably to equip a main base in the Philippines or elsewhere in the western Pacific and a subsidiary support base closer to Japan.[13] When Assistant Secretary of the Navy Theodore Roosevelt Jr called for a report on the Navy's readiness to relieve the Philippines, the major deficiencies listed by the War Plans Division included the lack of floating dry-docks capable of taking the heaviest ships, 40 cruisers, 48 submarines and five distilling ships, and a personnel shortage of more than 50 per cent.[14]

The urgent problem confronting American war planners after 1922 was to devise an Orange Plan to overcome the obstacles to operations in the western Pacific imposed by Article XIX of the treaty. Since Guam would almost surely be lost at the outset of an Orange war, the naval planners shifted their attention to the Philippines, where the United States had already built fortifications commanding the entrances to Manila Bay and neighbouring Subic Bay. It was hoped that the 14-inch guns on the islands at the entrances to Manila Bay would deny the bay to the Japanese Navy and perhaps save it for the Americans until the arrival of the United States Fleet from the eastern Pacific. Moved in part by pressure from the Navy, the Joint Board in May 1922 adopted an interpretation of Article XIX that left room for later upbuilding of military and naval forces in the western Pacific: that Article XIX imposed no restriction on mobile land and sea forces, that 'as a matter of policy', however, it was inadvisable to build up mobile forces in the Philippines at that time, and that Article XIX should be strictly carried out so far as naval shore facilities and fortifications were concerned. Proponents of a determined defence of the Philippines also won a further victory shortly thereafter when the Joint Board decided that Panama, Hawaii, and Manila were the three most vital coast positions to be defended.[15] From the Philippines, Admiral A.E. Anderson, the Commander-in-Chief of the Asiatic Fleet, joined with Governor-General Leonard Wood to demand the utmost endeavours to hold the islands as a base for the United States Fleet. Anderson claimed that with but small forces added to the light units of his command, he could gravely hamper if not deter Japanese operations against the Philippines and even Guam.[16]

A full reconsideration of the Philippines in the strategy of an Orange war was precipitated in June 1922 when Theodore Roosevelt Jr ordered the General Board working with the War Plans Division to survey the 'Grand Strategy of the Pacific' and to prepare estimates upon which to base 'plans for the execution of decisions already arrived at'.[17]

In September 1922 the naval war planners completed a 27-page estimate of the Blue–Orange situation in which they concluded that the United States could only force Japan to accept American terms by blockading the Japanese home islands from an advanced base within 500 miles of Tsushima. The planners anticipated a struggle by the United States to prevent Japan from establishing her 'suzerainty' in the Far East. Since the United States Navy was superior to the Japanese in all classes save cruisers, the basic American problem was to move the United States Fleet to the Far East and to establish base facilities there *after* the outbreak of war. Japan's objective, on the other hand, would be to secure her vital sea communications by denying the western Pacific to the United States after capturing the Philippines and Guam. The war planners estimated that the Navy would require the services of 35 per cent of the American merchant marine and of all American tankers just to supply the fleet on its trans-Pacific movement. To support the fleet in the western Pacific, the Navy would be forced to fabricate a base, the most vital elements of which would be floating dry-docks built in and moved from the United States. To construct a floating dry-dock capable of handling the largest warships would require 18 months.

The war planners devoted a good part of their estimate to the various means by which the United States might establish a superior fleet in the western Pacific: by keeping it there during peace, by dispatching it directly to the Philippines either during strained relations or immediately after the outbreak of war, by moving the fleet east through the Mediterranean or around Cape Horn, by sending it across the Pacific on a northern or southern route, or by moving it in stages across the central Pacific. The staged 'step-by-step' advance across the central route was judged in the September estimate to be the safest and surest of success. If Britain's Singapore base were available, the planners believed that the United States Fleet could sail directly to the western Pacific and rely on local British sources of support.[18]

The war planners' conservative estimate was far more cautious than the brief, aggressive 'Strategic Survey of the Pacific' completed by the General Board in April 1923. The General Board called for a vigorous offensive in its *General Concept*:

> An offensive war, primarily naval, directed towards isolation of Japan through control of all waters around Japan, through the equivalent of blockade operations, and through the capture and occupation of all outlying Japanese islands intensified by an air war against Japanese territory.

The board declared that the 'first and governing concern' was to secure a base for the fleet in the western Pacific and that Manila Bay was 'the best suited of all available sites for a primary advanced base'. To carry out its 'General Concept', the General Board proposed a war strategy based on an 'immediate naval advance with available land reinforcements for Manila', a subsequent movement to Japan's home waters, the transport of 250,000 troops to the western Pacific, and occupation or control of all anchorages in the Japanese mandates and in the Philippines. As part of its peace strategy, it called for construction of mobile base equipment and cultivation of 'good relations' with Far Eastern powers likely to adopt benevolent neutrality toward the United States: Holland, China, and a 'regenerated Russia'.[19]

The General Board's strategy, including its stress on the Philippines, was fully approved by the Navy Department. At the suggestion of Admiral Coontz, Britain was also designated as a power whose friendship the United States should cultivate in the Far East.[20] The war planners quickly modified their September Blue–Orange estimate to include a statement that the Philippines constituted a position of 'greatest strategic importance' whose retention was of 'utmost importance'. The security of the islands, observed the planners, was dependent on the 'timely arrival of a joint Army and Navy reinforcement', the naval contingent of which should be at least 25 per cent superior to the Japanese Navy. Although an early reinforcement would divide American naval strength and place a major portion of the fleet in the western Pacific without dry-docks and secure supply, the war planners now judged the importance of holding the Philippines sufficient to justify the risk. Their amended estimate, however, reflected ambivalence in American naval thinking. Whereas the estimate still described a step-by-step advance as the surest road to ultimate victory, it also approved an immediate westward dash to save Manila Bay as the site for the Navy's main base in the western Pacific.[21]

The General Board's strategic survey was incorporated practically without change in a Joint Board paper of July 1923 entitled 'Synopsis of Joint Army and Navy Estimates of the Orange Situation',[22] and the Joint Board's 'Synopsis' provided the basis for the Navy's Basic War Plan Orange (WPL-9) of February 1924 and the first Joint Army and Navy War Plan Orange of August 1924. The sequence of these estimates and plans suggests that the Army was largely content in 1922–24 to ratify the strategy proposed by the Navy. While the Navy's War Plan Orange stressed the importance of moving quickly to Manila, it also left to the Commander-in-Chief of the United States Fleet '*When* and *how* and *whether* Manila shall be relieved'. The prime objective of the plan was to establish American naval superiority over Japan in the western Pacific so that Japan could be isolated and blockaded in accordance with the General Board's 'General

Concept'. Destruction of the Japanese fleet 'whenever and wherever met' would 'contribute most' to success. To assure the Commander-in-Chief of freedom of choice, the Navy's 1924 Orange Plan included two logistic schemes: one for a step-by-step movement and the other for a quick dash across the Pacific. Insufficient personnel was termed 'the most serious difficulty in execution' of the plan; the lack of underwater repair facilities and of distilling ships, 'the most serious material difficulty'.[23]

The Joint Army and Navy War Plan-Orange completed by the Joint Board in August 1924 summed up the main features of the other post-Washington Conference plans and assigned missions to the Army as well as the Navy. Repeating the 'General Concept' of the General Board, the Joint Board anticipated a three-phased war, initially to establish the vital western Pacific base, secondly to isolate Japan by cutting her sea communications, and finally to press such further unspecified operations as might force Japan to submit. The Navy's interest in the first two phases was declared paramount, and the requirements of the service with paramount interest were to be governing. The board predicted 'a long war, primarily naval' that should be 'conducted with boldness from the earliest stage'. Apart from increasing the garrisons at Panama and Hawaii, the Army would provide troops for the 'United States Asiatic Expeditionary Forces' that would accompany the fleet. The plan also authorized the Army to mobilize troops in the continental United States; this was deemed necessary in order to meet 'unforeseen entanglements', that is, invasions from Canada and Mexico. In addition to building up the fleet, the Navy was to provide 'adequate mobile base facilities, particularly floating docks and fuel supply'. Timing in the plan was based on the Navy's Zero-Day schedule.[24]

The war planners, inspired by the heroic strategy of the General Board, had allowed valour to overcome sound judgement when they drew up their Pacific war plans in 1923–24. Naval men knew from experience that the civil authorities were unlikely to allow significant ship movements before the outbreak of war (Zero-Day) lest these movements themselves provoke war. Admiral Edward W. Eberle, the Chief of Naval Operations, conceded in late 1924 that, given the parsimony of Congress, the Navy would be unable for some years to progress toward the standards of readiness specified in the war plans.[25]

Confronted by these grim facts, Roosevelt concluded that the fall of the Philippines early in an Orange war was 'more than probable'. It was 'possible' that the United States might secure the use of a foreign base in the Far East, but Roosevelt judged it 'dangerous in the extreme to count on such a contingency'. Once the Philippines had fallen to Japan, the Assistant Secretary expected an 'irresistible demand' from the American people to rush the superior American fleet to Asiatic waters without 'the all important essential' for such a move, a Class A floating dry-dock capable of handling the largest ships.[26] The obvious importance of this key element for a mobile base notwithstanding, the General Board was unwilling to give priority to a dry-dock over ships, since it deemed that ships were also 'vital and essential' for a Pacific campaign.[27]

As Commander-in-Chief of the United States Fleet, in late 1924, Admiral Coontz strongly insisted that the greatest need of the fleet was a mobile base with floating dry-dock facilities. 'Convinced that a bold move would contribute largely to victory', however, Coontz was determined to sail westward quickly in an Orange campaign, even if the fleet train were smaller than planned.[28] Indeed, assuming that the Philippines would not fall to Orange before Zero-Day plus 60 days, and that the 16 battleships plus other basic elements of the initial expedition could assemble at Hawaii by Zero-Day plus ten days, the Commander-in-Chief opted for a direct movement to the Philippines in his Contributory Orange Plan (Plan 0–3 Orange). Although the Bureau of Navigation could not promise exactly the forces requested by Coontz for the initial expedition, it volunteered to provide a fleet of equivalent strength, including 18 battleships, on 30 days' notice.[29]

Meanwhile, during Admiral Coontz's tour as CINCUS, 1923–25, the fleet engaged in a series of fleet problems designed to test or to prove its ability to conduct trans-Pacific operations. In Fleet Problem No. 2, the fleet sailed south from California to the Gulf of Panama, simulating a dash from Hawaii to the Philippines with the west coast of Mexico and Central America substituted for Japan's Pacific island mandate; in Fleet Problem No. 4 it moved from Panama to capture a base at Culebra, an approximation at least of the distance to be covered by an expedition from the Philippines northward to seize a base at Amami Oshima, with Haiti substituted for Japan.[30]

Fleet Problem No. 5 was intended to test the ability of the fleet to protect its train against attack by an intercepting raiding force, an exercise that fell short of success, since fleet and raiding force failed to meet.[31] Perhaps the most interesting innovation during these fleet problems was the United States Fleet Cruising Disposition (or Screening Formation) No. 2, in which the fleet would be organized in four concentric circles for protection of the fleet train, including the mobile base if available, during its passage across the Pacific: an outer circle of submarine scouts enclosing circles of destroyers, of cruisers, and finally of battleships. The flagship of the officer in tactical command (OTC) would occupy a position within the inner ring of battleships, from which the tactical commander could signal shifts in direction that would be accomplished without breaking formation, as would necessarily be the case should the fleet be organized in rectangular formation. This circular formation was seen as the most effective instrument for resisting attrition from enemy raiding attacks as the Blue fleet moved slowly westward across the Pacific.[32] Finally, in the summer of 1925, Admiral Coontz led a fleet of 56 vessels, including 12 battleships of the Battle Fleet, on a spectacular cruise from Hawaii to Australia and New Zealand, roughly the distance from Pearl Harbor to Manila, that the Admiral hailed as a demonstration of the fleet's capacity to maintain itself at a great distance from its home sources of shore support.[33] Doubtless in deference to Japan, the Navy Department never sent the fleet on a trial run to the Philippines.

Vital to the success of the offensive strategy of the 1924 Orange plans was the assumption that the United States would hold the site for a base in the Philippines until the arrival of the United States Fleet. The primary mission for the Army and the Navy under the contributory Combined (Philippine) Army and Navy War Plan Orange of January 1925 was to defend Manila and Manila Bay 'by operating on the offensive and defensive against enemy forces in the Luzon area'. Naval forces from the weak Asiatic Fleet available to the defence were estimated at 18 destroyers, six submarines, and nine planes.[34] The army hoped through recruitment to expand by 10,000 men its peacetime garrison of approximately 13,000 officers and men. Of the utmost importance were the great guns mounted on Corregidor and neighbouring islands at the entrances to Manila Bay, including eight 14-inch guns, eight 12-inch rifles, 24 12-inch mortars, 11 six-inch gun batteries, and an elaborate system of searchlights. These awesome guns were the principal elements for holding an ultimate defence area embracing Bataan Peninsula and the islands at the bay's entrances. Outside the ultimate defence area were the small naval stations at Cavite on Manila Bay and Olongapo on Subic Bay.

It became increasingly clear that the United States would not be able to hold Manila Bay outside the ultimate defence area until the arrival of reinforcement in an Orange campaign, but local Army and Navy exercises in 1925 and 1926 demonstrated that naval facilities even within the ultimate defence area would be threatened with destruction by long-range enemy bombardment.[35] This and other factors led the Joint Board in 1928 to seek a new mission for American forces in the Philippines, on the assumption that Manila Bay could not be held as a base for the American battle fleet in an Orange war. Army officers in the islands then estimated that the forts at the bay's entrances could hold no longer than 90 days against Japanese attack, and they recommended a revised mission: 'To hold the entrances to Manila Bay until the arrival of the United States Fleet'.[36] This suggested an effort to deny the bay to the Japanese fleet without any attempt to hold the bay area as a base for the American fleet. Prompted by the Navy, which could not accept with equanimity the abandonment of the Philippine base, the Joint Board adopted a compromise mission, to encourage defence of the Manila Bay area, so long as the primary objective of holding the bay's entrances was not jeopardized:

> PRIMARY MISSION: To hold the entrances to Manila Bay.
> SECONDARY MISSION: To hold the Manila Bay area as long as possible consistent with the successful accomplishment of the Primary Mission.[37]

In the autumn of 1926 the Joint Army and Navy Board and its attendant Joint Planning Committee began a full review of its 1924 War Plan Orange, to clarify the timing and to establish more definite stages of mobilization. It was a review in which the Army would be heard. In place of the Navy's Zero-Day, by which time the Navy hoped to attain a degree of preparation contingent on a 40-day advance warning, the Joint Planning Committee adopted the Army's M-Day (Mobilization Day) as a firm starting time from which planners could establish stages of mobilization with confidence. The Joint Board also decided that the Japanese forces operating against Manila could render the bay untenable for the United States Fleet before its arrival, that it would be necessary to seize an outlying base in the western Pacific other than Manila Bay, and that no expedition should be launched across the Pacific without authorization from the President.[38]

These decisions clearly reflected fears from Army planners that the Navy's pressure for an early offensive would lead to disaster. In December 1926 the Army members of the Joint Planning Committee protested to the Joint Board that the 1924 War Plan Orange would 'commit the United States to a far reaching decision – the immediate movement of our forces to the Far East –' without indicating what further operations would be necessary to ensure Japan's submission. The Joint Board thereupon approved a proposal from General C.P. Summerall, the Army Chief of Staff, that the 1924 War Plan Orange be revised after 'comprehensive studies of the military, naval, political, psychological, and economic aspects' of the 'several courses of strategic action' likely to ensure success.[39]

The Joint Planning Committee laboured for more than a year to complete an 82-page, single-spaced estimate of the Blue-Orange situation that became the basis for an entirely new Joint Army and Navy War Plan Orange. As did other military papers of the time, the committee's 1928 estimate predicted possible conflict between the United States and Japan over China, immigration, the security of the Philippines, and Japan's quest for unchallenged naval domination of the Far East. While the British Dominions of Australia, New Zealand, and Canada would be wholly sympathetic toward the United States, Britain herself was expected by the planners to strive hard for neutrality. Indeed, the committee declared that Japan would not risk war with the United States unless Britain were 'seriously involved elsewhere' or had given other assurances of non-interference. Partly out of fear that Britain would oppose American naval operations to isolate Japan, the planners proposed to keep a reserve of 500,000 troops in the United States to watch the Canadian border. It also seemed that the anti-capitalist masters of the Kremlin and the self-serving warlords of China would incline toward Japan. France was believed to have entered a secret pact with Japan. Only from Holland did the war planners hope for benevolent neutrality, which would secure oil from the Dutch East Indies for American forces based in the Philippines.

The Joint Planning Committee still aimed to force Japan's acceptance of American will by isolating the Japanese home islands and defeating the Japanese fleet. It saw for the Army a role essentially as support for the Navy's campaign to isolate Japan, as it seemed impractical for the United States to invade the Japanese main islands or to operate on the Asian mainland. Air power, but little noticed in 1924, figured prominently in the 1928 estimate. Eventual American supremacy in the air seemed assured from the fact that the United States within 13 months could expand production to an estimated 1,500 planes a month, as compared with Japan's expected top production of only 700 planes a year.

Manila was still regarded as the best position for an advanced main base for the United States Fleet. Should Japan be able to deny Manila Bay as a base, the Joint Planning Committee favoured establishing a wholly new base elsewhere in the Philippines, preferably at Dumanquilas in Mindanao. It would leave to the Commander-in-Chief of the fleet whether to advance directly to the Philippines or to adopt a more cautious step-by-step strategy. The committee outlined a further northward movement by stages to Amami Oshima, the most promising location for a base for close investment of Japan. The committee was unwilling, however, to risk precious heavy American units in an assault on Amami Oshima until the Navy had built and moved to the Philippines one large floating dry-dock. This would delay the Amami Oshima operation to about M-Day plus 450 days. Proposed subsequent operations included the capture of Tsushima and of lesser islands to win access to the Japan Sea, from which to launch air strikes against Japan proper.

The Army members of the Joint Planning Committee pointedly refused to subscribe to the decision by the Navy members that it would be necessary to mount a strategic offensive in the western Pacific designed to force Japan's submission through economic pressure. Nor would the Army members endorse the decisions by the Navy committeemen that outlined an offensive war in terms strikingly similar to those of the 1924 War Plans Orange. The Joint Board, however, directed the planning committee to prepare a new Orange Plan 'based on the strategic offensive'.[40]

The Joint Board debated the details of the new Joint Army and Navy War Plan Orange for still another year before it was finally issued to the services in January 1929. Modified only slightly from the General Board's wording of 1923, the 'concept' of the 1929 plan still predicted a primarily naval war to isolate and exhaust Orange, but with the provision that the Army might be employed in major operations. First of the joint decisions in the new plan was to establish at the earliest possible date Blue sea power in the western Pacific superior to that of Orange. To this end, the 1929 plan called for an expedition with naval forces superior to those of Orange to secure an advanced base at Manila Bay or elsewhere. The second major decision in the 1929 plan was to hold Manila Bay as long as possible with forces in the western Pacific, so that the area would be denied to Orange as a naval base even if it could not be secured for Blue. Other decisions too numerous to repeat provided for defence of such key positions as Hawaii and Panama, protection of vital Blue lines of supply, and operations to win for Blue control of Orange home waters. An intricate arrangement based on the principle of paramount interest assured the Navy of the power to coordinate all forces in the Hawaiian and Asiatic theatres during the presence of the main Blue fleet. The entire trans-Pacific movement, however, would await authorization from the President rather than depend upon the discretion of the Commander-in-Chief of the United States Fleet.

Much of the 1929 War Plan Orange provided mobilization schedules that stipulated progressive assembly of army units at Pacific Coast ports, and of warships at Hawaii. By M-Day plus 60 days, the Navy was to have concentrated in Hawaiian waters a fleet roughly equivalent to that provided in the 1924 plans for Zero-Day plus ten days. Ultimately, the Army was to mobilize 1,200,000 men. Except for the initial decisions, the stress of the 1929 plan was toward an orderly build-up of forces rather than a hasty, dangerous offensive.

The plan reflected years of deliberate planning, consulting and esti-
mating by both services, in contrast to the hastily conceived generali-
ties in the 1924 joint plan, which were derived from the earlier, still
more general synopsis of the General Board.[41] With numerous modi-
fications, the 1929 plan remained the Joint Army and Navy War Plan
Orange until 1938, when it was replaced by a wholly new plan in
which, at the insistence of the Army planners, stress was placed on
defence of the eastern Pacific, with only modest reference to an
advance by the fleet to the west of Hawaii.[42] In March 1929, two
months *after* the Joint Army and Navy War Plan Orange was distrib-
uted, the Navy issued its new Navy Basic War Plan Orange based on
the joint plan, a distinct reversal in order from the 1924 practice.[43]

From Orange, the services turned to plans for war against Red
(Britain), and then against a Red–Orange (Anglo-Japanese) coalition.
The Anglo-American deadlock over cruisers at the Geneva Naval
Conference in 1927 left the Navy's War Plans Division uncertain
whether war was more likely in the Atlantic or in the Pacific, and
watchful for evidence of an Anglo-Japanese understanding. The division held in its 1928 annual estimate of the situation that, since
Japan was unlikely to attack the United States alone, Japan would
probably only fight the United States if she had a European ally.[44]

The Joint Army and Navy Board completed its War Plan Red in
1930, essentially a defence of the western hemisphere from attack by
Red (Britain) in the Atlantic.[45] Materials survive for a Red–Orange
plan that remained unfinished on the Joint Board's agenda until it was
finally dropped in 1939.[46] Indeed, Red as a possible enemy practically
disappeared from the estimates of the naval war planners after the
successful conclusion of the London Naval Conference of 1930.
When the United States Fleet was concentrated in the Pacific in 1932,
however, it joined with the Army in an elaborately conceived exercise, Grand Joint Exercise No. 4, that related to a hypothetical war
against a coalition designated Black, clearly a Red–Orange (Anglo-
Japanese) combination. Assuming that the enemy in the Pacific had
captured Hawaii while the United States Fleet was defeating its more
powerful enemy in the Atlantic, the task of the fleet and the Army in
the exercise was to undertake an amphibious assault on Oahu. The
attack included air strikes against Oahu from the Navy's fine new
carriers *Lexington* and *Saratoga*, perhaps a harbinger of the Japanese

attack on Pearl Harbor in 1941.[47] The exercise itself, however, was conceived within the framework of the years 1919–1931, when Britain and Japan were the primary concerns of American war planners.

It is ironic that the United States Fleet was concentrated in the Pacific in 1932 to play out a Red–Orange (Anglo-Japanese) scenario at the very time when statesmen in Washington and London were anxiously searching for means to prevent the Japanese in Manchuria and at Shanghai from breaking up the Washington Conference system. Reflecting the progressive demise of that system, except for visits to the Atlantic in 1935 and 1939, the United States Fleet remained concentrated in the Pacific as a caution to Japan until the outbreak of the Second World War. Britain, after 1932, was gradually restored in American naval thinking to her pre-1919 role as guardian of the Atlantic.

From 1919 to 1931, the Anglo-American–Japanese system of naval power provided American military and naval planners with valuable opportunities for testing and revising their plans, through the playing out of games, problems, and other exercises. Planning for an Orange campaign was most challenging to naval planners in Operations, in the fleet, and at the Naval War College, for the very reason that the problem was so difficult, if not impossible, to solve. Conversely, the Army planners were attracted to Red and Red–Orange campaigns because they gave credibility to their plans for mobilizing a mass army for defence of the United States against invasion, an undertaking that held no appeal for the Navy whatsoever.

The plans for naval operations against Orange (Japan) were worked out and revised in response to changing circumstances and lessons learned over time. As previously noted, it seemed from the lessons derived from Fleet Problem Nos. 2, 4, and 5 between 1923 and 1925 that the Navy had solved the logistic problem of how to overcome the obstacles imposed by the Five-Power Naval Treaty of 1922 and get the United States Fleet to the western Pacific, if the civilians in government would provide money for ships and mobile base equipment, especially floating dry-docks. The scheme for a quick movement in the 1924 Orange plans, however, was seriously undermined by the inability of the Army to guarantee the security of a protected site for a base in the Manila Bay area until the arrival of the fleet. The 1924 plans were consequently followed by the more conservative and thoroughly reasoned 1929 Joint Army and Navy War Plan Orange, which was probably a more truly joint Army and Navy Orange plan than any previous Orange plan. The moderating influence of the Army on operational planning for the Pacific became progressively stronger through the 1930s.

University of Texas

NOTES

1. For materials on introductory statements, see W.R. Braisted, *The United States Navy in the Pacific, 1897–1909, 1909–1922* (2 vols.: Austin, University of Texas Press, 1958, 1971). For an original interpretation of American planning for war against Japan, see E.S. Miller, *War Plan Origin: US Strategy to Defeat Japan, 1897–1945* (Annapolis Naval Institute Press, 1991). Miller interprets that planning as a competition between two factions, the 'thrusters' who advocated an immediate advance by the United States Fleet across the Pacific, and the 'cautionaries' who favoured a step-by-step movement.
2. General Board draft programme, 22 Sept. 1922, National Archives, Record Group 80, General Board Papers, GB 420–2.
3. James H. Oliver to Chief of Naval Operations (CNO), 8 June 1920, NA, RG 80, Secret-Confidential Correspondence of the Secretary of the Navy, 1919–1927, PD 198–2 and PD 138–2.
4. Coontz to Secretary of the Navy (Secnav), 27 Feb. 1920, ibid., PD 198–2.
5. Daniels to CNO, 15 April 1920, ibid., PD 138–1. Although the plans in this war portfolio apparently have not survived, their outlines can be determined from other correspondence. For the War Plans Division's listing of its studies, 1919–1921, see ibid., PD 100.
6. Lecture by Lt. Com. H.H. Frost on Red–Orange Campaign, 25 Oct. 1920, Naval War College Archives.
7. Ibid.
8. Oliver to CNO, 22 Oct. 1919, NA, RG 80, Secnav's Secret-Confidential Correspondence, 1919–1927, PD 198–2.
9. Peyton C. March to Secnav, 18 Dec. 1919, ibid., PD 196–7.
10. Coontz to Secnav, 15 July 1920, ibid., PD 190–6:1.
11. For the Navy at the Washington Conference, see Braisted, *US Navy in the Pacific, 1909–1922*, pp. 567–666; T.H. Buckley, *The United States and the Washington Conference, 1921–1922* (Knoxville: University of Tennessee Press, 1970); Roger Dingman, *Power in the Pacific: the Origins of Naval Arms Limitation, 1914–1922* (Chicago: University of Chicago Press, 1976).
12. William R. Shoemaker to CNO, 17 March 1924, NA, RG 80, General Board Papers, GB 425.
13. Basic Readiness Plan (WPL-8), Feb. 1923, Appendix F to Basic Readiness Plan, Dec. 1923, NA, RG 80, Secnav's Secret-Confidential Correspondence, 1919–1927, PD 198–1.

14. Shoemaker to CNO, 17 Jan. 1924, ibid., PD 196–15.
15. Braisted, *US Navy in the Pacific, 1909–1922*, pp. 681–2; Joint Planning Committee to Joint Board, 20 May 1922, NA, RG 225, Joint Army and Navy Board Records, JB 303 (Serial 184).
16. Braisted, *US Navy in the Pacific, 1909–1922*, pp. 683–5.
17. Roosevelt to General Board, 13 July 1922, NA, RG 80, General Board Records, GB 425.
18. War Plans Divisions Estimate of the Situation, Sept. 1922, Naval Historical Center, Archives. In his *War Plan Orange* (p. 115), Edward Miller holds that the author of this estimate was Rear-Admiral C.S. Williams, the Director of War Plans, and that Williams was the leading thinker in a group that worked for a cautionary strategy.
19. W.L. Rodgers to Secnav, 26 April 1923, NA, RG 80, General Board Papers, GB 425 (Serial 1136).
20. Memorandum by Coontz, 10 May 1923, with approval by Secnav Edwin Denby, NA, RG 80, Secnav's Secret-Confidential Correspondence, 1919–1927, PD 198–26.
21. Sinclair Gannon to CNO, 9 June 1923, approved by Coontz, 10 July 1923, Naval Historical Center, Archives, Orange Studies, Folders 802–3.
22. Memorandum for the CNO, 7 July 1923, NA, RG 225, Joint Army and Navy Board Records, JB 325 (Serial 207).
23. Navy Basic War Plan Orange, Feb. 1924, Naval Historical Center, Archives.
24. Joint Army and Navy War Plan Orange, 15 Aug. 1924, NA, RG 225, Joint Army and Navy Board Records, JB 325 (Serial 228).
25. Eberle to Commander-in-Chief, US Fleet, 11 Oct. 1924, NA, RG 80, Secnav's Secret-Confidential Correspondence, 1919–1927, PD 198–13.
26. Roosevelt to General Board, 25 July 1924, ibid., PD 196–15.
27. Endorsement by H.P. Jones, 22 Sept. 1924, ibid.
28. Coontz to CNO, 23 Oct. 1924, ibid., PD 198–13.
29. US Fleet Contributory Orange Plan, 18 Jan. 1925, Shoemaker to CNO, 8 Nov. 1924, ibid.
30. Materials Relating to Fleet Problem Nos. 2, 3, and 4, ibid., PD 162–78:4.
31. Materials Relating to Fleet Problem No. 5, 1925, ibid., PD 198–35:3.
32. *General Instructions United States Navy, F.T. P. 45* (Washington: Government Printing Office, 1925), Naval Historical Center, Archives. Another version entitled 'United States Fleet Cruising Disposition No. 2' may be found in NA, RG 80, Secnav's Secret-Confidential Correspondence, 1919–1927, PD 162.
33. W.R. Braisted, 'On the 1925 Australian Cruise of the American Fleet', *Pull Together: Newsletter of the Naval Historical Center*, XXIX (Spring–Summer 1990), pp. 1–4.
34. Combined Army and Navy War Plan Orange, 1925, the Philippines, Naval Historical Center, Archives, Strategic Plans Division Records, Box 64.
35. Commander-in-Chief Asiatic Fleet, C.S. Williams, to CNO, 1 March 1927, NA, RG 80, Secnav's Secret Confidential Correspondence, 1919–1927, PD 168–78:14.
36. Army Members, Joint Planning Committee, Manila, to Adjutant General, 17 March 1928, Major General F.W. Sladen to Adjutant General, 26 March 1928, NA, RG 225, Joint Army and Navy Board Records, JB 303 (Serial 298).
37. Memorandum by Schofield, 12 June 1928, Hughes to Secnav, 14 June 1928, ibid.
38. Memorandum by Joint Planning Committee, 11 Oct. 1926, Memorandum for Joint Planning Committee by Jarvis Butler, 23 Oct. 1926, ibid., JB 325 (Serial 280).
39. Memorandum for Joint Planning Committee by Butler, 26 Jan. 1928, ibid.
40. Joint Estimate of the Blue–Orange Situation, Jan. 1928, Memorandum by Butler, 26 Jan. 1928, ibid.
41. Joint Army and Navy War Plan Orange, 1929, ibid.

42. Louis Morton, 'War Plan Orange: Evolution of a Strategy,' *World Politics*, XI (Jan. 1959), pp. 247–8.
43. Navy Basic War Plan Orange, March 1929, Naval Historical Center, Archives.
44. Schofield to CNO, 13 April 1928, 10 April 1929, NA, RG 80, Navy Department Confidential Records, 1927–1939, Ll-l File.
45. C.F. Hughes to Secnav, 8 May 1930, NA, RG 225, Joint Army and Navy Board Records, JB 225 (Serial 435); W.R. Braisted, 'On the American Red and Red-Orange Plans, 1919–1939', in Gerald Jordan, *Naval Warfare in the Twentieth Century, 1900–1945, Essays in Honour of Arthur Marder* (London: Croom Helm, 1977), pp. 167–8.
46. Drafts of Red–Orange Estimates, Naval Historical Center, Archives.
47. Materials on Grand Joint Exercise No. 4, 1932, NA, RG 80, Navy Department Secret Confidential Correspondence, 1927–1939, A16–3 (9) ND–14.

The Icarus Factor: the American Pursuit of Myth in Naval Arms Control, 1921–36

THOMAS H. BUCKLEY

Daedalus, the ancient Greek craftsman, watched his son Icarus, imbued with too much hubris as he flew toward the sun, exceed the limits of his father's art, and then plunge from the heavens into the sea. Like Daedalus, the American statesmen who constructed the Washington 'system' saw their creative accomplishment destroyed by their successors who, mired in their own distinctive hubris, so concentrated on the technical issue of numerical ratios to the exclusion of political considerations that they failed to secure either effective arms control or lasting peace. As the increasing heat of political conflict grew more intense, the waxwork of political webs that had held together the original quest for disarmament in 1922 began to shift by 1930, tear asunder in 1936, and melt away before the Rising Sun in 1941. American statesmen, responsive to a public disillusionment with the results of the First World War, followed policies of political isolationism that encompassed an avoidance of the League of Nations, unilateral disarmament, moral pronouncements against that notorious outlaw, war, and righteous indignation against nations that had not only failed to pay their previous war debts, but now purchased further arms. Naval arms control, strongly supported by an American public opinion more interested in diminishing the cost of a war machine than in any altruistic desire to end war, stood as the dramatic centrepiece of American policy. However, the Icarus Factor of disarmament – that arms control, unsupported by a web of political arrangements, can neither secure nor maintain peace – doomed both arms control and peace when the former, never containing within itself the power to capture peace, perished in the fire of conflict.

I

When the United States failed to join the League of Nations in 1919–1920, it decided not to travel the crowded road of collective security, with its perils of unknown destinations, fellow riders who had not even paid their fare for the previous ride but were now again travelling on American credit, and other travellers with whom the United States would eagerly trade goods at any roadside stand but not negotiate political arrangements. The United States, therefore, would proceed on its own traditional, independent path, meeting each problem as it came up and seeking its own unique solutions. In that vein, President Warren G. Harding had suggested during the presidential campaign of 1920 that a non-permanent, voluntary association of nations might gather periodically to discuss common problems and perhaps seek solutions without, of course, committing themselves in advance to any action directly weakening any nation's right to take independent steps.[1] Disarmament, he believed, might well serve as the topic of the initial meeting of such an association of nations.

Urged on by a congressional resolution proposed by Senator William E. Borah, calling for a 50 per cent cut in the naval building programmes of the United States, Great Britain, and Japan, President Harding and his Secretary of State, Charles Evans Hughes, combined Harding's vague hopes for an association of nations, widespread public support for disarmament, and an opportunity to settle some problems with Japan, into a call for a conference to be held in Washington, DC, on 11 November 1921.[2] Politics at home, unsettled conditions in the Pacific and China, and a naval race with Great Britain and Japan prompted the convocation of the Washington Conference on the Limitation of Armaments.

What problems faced the Harding Administration at home and

abroad? The bitter struggle over the League of Nations forced the Republicans to develop a positive programme. Negative attacks on the Woodrow Wilson Administration had worked quite well in opposition, but once the Republicans were in power positive steps had to be taken. Harding, to use a favourite word of his, wanted to do something 'becoming' in world affairs.[3] After the high costs of the war and the short economic recession that followed, the American public wanted relief from high taxes and the burden of maintaining a large, expensive military establishment. Agitation from organized, growing pacifist groups in the United States peaked, but the dominant attitude of the public centred on the question of tax relief, not on the prevention of war.[4] Through naval disarmament, the Harding Administration could tie itself to a popular movement, and gain, it hoped, not only a cut in military spending but also the resolution of naval and political problems with Great Britain and Japan.

In 1916, on the eve of the American entrance into the First World War, the United States had begun a naval construction programme that included the building of 156 vessels; 16 capital ships (battleships and battle cruisers) anchored the powerful core of the programme. Under the pressures of war, since the German battle fleet seldom ventured far from the safety of home, the United States concentrated on the building of destroyers for convoy duty, to meet the submarine threat, rather than on battleships and battle cruisers. In the autumn of 1921, 15 of the 16 capital ships, still under construction, and from roughly four per cent to 86 per cent finished, stood on the building stocks. Upon their completion, the United States would have the most modern and powerful capital ship fleet in the world. American admirals and some political leaders, like the former Senator Harding, had long talked of a navy 'second to none'.[5]

The British, of course, occupying the number one position in 1920, had met many previous challenges to that rank, and announced that they would build a fleet equal or superior to that of any other nation. Japan, by beginning an 8–8 programme designed to construct eight battleships and eight battle cruisers, displayed its intention to match the American fleet. Considerable American opinion held that neither Great Britain nor Japan had the immediate funds to complete her programme, unlike the United States, which had ended the war as a creditor nation. Serious doubts, however, existed in the Harding

Administration about the willingness of Congress to vote the necessary funds to complete the unfinished capital ships, let alone vote
additional funds for either their maintenance or the construction of
the necessary supporting auxiliary ships. Congress in the 1920s did in
fact display more interest in paying off the national debt than in
funding high cost naval projects.[6]

A further complication revolved around the ties that bound the
British and the Japanese together in the Anglo-Japanese Alliance, due
to expire in 1921. Originally signed in 1902 and aimed against
Russia, renewed in 1911 and then centred against Germany, it had
served useful purposes for Great Britain and Japan. In 1921, both
governments wanted a renewal, but the United States had indicated
that such a continuation would, at the very least, give the appearance
of an alliance against the United States. The Harding Administration
did not fear that the alliance would lead the United States into a war
with Great Britain. It did believe that the Japanese used the pact to
advance their interests in Asia, with either open or silent British
support. Japan, for example, had received the former German islands
in the Pacific as League of Nations mandates through a prior secret
Anglo-Japanese agreement followed by an open British confirmation
of that arrangement in the Versailles Treaty. The British, however,
found themselves under severe Canadian pressure against renewal in
1921. The Canadians feared that any dispute between the United
States and Japan that might draw in Great Britain, even as a neutral,
could also put Canada in a position vulnerable to American
retaliation.[7]

Great Britain and the United States in the interwar period had an
uneasy, often adversarial relationship. Most Americans, and many
scholars, have forgotten how deep the suspicions of Great Britain ran
in the United States in the 1920s and 1930s. Some Americans believed
that the image of Perfidious Albion reflected reality, that the British
worked only for their own interests and would always make sure that
they gained in every situation, and that the United States would
always lose in any negotiation with the British. Other Americans
came to believe that the British had somehow manipulated the United
States into the First World War to save British commercial interests.
Since control of the seas appeared to be the foundation of British
power, to stand on an equal plane with the British, the United States

must build a fleet superior or at least equal to the Royal Navy. While few wanted a war with Great Britain, or predicted the likelihood of one, many saw the British as arrogant competitors whose pretensions of leadership failed to recognize the realities of either their own declining power or the rise of American power. Britain's broader world interests often clashed with the narrower American goals, especially in Asia, and neither had much appreciation of the other's difficulties. Such feelings permeated both naval and foreign policy debates, and created serious hurdles for those in both governments who sought a closer relationship.[8]

If war with Great Britain appeared unlikely, war with Japan was not inconceivable. With the Japanese defeat of Russia in 1904, the United States changed from a quiet admirer of Japan to a vocal critic. Japanese actions in Korea, China, and the Pacific islands from 1904 to 1920 appeared aggressive and threatening to American interests in those areas. Looming behind the specific threat to the Philippines, in the eyes of naval officers, lay the even more general, ambiguous problem of China. Many Americans had a sentimental attachment to China as well as high hopes of cracking a market of over 400 million potential customers. Japanese expansion into Manchuria, Shantung, and even into Russian Siberia raised questions about Japan's ultimate intentions. Its acquisition of the former German islands (the Marshalls, Marianias, and Carolines) in 1919 added further strategic dimensions in the South Pacific. War Plan Orange grappled with the problems and opportunities, offered to both Japan and the United States, that those islands presented.[9] Books predicting war between the United States and Japan appeared with regularity from 1915 to 1925.[10]

The Harding Administration thus faced a domestic political question – how to demonstrate leadership in foreign affairs after the defeat of the League, how to placate an American public that wanted tax relief from the funds required to build naval ships, and how to take advantage of the fact that Congress might well not vote the appropriations even to finish the ships already under construction. It also faced an international question – how to gain naval parity with Great Britain without further building, how to restrain Japanese building, and how to prevent further Japanese inroads into American interests in the Pacific and China.

The Harding Administration in 1921 had five options – some clearly unrealistic, others in the realm of possibility:

1. It could complete the 1916 programme for capital ships, meet any further challenges ship for ship, and aggressively build up American fortifications in the Pacific. This option, a type of imperial America, assumed that Congress would indeed vote the necessary appropriations for both naval construction and the fortification of the Philippines and the Wake and Guam islands (although neither was a desirable alternative either politically or militarily), as well as increasing the status of the then largely undeveloped Pearl Harbor. Under those circumstances, the United States also had to assume that certainly Japan, which would have viewed such offensive actions as a direct threat, and possibly Great Britain, would complete and perhaps even expand her fortifications and building programmes. Just the completion of the three original programmes would have brought an estimated ratio of capital ship tonnage in 1928 of 10(US):11(GB): 9(J). Not only Congress but also the American public would have to support an expensive alternative that might lead to war. The Harding Administration correctly concluded that neither Congress nor the public would support such an option.

2. It could complete only the 1916 programme and not build auxiliaries or further fortifications. While this would have cut some expense, it would not, in all probability, have prevented the British construction, although it might have influenced the Japanese to slow down or make a small cut in their programme. Again, there is no indication that Congress or the public would have rallied to support this alternative. One can argue, however, that the calling of a conference *after* the completion of the programme might well have eliminated the type of criticism (that is, that the United States gave up too much without corresponding reductions by Great Britain and Japan) that developed during the late 1920s. While such a tactic might have put the United States in a stronger bargaining position, say in 1926, building an expensive fleet only to scrap it for arms control purposes appeared nonsensical at that time and few would have supported such an outrageous proposal.[11]

3. It could complete none of the 15 ships, replace only a small number of auxiliary ships, provide no further funds for the expansion of fortifications, and negotiate no international treaty. This option, in

effect a planned unilateral disarmament with no consideration of the impact of other naval powers or American political interests in the Pacific, would have addressed the financial concerns of Congress and the public, but would have left the British and Japanese free to build as they wished and doomed any hopes whatsoever either of parity with the British or of any restraint, other than words, on Japanese expansion. The United States would have withdrawn into itself and gambled that in the foreseeable future no threats requiring a military response would occur; after all, who would, or could, attack the United States? It would also have abandoned any American hopes of greatly influencing either Great Britain or Japan in East Asia. While the naval aspects of this option may have had some appeal, the political side did not. This was not the basic policy chosen in 1921, but aspects of this alternative actually occurred when Congress failed to vote the funds for even a treaty navy.

4. It could complete part of the uncompleted capital ships, join the Anglo-Japanese Alliance, and in effect draw formal spheres of influence in Asia between the three powers.[12] While this option would have cut down on naval expenses, it would have met the same fierce resistance in Congress that the League of Nations encountered. Such an alliance could not have gained the political support of either Congress or the American people in 1921; such an act of *realpolitik* appeared neither American nor legitimate. It would not only have involved a far more active role in world affairs, but also have severely restricted American independent actions.

5. It could stop the naval construction programme in return for the end of the Anglo-Japanese Alliance, negotiate an end to the British and Japanese programmes, and sign political arrangements that would restrict Japanese expansion. If the United States had no intention of finishing either the ships or the fortifications, it could gain a relative, rather than an absolute, measure of security by holding its competitors to a lower level of power than in all probability could have been achieved by building. This option might not only solve the funding problem but actually gain the United States a better political position. Political concessions might well be secured from the British and Japanese in return for the United States not completing its capital ships. The option appeared largely achievable; not only did it offer the possibility of gaining strong public support, but both the British

and the Japanese might find advantages in such a proposal.

The fifth alternative, of course, became the foundation of the plan chosen by the Harding Administration. An American delegation, led by Hughes and composed of Senator Henry Cabot Lodge, chairman of the Senate Foreign Relations Committee, Senator Oscar W. Underwood, the Senate minority leader, and ex-Secretary of State Elihu Root, ably assisted by Assistant Secretary of the Navy Theodore Roosevelt Jr, developed a 'stop now' proposal for naval arms control that Hughes dramatically presented at the opening session of the conference on 12 November 1921.[13] The Secretary of State proposed that the three major naval powers scrap their capital ship construction programmes (under way or proposed), build no capital ships for ten years, have a naval ratio of 5(US):5(GB):3(J) in total capital ship tonnage (approximately 500,000 tons for the United States and Great Britain, with 300,000 for Japan), and provide lesser amounts of tonnage for both France and Italy.[14] By seizing the public initiative, Hughes focused world public opinion, and made it difficult, but not impossible, for Great Britain and Japan to reject the proposals totally.

In almost three months of hard negotiations, the delegations hammered out the Five-Power Naval Treaty. Alterations in the original proposal did occur. Japan asked for a higher ratio (10:10:7 rather than 10:10:6), and the resulting compromise kept the 5:5:3 capital ship ratio, but also provided for no further fortification of the Western Pacific Island territories of the signatories. The United States and Great Britain received the right to have 135,000 tons (Japan 81,000) of aircraft carriers now designated as capital ships; the United States turned two of its uncompleted battle cruisers into carriers (the *Lexington* and the *Saratoga*), but the French caused the decisive change. Hughes clearly expected to apply the 5:5:3 ratio not only to capital ships but also to auxiliary ships (cruisers, destroyers, and submarines). Hughes, however, had wounded French pride in his original proposal by not assigning them the same capital ship ratio as that of the United States and Great Britain. Hughes had suggested a 1.75 ratio. France would accept the assigned capital ship ratio only if defensive ships, the French definition of all auxiliary ships, had no numerical limits placed on them.[15] Unknown to the others, the British, who had publicly argued on behalf of the abolition of the submarine, would also probably have scuttled the auxiliary ship clause because they wanted more cruisers, but the French saved them the necessity of raising the issue.[16] The auxiliary ship exception grew into a serious problem at future naval arms control conferences as a naval race in cruisers occurred.[17]

The United States insisted that political arrangements become a part of the final settlement. While to the relief of the Japanese delegation, and probably also the British, the Americans did not present a surprise proposal on Pacific and Asian affairs as they had done on the naval side of the conference, few doubted that at the very least the United States wanted an end to the Anglo-Japanese Alliance.[18] Prior to, during, and after the conference, the Harding Administration tied the end of the alliance to the American accept-ance of the naval treaty. The Four-Power Treaty (United States, Great Britain, Japan, and France) formally terminated the alliance and called for consultation between the powers if any dispute arose between them in the Pacific. This killed the alliance, the United States made no commitments except to consult, and the treaty included no formal recognition of either British or Japanese spheres of influence. Senator Lodge made the tie between the naval treaty and the Four-Power Treaty very explicit by scheduling the vote on the latter treaty first and by stating that its ratification must precede that of the naval treaty.[19]

Two other major political treaties emerged from the conference. The Nine-Power Treaty (United States, Great Britain, Japan, France, Italy, Belgium, Portugal, the Netherlands, and China) provided that trade with China should be open on an equal basis to all of the signatories. In effect, it wrote the American open-door policy into formal treaty form for the first time. The weakest link of the confer-ence political treaties, the Nine-Power Treaty fell first despite later American diplomatic attempts to get Japan to comply with its terms. The fourth treaty dealt with Chinese customs in an attempt to raise the effective tariff rate, and to provide the central Chinese Government with more funds, and eventual tariff autonomy (secured in 1930). Provisions to establish committees to study recommen-dations for the revision of foreign extraterritorial rights in China and the Chinese judicial system completed the formal political arrangements.[20]

In three steps taken outside the conference, but made possible because of the conference gathering and American pressures, the Japanese and Chinese made an agreement that in effect returned political control of the Chinese province of Shantung to China (something Woodrow Wilson had failed to accomplish), but allowed the Japanese to retain some economic privileges (control of the Shantung railroad, eventually to return to China). The Japanese also agreed to withdraw their troops from Siberia, and finally, in a third agreement, the United States and Japan settled the question of communications rights on the island of Yap.

The treaties then went before the United States Senate. Brilliantly shepherded by the team of Hughes, Lodge, and Underwood, the agreements sailed through the ratification process. Controversy centred only on the Four-Power Treaty, which, opponents such as Borah and Hiram Johnson argued, had not appeared on the conference agenda and had been negotiated and signed in secret, its existence being announced without warning. Under such suspicious circumstances, they believed that the treaty must include, either explicitly or implicitly, secret understandings that either made it an alliance or at least recognized British and Japanese interests. Harding, with reluctance, agreed to a reservation that stipulated that no such conditions existed, and the Four-Power Treaty received a winning vote of 60 to 25. All the other treaties sailed through with only a total of two votes cast against them.[21]

The debate over the extremely popular Five-Power Naval Treaty is worthy of further note. Remarkably, no hearings took place before either the Senate Foreign Relations Committee or the House Committee on Naval Affairs. Opponents, in particular naval officers, never got a chance to testify about their concerns. The Foreign Relations Committee gave its unanimous approval after just a few hours' discussion. Lodge, not only chairman of the Foreign Relations Committee but also the majority leader of the Senate, steamrollered the treaty through the Senate itself. The debate lasted only a few days.[22] Lodge, in reply to a question as to the role of naval advisers, testified that such advisers had a role similar to that of experts testifying on tariff bills. They acted only as technicians; the President and Congress, not advisers, made policy.[23] A few words sum up the little debate that actually took place – shallow, cursory, and largely uninformed. Neither the strengths nor the weaknesses of the treaty received an intelligent or full discussion. Lodge had the votes, enormous public enthusiasm, and the support of a president who had just won the largest percentage of the popular vote that any president had received in American history. Only one senator voted against the treaty.

What did the United States achieve with the Washington Conference treaties as ratified in 1922? First, the Five-Power Treaty averted a potentially expensive and possibly dangerous naval race in capital ships. Anglo-German competition at a lower numerical level had greatly added to the tensions that eventually exploded into the First World War. Second, the United States, through arms control, attained a better relationship with its major naval competitors at a lower, less expensive level than it would have achieved had it, and they, completed their building programmes. Third, the United States achieved a rough equality, but not parity, with Great Britain and a superiority over Japan that also restricted fortifications on Japanese islands (this did not include, of course, Japan proper). Fourth, it forced the termination of the bothersome, if not really threatening, Anglo-Japanese Alliance; Great Britain would no longer, either directly or indirectly, act as an ally of Japanese ambitions. Fifth, the Japanese, for the only time in the interwar period, withdrew from overseas areas in Shantung and Siberia. Sixth, in the Nine-Power Treaty the United States for the first time received formal treaty approval of its open-door policy. Seventh, Harding and Hughes took a naval programme that neither Congress nor the public wanted to continue and turned a potential weakness into a diplomatic asset. The Harding Administration took advantage of a propitious time in history – the end of a major war, with an international desire for a cutback in weapons, and a Japanese Government willing to try cooperation rather than confrontation – to tie a popular naval arms control into a package that included political agreements advantageous to the United States.

Weaknesses include: First, after the conference the Harding Administration, abandoning its original limited goals, oversold both itself and the American public on the accomplishments of the conference. While indeed substantial, the Naval Treaty, for example, did not 'end, absolutely end, the race in competition in naval armament'.[24] A naval race in auxiliary ships, with cruiser construction as the key point, immediately started when the Japanese and the British began large cruiser construction programmes. Second, the United States did not build up to treaty strength in capital ships; it did, however, complete the ten 7,000-ton *Omaha* class light cruisers from the 1916 programme and build eight 10,000-ton heavy cruisers by the end of the 1920s. As a result, in 1930 the United States did not have parity with Great Britain in capital ships (a careful reading of the Washington Treaty would reveal that such a result was not actually intended until 1942), and while Congress authorized 15 cruisers in 1929, that programme was not near completion by the London Conference of 1930. In large part, the 1929 programme represented an angry response to the failure of the Geneva Conference of 1927, rather than any great desire to build. The presidents did not push for further construction funds, and Congress appeared in no mood to vote them (with the exception of the cruiser bill) even if asked. Third, there is at least some question as to the extent of funds saved by not completing the capital ships. It is a complex question, so far un-answered by any historian, for while it is true that funds were saved by not completing the 1916 programme, with its additional costs of maintaining, repairing, and staffing the resulting vessels in the 1920s, these were short-term savings. One could argue, in the long term, that these ships then had to be replaced in the late 1930s at a slightly higher cost. On the other hand, the later ships were more modern and powerful. Such costs as those involved in the cutting back or closing of naval construction yards immediately after the Washington Conference, the loss of skilled workers, and the later reopening of the yards and training of new workers are important facets not yet taken into account. Annual naval appropriations in the 1920s hovered around $350 million, and did not significantly decrease or increase. Historian William R. Braisted wisely suggests that funds saved by not constructing the battleships were not so much saved as moved else-where to support the building of the two carriers and the growth of the Naval Air Arm.[25] Fourth, the absence of verification procedures left the door ajar to small and large violations of both the spirit and the letter of the treaty; most major transgressions occurred in the 1930s rather than the 1920s.[26] Fifth, and quite importantly, American statesmen came to resent the actions of the other powers in building auxiliary ships beyond the 5:5:3 ratio as unfair, unsporting, and contrary to the spirit of the Washington Treaty.[27] The other powers, of course, had a perfect legal right to build, since the treaty did not include auxiliary ships. That bad feeling on the part of the Americans, much akin to the sort of resentment that resulted from the failure of the former allies to repay their First World War debts, intensified when several nations who had not paid back their war debts to the United States, such as Great Britain, France, and Italy, began to build all those auxiliary ships.

Finally, and most importantly, a feeling, soon transformed into policy, came out of the conference that made the numbers 5:5:3 sacred. This led to an American obsession with the idea that a large part of American security somehow resided in those magic numbers. Parity with Great Britain, and 40 per cent superiority over Japan, became an incantation that would ward off any potential disaster and which, by itself, would solve all problems. This obsession obscured the equal importance of political considerations. Few American leaders took notice of the changing political conditions in the Pacific or Asia. Presidents Calvin Coolidge and Herbert Hoover, as we shall see, were both willing to accept arms control treaties at Geneva and London totally devoid of political arrangements; Hughes had not made that error. The political web that held the Washington structure together, unreinforced, under severe strain by 1930, soon broke. For that, American statesmen of the interwar period bear a heavy responsibility.

In most respects the Washington 'system', in the sense that most political scientists and some historians have argued, never existed.[28] The United States had limited goals. The American delegation had no design to establish even a regional system, let alone a new world order. The Harding Administration at the Washington Conference had an interest in attempting to solve specific, limited problems amenable to solution at that specific time in history when there existed a favourable political, economic, and military equilibrium. Harding's whole concept of an association of nations revolved around the idea of specific, voluntary conferences designed to solve immediate issues, not indefinite, vague ones reaching far into the future. None of the political arrangements made specific future commitments, except to talk and consult, on the part of the United States. The refusal to bind itself to future actions was, after all, the very reason why the United States did not join the League of Nations in 1919 or thereafter.

II

The succeeding naval conferences from 1927 to 1936 stand as monuments to the futility of seeking arms control without connecting political arrangements. None of the conference delegates practised the major political lessons of the Washington Conference, nor did they succeed even in reducing naval armaments or stopping construction. On the part of the United States, the quest for parity with Great Britain became a parody, superiority over Japan an illusion, and increased security a chimera.

President Calvin Coolidge attempted to expand the capital ship ratios to auxiliary ships at the Geneva Conference of 1927. Since, in the minds of the Americans, only one aspect mattered – the application of the 5:5:3 standard to cruisers, destroyers, and submarines, something that should require only minor technical adjustments – naval experts rather than diplomats took the centre stage; political discussions stood outside the pale. The 'minor' naval adjustments, however, soon turned into a full-scale controversy between the United States and Great Britain over the number and size of cruisers (heavy: 10,000 tons, and light: 7,000 tons). Unknown to the Americans, Lord Balfour, the British delegate at the Washington Conference, had then had instructions that Great Britain, to protect its far-flung Empire, should not restrict the numbers of cruisers. Because of the French opposition to any numerical restrictions on auxiliary ships, the question of the number of cruisers did not come up at Washington, and the British did not have to reveal their position; nor did the Japanese. Within a few short years, however, both the British and Japanese had large cruiser programmes under way. The United States had not responded with similar cruiser construction programmes (although it had completed the ten *Omahas*, six-inch guns, 7,000 tons, from the 1916 programme); it hoped to stop that particular race at Geneva. Despite its lack of cruisers, and of an authorized, funded building programme, and despite the fact that the United States would have to build to raise itself to a 5:5:3 ratio, the American delegation pushed ahead with its demand for the ratio.

Since the British believed that they needed at least a combination of 50 to 70 light and heavy cruisers and the United States found this completely unacceptable at a conference designed to reduce armaments and spending, not increase them, the conference failed to sign a treaty.[29] The Japanese, who favoured the British position, remained quiet and let the British shoulder the blame for the failure. President Coolidge then asked Congress for authorization to build 15 10,000-ton heavy cruisers armed with eight-inch guns, but with the stipulation that if another arms control conference materialized, the United States might suspend that programme.[30]

The torch of carrying on the Washington idea was then handed on to the Herbert Hoover Administration in 1929. There is little doubt that Hoover and his Secretary of State, Henry L. Stimson, wanted to extend the ratio to 5:5:3 in all categories and prevent as much building as possible. Both saw that hope as intimately linked to the just concluded Kellogg–Briand Pact. Hoover began preliminary discussions with Prime Minister Ramsay MacDonald of Great Britain. MacDonald promised 'parity in full measure' and then finalized plans for the London Conference of 1930.[31] The United States went to London in a hopeful mood, only to run into a British hard line. The American delegates also discovered the difficulties of negotiating on arms control without large numbers of ships already in hand or close to completion, as both Great Britain and Japan had stolen a march on the United States with their auxiliary construction programmes.

In the London Treaty of 1930, all five nations agreed to refrain from laying down the capital ship replacement tonnage (new construction replacing capital ships that according to the Washington Treaty would become overage from 1931 to 1936). The agreement also provided for a low level continuation of scrapping; the United States, Great Britain and Japan would demolish a total of nine capital ships. Critics argued that the resulting ratio for capital ship tonnage in 1936 would still rest below the desired 10:10:6 level. But if the major nations in 1936 applied the 20-year age limit of the Washington Treaty, ten of the 18 American capital ships would qualify as overage, as would 16 of the British 18 and five of the Japanese nine.[32] All three of the major powers could then decide to build large numbers of capital ships; this, of course, would end naval arms control.

In the category of auxiliary ships, both Great Britain and Japan would retain their high ratios, which exceeded 5:5:3 for several years.[33] France and Italy did not accept any limitations on auxiliary ships. To provide for the possibility of either France or Italy constructing auxiliary fleets that might challenge the position of any (read Britain) of the three major signatories, the British insisted on the inclusion of an escalation clause. Designed to continue Great Britain's two-power standard in European waters, the clause specified that if France or Italy should build auxiliary ships that challenged the position of the three major naval powers, any one of the latter could then begin to construct ships to meet the challenge; if that one signatory power built, the other two signatory powers could then construct auxiliary ships with the same proportional increases. This clause clearly opened the possibility of almost unlimited building in auxiliary ships.

Again, no political arrangements marred the technical purity of the London Conference. As Senator David A. Reed, an American delegate at the gathering, later explained:

> We did not want any political arrangement whatsoever in the treaty . . . we did not want the sovereign action of the United States to be limited by the future agreement of some other countries. It would be the old League of Nations business over again, and we were not going to get into it sideways or backwards.[34]

The treaty met a firestorm of opposition when President Hoover called a special session of Congress, in the heat of the unairconditioned summer of 1930, to consider ratification. A struggle occurred in the Senate Foreign Relations Committee, headed by Borah, who favoured the treaty, and Hiram Johnson, who spearheaded the opposition. Hearings took place before both the Foreign Relations Committee and the Committee on Naval Affairs, and a long and sometimes bitter debate took place on the Senate floor. This time the naval establishment got ample opportunity to fire its salvos, which it had not had in 1922; almost all of the testimony, with the exception of that of Admiral William V. Pratt and Secretary of the Navy Charles F. Adams, attacked not only the London Treaty but the Washington Treaty.

It is worth noting some of the vitriolic comments on the

Washington Treaty made by the opposing senators. Hiram Johnson found that Hughes and his fellow delegates in 1921 had acted 'egregiously in error . . . [and were] outrageously fooled'.[35] Harding had 'made promises to the American people which were never fulfilled', charged Claude Swanson.[36] Kenneth D. McKeller, with considerable hyperbole, concluded that

> there was never in all the history of time such a naval victory as Great Britain won over the United States in the naval victory of 1922 at the Washington Conference. The sinking of the Armada was insignificant . . . the battle of Trafalgar was of infinitesimal importance

in comparison.[37] The senator from Tennessee felt that 'Admirals' Hoover, Stimson, and Reed acted equally ineptly in the London Treaty when they ignored the advice of the General Board and agreed to further British and Japanese advances.[38]

At the heart of the storm of criticism lay an enormous resentment and antagonism toward Great Britain that permeated the debate. In sum, critical admirals and senators concluded that the clever and unprincipled British had taken advantage of the less intelligent and more principled Americans both at Washington and at London. The British, they argued, had never had any intention of accepting parity with the Americans; not in 1921, not in 1930, not in 1936, not in 1942, not ever. To American critics, when the British reduced the number of their capital ships, they then simply shifted their superiority to cruisers. When the United States tried to force cruiser parity on the British, the clever Admiralty, by restricting the majority of American cruisers to six-inch guns, had made sure that the British could arm all of their vast merchant fleet with those same six-inch guns and thus overwhelm the Americans with sheer numbers of armed merchant raiders. To many senators, the issue at stake centred around not just the number and size of cruisers, but the battle for world commerce. It further appeared to the senators that the Americans, not the British, had scrapped the ships and made the concessions. Ignoring the inconvenient fact that at London the American delegation had persuaded both the British and the Japanese to halt a large part of their auxiliary ship building until the United States got a chance to catch up, the critics even questioned the integrity and abilities of two of their own senators (Reed, R. – Penn, and Joseph T. Robinson, D. – Arkansas) who had taken leading parts in negotiating the London Treaty.[39]

Few of those senators present (about one-fourth to one-third of the Senate never did show up for the debates), whether in the ranks of the overwhelming number of supporters or of the small group of opponents, wanted to discuss the fact that no matter who won, Congress and the American taxpayers would have to come up with over a billion dollars' worth of naval construction even to reach the treaty levels. Damning Great Britain and Japan, and arguing over the technical details of different kinds of cruiser (heavy, light, six-inch or eight-inch) and whether they were more valuable as fleet auxiliaries or as convoyers of merchant ships, overshadowed any attempts at discussing or trying to understand the shifting world balance of power and its relation to naval arms control. Robert Wagner came closest to the truth when he said that the real issue in the Senate debate was neither political nor even technical over ratios; it was really between 'those who want big navies and those who desire bigger navies'.[40]

Japan, it also appeared, had advanced its interests at the London Conference, when it had received approval from the United States and Great Britain to exceed the 10:10:6 ratio in auxiliary ships. The Japanese having taken that step in 1930, few doubted that at the next conference, scheduled for 1936, they would push for an equal ratio of capital ships with the United States and Great Britain. To head that off, more than one senator suggested that the American delegation should simply have told the Japanese at London that the no further fortification of Pacific islands clause would no longer apply if the Japanese exceeded the 10:10:6 ratio. If the Japanese could not accept that ratio, then the United States should revoke the fortification clause,[41] but the Hoover Administration believed in a treaty at any price, and such a suggestion might well have broken up the conference. It might, however, have warned both the Japanese and the British of the limits of American cooperation, and had the London Conference then failed, as Geneva had in 1927, the United States would have had the option, under the terms of the Washington Treaty, of calling another Washington meeting in 1931.[42] The United States, having staked its position, might have faced a better negotiating situation, and a different world political scenario, and that might have forced a total reconsideration that brought back the ties between arms control and political arrangements.

The London Treaty of 1930, despite strong attacks by navalists in the United States, Great Britain, and Japan, secured ratification in all three countries and set the stage for the final conference in London in 1936. By that time, arms control treaties were indeed fragile reeds. Japan had already given its two-year notice in 1934 that it would leave the naval arrangements at the end of 1936, and also gave a similar warning on the League of Nations. Germany, which had signed the Anglo-German naval pact in 1935, had thus joined the European side of the naval arrangements, at least in the short term, but both France and Italy believed that they could no longer restrict themselves any further, if for different reasons.[43]

When the five naval powers met for the last time in London in 1936 no one, except the United States, wanted a continuation of the ratios. The British demonstrated the most flexibility when they called for an end to ratios and proposed instead that qualitative limits (involving the size of armaments and the total tonnage of individual types of ship by categories) become the standard rather than the ratio limits of the Washington Treaty. However, the Americans remained absolutely opposed, not only to the Japanese demands for parity, but basically to any increase in Japanese numbers that did not fit the Washington Treaty ratios. The final treaty, not signed by Japan, limited new capital ships to 35,000 tons and not over 14-inch guns (with provision for an increase to a 16-inch limit). New aircraft carriers were not to exceed 23,000 tons, and a six-year holiday was declared on the building of heavy cruisers, subject to an escalator clause that would void that clause if the Japanese built large numbers of cruisers. They did.[44] It is perhaps superfluous to point out again that no political arrangements came out of the last London Conference as the ratio system on which the United States had spent so much time, hope, and energy quietly slipped beneath the seas.

III

What long-term results came out of the Washington arrangements? Did the Washington treaties have an effect on or lead to the disaster at Pearl Harbor on 7 December 1941? Was it also true of the Washington Conference that, as Will Rogers said, the United States had 'never lost a war and never won a conference'?[45]

The United States Government in 1921 sought limited, specific goals. No attempts to make the world safe for democracy, no steps to participate in or establish a world organization, and no promises of the end of war, marred its initiation. The Harding Administration had specific, attainable goals in mind. Hughes wanted to stop or slow down the capital ship race with Great Britain and Japan at a level that would ensure American security against attack and also meet the public demand for a cut in naval expenditures which the Administration believed Congress would never support in the first place. The Secretary of State wanted to end the Anglo-Japanese Alliance which had operated to both Great Britain's and Japan's benefit in the Pacific and East Asia. He hoped to encourage the Japanese to understand that their interests were not threatened by the United States and that they would be better off in a mutual cooperation arrangement. And, finally, he sought to get the powers in China to agree formally to the American open-door policy. He largely succeeded in attaining the first three goals; the fourth, apparently achieved in the Nine-Power Treaty, proved a mistaken goal beyond the capacity of American power to achieve.

Critics have argued that the United States gave up naval supremacy at the Washington Conference. This is nonsense; the United States, at best, gave up potential naval supremacy, not actual superiority. There is an enormous difference between actual and potential power. Potential superiority, in particular, assumes that America's competitors would allow her to become number one, and that both Congress and the American people would support the goal of a navy second to none. It took the Second World War to achieve that goal, at enormous cost in lives and funds. Hughes achieved a better relative ratio for the United States by not building, while restricting his competitors' programmes, than he would in all probability have secured by building. The very essence of modern arms control is to achieve that perceived goal.

Three presidential administrations chose not to build up to the treaty limits. While a desire not to spend funds on naval construction had strong public support, it is also true that the United States could have afforded to designate $100 million, or more, a year for the Navy above the approximately $350 million a year that was in fact spent in the 1920s. It was a matter of choice. The administrations and the public preferred to spend their funds elsewhere. The latter, for example, had spent about three billion dollars a year on alcohol consumption prior to prohibition; while prohibition cut the figure down appreciably, it is also safe to say that Americans continued to spend large sums of money on drinking.[46] Congress and the administrations preferred to pay on the national debt and lower taxes. No serious threat of war loomed on the horizon. Without funds, and without more ships, diplomacy had to protect what non-existent naval forces could not.

Hughes's major accomplishment resided in his use of arms control to support a political structure which in turn mutually strengthened the quest for arms control. To have dealt only with arms control would have required dealing only with the surface and not going beneath it to the antagonisms that had caused the nations to build the capital ships in the first place. To have dealt with the former and not the latter would eventually have jeopardized the security of all concerned. Arms control by itself cannot provide a permanent structure because the political structure is constantly shifting and changing, always in transition. Hughes had recognized this; those who followed did not.

The Washington treaties, encompassing necessary *first* steps in an auspicious *detente* of pragmatic advantage and reciprocity, offered tangible political and naval advantages to every group at the Washington Conference. Each nation gained something at the conference in exchange for giving up something else. The reduction of military and political tension purchased breathing space, but no one, neither the United States nor the other powers, took advantage of it to solve other areas of conflict, let alone shore up the existing structure. It was foolish to hope that any temporary settlement, designed as only the first step, would in itself prove permanent. Never adequately politically reinforced, in time the Washington *political* and naval settlement, weakened by the American quest for technical ratios to the exclusion of political goals, died a slow, but sure death in the subsequent conferences.

University of Tulsa

NOTES

The author would like to acknowledge his appreciation of a shared grant from the Oklahoma Foundation for the Humanities and from the Henry Kendall College of Arts and Sciences of the University of Tulsa in support of this study. The author is also extremely grateful to William R. Braisted and Robert H. Ferrell for their critical readings and suggestions.

1. Harding's most important statement on the association can be found in the *Congressional Record*, 4 March 1921, pp. 4–6.
2. Thomas H. Buckley, *The United States and the Washington Conference, 1921–1922* (Knoxville, 1970), pp. 1–34; John Chalmers Vinson, *The Parchment Peace, The United States Senate and the Washington Conference, 1921–1922* (Athens, Ga., 1955) remains useful.
3. Buckley, *Washington Conference*, p. 16.
4. Charles L. Hoag, *Preface to Preparedness: The Washington Conference and Public Opinion* (Washington DC, 1941), p. 73.
5. Harold and Margaret Sprout, *Toward A New Order of Sea Power; American Naval Policy and the World Scene, 1918–1922* (Princeton, 1943); Buckley, *Washington Conference*, pp. 6–9.
6. *Congressional Record*, 18 July 1930, p. 241.
7. Buckley, *Washington Conference*, p. 27.
8. Thomas H. Buckley, 'The Washington Naval Treaties', in Michael Krepon and Dan Caldwell (eds.), *The Politics of Arms Control Treaty Ratification* (New York, 1991), p. 71; *Congressional Record*, 16 July 1930, p. 180.
9. The classic description of the naval and political background in the Pacific is William R. Braisted, *The United States Navy in the Pacific, 1909–1922* (Austin, 1971); Braisted points out how the islands became an Achilles heel to the Japanese in the Second World War. Edward S. Miller, *War Plan Orange: The U.S. Strategy to Defeat Japan, 1897–1945* (Annapolis, 1991), is a comprehensive book on its subject.
10. The most interesting example is Hector C. Bywater, *The Great Pacific War* (Boston, 1925). See also William H. Honan, *Visions of Infamy; The Untold Story of How Journalist Hector C. Bywater Devised the Plans That Led to Pearl Harbor* (New York, 1991).
11. *Congressional Record*, 21 July 1930, p. 370.
12. Sadao Asada argues, not convincingly, that such an arrangement was made in the Nine-Power Treaty, in 'Japan's Special Interests and the Washington Conference, 1921–22', *American Historical Review*, LXVII (Oct. 1961), pp. 62–70.
13. Buckley, *Washington Conference*, pp. 48–62.

14. Department of State, *Conference on the Limitation of Armament* (Washington DC, 1922), pp. 44–64.
15. Ibid.
16. *Congressional Record*, 18 July 1930, p. 256.
17. A second treaty, on Poison Gas and Submarines, was signed at the conference, but never went into effect because the French failed to ratify.
18. *Washington Post*, 11 Dec. 1921.
19. Buckley, 'The Washington Naval Treaties', p. 92.
20. Buckley, *Washington Conference*, pp. 145, 171.
21. Buckley, 'The Washington Naval Treaties', p. 102.
22. *Congressional Record*, 29 March 1922, pp. 4718–19.
23. Ibid.
24. *Conference on the Limitation of Armament*, p. 248.
25. William R. Braisted to author, 16 Aug. 1992.
26. Thomas H. Buckley, 'The Washington Naval Limitation System, 1921–1939', forthcoming, 1993.
27. *Congressional Record*, 18 July 1930, p. 303.
28. Emily Oppenheimer Goldman, 'The Washington Treaty System: Arms Racing and Arms Control in the Interwar Period', Ph.D. Diss., Stanford University, 1989, argues on behalf of an organized, structured system; Ian Nish, on the other hand, disagrees in *Japanese Foreign Policy* (London, 1977), pp. 141–2.
29. Limitation of Naval Armaments, *Records of the Conference for the Limitation of Naval Armament* (Washington, 1928), p. 161.
30. *Congressional Record*, 8 July 1930, p. 13.
31. Ibid., 16 July 1930, p. 188.
32. Buckley, 'Washington Naval Limitation System'.
33. Department of State, *Proceedings of the London Naval Conference of 1930* (Washington, 1931), pp. 215–17.
34. *Congressional Record*, 31 July 1930, p. 347.
35. Ibid., July 1930, p. 223.
36. Ibid., 8 July 1930, p. 23.
37. Ibid., 16 July 1930, p. 180.
38. Ibid.; and also 18 July 1930, p. 312.
39. *Treaty on the Limitation of Naval Armaments, Hearings Before the Committee on Foreign Relations* (Washington, 1930), p. 338. See also *Congressional Record*, 16 July 1930, p. 186.
40. Ibid., 21 July 1930, p. 354.
41. Ibid., 19 July 1930, p. 342.
42. Article XXI of the Washington Treaty.
43. Richard Dean Burns and Donald Urquidi, *Disarmament in Perspective: An Analysis of Selected Arms Control and Disarmament Agreements Between the World Wars, 1919–1939* (Washington, 1968), pp. 214–42.
44. Stephen E. Pelz, *Race to Pearl Harbor: The Failure of the Second London Naval Conference and the Onset of World War II* (Cambridge, Mass., 1974), pp. 196–211.
45. *Congressional Record*, 11 July, p. 111.
46. Ibid., 9 July 1930, p. 60.

From Washington to London: The Imperial Japanese Navy and the Politics of Naval Limitation, 1921–1930

SADAO ASADA

The decade of the 1920s seemed a tranquil era of arms limitation defined by the three naval conferences: at Washington in 1921–22, Geneva in 1927, and London in 1930.[1] Within the Japanese Navy, however, there was strong and growing opposition among officers, particularly those on the Naval General Staff, to the policy of arms limitation pursued by the leadership of the Navy Ministry. This essay examines, on the basis of the hitherto unused Japanese naval record,[2] the hidden moves and countermoves in the years after the Washington Conference that climaxed in a violent collision within Japanese naval circles in 1930 over the London Naval Treaty. In short, it examines the Japanese side of the 'prelude to Pearl Harbor'.[3]

Japanese Naval Traditions

The Five-Power Treaty of the Washington Conference, signed on 6 February 1922, met with a chilly, often hostile reception from professional Navy men among all the signatories, but none harboured as great an antipathy and indignation as those in the Japanese Navy. For them the Washington Treaty, 'imposing' on Japan an 'inferior ratio' of 60 per cent in capital ships (battleships) *vis-à-vis* the United States and Great Britain, was nothing short of a total negation of their naval traditions, which went back to 1907, the year in which an 'Imperial National Defence Policy' was sanctioned by the highest council of the state. By this time the Navy's views had been formulated into the following basic guidelines: (1) the need for a 70 per cent naval ratio as a strategic imperative; (2) its corollary, a building plan for an 'eight–eight fleet' (consisting of eight battleships and eight battle cruisers); and (3) the conception of the United States as the Japanese Navy's 'hypothetical enemy'. These doctrines were of course interrelated, and the abandonment of the first guideline at the Washington Conference jeopardized the other two. Therefore, a brief discussion of these doctrines will be in order here as a background for understanding Japanese naval policy during the 1920s.

The idea of a 70 per cent ratio as Japan's minimum defence requirement *vis-à-vis* the United States rested on the premise that the approaching enemy armada would need a margin of at least 50 per cent superiority over the defending fleet. This spelled a 70 per cent ratio for the Japanese Navy.[4] To the Japanese Navy, therefore, the seemingly minor difference between 60 and 70 per cent made the difference between victory and defeat. The great importance it attached to this issue explains the tenacity with which Japan demanded a 70 per cent ratio at the three naval conferences during the 1920s. This ratio that assured Japan of 'a strength insufficient to attack and adequate for defense' was believed to be imperative as deterrent to the United States. The idea of a 70 per cent ratio, reinforced by war games and manoeuvres in the Pacific, was in time crystallized into a firmly held consensus – even an obsession – within the Japanese Navy.

The conception of the United States as the Navy's 'hypothetical enemy' had first appeared in the Imperial National Defence Policy of 1907. At that time, however, it amounted to little more than a 'budgetary enemy' – a convenient pretext for demanding greater building appropriations. This manner of defining a 'hypothetical enemy' reflected the dictum of Alfred T. Mahan, who once wrote that the standard of naval preparedness should take into account 'not the most probable of dangers, but the most formidable'.[5] Similarly, Japanese naval strategists defined their 'hypothetical enemy' as 'any one power, whether friendly or hostile, that can confront Japan with the greatest force of arms'.[6]

By the time the Imperial National Defence Policy was revised in June 1918, an increasing number of Japanese naval officers had come to regard the United States as more than a mere 'standard for armaments'. Japanese–American relations had seriously deteriorated as Japan took advantage of the First World War to pursue a frankly expansionist policy in China and Siberia, and as the United States attempted to contain Japan. More fuel was added by the revival of the anti-Japanese movement in California. Against this backdrop the conviction grew in the Naval General Staff that 'the rival nation with which a clash of interests is most probable – in other words, the potential enemy – is the United States'.[7]

However, Navy Minister Kato Tomosaburo[8] declared at a cabinet meeting on 26 July 1917 that it was '*from the viewpoint of naval armaments* that America is regarded as hypothetical enemy number one'.[9] Kato's statement, in line with the traditional conception of a 'budgetary enemy', is to be understood as an expression of Japan's effort to maintain a naval balance with the United States, which had ambitious plans for a navy 'second to none'. And the 'eight–eight fleet' plan was Japan's attempt to cope with the American building programme.

As early as 1917 the Japanese Navy seems to have acquired fairly accurate information about the emerging war plan (Plan Orange) of the United States Navy. In October 1920 Tokyo obtained a copy of a confidential war plan jointly drafted by three brilliant young planners – Harry E. Yarnell, Holloway H. Frost, and William S. Pye – outlining the operations for a transpacific offensive. From such intelligence reports the Japanese Naval General Staff gathered that the American Navy required at least a three-to-two superiority over Japan in order to advance its main fleet to the western Pacific and cut off Japan's vital seaborne traffic for an economic blockade that would lead to final victory.[10] To counter such a Pacific strategy the Japanese Navy spelled out in more detail its war plans in the Outline of Strategy that accompanied the 1918 Imperial National Defence Policy. It stipulated that after having captured the American naval base in Luzon in the initial phase of hostilities, the Japanese fleet must 'intercept' the approaching American fleet in the western Pacific and annihilate it in an all-out 'decisive encounter' recalling the Battle of Tsushima.[11]

Offensive operations, early engagement of the enemy in a main encounter, and a quick and decisive showdown – these were to remain the precepts of Japanese naval strategy throughout the 1920s and beyond, and they had a definite Mahanian stamp. Indeed, Admiral Kato Kanji, one of the key naval figures and a dogged opponent of the Washington Naval Treaty, may well have had Mahan in mind when he took special note of the fact that 'the Japanese navy's studies on strategy tallied exactly with their American counterparts'. It was only natural, he explained, that

> strategic planning in any nation, even that bearing on the most secret aspects of national defence, should lead to identical conclusions if based on the same premises and reliable data . . . This is precisely the reason why the United States tries to impose a 60 per cent ratio on us and we consistently demand a 70 per cent ratio.

The universality of Mahan's doctrines was acknowledged by Fleet Admiral Togo Heihachiro, the hero of the Battle of Tsushima and the venerated naval Genro during the 1920s. In 1918 he wrote: 'I express my deep and cordial reverence for his [Mahan's] far-reaching knowledge and judgement'.[12]

Japan's apparent success in adopting Mahan's teachings caused an alarmed reaction in American naval circles. For example, William Howard Gardiner of the Navy League wrote to Admiral William S. Sims in 1920–21:

> I'll warrant every Japanese flag officer knows them [Mahan's sea power series]. . . . Mahan is a perfect guide book to the imperial policy of Japan.

What particularly worried Gardiner was that Japan was systematically applying Mahan's 'principles of overseas expansion' to conditions in the Pacific.[13]

It was precisely because of these shared naval doctrines that a fundamental conflict arose and intensified over the formula of naval limitation. This essay, then, is predicated on two general assumptions: first, that the technical–professional precepts of Japan's naval planners did not exhibit any peculiarities owing to its national psychology or culture,[14] and, second, that the political process of formulating naval policy – particularly with respect to arms limitation – was heavily influenced by the Japanese mode of decision-making, organizational set-up, and factionalism.

The Washington Conference

Taking account of the developments of the First World War, the Imperial National Defence Policy, revised in 1918, stipulated that 'the determination and preparations for enduring a long drawn-out war will be required'.[15] What kind of armaments would Japan need in this new age of total war? The fundamental conflict of views over this question was at the heart of the dissension within the Japanese Navy over arms limitation.

The 'battle of the two Katos' at the Washington Conference, with all its drama and human poignancy, has been narrated elsewhere; a summary account of their respective positions should suffice here.[16] Cognizant of the new realities of total war, Navy Minister Kato Tomosaburo held that no amount of armament would be adequate unless it was backed up by overall national strength, whose essence consisted in industrial and commercial power. Squarely facing Japan's limitations in this respect, he concluded that it would have to be content with 'a peacetime armament commensurate with its national strength'.[17] Kato Tomosaburo had arrived at this broad view of national defence as a Cabinet member participating in the formulation of national policy since 1915.

In sharp contrast, Vice-Admiral Kato Kanji, representing staff and line officers, gave the highest priority to military-strategic considerations, and the particular 'lessons' that he drew from the First World War were markedly different. He held that the United States, with its 'huge wealth, resources, and gigantic industrial power', could speedily turn its war potential into actual fighting forces once hostilities broke out. Hence it could meet its security needs with

peacetime preparations on a par with a 'have-not' nation like Japan.
Conversely, Japan required a large peacetime armament. Another
'important lesson' of the First World War, he held, was the need to
bring about a decisive encounter early in the war; failure to do so
would turn the conflict into a drawn-out war of economic attrition, to
Japan's disadvantage.[18] Thus the Japanese Navy faced the dilemma
of 'expecting' any future war to be a prolonged one while at the same
time realizing that its chance of victory rested on a quick showdown.
This predicament prompted Japan to accelerate its naval build-up,
and this in turn aggravated the vicious circle of the arms race in
the Pacific.

It was Navy Minister Kato Tomosaburo – the architect of the
'eight–eight fleet' plan – who was the first to recognize that this
programme was destined to be a paper plan. In 1919–1921 Japan
was chafing under a postwar recession. At the budget subcommittee
of the Diet in February 1919, Kato frankly admitted: 'Even if we
should try to compete with the United States, it is a foregone conclusion that we are simply not up to it'.[19] He knew very well that a
continued naval race with the United States spelled financial ruin for
Japan. For Kato, hoping for a convenient occasion to halt the dangerous armaments race, the invitation to the Washington Conference
must have seemed a godsend.[20]

As was to be expected, however, violent objections came from the
Navy men in charge of operational matters. An important 'resolution'
of the special committee on arms limitation, submitted to Navy
Minister Kato in late July 1921, categorically stated that Japan
'absolutely requires a naval ratio of 70 per cent or above *vis-à-vis* the
American Navy', thus reconfirming the Navy's longstanding consensus about its security requirement.[21] Kato simply ignored this position paper because he was determined to maintain a completely free
hand in his negotiations at Washington. He had been appointed as
chief of the Japanese delegation because Prime Minister Hara Kei
believed that this naval leader was the only individual capable of
restraining the Navy's demands; civilian delegates would simply be
unequal to the task.[22] Paradoxically, Kato – the Navy Minister and
an Admiral on active duty – was expected to exercise 'civilian' control
by proxy.

At Washington Kato was prepared to take a flexible position. He felt that the question of America's advance bases in the Philippines and Guam was more crucial to Pacific strategy than hairsplitting bargains over fleet ratios. Even so, he was 'dumbfounded' by the dramatic Hughes proposal at the opening session of the conference, offering an itemized plan for the drastic reduction of capital ship strength according to the ratio of 10:10:6 for the United States, Britain, and Japan. Kato at once decided that Japan had no choice but to accept it. His was an 'intuitive decision' aimed first and foremost at improving Japanese–American relations. Defining security in broad terms, he held that 'avoidance of war with America through diplomatic means is the essence of national defence'. The prudent course, then, was to accept the American proposal and stop the risky naval competition.[23] Kato thus subordinated military-strategic needs, however imperative, to higher political considerations. In return for the status quo regarding fortifications in the Philippines and Guam, he accepted the 60 per cent ratio in capital ships.

This decision was vehemently resisted by Vice-Admiral Kato Kanji, the chief naval expert in the Japanese delegation. Being a typical 'sea warrior' of the blue water school, he adamantly opposed any compromise and pressed for a 70 per cent ratio from a strategic standpoint. His view was reinforced by the doctrine of 'the equality of armament' and 'points of national honour'. He held that Japan, as a sovereign nation, was inherently entitled to parity – a 'ratio of 10:10'. Thus viewed, the 70 per cent ratio already represented Japan's maximum concession.[24]

Further, Kato Kanji saw behind America's proposal an 'unreasonable' demand to freeze the status quo and to 'deprive the Imperial Navy of its supremacy in the Far East', substituting America's own 'hegemony'. The United States, he felt, was 'dictating' an 'unequal treaty' to Japan. Embittered to see the British delegates aligning with the Americans, Kato Kanji warned that submission to 'Anglo-American oppression' would not only be an 'unbearable humiliation', but also result in 'the most serious threat' to Japan's security.[25]

These views were, of course, contrary to those held by Kato Tomosaburo. He wired to Tokyo that 'Anglo-American coercion is a fantasy which has never even occurred to us delegates in Washington'.[26] The senior Kato, a controlling figure who exercised charismatic leadership, simply defied any challenge from his subordinates. He did meet Kanji's violent opposition with cogent arguments, but when these proved unavailing, he forcefully overruled and silenced the junior Kato.

The relentless Kanji, however, attempted to subvert his chief's decision: going behind Tomosaburo's back, he disregarded the regular procedure and directly ordered the telegraph officer to wire to the Naval General Staff his dissenting views, drafted by his confidant, Captain Suetsugu Nobumasa.[27] Such backstairs machinations did not confuse or mislead the naval authorities in Tokyo. With his usual foresight, the senior Kato had already wired them through a direct pipeline to his Vice-Minister, Ide Kenji, and obtained the approval of the Government and the naval Genro, especially Fleet Admiral Togo, for his decision to accept the 60 per cent ratio. At the Washington end, the only officer who was permitted to handle these 'top secret dispatches' was Captain Nomura Kichisaburo, the senior Kato's devoted aide.[28]

The most notable feature of Kato's decision-making style was the extent to which he ignored or commanded his unruly subordinates at Washington. Such a mode of policy-making, quite unusual in Japan where consensus-building is the norm, was especially effective in coping with a crisis situation, which Kato saw in the ongoing naval race. In short, it was triumph of 'rational decision-making' over 'bureaucratic politics'.[29]

On the other hand, there was the drawback of overburdening an individual leader. Already suffering from cancer of the colon, Kato had to endure enormous strains that were to shorten his life. Another disadvantage was that no matter how powerful a leader he was, his individualized decision-making went against the strongly held bureaucratic norms of the naval establishment and was destined sooner or later to fail. As 'the battle of the two Katos' showed, the senior Kato did squash the junior Kato's spirited opposition, but the latter remained unreconciled to the 60 per cent ratio. On the day Japan accepted the 60 per cent ratio, Kato Kanji was seen shouting, with tears of chagrin in his eyes, 'As far as I am concerned, war with America starts now. We'll get our revenge over this, by God!'[30] Thus the *political* decision to accept the compromise settlement failed to take root in Japan's subsequent naval policy; on the contrary, the reaction from naval men, if anything, reinforced their obsession with the 70 per cent ratio and their notion of the United States as the hypothetical, even inevitable, enemy.

Foreseeing some such development, Kato Tomosaburo had already begun during the Washington Conference to contemplate drastic institutional reforms, including 'a system of civilian navy ministers'. Apparently he had been contrasting the Anglo-American type of civilian control with Japan's anomalous system, which imposed on him, a full Admiral and Navy Minister, the onerous task of going against the organizational mission of the service that he himself headed. The second institutional reform Kato had in mind was firmly to subordinate the Naval General Staff to the Navy Minister.[31] Did Kato already foresee the collision between the Navy and the Government, as well as an internal conflict between the Navy Ministry and the Naval General Staff, that ensued from the 1930 London Naval Conference?

At the time of the Washington Conference no clear pattern of internal conflict had emerged between the Navy Ministry and the Naval General Staff. Yet it is significant that the 'intractable' rebels against the Washington Naval Treaty centred in the Naval General Staff; these 'hot blooded' junior officers were the disciples of Kato Kanji and Captain Suetsugu. And the latter now occupied a key post as chief of the Operations Section of the Naval General Staff.

Turning to the Naval Ministry, officers who had faithfully supported Kato Tomosaburo – Captain Nomura, Commander Hori Teikichi, and Captain Yamanashi Katsunoshin – all occupied Navy Ministry posts. These men, as self-conscious 'heirs' of Kato Tomosaburo, remained firmly committed during the 1920s and beyond to what has come to be called 'the Washington Treaty system'.[32]

The conventional interpretation (to which the present writer has contributed in the past) holds that the senior Kato's views of national security and naval limitation were handed down through these 'heirs' as 'naval orthodoxy' into the 1920s and 1930s. When viewed in the context of the foregoing analysis, however, quite a different picture emerges. After all, was it not Kato Tomosaburo himself who abandoned the three basic guidelines of the Imperial Japanese Navy since 1907 – a 70 per cent ratio, the 'eight–eight fleet' plan, and the notion of the United States as the 'hypothetical enemy'? Rather, it was Kato Kanji and his followers in the Naval General Staff and the fleets who would soon claim to occupy the 'mainstream' of the Japanese naval establishment by denouncing the Washington Treaty.

From Washington to Geneva, 1922–1927

Appointed Prime Minister in June 1922, Kato Tomosaburo served concurrently as Navy Minister for nearly a year. His immediate task was to implement the Washington treaties, but the more difficult problems were the Navy's institutional reforms and the revision of the Imperial National Defence Policy to accord with the new course he had set at Washington. But alas, his health, so severely taxed at Washington, failed him at this critical juncture, and his premature death was to doom all but the first of these tasks to failure.

Drastic personnel retrenchment, necessitated by the naval reductions, caused even greater discontent among naval men than the scrapping of ships, built and under construction. Still greater was the shock administered by the sharp cut in enrolment at the Naval Academy: the entering class of 1922 numbered less than one-fifth of the previous class. The demoralizing effects were profound. (It was no accident that three of the young officers later to be involved in the 'May 15 [assassination] Incident' of 1932 came from the classes that had acutely felt this impact.)

The second task of institutional reform had little chance of success. Kato Kanji, who had been promoted to Vice-Chief of the Naval General Staff in May 1922, was of course absolutely opposed to any system of civilian Navy Ministers. In the end, Kato Tomosaburo's reform plan backfired: it simply provoked the Naval General Staff into taking preemptive action.

This is seen in the third and most important task, revision of the Imperial National Defence Policy. It was only after the Navy and Army General Staffs had reached an agreement on the new national defence policy that they 'consulted' the ailing Kato Tomosaburo, who had no choice but to give his reluctant consent.[33]

Officially sanctioned in February 1923, the revised national defence policy negated the senior Kato's basic principle of 'avoidance of war with America' and instead adopted the junior Kato's notion of inevitable war. This document singled out the United States as the common 'hypothetical enemy' number one for *both* the Navy and the

Army (which had hitherto placed priority on Russia). Its underlying perception of the international situation went directly counter to the views of the senior Kato and the liberal diplomat Shidehara Kijuro, soon to become Foreign Minister, who envisaged an era of peaceful cooperation under the Washington Treaty system. The new national defence policy of 1923 saw the East Asian scene as still riddled with 'sources of conflict'.

> The United States, following a policy of economic invasion in China, menaces the position of our Empire and threatens to exceed the limits of our endurance. . . . The longstanding embroilments, rooted in economic problems and racial prejudice [discrimination against Japanese immigrants], are extremely difficult to solve. . . . Such being the Asiatic policy of the United States, sooner or later a clash with our Empire will become inevitable.[34]

The main motifs of economic determinism and a fatalistic belief in the coming of war with America unmistakably bore Kato Kanji's stamp, with his peculiarly narrow and ethnocentric perspective on the external world. For him the United States was the arch-antagonist with whom hostilities were unavoidable 'in the near future'. It is an irony of history that such an idea was officially adopted in the top-level policy document just when the Washington Naval Treaty made it strategically infeasible for either navy to wage offensive warfare across the Pacific.

The background of these developments was the remarkable ascendancy of Kato Kanji in the Naval General Staff. Outweighing his mild-mannered chief, Admiral Yamashita Gentaro, he wielded such great power that he 'often tended to overwhelm the administrative branch [the Navy Ministry]'.[35] Kato Tomosaburo's untimely death in August 1923, removing effective control over the insurgent elements, caused a crack in the Washington Treaty system as far as the Japanese Navy was concerned.

Significantly, the profound effect of Kato Tomosaburo's death on Japanese–American relations was seen most clearly by the American Admiral William V. Pratt, whose exertions on behalf of naval limitation had placed him 'outside the mainstream of navy opinion'.[36] Upon hearing about Kato's death, a 'greatly shocked' Pratt hastened to send his old friend, Rear-Admiral Nomura Kichisaburo, a long and moving letter of condolence:

> I feel that not only Japan lost one of the greatest broad minded men but that we in the United States have lost a sincere friend and a man who understands us far better than the average man can. . . .
>
> During the course of the conference in Washington I watched Baron Kato very closely; I wanted, if possible, to find out the kind of a man he was. . . . I became thoroughly convinced in my mind at that time that Baron Kato was one of the finest, biggest, and most courteous gentlemen that I ever had the honor of meeting. I felt that so long as he [Kato Tomosaburo] had the direction of affairs in his hands no misunderstanding could arise between your country and mine which could not be settled through amicable arrangements.[37]

The succeeding Navy Minister, Takarabe Takeshi – who served from 1923 to 1927 (excepting a short interval) and again during 1929 to 1930 – simply did not possess the kind of charismatic leadership qualities, broad internationalist outlook, and powerful personality that distinguished Kato Tomosaburo. Nor would Takarabe pursue Kato's policies. With Kato's towering presence gone, the vagaries of bureaucratic politics and 'competition among mediocrities' came to the fore.

For his part, Kato Kanji had been building up a cohesive faction. He and Suetsugu cultivated a strong following among 'hot-blooded young officers' in the Naval General Staff. In the Navy Ministry, Vice-Minister Abo Kiyokazu (1924–25) and Osumi Mineo (1925–28) were Kato's close allies and were the opponents of the Washington Naval Treaty.[38] It was against the background of such a factional alignment that policy regarding naval limitation unfolded in the mid-1920s.

As early as 1923 the Japanese Navy had come to expect that sooner or later the United States would propose a second naval conference, this time to halt the incipient race in the auxiliary vessels – cruisers, destroyers, and submarines – which were not restricted under the Washington Treaty. To prepare for it, the Navy's committee on arms limitation drafted a careful policy study. Appropriately enough, this report began with a discussion of the 'Lessons of the Washington Conference', and it clearly reflected Kato Kanji's views.[39]

The major lesson was that Japan's 'failure' at Washington was largely due to inadequate preparation. In anticipation of a second conference, therefore, Japan must establish 'a firm, concrete, and clear-cut policy' well in advance and demand preliminary negotiations with the other participating powers so as to obtain prior recognition of Japan's demands. The second 'lesson' was that its position must be publicized at home in order to 'educate, unify, and firm up' domestic public opinion behind the delegates. This was a point particularly stressed by Kato Kanji: he bitterly recalled how he had been 'handicapped' by the lack of domestic support at the time of the Washington Conference. The third 'lesson' was that 'the utmost caution must be taken never again to be confronted by joint Anglo-American coercion'.

The Japanese Navy took it for granted that the American aim in calling a second conference would be to extend the Washington ratios of 10:10:6 to auxiliary vessels as well. Of course, the Japanese Navy was 'absolutely opposed' to such a formula. As to the all-important ratio question, the report stated that Japan would be justified in first proposing the 'principle of parity' (10:10), but, anticipating Anglo-American opposition, that it would be prepared to 'compromise' with an 80 per cent ratio. Such a conference strategy again reflected the thinking of Kato Kanji, an advocate of 'the right of equality'. This line of argument was considered to be particularly applicable to auxiliary vessels, which the United States with its huge industrial might could build rapidly and in large numbers once hostilities started. However, the recommendation for an 80 per cent ratio was rejected by those committed to the long-standing policy of a 70 per cent ratio, and the latter 'orthodox policy' was to be steadfastly pursued by the Japanese Navy thereafter.[40]

The final point raised by the committee's report was the timing of the next conference. It would be to Japan's advantage if it could synchronize with the completion of its current 'auxiliary replacement plan' in fiscal 1928. Anxious to secure a vantage ground at the next conference, the Naval General Staff urged an acceleration in the current building programme.[41]

What was most noteworthy about this programme was the great

stress placed on the number of large submarines. The effort to break
the strategic deadlock in the Pacific under the Washington Treaty had
resulted in major innovations in Japan's naval technology and
strategic planning. A new feature added to the Outline of Strategy
(accompanying the 1923 version of the Imperial National Defence
Policy) was an 'attrition strategy' that was to precede the 'interceptive
operations'. This strategy assigned to large, high-speed submarines
the important mission of wearing down the enemy's main fleet on its
transpacific passage. In addition to patrolling and defending the
western Pacific, the submarine squadrons were to engage in relentless
attacks on the enemy's approaching main fleet. It was Rear-Admiral
Suetsugu who worked out this strategy, as commander of the First
Submarine Squadron in 1923–25.[42]

As the radius of action and line of naval defence had been extended
for both navies by rapid advances in technology and weaponry, war
plans began to take more concrete shape on both sides of the Pacific
in the mid-1920s. The Japanese Navy hypothesized, correctly, that
America's main fleet would in all probability advance by the central
route from Pearl Harbor to the Gilbert Islands, Guam, and then
Manila Bay. On this transoceanic passage the American forces would
try first to seize the intervening islands under Japanese mandate – the
Marshall and Caroline Islands – and then carry their offensive into
Japan's home waters.[43] It was on such a scenario that Japan's 'interceptive operations' were predicated.

There was, however, considerable speculation among Japanese
planners as to America's timing in sending its main fleet to the
western Pacific. The dominant view in the Naval General Staff held
that the Japanese capture of the Philippines would so provoke the
American people as to compel immediate dispatch of their main fleet
to relieve Manila.[44] Unaware of the ambivalence in American naval
thinking in this regard, Kato Kanji observed:

> The fundamental guideline of American strategy is the principle
> of the quick-and-decisive battle. It is bent on promptly forcing
> an encounter with the Japanese fleet and deciding the issue in
> one stroke.[45]

However, there were those in the Japanese Navy who questioned
whether the American Navy would begin 'a quick westward dash

without full preparations'. What if the United States chose to hold back its main fleet until it had secured overwhelming strength and the essential logistic support? In that case, Japanese efforts to keep up the naval ratio *vis-à-vis* the United States would all come to naught.

To overcome such strategic weaknesses, Kato Kanji, appointed Commander-in-Chief of the Combined Fleet in December 1926, ordered his fleet to conduct relentless night drills. Such were the risks involved that a double collision of four cruisers occurred one moon-less night in August 1927, resulting in 120 casualties. After this disaster Admiral Kato grimly addressed the assembled commanders: 'We must devote ourselves more and more to this kind of drill, to which our navy has applied all its energies ever since the acceptance of the 10:10:6 ratio'. This was language calculated to inflame anti-pathy to the Washington Naval Treaty. The mounting indignation with the 60 per cent ratio had crystallized into the conviction that 'only through these hard drills can we expect to beat America!'[46]

On the other hand, the United States Navy may, however unwitt-ingly, have added to such antagonism in Japanese naval circles. During the first half of 1925, Admiral Robert E. Coontz, Commander-in-Chief of the United States Fleet, led 56 vessels (in-cluding 12 battleships of the Battle Fleet) on a spectacular cruise to Australia and New Zealand.[47] Their manoeuvres, on an unprece-dented scale, provoked Kato Kanji and his subordinates, who took them to be 'a naked demonstration of American naval buildup against Japan' and a full dress rehearsal for a transpacific offensive.[48]

The discontent which had been building up among fleet officers ever since the Washington Conference found hyperbolic expression in a letter of protest written later by Admiral Yamamoto Eisuke (not to be confused with Yamamoto Isoroku), who was to be the Commander-in-Chief of the Combined Fleet at the time of the 1930 London Naval Conference. As the nation's 'first line of defence', he protested, the fleet was engaged day and night in relentless exercises to overcome deficient armaments, but the top leaders of the Navy Ministry were all too ready to make 'political compromises' when confronted with budgetary problems, seemingly oblivious to the ser-ious defects in armaments they brought about. These 'moderate leaders' in Tokyo had 'come to resemble civilian desk officers rather than real sailor-warriors'. Venting his 'violent resentment', Admiral

Yamamoto traced this 'deplorable' condition to the Washington Conference, Kato Tomosaburo's 'despotic' rule, and his 'emasculation' of the Navy.[49]

Such strong sentiments bespoke a deep split that had come to plague the Japanese Navy. The late 1920s saw the confluence of two undercurrents that had been building up ever since the Washington Conference. First, there was rivalry and antipathy between the 'fleet faction' led by Kato Kanji and the 'administrative faction' adhering to Kato Tomosaburo's legacy of naval limitation. The latter occupied some of the key posts in the Navy Ministry.

Second, there was a growing sense of crisis, among fleet officers and the Naval General Staff, concerning the 'grave defects in national defence' caused by the policy of naval limitation pursued by the 'administrative faction'. The conflict along organizational lines would suddenly explode over the London Naval Treaty of 1930. Previous to this culmination, however, Japan participated in a second naval conference, at Geneva.

The Geneva Naval Conference, 1927

When the American invitation to the Geneva Conference came in February 1927, the Japanese Government, headed by Wakatsuki Reijiro, decided to participate because it put a premium on the political necessity of cooperating with the United States. Japan's reply stated that it would be happy to join a conference 'calculated to complete the work of the Washington Conference'. To this phrasing the Navy registered stiff opposition, objecting to the American plan to apply the Washington ratios of 10:10:6 to auxiliary vessels. In the end, however, the Navy unwillingly acquiesced in the Government's decision.[50] Thus a head-on collision with the United States seemed unavoidable.

As it turned out, the entire parley at Geneva was so plagued with Anglo-American differences over the question of cruiser types and tonnage that Japanese–American conflict never came to the surface. The civilian delegate Ishii Kikujiro later reflected: 'Had the negotiations continued for a little while longer, at the least a violent controversy with America over the ratio issue would have become inescapable'. This is corroborated by Commander Nomura Naokuni, a naval member of the delegation: 'Although Japan had taken a very rigid stand [on the ratio issue], Anglo-American antagonism so dominated the conference that it broke up without going into the issues at stake with Japan'.[51] As far as the Japanese Navy was concerned, therefore, the historical significance of the Geneva Conference was that it amounted to a preliminary skirmish with the United States, a prelude to the major confrontation at the London Naval Conference of 1930. Since there exists no study of the Japanese Navy and the Geneva Naval Conference, the subject deserves to be treated here in some detail.[52]

The general instructions given to the Japanese delegates contained no specific mention of the ratio matter, but the instructions handed to the chief naval adviser, Vice-Admiral Kobayashi Seizo, revealed that the naval authorities in Tokyo maintained a rigid stand on the 70 per cent ratio. However, the chief delegates – Admiral Saito Makoto and the veteran diplomat Ishii – interpreted the 70 per cent formula rather flexibly, as 'a mere criterion for negotiations', and not as a 'strict mathematical figure absolutely required for national defence'.[53] As had been the case at the Washington Conference, much would depend on the head delegate – his personality, quality of leadership, and international outlook.

The great importance that Prime Minister Wakatsuki attached to the success of the forthcoming conference, rendered all the more urgent by the financial crisis of March 1927, is clear from his selection of Admiral Saito as head delegate; one-time Navy Minister and the incumbent Governor-General of Korea, he was regarded as 'a great figure of superdreadnought caliber'.[54] The move to appoint Saito greatly alarmed Kato Kanji, then Commander-in-Chief of the Combined Fleet. He hastened to write Saito a long, presumptuous letter, urging him to withdraw his acceptance. Kato invoked the 'bitter lesson' of the Washington Conference. 'From the navy's standpoint', Kato opined, 'it is undesirable to appoint a great naval figure as the chief delegate to discuss naval questions'. Obviously, what Kato feared was that an 'admiral-statesman' like Saito might overrule naval-strategic views to reach a political compromise, just as Kato Tomosaburo had done at Washington. Rather condescendingly Kanji went on to explain that a free and extemporaneous give-and-take in international conferences required a certain practical experience and skill which, he insinuated, Saito lacked. Matters of substance were best left to naval experts in the delegation.[55] Kato vastly underestimated Saito's diplomatic acumen: in reality, Saito had accumulated considerable political experience through 16 years of service as Navy Minister and Vice-Minister and, since 1919, as Governor-General of Korea.

In the negotiations at Geneva, as it turned out, Admiral Saito showed that he was a master of diplomacy and commanded the respect of the American and British delegates for his impartiality and genuine devotion to naval reduction. Under the leadership of Saito, ably assisted by his chief naval adviser, Vice-Admiral Kobayashi, the naval members of the Japanese delegation worked 'in a shipshape manner'.[56]

This is not to say, of course, that there were no differences within the delegation. In formulating conference strategy the naval members became involved in heated arguments. Hardliners, representing Kato Kanji's views, maintained that Japan must take the initiative, resolutely declaring and adhering to its position even at the risk of breaking up the conference. Saito admonished them, saying that it would be impolitic for Japan to bluff. 'The essence of preparedness' consisted in 'gradually enhancing our national strength – our economic and industrial power – while winning greater respect and understanding from the rest of the world'. In view of Japan's limited resources, Saito warned, 'we should not opportunistically attempt a sudden expansion of our navy . . . in one conference or two'. Saito's words settled the argument, and they remind one of Kato Tomosaburo's views on national defence.[57]

However, Saito's decision-making at Geneva was hampered by the lack of coordination with the naval authorities in Tokyo. Departing from the procedure set at the time of the Washington Conference, the Navy decided that instructions should be sent from the Navy Vice-Minister to the chief naval adviser, not to the head delegates. Thus Saito seldom received specific instructions directly from the Government or the naval leaders.[58] This procedural change may have been designed to tie Saito's hands. Furthermore, Navy Vice-Minister Osumi was Kato Kanji's confidant. Regarding the Washington Conference as 'a most flagrant oppression' of Japan, Osumi harboured a deep distrust of the United States.[59] On the other hand,

Vice-Admiral Kobayashi, the chief naval adviser, was a man of broad international outlook similar to Admiral Saito's. And Kobayashi was assisted by Captain Hori Teikichi, an advocate of naval limitation ever since he attended the Washington Conference. Thus a clash of views between the delegates and the naval leaders in Tokyo was inevitable.

The greatest obstacle the Japanese faced at Geneva was, of course, the rigid position taken by the American delegates on the 10:10:6 ratio. The most outspoken among them was Rear-Admiral Hilary P. Jones, a 'die-hard' and advocate of 'the Big Navy school', who, as a senior naval adviser, seemed to control the civilian delegate, Hugh Gibson. Even before the conference opened on 20 June, Jones had, in his informal talks with the Japanese, blurted out a 'threatening' remark: 'If the application of the 10:10:6 ratio [to auxiliary vessels] should fail to materialize, the United States will achieve it through a naval race backed by its unlimited wealth'. He insisted that, since a quota of 50 per cent would practically assure Japan of parity in its home waters, the 60 per cent ratio was already overly generous. A 70 per cent ratio was simply out of the question: it would destroy the naval balance. The United States, he said, did not wish to allow Japan naval superiority in the western Pacific – the anticipated theatre of hostilities in the future. This, of course, was the position of the United States Navy throughout the 1920s, but it had never before been so bluntly stated to the Japanese.[60]

However, circumstances were quite different from those of the Washington Conference. In auxiliary vessels (especially in cruisers) built and planned, the United States did not have the overwhelming superiority over Japan that it had had at the Washington Conference.

From the beginning, the Japanese delegates proposed to take as the standard of naval reduction Japan's existing strength plus its authorized building programme, which would place its ratio somewhat above 70 per cent of the United States, but about 65 per cent of Britain. The Japanese delegates were so preoccupied with their ratio question that they did not fully recognize how serious the Anglo-American impasse over the cruiser issue had become. Instead, the Japanese had an excessive fear that the British would finally yield to the Americans and then form a combined front against Japan to impose a 60 per cent ratio – a fear that was fuelled by their subjective memory of 'Anglo-American coercion' at the Washington Conference.[61]

Anxious to forestall such a development, the Japanese delegates entered into bilateral talks with the British, who seemed more accommodating on the ratio issue, to work out some compromise formula that might help to break the three-cornered deadlock. On 16 July a broad Anglo-Japanese 'compromise formula' emerged out of informal exchanges between Vice-Admiral Kobayashi and the British delegate Vice-Admiral Frederick Field, and it was provisionally endorsed by Saito. Most notably, in this 'compromise formula' the Japanese conceded the lowering of the acceptable ratio to 65 per cent in 'surface auxiliary vessels' (cruisers and destroyers).[62]

Why was it that the Japanese delegates proposed this important concession, despite renewed instructions from Osumi 'to do their utmost' to obtain the 70 per cent ratio? According to Kobayashi's reports and reminiscences,[63] the Japanese delegates believed it to be most urgent to remove the Anglo-American 'fixation' with the Washington ratio system and reach any agreement, be it 62 or 63 per cent, that would do away with the 60 per cent ratio.[64] Computing from a 65 per cent ratio for surface auxiliaries and the parity of 60,000 tons for submarines, the delegates showed that Japan would attain the overall figure of 68.7 per cent for auxiliary vessels – only 1.3 per cent short of their original instructions.

On Saito's behalf, Kobayashi hastened to wire to Navy Vice-Minister Osumi an important policy recommendation, listing four reasons for speedy acceptance of the proposed compromise:

(1) Naval limitation on the basis of the Anglo-Japanese plan would not be disadvantageous to Japan's national defence.
(2) Rupture of the conference would inevitably accelerate a naval race, causing international instability.
(3) If Japan were to be held responsible for the breakup, its international position would be adversely affected.
(4) A more favourable opportunity for naval limitation would not recur in the near future.[65]

This 'wide view', urging compromise in the interests of larger political considerations, bore a striking resemblance to Kato Tomosaburo's position at the Washington Conference.

However, the naval authorities in Tokyo rejected out of hand any formula that deviated from their original instructions. Osumi directed the delegates to withdraw the 'compromise formula' immediately, wiring Kobayashi: 'We feel it most deplorable that the delegates have proposed to sacrifice the 70 per cent ratio which has been Japan's long-cherished desire'. Such a concession would be 'especially painful from the standpoint of our relations with the United States'.

> The delegates must persist to the bitter end in their demand for a 70 per cent ratio. If this demand cannot be met, public opinion will certainly be aroused, and the resultant treaty will have little chance of being approved by the cabinet or being ratified. . . . Depending on the attitude of Britain and the United States, a worst case scenario might arise, ultimately forcing us to *resolve to fight to the death*.[66]

In these scathing words, as Kobayashi later wrote, Osumi 'rebuked and denounced Kobayashi as if he were a traitor who endangered Japan's national defence'.[67]

From the beginning the Anglo-Japanese compromise was doomed to failure, because it encountered stiff opposition not only from Tokyo but also from the American delegates. As the Japanese delegates had suspected they would, the American naval advisers opposed the 65 per cent ratio as 'gravely endangering America's position in the western Pacific'. However, the American delegates had studiously 'evaded' Japanese attempts to ascertain their stand on the ratio question. The Japanese sensed the American ploy: for the moment the Americans needed their cooperation in countering Britain's demand, but once the latter yielded, the United States, supported by Britain, would 'turn all out against Japan to impose a 60 per cent ratio'.[68]

On 24 July Saito and Ishii wired Tokyo, expressing their worst fear. The time was fast approaching, they telegraphed, when Japan would be forced into confrontation with the United States over the ratio issue. (Their alarm was well-founded, for two days earlier Gibson had wired Washington that discussion of the ratios with the Japanese would be necessary 'at a very early date'.) The Japanese delegates felt certain that the United States would insist on 63, if not 60, per cent for Japan. Here was the dilemma as they saw it: on the one hand, if Japan should reject the American demand outright,

Japan would be held responsible for the collapse of the conference; on the other hand, if Japan should yield, an impression of 'surrender under American pressure' would be created at home. The only way out, the delegates urged Osumi, was 'to reach a compromise on the maximum ratio acceptable to the United States', which in their view was 63 per cent.[69]

As was to be expected, Osumi's reply was a flat refusal: 'If such is the case, the game is up; there will be no room for further negotiations whatsoever'. If Japanese demands should be rejected, 'the resentment of our people would become an eternal source of future trouble, and it would also destroy the morale of our navy'.[70]

Yet the worst did not materialize, and a head-on collision was narrowly avoided, because irreconcilable Anglo-American differences over the cruiser issue submerged the explosive ratio question. Vice-Admiral Kobayashi has written: 'The clash between the [Japanese] government and the navy did not occur, because Anglo-American differences broke up the conference'.[71]

On the public scene in Geneva, at least, the Japanese delegates managed to hold on to the legacy of Kato Tomosaburo, but within the Navy the forces of opposition personified by Kato Kanji were gaining momentum. According to Admiral Takarabe's later testimony, the Anglo-Japanese 'compromise formula' caused 'tumultuous controversies' within the Navy which apparently became unmanageable. Upon Saito's return, Vice-Admiral Yamanashi Katsunoshin, chief of the Naval Ordinance Division, vaguely intimated that 'knotty circumstances and irresistible pressures' were to blame for poor coordination between Tokyo and the delegates in Geneva.[72]

Presumably, these 'pressures' had to do with the exigencies of bureaucratic politics. The extremely intransigent stand taken by Navy Vice-Minister Osumi remains something of an enigma. To be sure, he was a protégé of Kato Kanji and a sworn enemy of naval limitation, but most of the other high-ranking naval leaders belonged to the 'moderate group' that supported the Washington and, later, London naval treaties. Among the latter were: Navy Minister Okada Keisuke; Nomura Kichisaburo, Vice-Chief of the Naval General Staff; Vice-Admiral Yamanashi; and Rear-Admiral Sakonji Seizo, chief of the Naval Affairs Bureau. However, even their collective leadership could not match the overwhelming control exercised by Kato Tomosaburo at the time of the Washington Conference. Under the circumstances, the vociferous opponents of naval limitation – Kato Kanji, Suetsugu (then head of the Navy's Education Bureau), Yamamoto Eisuke (head of the Naval Aviation Division), and their confreres – rallied to a man behind Navy Vice-Minister Osumi.

The balance between the two camps – the one committed to the Washington Naval Treaty and the other to overturning it – was, indeed, a precarious one. Before it came to a showdown at the London Naval Conference in 1930, the former attempted to reinforce their position.

The Road to London, 1928–1930

Only two months after the debacle of the Geneva Conference, Navy Minister Okada ordered the committee on arms limitation to make a comprehensive study that would guide not only preparation for the next naval conference but also building programmes in the broad context of Japanese–American relations, present and future. Headed by Vice-Admiral Nomura Kichisaburo, this committee (commonly referred to as the Nomura Committee) was dominated by the supporters of naval limitation, including Rear-Admiral Sakonji, the chief of the Naval Affairs Bureau. The strictly confidential report of the committee, submitted to the Navy Minister in September 1928, was an authoritative document which was to provide the basis for future naval policy.[73]

The first point to be noted in this report is the reaffirmation of the Washington Naval Treaty. This would seem to indicate that, Osumi's rigid attitude toward the Geneva Conference notwithstanding, the thinking of the upper echelons was still fluid in 1928. Under existing conditions, the report concluded, the Washington Naval Treaty was 'on the whole advantageous' to Japan, financially as well as strategically. Kato Tomosaburo's philosophy of naval security was restated in the following passages:

> Since Japan's national strength in relation to the Anglo-American power is vastly inferior, it would be to our advantage to keep them tied down to the capital ship ratio of 10:10:6, even though Japan was assigned an inferior strength. . . . Vis-a-vis

great industrial powers like the United States and Britain, the utmost effort must be made to avoid a war whose outcome would be decided by an all-out contest of national strength.[74]

The report saw Japan's naval armament as a 'silent power' with which to deter the United States from 'obstructing' Japanese policy in China.[75] Here was an explicit reiteration of Kato's view of the Navy as an instrument of deterrence.

Secondly, the Nomura Committee's report presented a highly optimistic view of Japanese–American relations, present and future. Its fundamental premise was that ever since the Washington Conference their mutual relations had been 'so greatly improved' that there no longer existed any problems of such magnitude as to provoke a war. As to China, Americans were finally awakening to its 'chaotic and hopeless condition' and therefore becoming more sympathetic and cooperative towards Japanese policy. 'Therefore the United States is quite unlikely to collide head-on with our efforts to make peaceable inroads into China'. Japan, for its part, fully realized the importance of closer economic relations with the United States.[76] Such views were almost identical with the liberal outlook that informed Foreign Minister Shidehara's policy.

In sharp contrast to such sanguine views, the dissenting opinion attached to the committee's report reechoed Kato Kanji's convictions. In strong language similar to that of the 1923 Imperial National Defence Policy, the dissenting view held that conflict over the China market must 'lead to the outbreak of war between Japan and the United States'. At the zenith of its prosperity, the United States was 'increasingly showing its true colours as an economic imperialist' in China.[77]

While the report of the Nomura Committee and the dissenting opinion were diametrically opposed in their estimates of Japanese–American relations, both agreed on the necessity for a 70 per cent ratio for auxiliary vessels. This position did not necessarily contradict the committee's support for the Washington Naval Treaty. As the report explained, at the Washington Conference Japan had conceded the 60 per cent ratio in capital ships only in return for the status quo regarding Pacific fortifications; this being the case, it was by no means to be construed as 'abandonment' of the long-standing consensus on the 70 per cent ratio. The committee's report reconfirmed that a 70 per cent ratio for auxiliary vessels was 'absolutely necessary for the nation's defence, nay, for its very existence'; there must be no bargaining over this at the next conference.[78]

Meanwhile, Kato Kanji had become convinced that 'even the 70 per cent ratio was insufficient'. By this time he had come to realize the error of 'relying too heavily on intangible forces', by which he meant excessive drilling. The immediate occasion for his rethinking was the emergence of 10,000-ton cruisers carrying eight-inch guns (the maximum allowed under the Washington Treaty) as the main prop of auxiliary strength.[79] The Japanese Navy had come to recognize the superiority of these high-speed, heavily armoured heavy cruisers, regarding them as 'semi-capital ships'. In the report of the Nomura Committee heavy cruisers were given special importance. In pursuance of the 'attrition strategy' and 'interceptive operations', the Naval General Staff assigned heavy cruisers the crucial mission of wearing down America's main fleet in its transpacific passage before it could reach the anticipated theatre for a decisive encounter.[80]

A lengthy staff study, prepared in late 1929 by the Operations Division of the Naval General Staff, spelled out in detail the 'formidable power' of the 10,000-ton cruisers. First, they excelled in speed; second, they were equipped with great striking power (eight-inch guns had twice the firepower of six-inch guns); third, and most importantly, their great cruising capacity was a vital element in transoceanic operations. According to this study, America's strategic outposts which had hitherto been isolated from each other – the Philippines and Guam in the west, Hawaii at the centre, Samoa in the south, and the Aleutians in the north – could now be closely linked thanks to the long radius of these heavy cruisers. Thus the Pacific had been 'seemingly reduced to an American lake'. Japan, for its part, was rapidly losing its geographic advantages. For these reasons Japanese naval planners emphasized that their demand for a 70 per cent ratio in heavy cruisers left 'absolutely no room for compromise'.[81]

Whereas *relative* strength, or ratio, was all-important with regard to the heavy cruiser, *absolute* strength (total tonnage irrespective of the ratio) was the paramount consideration in respect of the submarine. Unlike heavy cruisers, submarines were never meant to fight the enemy's counterparts but were to be deployed to wear down the enemy's main fleet. At the coming London Conference, therefore, the Navy decided to demand 78,000 tons – Japan's submarine strength upon the completion of the building programme at the end of fiscal 1931.[82]

The Denouement: The 1930 London Naval Conference

Existing studies on the London Naval Conference, based mainly on the records and testimonies of the 'administrative faction' in the Navy Ministry, tend to slight the views of the 'command faction' in the Naval General Staff. Nor have they clarified the internal complications and clashes (a) within the Japanese delegation in London, and (b) between the delegates and the naval authorities in Tokyo.[83] The account that follows will highlight some of these neglected aspects.

Preparations for the London Conference began as early as June 1929, when Navy Minister Okada obtained the Cabinet's approval for the Navy's 'three basic principles': (1) a 70 per cent ratio with the United States in total auxiliary tonnage; (2) the special importance of the 70 per cent ratio with regard to 10,000-ton, eight-inch-gun cruisers; and (3) the submarine tonnage of 78,000.[84] The key figure in promulgating and insisting on these demands was, of course, the chief of the Naval General Staff, Kato Kanji.

On 18 November Kato pressed upon Prime Minister Hamaguchi Osachi that the 70 per cent ratio was 'the rock-bottom ratio' and constituted 'a matter of life or death for our navy'. This overriding goal had 'stiffened the navy's morale and sustained its determination through unspeakable hardships' ever since the Washington Conference; Japan would 'rather do without any new agreement' than yield on this. In his conversations with Foreign Minister Shidehara, Kato urged the 'pressing need of obtaining a prior commitment to a 70 per cent ratio' for auxiliaries in preliminary negotiations with the United States and Britain. Uppermost in his mind was a determination 'never to repeat the mistake of the Washington Conference'; only by such an understanding could 'joint Anglo-American coercion' be forestalled.[85] However, preliminary diplomatic efforts in Washington and London, continued until the eve of the conference, failed to yield any prior understanding.

As the chief delegate to the conference Prime Minister Hamaguchi chose Wakatsuki Reijiro, twice Finance Minister, and Prime Minister at the time of the Geneva Naval Conference, trusting that he would carry out the Government's twin goals of fiscal retrenchment and friendly cooperation with the Anglo-American powers. Wakatsuki knew full well that Japan's limited financial capabilities ruled out a naval race, and for this reason he had once supported the Washington Naval Treaty. At the coming conference, he believed, it would be 'unwise to persist uncompromisingly in the 70 per cent ratio'; he favoured 'concluding a treaty within negotiable limits, say 65 or 67 per cent'.[86]

The choice of Wakatsuki as the civilian delegate posed a problem for the Navy. Navy Minister Takarabe was all too willing to go to London, but within the Navy he had the reputation of being 'unreliable'. Kato Kanji was worried that Takarabe was no match for a powerful brain like that of Wakatsuki. He consulted with the naval Genro, Fleet Admiral Togo, and decided to send as 'the highest naval adviser' Admiral Abo, his intimate friend and a member of the Supreme War Council, who was a hard-liner in the 'command faction'. Abo was to be Kato's spokesman in London and a 'chaperon' for the 'untrustworthy' Takarabe in Washington. The second-ranking naval expert member, Rear-Admiral Yamamoto Isoroku, of whom Kato had a very high opinion, was counted on to take a firm stand in London. Among junior naval members Kato took special care to include Captain Nakamura Kamesaburo, chief of the Operations Section of the Naval General Staff and a steadfast 'hawk'.[87] Such a line-up in the naval delegation tended to isolate and overpower Vice-Admiral Sakonji, chief naval adviser, whose moderate views on naval limitation placed him among the successors of Kato Tomosaburo.

During Takarabe's absence, Prime Minister Hamaguchi served as acting Navy Minister, following the precedent established at the time of the Washington Conference. Under him, Vice-Minister Yamanashi assumed the onerous responsibility of controlling the Navy and keeping close contact with the Government. (Later, the Superintendent-General of Metropolitan Tokyo intimated to Yamanashi: 'You were in such a physical danger that I feared for the worst. You are lucky indeed to be alive at all!')[88]

Yamanashi was ably assisted by Rear-Admiral Hori, head of the

Naval Affairs Bureau, and Captain Koga Mineichi, the chief Navy Ministry adjutant, but these 'moderate' leaders were simply no match for Kato Kanji, a full Admiral, and his followers in the Naval General Staff. Later, when the fate of the naval treaty hung in the air, the Navy Ministry leaders turned to the naval elder Admiral Okada to be a mediator between the Government and the Navy on the one hand and between the two branches of the Navy on the other. It was believed that Okada – Kato's 'big senior', hailing from the same province – was the only man available to restrain the impetuous Kato Kanji.[89]

The mounting dissension between the Navy Ministry and the Naval General Staff may be partly explained by the Navy's personnel alignment. In 1930 the key policy-making positions in the Navy Ministry were virtually monopolized by officers with rich politico-administrative experience. In contrast, the crucial posts in the Naval General Staff were occupied by stout officers of the 'sea warrior' type, who had made their careers as line or staff officers. Neither Kato Kanji nor Suetsugu had held important posts in the Navy Ministry; they had served mainly in the Combined Fleet as well as in the Naval General Staff. In contrast, Yamanashi and Hori had had no important tours of duty in the fleet. Such divergence of career backgrounds naturally accentuated the differences between the 'administrative faction' and the 'command faction' in their approach to naval limitation.

With regard to procedures for deciding on the size of armament, Yamanashi and his subordinates in the Navy Ministry took a flexible position: 'Armament plans, drafted by the Naval General Staff from strategic-operational viewpoints, are not fixed absolutes; they must be agreed upon between the Navy Ministry and the Naval General Staff, on the basis of a broad outlook that takes all factors into consideration'. Head of the Naval Affairs Bureau Hori went further, and believed that decisions on armament were *political* matters involving budgetary appropriations; responsibility hence lay with the Government.[90]

The leaders of the Naval General Staff, for their part, believed that they were performing their assigned duty in pressing for their estimated security needs. Taking an absolute stand on 'the three basic principles', these leaders burned their bridges when they clamorously appealed to public opinion. Kato bitterly recalled that at the time of the Washington Conference he had lacked domestic public support and was determined not to have that happen again, but his public campaign annoyed and embarrassed chief delegate Wakatsuki, whose diplomatic hands were thus tied.[91]

Kato Kanji reacted violently to the Anglo-American position on the ratio issue – if a 60 per cent ratio was acceptable to Japan at Washington, why not at London? The naval situation, Kato retorted, had greatly changed since the days of the Washington Conference. Why should Japan accept the Washington Treaty ratio when its existing auxiliary strength was 74 per cent and its heavy cruiser strength was above 80 per cent of the United States? In addition to strategic considerations, Kato was led by twin 'convictions' that had governed his views ever since the Washington Conference: the doctrine of 'the equality of armament' and the dictate of Japan's 'national prestige'. He held that a 70 per cent ratio would already be a substantial concession on Japan's part. 'The more humbly Japan acquiesces in the 70 per cent ratio *despite its sovereign right of equality*, the more flagrant the United States becomes in flaunting its high-handed and coercive attitude'.[92]

In support of his demands, Kato forcefully presented his views on their foreign policy implications to Prime Minister Hamaguchi and Foreign Minister Shidehara. American ambitions in China, he claimed, must 'inevitably lead its diehards to clamour for forcible settlement of the China question by naval strength'. The United States was being inhibited 'only by Japan's armament and by America's lack of offensive capability'. America's real design was to bind Japan to an inferior naval ratio so that it could pursue its 'domination' of China without hindrance.

In a similar vein, Kato wrote on 5 February to Admiral Abo in London: 'The real issue at stake is no longer our naval power per se but *our national prestige and credibility*'. In these emotional outbursts Kato subordinated the material factor of ratios and tonnage figures to such intangibles as national dignity and a valiant self-image. In the same letter he requested Abo to send home 'more and more telegrams about Anglo-American oppression', which he assured him would stir up public sentiment and 'force the government to stiffen its attitude'.[93]

In London, however, the prospect of attaining the Japanese terms seemed to be getting dimmer and dimmer. As early as 12 August 1929 – several months before the conference opened – Ambassador Matsudaira Tsuneo (appointed one of the delegates) wired a very pessimistic forecast: 'It is totally impossible to win British and American consent; on the contrary, our demands will only provoke their antipathy'.[94] Ambassador Matsudaira followed up this dispatch with another one, warning Shidehara that if Japan should insist, to the bitter end, on a 70 per cent ratio, clashes with the United States and Britain would be inevitable, and they would conclude a bilateral treaty to the exclusion of Japan. Similarly discouraging dispatches came from Ambassador Debuchi Katsuji in Washington. In reply, Shidehara 'strictly forbade' the ambassadors to take a defeatist view, urging them to redouble their efforts to win the 70 per cent ratio.

Against this diplomatic background, chief delegate Wakatsuki arrived in London on 17 November 1929. It did not take long for him to conclude that 'further perseverance in the same hard-line demands must inevitably result in an angry parting with America and Britain'. On 25 January 1930, only four days after the conference opened, he drafted a telegram to this effect: 'We are at our rope's end; the time has now come to request the government to apprise us of the terms of compromise'. Meeting staunch opposition from Admiral Takarabe and his naval advisers, this telegram was shelved.

In mid-February, when the conference seemed to founder on the reef of a Japanese–American deadlock, Wakatsuki confidentially wired to Foreign Minister Shidehara, urging the Government to take the utmost precautions 'so as not to drive the issue to the last extremity'. The break-up of the conference would place Japan in an 'extremely difficult position internationally'.[95]

Shidehara and Hamaguchi were daily exposed to the rigid stand of the Naval General Staff, which was dead set against any compromise, so they directed Wakatsuki to follow 'the logical steps of first consulting with delegate Takarabe and jointly working out some appropriate solution'. For Wakatsuki, however, such 'consultation' with Takarabe had become totally impossible. In fact, the civilian and naval delegates had become locked in irreconcilable differences. Later, when the Japanese–American negotiations reached a critical point, Wakatsuki complained to Shidehara about Takarabe's intransigence in these bitter words:

> Although I have urged delegate Takarabe to rise resolutely to the occasion as a statesman and take broad-minded measures to save the situation, he disagrees with me in every instance and has instead aligned himself with Admiral Abo and naval advisers. . . . To my great distress, it has proved beyond my power to persuade him despite my repeated efforts.

In sending these secret dispatches, Wakatsuki resorted to the most confidential telegraphic channel in order to circumvent the naval members of the delegation: a special route through his co-delegate Matsudaira Tsuneo, who alone could handle the codes as Ambassador to London. This attempt to keep the navy side in the dark failed, because Matsudaira's 'top secret' telegrams were easily deciphered by the Navy's decoding experts, and the upshot was further to enrage the naval representatives.[96]

To compound matters, Wakatsuki's acts of 'nonconfidence' were reciprocated by the naval advisers in London. For their part, they had been wiring their dissenting views directly to naval authorities in Tokyo without informing chief delegate Wakatsuki. In addition to the Navy's formal channel of communication – that between Navy Minister Takarabe and his Vice-Minister Yamanashi – a tangle of irregular lines extended from London to Tokyo. When Admiral Abo, the highest naval adviser, sent his confidential telegrams to Kato Kanji, it was chief naval adviser Sakonji who personally ciphered his telegrams in order to prevent a leak. (In one of them Abo urged that special watch must be kept over Wakatsuki, who was all too ready to succumb to 'Anglo-American coercion'.) In the next echelon, Sakonji was sending secret dispatches to Vice-Minister Yamanashi and Naval Affairs Bureau chief Hori. On lower levels, junior naval members, who represented the 'hot-blooded young officers' of the Naval General Staff, telegraphed to their home office without even the permission of their superior, Sakonji.[97]

This jumble of telegraphic channels bespeaks a serious failure of communication within the Japanese delegation, a situation that was largely due to Takarabe's lack of leadership as Navy Minister and a delegate. Even at the critical stages of negotiations he remained strangely passive, making himself most unpopular with his subordinate officers. Admiral Abo, Rear-Admiral Yamamoto, and high-spirited junior officers would rather argue directly with civilian delegate Wakatsuki than deal with an 'indecisive and vacillating' Takarabe. In appointing the Navy Minister as a delegate, the precedent of the Washington Conference had been followed without much thought; Takarabe was simply not of the calibre to reenact Kato Tomosaburo's role at Washington.[98]

From the Navy's viewpoint, the 'grave error' revolved around the 'Reed–Matsudaira compromise' that was reached on 13 March between Matsudaira and Senator David A. Reed, an American delegate. The two civilian delegates had entered into informal talks in order to find a way out of the Japanese–American deadlock, but Wakatsuki had reassured the naval advisers time and again that any formula to come out of these conversations would be merely a 'private plan'; that he would decide on it 'only after consulting with the navy side'. Meanwhile, however, the impasse reached in the negotiations had forced the Japanese delegates to commit themselves to the 'Reed–Matsudaira compromise'. To the Japanese naval experts the 'Reed–Matsudaira compromise' came as 'a bolt from the blue'. It conferred on Japan: (1) an overall ratio of 69:75; (2) a 60 per cent ratio in heavy cruisers, with a proviso that assured Japan of a ratio slightly above 70 per cent (the United States promising not to complete three of its heavy cruisers during the life of the treaty, that is until 1936); and (3) parity in submarine tonnage, which was set at 52,700 tons.

On the day this compromise plan was reached, Wakatsuki hastened to wire Foreign Minister Shidehara, categorically stating that there was 'no prospect of obtaining more favourable terms' and pleading with the Government to 'make the final determination' to accept them. On the other hand, Takarabe – ever mindful of the stiff stand taken by Kato and Suetsugu, and faced with strong objections by his technical advisers – demurred, saying that the compromise plan would not be acceptable to the Naval General Staff. Takarabe and the naval advisers said that they would dispatch a separate and dissenting telegram to the Government. However, on 14 March Takarabe reluctantly joined the civilian delegates in sending an important dispatch to Tokyo over all their signatures. In effect, this dispatch requested the Government to accept the 'Reed–Matsudaira compromise'. Uppermost in Wakatsuki's mind was the importance of avoiding a clash with the Anglo-American powers and of forestalling a ruinous naval race, and on this stand he would stake not only 'his position as chief delegate but also his life itself'.[99]

However noble Wakatsuki's resolve may have been, the fact remains that the 'Reed–Matsudaira compromise' negated the Navy's long-standing armament policy. Wakatsuki honestly believed that this plan was not only acceptable but also advantageous to Japan. After all, did it not to all intents and purposes meet the demand for a 70 per cent ratio? Did the United States not make 'an enormous concession' by agreeing to parity in submarines? Had he not obtained the substance, if not form, of all of the three objectives of the Japanese Government? Wakatsuki was prepared to resign immediately if the Tokyo Government should disapprove of the 'compromise' or send a new instruction at variance with it.[100]

However, Wakatsuki overlooked the import of restricting submarine strength to 52,700 tons. In the expert eyes of the Navy men, Wakatsuki's 'amateurish' reasoning ignored Japan's strategic imperatives. Chief naval adviser Sakonji was a supporter of naval limitation, but even he opposed the 'Reed–Matsudaira compromise'. It gave Japan, he said, a mere token – an overall 70 per cent ratio, the least important of its demands – while denying the 'essence' regarding the all-important categories of the heavy cruiser and the submarine. Rear-Admiral Yamamoto was furious at the compromise plan. Staking his own position, he forced on Takarabe his opposing views. So vehement did Yamamoto feel toward the weak-kneed delegates that, one witness noted, he 'almost seemed intent to do them in'.[101] When Kaya Okinori, a Ministry of Finance representative, emphasized the financial factors involved in naval limitation, Yamamoto shouted: 'Say another word and you will get a smack in the face'.

In Tokyo, Kato Kanji angrily declared: 'The American [Reed–Matsudaira] plan[102] is a most high-handed one, offering us, as it were, only the crust of a pie without filling'. On 19 March, as 'one responsible for national defence and strategic plans', he visited Prime Minister Hamaguchi and in a most unbending manner talked for more than an hour, insisting vehemently that he was 'absolutely opposed' to the compromise. Kato emphasized that its acceptance would undermine Japan's operational plans since (1) the shortage in submarine strength would impede Japan's capture of the Philippines and cripple its patrolling as far as Hawaiian waters, not to mention its attrition strategy in the Pacific, and (2) the concession on heavy cruisers would cause 'grave defects' in a main fleet encounter, making it impossible to make up for the 60 per cent strength in battleships.

In this rigid position Kato was powerfully backed by Fleet Admiral Togo, deified as 'the Nelson of Japan', who said he would rather break up the conference and walk out than yield one iota. These strong words Kato hastened to send to Takarabe in London to put further pressure on him.[103]

From London, Sakonji (perhaps conveying Abo's views) wired the naval authorities in Tokyo that acceptance of the compromise plan, entailing a 'crisis' in naval defence, was 'simply out of the question'. On 15 March, learning about the 'Reed–Matsudaira compromise', an incensed Admiral Abo flew out at Takarabe, accusing him of having been brought over to the side of the civilian delegates. Abo threatened to resign from the Supreme Military Council if the compromise should be accepted. Rear-Admiral Yamamoto was equally vehement in his opposition to 'any unwarranted political retreat'. Even more extreme were agitated junior officers like Captain Nakamura, who directly appealed to delegates Takarabe and Wakatsuki for 'a firm and resolute stand'. Failing to obtain a satisfactory response, these young officers proposed, as the last resort, to send their strongly worded dissenting views directly to the chief of the Naval General Staff, Kato, and the Navy Vice-Minister, Yamanashi. Their aim was to force some 'drastic' new instructions from Tokyo that would turn the tables at the conference and reverse the 'defeatist policy' of Wakatsuki and his fellow travellers. In a gesture to mollify the young 'hawks', Yamamoto wired his friend Hori, head of the Naval Affairs Bureau, apprising him of these strong pressures from below.[104]

It must be emphasized that the naval leaders in Tokyo, such as Yamanashi and Hori, were by no means entirely satisfied with the 'Reed–Matsudaira compromise', but it was their responsibility to take careful measure of the diplomatic, political, and fiscal consider-ations that compelled a compromise settlement. In order to bring about a successful naval treaty, Admiral Okada backed up these moderate leaders, using his considerable political influence and tact to mediate between the Navy Ministry and the Naval General Staff on the one hand, and between the Navy and the Government on the other.[105] Okada, whose views on naval limitation were heavily influenced by Kato Tomosaburo's, took a very flexible stand on the ratio matter and naval armament.

At the conference of naval leaders on 25 March, Prime Minister Hamaguchi told Yamanashi that the Government had made up its mind not to run the risk of breaking up the conference: 'Though I lose the prime ministership, though I lose my life itself, this decision is unshakable'.[106] On 27 March Hamaguchi had an audience with Emperor Hirohito, to 'explain the progress of the London Naval Conference'. The emperor told him 'to make every effort to speedily conclude [the London Treaty] in the interest of world peace'. These words had an electrifying effect on Hamaguchi,[107] and from that time onward Hamaguchi's determination was immovable. Later in the day, Hamaguchi called Kato Kanji, Okada Keisuke, and Yamanashi to his official residence, and in their conversations he alluded to the source of his renewed resolve.

Until 26 March there still remained a modicum of harmony, but the arrival on that day of two separate and conflicting telegrams from Wakatsuki and Takarabe caused great confusion in Tokyo. Wakatsuki once again urged a speedy and full acceptance of the compromise plan, while Takarabe withdrew what he had said in the telegram of 14 March and urged the Government to persist at the risk of breaking up the conference. These dispatches from London precipitated a violent split within the Japanese Navy as well as one between the Government and the Navy. In the words of Ikeda Kiyoshi, the leading Japanese naval historian, thus began 'an upheaval unprecedented in the history of the Imperial Japanese Navy'.[108]

How it became politicized and developed into a national crisis, involving the 'right of Supreme Command', needs no retelling here.[109] Suffice it to note that Takarabe, placed in a dilemma between his duty as the Navy Minister and his political responsibility as a member of the Hamaguchi Cabinet, continued to vacillate and temporize to the last. His contradictory behaviour bewildered Tokyo and compounded the confusion. Even as the Government's 'final instructions' – directing the delegates to accept the treaty along the lines of the 'Reed–Matsudaira compromise' – were being dispatched to the delegates in London, an apprehensive Yamanashi wired Takarabe to urge 'utmost prudence' and 'circumspection':

> It is feared that in the event that you should take actions at odds with Wakatsuki, they will divide our delegation in London to the detriment of its negotiating power, and at home such actions will cause grave political difficulties, driving the navy into a most inimical and self-damaging predicament.[110]

Yamanashi's warning against any rash action betrayed his fear that at the last moment Takarabe might still be swayed by his extremist naval advisers, who demanded 'one final thrust' to wrench further concessions from the United States.

Tokyo's final instructions, arriving in London on 1 April, produced quite a commotion among naval representatives, especially junior staff officers. Suddenly informed of the Government's decision for compromise, excited young officers denounced and reviled Wakatsuki and plotted to storm Takarabe's suite. (Indeed, such was their excitement that they forgot themselves and gave a bloody nose to a civilian representative.)

On the following day, Rear-Admiral Yamamoto admonished his subordinates 'not to commit a breach of service discipline', but he himself proceeded to contradict his orders to his subordinates. He put extraordinary pressure on his chief, even asking Navy Minister Takarabe to take responsibility by resigning immediately:

> The last and the only way left for the navy minister to preserve honour after this defeat at the conference is to resign in protest as befits the occasion and to prove to the Japanese people that 'the navy has not betrayed' their trust.

He went on to warn that public surrender to the American demands would 'shock our entire navy, destroy its morale, and bring about some untoward incident'. (The above account should modify the prevalent notion of Yamamoto as a member of the 'treaty faction'.)[111]

Prelude to Catastrophe

On 22 April the London naval treaty – along the lines of the 'Reed–Matsudaira compromise' – was signed at the Court of St James.

Success in steering this treaty safely to its signature and ratification meant victory for the 'administrative faction' and defeat for the 'command faction'.

However, ironically enough, the outcome of the domestic commotions it triggered actually enhanced the power of the latter group. The struggle over the London naval treaty brought into the open a violent split within the Navy between the pro-treaty and anti-treaty camps – a split that was to plague the Japanese Navy during the subsequent decade. How the treaty issue was made a football of party politics; how it brought about a head-on collision between the Government and the Navy; and how it triggered a series of political assassinations, starting with the fatal attack on Prime Minister Hamaguchi in November 1930 – these are questions that fall outside the purview of this study of naval policy.

For our purpose, however, it is important to underscore that the London naval treaty, just at the time when Japan concluded it, was already being sabotaged by the anti-treaty forces in Japan; the treaty was destined to be short-lived. The Navy held that the London treaty, 'seriously jeopardizing national defence, must not be allowed to last long'. Emperor Hirohito, who had earnestly desired the conclusion of the treaty, astutely surmised the Navy's intent, and tried to obtain an assurance that the 'Navy's policy would not bind Japan's position at the next naval conference of 1935'. This caveat notwithstanding, the Supreme Military Council went ahead to state in its 'official reply to the Throne' on 23 July that the Navy was opposed to the continuation of the London naval treaty beyond its expiration in 1936. Suetsugu expressed the prevailing naval view when he wrote to Kato: 'As things stand now, there is no way left but to force our way to the abrogation of the fatal treaty'. Kato had also been venting his indignation: 'It is as if Japan were bound hand and foot and thrown into jail by the Anglo-American powers!'[112]

With the advantage of historical hindsight, the tragedy of the London Conference may be said to have been that it contained the seeds of subsequent developments in the 1930s. First, the so-called 'Osumi purge' forced out or prematurely retired brilliant senior officers who had been committed to the 'Washington system' and naval limitation: Yamanashi, Sakonji, Hori and others. Osumi Mineo, Navy Minister from 1933 to 1936, was a stiff opponent of naval limitation, and he had the strong backing of Kato Kanji and his 'fleet faction'. Second, Japan abrogated the Washington Naval Treaty in 1935 and withdrew from the second London Naval Conference in 1936. This led to the resumption and escalation of the naval race, which one American historian has called 'the Race to Pearl Harbor'.[113]

When one traces the historical origins of the collision course, however, the forces of opposition that had been building up since the Washington Conference loom large. In 1933 Prime Minister Saito Makoto stated succinctly, 'The present commotions have their roots in Kato Kanji's antipathy toward [the policy of] Admiral Kato Tomosaburo, the chief delegate at Washington'.[114] No contemporary Japanese leader was better qualified to make this assessment. Kato Tomosaburo's success in 1921–22 proved to be a Pyrrhic victory. Heralded at the time as 'a new order of sea power',[115] the Washington and London treaties – or rather Japan's response to them – were signposts on the Japanese Navy's road to the Pacific War.

Doshisha University

NOTES

1. This paper is adapted from Chapter 4 of my forthcoming book, *Ryo-taisenkan no Nichi-Bei kankei – Kaigun to seisaki kettei katei* [Japanese–American Relations Between the World Wars: Navies and the Decision-Making Process] (Tokyo: University of Tokyo Press, 1993). In preparing this paper I am greatly indebted to the professional advice and assistance of Nomura Minoru and Suekuni Masao (retired from the War History Office, Defense Agency). The late Arthur J. Marder and Joseph Frankel made valuable suggestions on an earlier version of this paper.
2. The single most important record for the purpose of this essay is the splendid collection of the late Enomoto Juji (Professor of the Naval Staff College, Imperial Japanese Navy, and international legal adviser to the Navy), who attended all the interwar naval conferences as expert adviser. I was privileged to examine his papers and interview him at his residence while he was alive. Portions of the Enomono papers are now deposited at (1) the Library of the Institute of Defense Studies, the Defense Agency, the War History Department (hereafter cited as Institute of Defense Studies); and (2) the Library of the Maritime Self-Defense Force Staff College. Also important are the papers of Hori Teikichi, which I examined at the Institute of Defense Studies.
3. Cf. Gerald E. Wheeler, *Prelude to Pearl Harbor: The United States Navy and the Far East, 1921–1931* (Columbia, Missouri, 1973).

4. Boeicho Senshishitsu (War History Office, Defense Agency) (ed.), *Senshi sosho, Daihon'ei kaigunbu: Rengo kantai* [War history series: Imperial Headquarters: Navy], I, pp. 156–9; Nomura Minoru, 'Tai-Bei-Ei kaisen to kaigun no tai-Bei shichiwari shiso' [The outbreak of war with the United States and Great Britain, and the idea of a 70 per cent ratio], *Gunji shigaku*, Vol. 9, No. 3 (1973), pp. 26–7.

5. Alfred T. Mahan, *The Interest of America in Sea Power, Present and Future* (Boston, 1897), p. 180.

6. Sato Tetsutaro, *Teikoku kokubo shiron* [A historical treatise on the national defence of the Japanese Empire] (Tokyo, 1908), pp. 724, 748, 760.

7. Naval General Staff (ed.), 'Taisho 4 naishi 9-nen sen'eki kaigun senshi furoku dai-6-hen: Kimitsu hoshu' [A history of naval battles in 1915–1920, Appendix 6 – confidential addendum], Institute of Defense Studies.

8. Throughout this essay I have adopted the normal Japanese practice of giving family names first, except for the two Katos, where first names alone are occasionally used to avoid confusion.

9. Navy Minister's Secretariat (ed.), *Kaigun gunbi enkaku* [The development of naval armaments], I (1934, reprinted, Tokyo, 1970), p. 220 (italics added).

10. Takagi Sokichi, *Shikan Taiheiyo senso* [A personal interpretation of the Pacific War] (Tokyo, 1969), pp. 64–6. My search in the US naval records has failed to pinpoint the document in question, but its contents are very similar to Admiral R.E. Coontz to Secretary of the Navy, 17 Feb. 1920, P.D. 198–2, RG 80, National Archives.

11. Although the text of the 1918 Imperial National Defence Policy has not yet been discovered, it can be reconstructed in an outline form on the basis of collateral sources. Boeicho Senshishitsu, *Senshi sosho: Kaigun gunsenbi* [War history series: Naval armaments and preparations], I (Tokyo, 1969), pp. 64–7, 146; *Senshi sosho: Daihon'ei rikugunbu* [War history series: Imperial Headquarters, Army], I (Tokyo, 1967), pp. 217–23, 248, 319; *Rengo kantai*, I, pp. 164–70; Shimanuki Takeharu, 'Nichi-Ro senso iko ni okeru kokubo ho-shin, shoyo heiryoku, yohei koryo no hensen' [The development of the Imperial National Defence Policy, the Estimate of Requisite Armament, and the Outline of Strategy since the Russo-Japanese War], *Gunji shigaku*, Vol. 8, No. 4 (1973), pp. 2–11.

12. 'Gunshuku shoken' [My views on naval limitation], presented by Kato Kanji to Saito Makoto in 1930 [hereafter cited as Kato, 'Gunshuku shoken'; Naval General Staff's memo on American naval armaments since the Washington Conference, 14 Dec. 1929, Papers of Saito Makoto, Kensei Shiryo Shitsu (The Depository for Documents on Political and Constitutional History), Diet Library (hereafter cited as Saito papers).

13. W.H. Gardiner to W.S. Sims, 17 June 1921, Papers of William Howard Gardiner, Houghton Library, Harvard University.

14. Bernard Brodie convincingly argues that since 'the professional lore of naval men is highly internationalized', the Japanese Navy received its 'tuition as well as its naval designs and ordnance' from Anglo-American sources. *A Guide to Naval Strategy* (rev. edn, New York, 1963), pp. 114–15, 160–61.

15. *Rengo kantai*, I, p. 168; *Kaigun gunsenbi*, I, p. 146.

16. Asada, 'Japanese Admirals and the Politics of Naval Limitation: Kato Tomosaburo vs Kato Kanji', in Gerald Jordan (ed.), *Naval Warfare in the Twentieth Century, 1909–1945: Essays in Honour of Arthur Marder* (London, 1977), pp. 141–66 (hereafter cited as Asada, 'Japanese Admirals'.)

17. Nihon Kokusai Seiji Gakkai (Japan Association of International Relations) (ed.), *Taiheiyo Senso e no michi: Bekkan shiryohen* [The Road to the Pacific War: Supplementary volume of documents] (Tokyo, 1963), pp. 3–7 (hereafter cited as *TSM*); Terashima Ken Denki Kankokai (ed.), *Terashima Ken den* [Biography of Terashima Ken] (Tokyo, 1973), p. 147.

18. Kato Kanji Taisho Denki Kankokai (comp.), *Kato Kanji taisho den* [Biography of Admiral Kato Kanji] (Tokyo, 1941), pp. 756–7.

19. Minutes (5 Feb. 1919) of the 4th Subcommittee for Budget, Lower House of the Imperial Diet (41st session), Institute of Defense Studies; Yamanashi Katsunoshin Sensei Kinen Shuppan Iinkai (ed.), *Yamanashi Katsunoshin sensei ihoroku* [Memoirs of Admiral Yamanashi Katsunoshin] (Tokyo, 1968), pp. 66–7 (hereafter cited as *Yamanashi ihoroku*); Yamanashi, *Kato Tomosaburo gensui o shinobu* [Fleet Admiral Kato Tomosaburo in reminiscence] (Tokyo, 1967), p. 8; Kurihara Hirota (ed.), *Gensui Kato Tomosaburo den* [Biography of Fleet Admiral Kato Tomosaburo] (Tokyo, 1928), pp. 87–8.

20. For the Washington Conference, see William Reynolds Braisted, *The United States Navy in the Pacific, 1909–1922* (University of Texas Press, 1971), Chapters 28–41; Roger Dingman, *Power in the Pacific: The Origins of Naval Arms Limitation, 1914–1922* (University of Chicago Press, 1976).

21. Kaigun Kokusai Remmei Kankei Jiko Kenkyukai [Navy Ministry's committee to investigate League of Nations affairs], 'Kafu kaigi gunbi seigen mondai ni kansuru kenkyu' [Studies on the arms limitation question at the Washington Conference], 21 July 1921, Enomoto papers.

22. Hara Keiichiro (ed.), *Hara Kei nikki* [Diary of Hara Kei] (Tokyo, 1965), Vol. 5, p. 435.

23. Navy Minister to Navy Vice-Minister, 12 Nov. 1921 (Strictly confidential), Enomoto papers; *TSM: Shiryohen*, pp. 3–4.

24. Vice-Admiral Kato Kanji to Navy Minister and Chief of the Naval General Staff, 24 Nov. 1921, IJN Archives; *Kato Kanji taisho den*, pp. 746–49.

25. Kato Kanji to Navy Vice-Minister and Vice-Chief of the Naval General Staff, 4 Dec. 1921, Institute of Defense Studies.

26. Navy Minister to Navy Vice-Minister, 16 Jan. 1922, IJN Archives; *TSM: Shiryohen*, p. 7.

27. Hori Teikichi's memo on the Washington Naval Conference, n. d., Hori papers.

28. Navy Minister to Navy Vice-Minister, 4 Dec. 1921; Captain Nomura to Navy Vice-Minister, 15, 18, 28 Nov.; 1, 9 Dec. 1921, Enomoto papers and Institute of Defense Studies.

29. A full theoretical analysis of Kato's negotiation and decision-making behaviour is Asada, 'Washinton kaigi o meguru Nichi-Bei seisaku kettei katei no hikaku: Hito to kiko' [A comparative study of the Japanese and American decision-making process at the time of the Washington Conference: Decision-makers and mechanisms] in *Taigai seisaku kettei katei no Nichi-Bei hikaku* [Comparative studies of the foreign policy decision-making process in Japan and the United States] edited by Hosoya Chihiro and Watanuku Joji (Tokyo, 1977), pp. 419–64; and Asada, 'Japanese Admirals'.

30. Mori Shozo, *Sempu nijunen* [Twenty tumultuous years] (Tokyo, 1968), p. 50.

31. *TSM: Shiryohen*, p. 7.

32. Yamanashi Katsunoshin sensei kinen shuppan iinkai (ed.), *Yamanashi Katsunoshin sensei ihoroku* [Yamanashi's memoirs] (Tokyo, 1968), passim (hereafter cited as *Yamanashi ihoroku*).

33. *Rengo kantai*, I, pp. 196, 202–3, 234; *Kaigun gunsenbi*, I, pp. 68–73.

34. Shimanuki, 'Daiichiji sekai taisen igo no kokubo hoshin, shoyo heiryoku, yohei koryo no hensen' [The development of the Imperial National Defence Policy, the Estimate of Requisite Armament, and the Outline of Strategy since World War I], *Gunji shigaku*, Vol. 9, No. 1 (1973), pp. 65–74.

35. *Kato Kanji taisho den*, pp. 767–68, 770–72.

36. Gerald E. Wheeler, *Admiral William Veazie Pratt* (Washington DC: Naval History Division, Department of the Navy, 1974), pp. 182–7.

37. Pratt to Nomura, 25 Aug. 1923, Papers of Admiral William V. Pratt, Naval History Foundation, Washington Naval Yard, Washington DC.

38. *Kato Kanji taisho den*, p. 768; Yamaji Kazuyoshi, *Nihon kaigun no kobo to sekinin-sha tachi* [The rise and fall of the Japanese Navy and its leaders] (Tokyo, 1959), p. 175.

39. Gunbi Seigen Kenkyu Iinkai [Investigatory committee on naval limitation], 'A study on a second naval limitation conference', 10 May 1925, Enomoto papers [Hereafter the titles of Japanese manuscript materials are given in English translation.]

40. Draft instruction to the Japanese naval representative at the League of Nations, 17 Nov. 1924, Japanese Ministry of Foreign Affairs (hereafter cited as JMFA), Diplomatic Record Office; Hori Teikichi, 'Explanations of ratios in auxiliary vessels', n.d., Hori papers; *Kato Kanji taisho den*, pp. 746–60.

41. Navy's revised instructions to the naval representative at the League of Nations, 17 March 1926, JMFA; Gunbi Seigen Kenkyu Iinkai, loc. cit.; *Kaigun gunsenbi*, I, pp. 332–41.

42. Ibid. pp. 148–9, 152–8; Naval General Staff, 'Memo for an oral presentation', n.d. (1930), apparently prepared by Kato Kanji; Nagai Sumitaka, 'Kokubo hoshin to kaigun yohei shiso no hensen' [The development of the Imperial National Defense Policy and naval strategic thought], May 1962, part 13, pp. 3318–27, 3335–8, War History Department, Institute for Defense Studies; Ikeda Kiyoshi, *Nihon no kaigun* [A history of the Japanese navy] (Tokyo, 1967), Vol. 2, pp. 137–9.

43. Nagai, op. cit., pp. 3329–31; *Kaigun gunsenbi*, I, pp. 150–51; Naval General Staff, 'Memo for an oral presentation'; Kato Kanji's memo, 'My views on arms limitation'; Memo on American armaments since the Washington Conference, Enomoto papers. Cf. William Reynolds Braisted, 'On the United States Navy's Operational Outlook in the Pacific, 1919–1931', unpublished paper presented to the Kauai Island Conference on the history of Japanese–American relations (1918–1931), 5–9 Jan. 1976; and Wheeler, *Prelude to Pearl Harbor*, pp. 77–91; Edward S. Miller, *War Plan Orange: The US Strategy to Defeat Japan, 1897–1945* (Annapolis, Maryland, 1991).

44. The 'Annual Operational Plan' of 1926 estimated that the main fleet encounter would take place about 45 days after the outbreak of war, and this estimate remained the same until 1930. Nagai, op. cit., p. 3328.

45. Kato Kanji's memo, 'My views on arms limitation'; *Kaigun gunsenbi*, I, p. 150. For the Pacific strategy of the United States Navy, see Miller, *War Plan Orange*.

46. *Kato Kanji taisho den*, pp. 846–57, 918–19; Kato Kanji, 'Secret memoirs of the London Naval Treaty', IJN Archives; Kato to Makino Nobuaki, 29 Jan. 1930, Makino papers.

47. Braisted, 'On the United States Navy's Operational Outlook in the Pacific'.

48. Kato Kanji's memo, 'My views on arms limitation'; Naval General Staff, 'Memorandum for an oral statement'.

49. Kido Nikki Kenkyukai (ed.), *Kido Koichi kankei monjo* [Papers relating to Kido Koichi] (Tokyo, 1966), pp. 263–6.

50. *Rengo kantai*, I, p. 218; United States Department of State, *Foreign Relations of the United States, 1927* (Washington DC, 1942), I, pp. 4, 13–14, 28 (hereafter cited as *FRUS*).

51. Ishii Kikujiro, *Gaiko yoroku* [Diplomatic commentaries] (Tokyo, 1930), p. 234; Nakamura Kikuo (ed.), *Showa kaigun hishi* [Secret history of the Navy during the Showa era] (Tokyo, 1969), pp. 33–4.

52. Stephen Roskill's majestic study of *Naval Policy Between the Wars, Vol. 1: The Period of Anglo-American Antagonism, 1919–1929* (New York, 1968), and Wheeler's *Prelude to Pearl Harbor* do not examine Japanese policy. Unno Yoshiro, *Nihon gaikoshi, Vol. 16: Kaigun gunshuku kosho, fusen joyaku* [Japanese diplomatic

history, Vol. 16: Naval limitation negotiations / the Kellogg – Briand Pact] (Tokyo, 1973) contains an account of Japan at the Geneva Conference, but it is based on the Foreign Ministry Archives and does not analyse naval policy and politics.

53. Instructions to the chief delegates to the Geneva Conference, Cabinet decision, 15 April 1927, JMFA; Navy Minister's instructions to chief naval aide, 19 April 1927, Enomoto papers.

54. Navy Minister Takarabe Takeshi to Saito, 17 March 1927, Saito papers.

55. Kato Kanji to Saito Makoto, 23 March 1927, Saito papers. Because of the 'most delicate nature of the problem', Kato requested Saito to 'destroy this letter upon reading'.

56. Kobayashi Seizo, Report on the Geneva Conference on Naval Limitation, submitted to the Navy Minister and the Chief of the Naval General Staff, n.d. (1927), pp. 191–2, Enomoto papers (hereafter cited as 'Kobayashi's report'); Yamanashi ihoroku, p. 119; Aritake Shuji, Saito Makoto (Tokyo, 1958), pp. 107–9; Shishaku Saito Makoto den, Vol. 3, pp. 78–9, 90–91.

57. Kato had served as vice-minister when Saito was Navy Minister, and they were on the best of terms. In July 1921, when Kato was first asked by Prime Minister Hara to head the Japanese delegation to the Washington Conference, he suggested that Saito was better qualified. Aritake, Saito Makoto., pp. 3–4; Shishaku Saito Makoto den, Vol. 3, pp. 71–3.

58. A senior adjutant to the Navy Minister, Memo on procedural matters relating to naval limitation conferences, n.d., Enomoto papers.

59. Yamamoto Eisuke (comp.), Danshaku Osumi Mineo [Biography of Baron Osumi Mineo] (Tokyo, 1943), pp. 407, 484–6, 760; Kiba Kosuke, Nomura Kichisaburo (Tokyo, 1961), p. 856.

60. Kobayashi to Navy Vice-Minister and the Vice-Chief of the Naval General Staff, 23 June, 18 July 1927; Kobayashi's report, pp. 101, 117–18, 134–5, 138; Delegates to Foreign Minister Tanaka Giichi, 24 July 1927, JMFA.

61. Delegates to Foreign Minister, 25 June, 6 July 16, 1927, JMFA; Kobayashi's report, pp. 101–2, 115–16, 127; FRUS, 1927, I, p. 76.

62. FRUS, 1927, I, pp. 92–3; Kobayashi to Navy Vice-Minister and Vice-Chief of the Naval General Staff, 15 July 1927, Enomoto papers; David Carlton, 'Great Britain and the Coolidge Naval Disarmament Conference of 1927', Political Science Quarterly, Vol. 83, No. 4 (1968), p. 586.

63. Ito Takashi and Nomura Minoru (ed.), Kaigun Taisho, Kobayashi Seizo oboegaki [Memos of Kobayashi Seizo] (Tokyo, 1981), pp. 12, 224 (hereafter cited as Kobayashi Seizo oboegaki).

64. Navy Vice-Minister to Kobayashi, 6 July 1927; Kobayashi to Navy Vice-Minister and Vice-Chief of the Naval General Staff, 18 July 1927; Kobayashi's report, pp. 101–3, 115, 128–32, Enomoto papers.

65. Kobayashi to Navy Vice-Minister and Vice-Chief of the Naval General Staff, 18 July 1927, Enomoto papers.

66. Navy Vice-Minister to Kobayashi, 17, 20, 22, July 1927 (italics added), Enomoto papers; Foreign Minister to the delegates, 19 July 1927, JMFA.

67. Kobayashi Seizo oboegaki, p. 62; Terashima Ken den, p. 134.

68. Kobayashi's report, pp. 113–32, 134–40; Delegates to the Foreign Minister, 24 July 1927, JMFA; W.H. Medlicott, Douglas Dakin, and M.E. Lambert (eds.), Documents on British Foreign Policy, Series IA, Vol. 3 (London, 1970), pp. 686–7, 691–3; FRUS, 1927, I, pp. 113–14, 123–4, 130–31.

69. Delegates to Foreign Minister, 24 July 1927, JMFA; FRUS, 1927, I, pp. 130–34.

70. Navy Vice-Minister to Kobayashi, 28 July 1927; Foreign Minister to the Delegates, 27 July 1927, Enomoto papers.

71. *Kobayashi Seizo oboegaki*, p. 224.
72. Takarabe's statement at the Privy Council, 1 Oct. 1930, summary minutes of the main session of the Privy Council, Enomoto papers; Yamanashi to Saito, 29 Aug. 1927; Saito Diary, entry of 18 Sept. 1927, Saito papers.
73. Navy Ministry, Gunbi Seigen Kenkyu Iinkai (Investigatory committee on naval limitation), Studies on policy regarding naval limitation, prepared in August 1928, Book I, Enomoto papers; *Kaigun qunsenbi*, I, pp. 350–67.
74. Gunbi Seigen Kenkyu Iinkai, Reports, Part B, pp. 133–4, 169–71.
75. Ibid., Part A–1, p. 1.
76. Ibid., Part B, p. 10; Part C-1, pp. 49–50.
77. Ibid., Part B, p. 10; Part C-1, pp. 48–9, 53.
78. Ibid., Part A-2, pp. 15–16, 36, 38; Part B-1, pp. 41–2, 58, 68–9, 76.
79. 'Kato Kanji hiroku'.
80. Reports, Part A-1, pp. 4–5; Part A-2, p. 39; Part B-1, pp. 65–6, 99, 206–7; *Rengo kantai*, I, p. 218.
81. Operations Division, Memo on the power of 10,000-ton, eight-inch-gun cruisers. 1 Dec. 1929, IJN Archives; 'The value of 10,000-ton, 8-inch-gun cruisers and the need to secure 70 per cent', n.d., Saito papers; *Kaigun gunbi enkaku*, pp. 162, 177.
82. Kato Kanji, 'My views on arms limitation'.
83. Most notably, see Kobayashi Tatsuo (translated by Arthur E. Tiedemann), 'The London Naval Treaty, 1930' in James William Morley (ed.), *Japan Erupts: The London Naval Conference and the Manchurian Incident, 1928–1932* (Columbia University Press, 1984), pp. 11–117, and Tiedemann's succinct 'Introduction', pp. 3–10. See also Ito Takashi, *Showa shoki seijishi kenkyu: Rondon kaigun gunshuku mondai o meguru sho seiji shudan no taiko to teikei* [A study of the political history of the early Showa period: Conflicts and alignments of political groups over the issue of the London naval limitation] (Tokyo, 1969); Watanabe Yukio, *Gunshuku: Rondon joyaku to Nihon kaigun* [Naval limitation: The London Treaty and the Japanese Navy] (Tokyo, 1988).
84. Cabinet decision on policy regarding naval limitation, 28 June 1929, JMFA.
85. Kato Kanji to Makino Nobuaki, 29 Jan. 1930, Makino papers.
86. Wakatsuki was to be assisted by another civilian delegate Matsudaira Tsuneo, then ambassador to London. At the time of the Washington Conference Matsudaira had supported Kato Tomosaburo as secretary general of the Japanese delegation. Wakatsuki Reijiro, *Kofuan Kaikoroku* (Memoirs) (Tokyo, 1950), pp. 334–5; *Yamanashi ihoroku*, p. 122; Harada Kumao, *Saionjiko to seikyoku* (Prince Saionji and politics) (Tokyo, 1950), Vol. 1, p. 19.
87. Koga Mineichi's diary, entry of 27 Sept. 1929, copy contained in the Hori papers; *Kato Kanji taisho den*, p. 887.
88. *Yamanashi ihoroku*, p. 129.
89. Wakatsuki, *Kofuan kaikoroku*, pp. 365–6; Ko Matsudaira Tsuisokai (comp.), *Matsudaira Tsuneo tsuisoroku* [Reminiscences of Matsudaira Tsuneo] (Tokyo, 1961), pp. 530–32; Morley (ed.), *Japan Erupts*, pp. 28–9.
90. Hori Teikichi, Memo on the London Conference and the problem of the right of the supreme command, 11 July 1946, Hori papers; Arima Kaoru, 'Takarabe denki shiryo' (Manuscript materials for the biography of Takarabe), Books 5 and 6, IJN Archives; Aritake Shuji, *Okada Keisuke* (Tokyo, 1956), p. 59; interviews with Enomoto Juji, August 1975.
91. Naval Affairs Bureau, A report on the 1930 London Naval Conference and related papers, Vol. 10, prepared in December 1930, Enomoto papers; *Saionjiko to seikyoku*, I, pp. 1, 74; Nakamura, op. cit., pp. 9, 34.
92. 'Kato Kanji hiroku'; Kato's memo, 'My views on arms limitation'; Memo for an oral

presentation (italics added). Naval General Staff, Memo on American armaments since the Washington Conference.

93. Kato Kanji to Makino Nobuaki, 29 Jan. 1930; *Kato Kanji taisho den*, pp. 890–92 (italics added).

94. Japanese Foreign Ministry (ed.), *Nihon gaiko bunsho: 1930-nen rondon kaigun gunshuku kaigi* [Documents on Japanese Foreign Policy: London Naval Conference of 1930] (Tokyo, 1983), I, p. 160, 186–88.

95. Matsudaira to Foreign Minister Shidehara, 20 Feb. 1930 (strictly confidential dispatch with a note: 'Please destroy upon reading'). JMFA; Sakonji, The report on the 1930 London Naval Conference, pp. 1, 22, 41–2 (hereafter cited as 'Sakonji's report'), Enomoto papers. This is a most revealing day-to-day record of the Japanese naval delegation, which was drafted by its secretary Enomoto and approved by Rear-Admiral Yamamoto. Although its contents were considerably revised and toned down by the chief naval adviser, Vice-Admiral Sakonji, the report was never submitted to the higher echelon of the navy for fear of aggravating 'domestic political unrest and complications within the navy'.

Captain Nakamura, 'Seikun ni itarishi jijo . . .' (Report on the circumstances leading to the request for the final instructions from the government), April 1930 (hereafter cited as 'Nakamura's report'), Hori papers.

96. Foreign Minister Shidehara to Ambassador Matsudaira, 21 and 22 Feb. 1930; Matsudaira to Shidehara, 24 March 1939, JMFA; 'Takarabe denki shiryo', Book 7; Koga diary, entries of 6 and 15 March 1930; *TSM: Shiryohen*, pp. 10–11, 31.

97. Abo to Kato Kanji, 6 March 1930; 'Takarabe taisho denki shiryo', Books 5 and 7.

98. Ibid., Books 6 and 7; Nakamura's report, pp. 7, 10, 14, 23, March 1930; Ando Yoshio (ed.), *Showa keizaishi e no shogen* [Witness account of the economic history of the Showa period] (Tokyo, 1966), Vol. 2, p. 267.

99. Sakonji's report, pp. 46–7, 63–5, 73, 88, 93; Nakamura's report, 13 and 15 March; 2 April 1930; Wakatsuki, 'Rondon kaigun kaigi' [Memoirs of the London Naval Conference], JMFA; Wakatsuki, *Kofuan kaikoroku*, pp. 350–54; *TSM: Shiryohen*, p. 12; Kobayashi Tatsuo and Shimada Toshihiko (eds.), *Gendaishi shiryo* [Documents on contemporary history], Vol. 7 (Tokyo, 1964), p. 35; Sato Naotake, *Kaiko hachiju-nen* [Eighty years in reminiscence] (Tokyo, 1964), pp. 246–9; Okada Taisho Kiroku Hensankai (ed.), *Okada Keisuke* (1956), p. 33.

100. Wakatsuki, *Kofuan kaikoroku*, pp. 356–7.

101. Wakatsuki, *Kofuan kaikoroku*, pp. 354–6; Sakonji's report, p. 72; Nakamura's report, 13 March 1930; Hanmachi Eiichi, *Ningen Yamamoto Isoroku* [Yamamoto Isoroku as a human being] (Tokyo, 1964), pp. 301–2.

102. It is significant that Kato and his subordinates chose to call the 'Reed–Matsudaira compromise plan' an '*American* plan' to the annoyance of Stimson and other American delegates.

103. *Saionjiko to seikyoku*, Vol. 1, p. 27; 'Kato Kanji hiroku'; Naval General Staff, 'Memo for an oral presentation'; Koga Diary, 24 March 1930; *TSM: Shiryohen*, p. 17.

104. Sakonji's report, p. 76; Nakamura's report, 13–16 March 1930; Rear-Admiral Yamamoto's memo, 'Personal views on conference strategy', 10 March 1930; Yamamoto to Hori, 17 March 1930, Hori papers; *TSM: Shiryohen*, p. 15; Ando, op. cit., Vol. 2, p. 264; Nomura Minoru, *Tenno, Fushiminomiya to Nihon kaigun* [The Emperor, Prince Fushimi, and the Japanese Navy] (Tokyo, 1988), pp. 142–54.

105. Okada Taisho kitoku henshukai, *Okada Keisuke* (Tokyo, 1950), passim; Okada Sadanori (ed.), *Okada Keisuke kaikoroku* [Memoirs of Okada Keisuke] (Tokyo, 1977), *passim*.

106. Morley (ed.), *Japan Erupts*, p. 35.

107. Ikei Masaru, Hatano Masaru and Kurosawa Fumitaka (eds.), *Hamaguchi Osachi nikki, zuikanroku* [Diary and memos of Hamaguchi Osachi] (Tokyo, 1991), p. 318.
108. Ikeda Kiyoshi, op. cit., Vol. 2, p. 99.
109. See, most notably, Morley (ed.), *Japan Erupts*, pp. 27–117. Ito Takashi, op. cit.; Ikeda Kiyoshi, 'Rondon gunshuku joyaku to tosuiken mondai' [The London Naval Treaty and the problem of the right of the supreme command], *Hogaku zasshi*, Vol. 15, No. 2 (1968), 1–35.
110. Sakonji's report, pp. 101–5, 111; *TSM: Shiryohen*, pp. 22, 37; Kobayashi and Shimada (eds.), *Gendaishi shiryo*, Vol. 7 (1964), p. 4.
111. Yamamoto's oral presentation, 2 April 1930; Yamamoto's memo on the problem of submarine strength (summary of oral presentation to the Navy Minister), 9 April 1930, Hori papers; Nakamura's report, 2 April 1930; Nakamura Takafusa et al. (eds.), *Gendai o tsukuru hitobito* [Men who shaped contemporary Japan] (Tokyo, 1971), Vol. 3, p. 51.
112. The Emperor's statement, 22 July 1930, Hori papers; *Saionjiko to seikyoku*, I, p. 40.
113. Stephen E. Pelz, *Race to Pearl Harbor: The Failure of the Second London Naval Conference and the Onset of World War II* (Cambridge, Mass, 1974). For Japan's naval policy and strategy from 1930 to 1941, see Asada, 'Japanese Navy and the United States', in Dorothy Borg and Shumpei Okamoto (eds.), *Pearl Harbor as History: Japanese American Relations, 1931–1941* (New York, 1973), pp. 225–59, 650–63.
114. *Saionjiko to seikyoku*, Vol. 3, p. 147.
115. Harold and Margaret Sprout, *Toward a New Order of Sea Power: American Naval Policy and the World Scene, 1918–1922* (Princeton, 1943).

The substance of the first half of this paper appeared as 'The Revolt against the Washington Treaty: The Imperial Japanese Navy and Naval Limitation, 1921–27', *Naval War College Review*, Vol. XLVI, No. 3 (Summer 1993).

France and the Washington Conference

JOEL BLATT

The Washington Conference came upon France at a moment of difficult naval adaptation to the world after the Great War, and ultimately to the twentieth century. The French Government scrambled to fit the demands placed on it at Washington into an evolving postwar French naval programme. French decisions at Washington also reflected various domestic political pressures. Although atavistic yearnings for a vanished past surfaced, by and large French policymakers maintained a realistic focus. Often perceived and portrayed in France at the time as a French defeat, only *amour propre* and not French interests suffered at Washington. French decisions there subsequently blended harmoniously into interwar French naval policy. An assessment of the French role at Washington may diminish, but does not completely destroy, the accomplishments of the conference.

As the First World War ended, the French gazed back longingly at the recent past for their naval basing point, while other major naval powers emphasized more the present. In the Washington context, each participant pursued its own advantage. For example, following the conclusion of the Washington Conference, the signatories attempted to persuade non-participants to limit their navies. According to Salvador de Madariaga, one Spanish admiral agreed to such entreaties, dependent upon the year fixed as a measure. His British counterpart offered '1921': the Spaniard replied '1588'.[1] Loyal to the same principle, the French Navy regarded the large naval programme of 1912 with nostalgia: before the Great War the French had ranked fourth behind Great Britain, Germany, and the United States, and had been followed by Japan and Italy. During the First World War they sacrificed the growth of their Navy to produce armaments, while the British, Americans and Japanese launched major naval construction campaigns. After the war, the French still ranked fourth, behind Great Britain, the United States and Japan, but their Navy was declining, Japan had passed them by, and Italy was closing the gap.[2] As the French turned to postwar planning, the Navy called its most extensive proposal the 'Normal Programme', perhaps a semantic linkage to their prewar halcyon days,[3] and they hoped that 1912–14 rather than 1921 would serve as a basis for discussions at Washington.[4] In this light, long before the conference, perceptions of national interests and colonial ambitions drove the French towards planning significant postwar naval construction.

Three factors guided postwar French naval strategy and dictated a Mediterranean focus. First, if French paranoia about the onset of another European war became reality then the Navy needed to be capable of carrying large numbers of colonial troops to the metropole.[5]

Second, the Mediterranean served as the imperial road to the whole far-flung French Empire, still the second largest in the world. A colonial lobby, partly hidden from view but with visible leaders, exerted enduring pressure for naval construction.[6] Georges Leygues became perhaps the most prominent spokesman for colonial interests, particularly in the eastern Mediterranean and Syria. As an influential deputy, briefly premier in 1920, and long-term Navy Minister, he shaped the interwar Navy as much as any other individual.[7] Wishing to become the Colbert of the Third Republic, in a speech of June 1920 Leygues repeated the words of Louis XIV's Minister: 'Without the navy one can neither sustain war nor profit from peace'.[8] As premier, he implored his parliamentary colleagues to secure for France 'political, economic, naval bases' in the eastern Mediterranean.[9] He called the Mediterranean 'the axis of its [French] policy'. Asia Minor, and particularly Syria, was 'the most important crossroads of world routes'.[10] Aristide Briand, Leygues' successor as President of the Council, the mediator of French policy during the Washington

Conference, also asserted the significance of the Mediterranean. Briand added another reason for holding Syria when he told the Finance Committee of the Chamber of Deputies that the 'one thing that counted' in foreign affairs was 'the "do ut des", when one has money for barter . . . the concrete and solid to offer'.[11] Briand may have been reflecting the impact of the colonial lobby, which promoted the interwar naval building programme.

Third, and closely related, the leaders of France, similarly to those of other industrialized countries, were becoming aware of the all but ultimate importance of oil for modern economies. Henry Bérenger, Georges Clemenceau's Commissioner for Gasoline and Oil and a highly influential French political figure, reported to the premier in December 1919: 'For the French, as for the English, oil has become the very condition for existence as a great nation. Not to possess it in one's own right is to lose more than territories, it is to lose industrial, commercial, maritime, and military independence'. Since 'only Asia Minor' could provide that resource for France, Bérenger urged focusing French policy in 'the Mediterranean Levant and the Black and Caspian Seas' on the priority of oil.[12] In 1921, the Foreign Affairs Committee of the Chamber of Deputies, presided over by Leygues, alerted Briand to be vigilant concerning oil issues at Washington.[13] Two years later a Minister of the Navy told the Conseil Supérieur de la Défense Nationale (CSDN – a rough equivalent in France at that time of today's National Security Council in the United States), 'The provisioning of oil . . . has as necessary condition the freedom of communications'.[14]

Rationales that combined appeals to national security, colonial empire, industrial survival, and prosperity, might potentially attract considerable political support in parliament, among the populace, and from industrial (including shipbuilding), financial, and commercial interests. In this context, in 1919 and 1920 the Navy developed its first postwar naval plans and programme.

A year after France concluded the First World War, with Italy as an ally, Admiral Ronarc'H, the chief of the French Navy General Staff in 1919, posited a 'most probable' future conflict against Italy or Germany, or both allied. The Navy's far from self-evident conclusions in 1919 were significant because they embodied strands of French thinking that recurred in subsequent years and influenced preparation for the Washington Conference. With the German Navy sharply reduced by the Versailles Treaty to 108,000 tons of active ships and 36,000 tons of reserve,[15] it was not easy to project a plausible short-term enemy in 1919. Ronarc'H assumed that Italy (even pre-Mussolini Italy) held a 'non acknowledged but certain ambition to dominate in the Mediterranean', while French 'interests' in that sea precluded acceptance of these 'pretensions'. Germany would 'undoubtedly' strive to recover, with the 'ineluctable consequence' of an Italo-German accord. Such a threat 'would be precarious' for France, requiring a substantial French Navy or diplomacy that avoided an Italo-German opponent. Ronarc'H drew the conclusion that the future French Navy should be equal to or stronger than the Italian, and, if possible, equal to the combined German and Italian navies. Observing warily possible future wars with Great Britain, or between Great Britain and the United States, the report propounded a French Navy of sufficient weight to affect the naval balance between larger fleets.[16]

Additional planning followed in 1920 that began to be converted into potential naval laws for parliament's approval. In March 1920, Ronarc'H's successor as Navy Chief of Staff, Vice-Admiral H. Salaun, viewed France's 'most pressing' need as the western Mediterranean. Of significance for Washington, Salaun acknowledged a French superiority over Italy in battleships, the largest ships, but claimed a 'grave inferiority' in lighter vessels. He advocated recovering 'mastery' in the western Mediterranean that had been lost to Italy 'silently' during the First World War.[17]

By September 1920, naval planning had coalesced into an important report, enunciating the first comprehensive postwar naval programme and laying bare many of the premises that served as foundation under the interwar French Navy. The primary mission would be defending France, North Africa, and the waters between Africa and the metropole, across which the 'immense reservoirs' of potential soldiers for the French Army might be moved. The Navy assumed a Germany bent on *revanche*, a hostile Soviet Union that might ally with Germany, a Great Britain retreating back into 'splendid isolation', and an Italy 'more ambitious than ever', with a 'dream of supplanting us [France] definitively as the major Mediterranean power'. The Navy would control Italian ambitions by establishing clear French naval superiority in the Mediterranean. To do so, the report suggested two programmes. First, a 'Normal Programme' would establish dominance over Italy and Germany in the Mediterranean and North Sea respectively, but was too expensive. The Navy proposed a 'Minimum Programme' against Germany or Italy, really focused on Italy given the postwar naval restrictions on Germany, which would be flexible depending on naval construction abroad. Since France already held a 25 per cent advantage over Italy in battleships, and both countries had limited finances, Salaun concluded that there was 'no urgent necessity' to build the largest ships. On the contrary, France's alleged 'inferiority' in cruisers required vigorous attention. More than a year before the Washington Conference, therefore, the French Navy played down and put aside construction of capital ships. Next, parliamentary committees reshaped naval laws in accord with political pressures and financial necessity.[18]

When navy ministers went courting support for naval laws in parliamentary committees, they received generally favourable but mixed receptions. The Navy Committee of the Chamber of Deputies offered encouragement. Gabriel Guist'hau, Navy Minister in 1921 and a friend of Briand's, told it that finances as well as common sense made it 'madness' to pursue Great Britain, the United States, and Japan down the path of 'formidable construction'. Concentrate on 'mastery' of the Mediterranean and 'superiority over Italy' in order to secure the transport of colonial troops and supplies, he advised.[19] Ernest Flandin, a Navy Committee member, worried that in wartime Italian ships might dart out from behind island concealment and 'interdict' oil-carrying vessels.[20] Strong, but not unanimous, support also emerged in the committee for construction of a 'flotte d'appoint' (fleet of balance or fleet of difference), sufficient to be taken into account by the largest naval powers.[21] An idiosyncratic factor influenced another aspect of the naval story. Count Gustave de Kerguézec, a persuasive member of the Navy and Finance Committees, implemented his *idée fixe* that submarines provided the key to French 'independence', while the battleship was 'absolutely out of date'.[22] De Kerguézec worked assiduously to slip considerable numbers of additional submarines into naval proposals, which aggravated the British; Admiral Grasset, Chief of the Navy General Staff in

1921, said that he would accept the extra submarines if Parliament wished the Navy to fight a coalition of Germany and Italy.[23]

Scepticism about a naval arms race emerged too, particularly in the Finance Committee of the Chamber of Deputies. Laurent Bonnevay, Deputy of the Rhône, suggested that 'a certain disarmament' might be appropriate after a war. 'What power do you fear?' he asked.[24] Marie Calary de Lamazière, Deputy of the Seine, wanted to know what made the Italian Navy 'so imposing', and added, 'Have you envisioned a limitation of armaments?'[25] Noting Italy's financial weakness, deputies urged negotiations.[26] However, in November 1920, Navy Minister Landry replied, 'A conversation with Italy would be completely inopportune at this time – she will ask us for the status quo. She is superior.'[27] Actually, a small number of influential voices, including Georges Leygues' and a high-ranking naval officer's, advised against regarding Italy solely as a potential enemy.[28] Pressure from the Finance Committee of the Chamber of Deputies, as well as financial constraints, provided other parts of Briand's luggage for the Washington Conference. I would speculate further that finance ministries and finance committees of legislatures, acting for practical reasons, have contributed substantially to arms limitation in the twentieth century where it has occurred.

Despite disputes over the naval laws, a consensus existed before Washington. Indeed, much of the disagreement remained behind closed committee doors because, as de Keguézec said, they must never discuss in the Chamber of Deputies who was the target of their programme.[29] More importantly, the Navy and the politicians concurred in relegating battleships to a lower priority than the lighter vessels deemed essential for domination of the Mediterranean. Geography, chronic conflicts of interests, a need for some tangible 'enemy', and a resurgence of Italian nationalism led a number of French policy makers to distrust France's southern neighbour.[30] How, then, can the accord at Washington that seemed to enshrine Franco-Italian naval equality be explained?

Among the myths that grew up around French participation at Washington was that their delegation arrived unprepared. In fact, Vice-Admiral Ferdinand de Bon, the chief French naval expert at the conference, brought along a mixed bag of instructions, reflecting temptations towards lost grandeur, atavistic anglophobia, and realistic analysis. One set of contingency plans suggested a future French tilt towards the United States in the event of an Anglo-American war, because the United States would agree more easily to continuing restraints on Germany. Implementation of this pro-American policy, since France lacked the financial means to build capital ships, required sufficient lighter vessels and submarines to tip the balance against Great Britain. Moreover, in such circumstances the English would ally with Italy; therefore France needed to be stronger than Italy in the Mediterranean. In order to preserve its colonies France should remain neutral if war broke out between the United States and Japan. On the other hand, a conflict involving the United States against Japan and Great Britain would cost France its colonies.[31]

More useful, and of great significance in deciphering French responses at Washington, was a 'Note on the Limitation of Armaments' developed by the Naval General Staff, approved by the Navy Ministry, and forwarded to Briand.[32] Before Washington, Navy Minister Guist'hau sketched the Navy's point of view, in conversation with the President of the Council.[33] The Navy resented making current naval levels the yardstick for arms limitation, since France would be locked into a position of 'inferiority'. 'Does France want to be a great nation' (the Navy asked) and have a Navy that could defend its policy? France might face German–Italian or German–Russian coalitions. The stronger the French Navy, the greater France's weight would be in 'world councils'. The note expressed latent anglophobia, a wish to compete with the British Empire. An earlier draft even anticipated potential American aid for French naval development as a balance against Anglo-Japanese cooperation. Adopting a 'politique du pauvre' (policy of the poor), the French Navy advocated one maximum global tonnage for all, sufficiently low that countries of sufficient means might reach it through 'sacrifice'. The French fall-back position would accept a slightly higher tonnage for Great Britain and the United States, with Japan, France, and Italy together on the next rung, at least two-thirds of the higher figure. Since the Japanese Navy had been smaller than France's fleet before the First World War, France would demand equality with it at Washington. France would accept Italy at the same level, in theory, as long as the tonnage was pegged sufficiently high that France's greater financial strength would guarantee *de facto* superiority.[34]

Regarding the Italian position, de Bon's instructions predicted, 'For Italy, seeking Mediterranean naval supremacy, the only interesting navy in its eyes is the French, which it proposes to equal, then to surpass. Italian naval construction depends on ours'.[35] Temporarily failing to accept diminished French financial resources, mistakenly projecting Anglo-American conflict, de Bon's guidance anticipated the Italian policy of parity with France. Although de Bon's guidelines strayed beyond the more practical focus of postwar naval planning, they were still potentially reconcilable with main postwar themes.

Aristide Briand, President of the Council of Ministers and Foreign Minister, personally led an impressive array of officials and military experts to the naval festival on the Potomac.[36] Briand had become a legend: the man who read little but understood everything, not a details person, not one to cross the t's or dot the i's (Philippe Berthelot often provided those services). As one observer wrote,

> Born improviser, Briand at the tribune had invisible antennae. This is the only orator whom I have ever seen capable of ending an oratorical phrase – in the face of certain murmurs – otherwise than he had begun, like a cat turning in flight to fall on its paws.[37]

In appearance before parliamentary committees, he provided pluralistic explications of his actions depending on the audiences. He was a master of politics. He made no gratuitous enemies. Nonetheless, he was more than just an opportunist: persistent, realistic and practical, concerned with French interests, at times idealistic too.[38] Briand's acute political instincts served him well as he scrambled to keep up with Washington's fluid events and adapt developments there to French domestic politics.

Why did Briand choose to attend the conference's opening sessions personally in spite of criticisms at home?[39] In the two years since the Paris Peace Conference, the second half of the central compromise in achieving the Versailles Treaty, Germany's retention of the Rhineland in return for an Anglo-American promise to guarantee French security, had disappeared. Left alone in the sea of their paranoia towards Germany, one of the major weaknesses in the structure of interwar international relations, the French sought repeatedly throughout the 1920s to recover the broken Anglo-American promises of 1919.

Briand may have hoped to probe delicately for the lost security guarantees, either through establishing a special relationship with the United States or through a mediation between the Americans and the British.[40] Other reasons for Briand's personal participation were his appreciation of the increasing weight of the United States on the world scene and his desire to protect and elucidate France's position on land armaments. The French assumption of an Anglo-American rivalry at Washington collapsed immediately. After, probably circumspectly, gauging the temper of American leaders,[41] Briand's acute psycho-political antennae told him at once that the path towards the United States was at least temporarily closed. With his usual oratorical virtuosity, on 21 November he defended France's need for a large army against Germany and a possible German–Soviet combination, unless the First World War Allies provided security guarantees.[42] Soon thereafter, while the conference was still in its early stages, he left Washington with a third of the French delegation.

On 12 November, Briand had listened to Secretary of State Charles Evans Hughes' stunning proposal for a 5-5-3 naval ratio between the United States, Great Britain, and Japan, and the scrapping of hundreds of thousands of tons of older ships, as well as new ones still rising in the dockyards.[43] Amid the panoply of the conference's opening, however, and during subsequent weeks, French prestige suffered a series of assaults. At the inaugural session, the British and Americans sat at the principal table, while the French delegation was placed amidst those of the British Dominions. Although this was quickly rectified, the French viewed the slight as symbolic of their mistreatment at the conference.[44] More substantively, in his opening speech Hughes excluded France and Italy from the first and decisive round of negotiations between the 'Big Three', citing their experiences in the First World War, apparently referring to their lack of recent large-scale naval construction.[45] In a third incident, on 23 November, after a vigorous but appropriate exchange of views on land armaments between Briand and Carlo Schanzer, the head Italian delegate, newspapers distorted the French premier's words, causing riots in Italy.[46]

For a month, while they 'cooled their heels' impatiently, awaiting the decisions of others, the French clarified their thoughts about naval arms limitation. They protested at their exclusion, and Hughes responded, 'Fear nothing and wait, France will be satisfied'.[47] De Bon told Briand that Hughes' plan would reduce the distance between France and the larger navies.[48] He also informed Paris of Italy's desire for parity with France at the lowest possible level.[49] Naval authorities in Paris instructed de Bon, and advised Briand, to demand at least equality with Japan in global tonnage, equality with the strongest nation in submarines, and to oppose parity with Italy.[50] De Bon also forewarned the Navy Ministry in Paris that their 350,000 ton figure for capital ships was in trouble: even Briand thought it 'excessive'.[51]

Finally, on 15 December 1921, the waiting ended as Hughes communicated to the French and Italians the famous battleship ratios and tonnages: 5, 5, 3, 1.75, 1.75 (525,000 tons, 525,000, 315,000, 175,000, 175,000). American experts had worked out the figures while taking the British point of view into account. At first, the Americans had granted France the same figure as Japan, but the British had wanted equality with the combined Japanese plus French fleets.[52] The American Secretary of State attempted to conciliate the French by including France, against British opposition, in the Four-Power Treaty for the Pacific that replaced the Anglo-Japanese accord.[53]

The French delegation immediately regarded their assigned tonnage and parity with Italy in capital ships with 'stupefaction', and reaffirmed their right to replace ten battleships over 20 years, 350,000 tons.[54] De Bon suspected that the 175,000-ton proposal represented a British and American goal of 'absolute supremacy' over the world lines of communication.[55] Earlier in November, the French naval expert had witnessed Hughes' displeasure when confronted with France's maximum demands. According to de Bon later, the French thought that Hughes had accepted a 280,000-ton figure, which the French had reached in conversations among themselves. The American Secretary of State may have mentioned 175,000 tons to Ambassador Jusserand.[56]

Since de Bon had sensed earlier the impracticality of the 350,000-ton figure and Briand's own scepticism regarding it, why did he reiterate a demand that threatened the Anglo-American–Japanese accord? Throughout the conference, the French delegation implored the conference to take into account France's 1914 position, wartime sacrifices, and 'needs' as the second largest empire.[57] In response to a parliamentary inquiry, the Navy Ministry answered that de Bon had simply followed orders to demand equality with Japan.[58] Albert Sarraut, head of the French delegation after 14 December, and Briand, later told the Chamber of Deputies that the French delegation had feared the extension of the ratios for capital ships to lighter vessels and submarines.[59]

Parity with Italy then became a decisive issue, as Italy immediately supported Hughes' ratios because they contained parity with France at a reduced tonnage.[60] Going farther, the Italians also asserted that Briand had agreed to the principle of Franco-Italian parity.[61] The French premier admitted that in a conversation with Schanzer he had concurred in parity on battleships, but not on lighter vessels; de Bon had gone along because the decision lacked 'importance'. At the end of 1922 Briand described his contacts with the Italians this way:

> The Italian Delegation let me know that, when the maximum figure for capital ships would be discussed, it intended to request a figure equal to that of France; this was for it a political necessity. It asked me: 'Will you oppose?' I consulted Admiral de Bon who answered: 'No inconvenience as long as the whole question of the second line fleet will be reserved.' I then informed the representative of the Italian Delegation that, if he touched that proposition lightly, I would not raise any objection. That was all. There was no other engagement.[62]

On 17 December 1921, Sarraut accepted 'the principle of parity', but not *de facto* equality. Italy could construct its Navy up to the French limit.[63] Sarraut clearly assumed that the French level for the ships that mattered most to them would be beyond Italy's financial capabilities, while Schanzer believed that he had gained the principle of parity with France on all categories of vessels.[64] On the same 17 December, Briand and his close colleague Philippe Berthelot stiffened the tone, if not the substance, of their message to their representatives in Washington, emphasizing that the French and Italian situations were 'not at all comparable' and that 'equality' would grant Italy 'real superiority in the Mediterranean'. Paris 'could' concede on 'offensive . . . and most costly' battleships if the conference recognized French demands for 330,000 tons of lighter vessels and 90,000 tons of submarines.[65] Parity provided the backdrop for the French response to the major crisis of the conference.

In a firm letter of 16 December, Hughes virtually compelled French compliance with the accord, warning that the higher end of the ratios depended on French and Italian acceptance of the 1.75 figure; therefore the burden for the success or failure of the conference fell temporarily on French shoulders. Hughes argued that France had gained from the reduction of larger navies. Italy had come on board showing the proper economic priorities, and France should reconstruct its country rather than build battleships. Not too subtly, the Secretary of State thereby threatened economic and financial reprisals from France's major creditor.[66] With alacrity, on 18 December Briand responded affirmatively, as long as the conference acceded to French demands on lighter ships. The premier warned that Parliament would turn his Government out if he accepted the extension of ratios to lighter vessels.[67] Later, de Bon condemned the personal exchange over the heads of the French delegation.[68]

The French position hardened as the conference moved to extend limits to other categories of ships. To some extent this reflected mounting domestic pressures. Alexandre Millerand, the President of the Republic, the Navy Committee of the Chamber of Deputies, the French Maritime and Colonial League, a pressure group, and De Kerguézec, who posed an interpellation in Parliament, all became restive.[69] Briand, in London from 18 to 22 December for conversations with the British Prime Minister, David Lloyd George, that opened the route to Cannes, Genoa and Locarno, was kept informed of Parisian sentiments by his friend Guist'hau, who thought additional concessions 'impossible'.[70] Paris forwarded at least some of the same information to Washington for Sarraut, who was also the Minister of Colonies.[71] Paris ordered Sarraut to adhere to the 330,000/90,000 tonnages.[72] Briand stated that Parliament would 'never' approve the sacrifice of 'defensive ships'.[73] With reference to Italy, the premier said, 'Concerning Italy on light ships and submarines, we present no obstacle to its obtaining the same figure as ours, but we do not accept that its figure serves as a base upon which to fix ours'.[74]

As the conference began to debate submarines on 22 December 1921, Hughes and the French delegation clashed again. On submarines, the British favoured abolition, the Italians parity with France, and the Americans ratios.[75] The Secretary of State heatedly wanted to know against whom the French targeted their submarines, while Sarraut replied bluntly in kind, demanding against whom the Americans and British planned to use their 525,000 tons of battle-ships.[76] Irritated by the Italians on a number of issues, the French opposed their entry into the Four-Power Pact in the Pacific.[77] French officials in Paris considered reducing their figure on lighter ships to 320,000 tons, but Briand vetoed the suggestion as too little or too much.[78] De Bon reported that French intransigence on submarines (a position he favoured) might create a 'rupture'.[79] The French delegation received directions to hold firm, awaiting decisions in Paris.

A decisive meeting of the Conseil Supérieur de la Défense Nationale on 26 December 1921 pulled together the diverse threads of French policy at Washington. First, Vice-Admiral Grasset, head of the Navy General Staff, regretted the reduced tonnage of capital ships, but emphasized lighter vessels against Germany or Italy. In its 'Note of presentation to the CSDN', the Navy General Staff asserted that in the event of a war with Italy it was 'absolutely indispensable' to secure French 'communications with North Africa'. Greater numbers of light ships and submarines than Italy possessed were essential to fulfilling the task. The tonnage had to be sufficiently high that, with 'the actual troubled status of its finances', Italy could not achieve it. The 330,000/90,000 figures would 'probably' be adequate. Briand advocated 'willing' compliance with the Washington tonnages of capital ships, since they prevented the gap between France and the larger naval powers from increasing and 'avoid armaments whose cost (poids) the parliament would never have accepted'. Basically, the premier defended France's position on lighter ships, but he revealed qualms at this moment and others. He worried that 'the rupture of the Conference of Washington will put us up against the English and American war debts'. Paul Doumer, Minister of Finance, a former Governor-General of Indochina, assassinated in 1932 as President of the Republic, emphasized fiscal realities. France could not afford to construct both ships of the line and large numbers of auxiliary vessels, nor could it have a huge army and a huge navy. Did the Navy really intend to build 330,000 tons of lighter ships and 90,000 tons of submarines? Doumer asked, and Briand reinforced the question.

Guist'hau, the Navy Minister, called the tonnages 'indispensable' and the costs 'inevitable'. Vice-Admiral Grasset now stated more un-equivocally his preference in new construction for lighter ships over battleships. Just because Washington granted France the right to 175,000 tons of capital ships, France did not have to build them, he remarked. Guist'hau added that he would not 'spend one centime to construct the 175,000 tons of capital ships accorded to France'. Briand 'regretted' not having been aware of these views earlier, for they would have facilitated trade-offs between capital ships and lighter vessels and submarines at Washington.[80]

The Council of Ministers ratified the conclusions of the CSDN. On 27 December 1921 Paris forwarded the following instructions to the French delegation in Washington:

> The figures of 330,000 tons for light ships and 90,000 tons for submarines remain definitively fixed and you have mandate not to cede on these figures. . . . If the government did not maintain that position, it is certain that the Parliament would not ratify the accord.[81]

After they had established their obduracy on lighter ships and submarines, the French serve kicked high and wide into the British court. A persistent British propaganda campaign pilloried the French throughout the conference.[82] As their hope for substantial reductions in submarines foundered, rather than accept the 330,000/90,000 French figures, the British shifted and refused to accept any limits on lighter vessels (particularly cruisers).[83] The decision freed France to build the interwar Navy that the Naval General Staff and civilian politicians had placed on the drawing board and that the country's finances permitted.

For the French, the remainder of the conference was anticlimactic. At moments, American and British anger towards French policies broke through; for example, Hughes grumbled that perhaps the United States might watch from the sidelines as France grappled with its 'economic situation'.[84] As the conference reached additional accords on ratios for aircraft carriers, on the size of cruisers, and in other areas, the French avoided giving addititional offence.[85] France also approved a proposal by Elihu Root condemning assaults by submarines on merchant vessels, which became an annex to the Treaty, but was never presented to the French Parliament.[86]

Briand made practical choices during the Washington Conference that could potentially find significant support in parliament and among domestic pressure groups. The French achieved their minimum demands at Washington, and the conference did not inhibit their naval development. Later, Briand proudly proclaimed Washington as an example of France's capacity to participate in an international conference and mollify potential allies, to offer concessions on a secondary issue while securing primary concerns, and to reach an accord that reduced armaments and costs while permitting France to construct a 'modern Navy'.[87] Finance Committees of the Chamber of Deputies and Senate, and the Finance Ministry, could accept Washington because it avoided blockbuster expenditures. The broad centre of the political spectrum, from the centre right to the centre left, could support Washington because it did not hinder what came to appear to be a practical naval policy. Even the parliamentary navy committees and colonial interests could go along with Washington, because it allowed construction of the ships they wanted for the Mediterranean.

In the short run, though, segments of the French right reacted negatively, toppled Briand's Government, and contributed to enduring misperceptions of the Washington Conference as a disaster for France. Charles Maurras, leader of the Action Française, symbolized the outrage of French nationalists when, later, he tersely wrote, 'The King of France would have had Briand shot on his return from Washington', and called the Conference 'Trafalgar II'.[88] Some of the French right resisted recognition of France's dire financial straits. Even moderate French conservatives resented French exclusion from decision-making, regarded parity with Italy as an indignity, and feared that parity might be extended to other categories of ships. Some exploited Washington for political gain. Raymond Poincaré, former President of the Council and President of the Republic, wrote of Briand's return from Washington, 'He opened his valise and loyally showed that it was empty'.[89] Poincaré then rode discontent with Washington and other factors back to power as premier in January 1922.

A more astute, skilful, and calculating politician than his commonly held image suggested, Raymond Poincaré dawdled, but still guided the Washington treaty through parliament. He knew that the accord posed no obstacles to French naval development. Beneath some public criticism, in private the French Navy could live with the Treaty, as long as the '0.33 coefficient' did not become permanent, and France defined parity with Italy narrowly.[90] The Navy also regarded as an 'error' the widely held opinion that France had 'consented to grave sacrifices' at Washington.[91] In the face of pressure from the right, some of which corresponded to his own views, Poincaré attached reservations to the Treaty:

> The French Government estimates, and has always estimated, that relations of global tonnages of ships of the line and aircraft carriers attributed to each of the contracting powers do not express the respective importance of the maritime interests of these powers, and cannot be extended to categories of ships other than those for which they have been expressly stipulated.[92]

During the parliamentary debate, the left as well as the right criticized the Treaty; for example, the Socialist Deputy, Alexandre Bracke (Alexandre Desrousseaux) stated:

> The pretended disarmament of the accords of Washington is not a disarmament of peace, but a disarmament of war. All the powers that participated have argued with the idea of being able, if the occasion arises, of making war in the best conditions and cheaper. In that which concerns us, we have arranged to keep our liberty of construction of light ships and submarines and that example suffices to establish that they have not seriously wanted a plan of disarmament.[93]

Still, in July 1923, large majorities in the Chamber of Deputies and Senate approved the Washington treaty, with reservations.[94] Conservatives were mollified by an extensive naval programme that was beginning to be put into effect.

Taking the Washington Conference into account, in 1922 the French Navy General Staff revised the 'Minimum Programme' of 1920 and developed a Naval Statute that guided construction of the interwar Navy and looked ahead as far as 20 years. Given France's

finances, which precluded building capital ships in the short run at
least, the Navy General Staff assessed that Washington posed little
hindrance. Only the principle of parity with Italy worried the Navy,
which recommended not renewing the treaty in 1935 unless France
could excise parity from it. Germany was 'the most probable
adversary', and Italy, given its geography athwart French sea-lanes to
North Africa, 'the most dangerous adversary'. The Navy General
Staff's report on the programme proposed a 25 per cent margin of
superiority over each, which, given the Versailles Treaty's restrictions
on Germany, was more difficult to achieve over Italy. Since France
already led Italy in capital ships, the Navy would postpone decisions
on those vessels unless faced with an initiative by a continental
power. They gave priority to the light fleet.[95]

A number of considerations determined that the Naval Statute
would never be discussed as a whole by Parliament and would be
implemented in slices over a long period. The Navy favoured such a
process because it could take into account changes in naval construction abroad.[96] French governments and politicians wished to avoid
the disruption of sensitive reparations and war debt negotiations that
would probably occur if the full extent of France's naval programme
became public knowledge. Legislators also guarded their prerogative
of annual approval of budgets. France's troubled finances favoured a
step by step approach. Finally, French leaders feared the harm to
foreign relations that might follow a frank public discussion of
potential enemies in future wars.[97]

The rise to power of the bellicose Fascist regime in Italy in October
1922 gave added impetus to the naval programme. The French left
was hostile to Italian Fascism on ideological grounds, which for many
probably facilitated support of naval construction. Even most of the
French right, regardless of its considerable sympathy for Italian
Fascism's domestic ideology and practices, was not prepared to sacrifice French interests and French colonies to bolster impassioned pleas
for closer French relations with Fascist Italy.[98] In some ways, as early
as 1919, 1920, and 1922, perhaps by 1924, certainly by 1929, French
naval officials assumed a potential German–Italian enemy.[99]

From 1922 to 1934, the French Navy and governments of different
persuasions proposed naval laws, French parliaments approved them,
and French arsenals constructed the interwar fleet:[100]

1924 – 31,000 tons	1928 – 2,258 tons	1932 – 37,500 tons
1925 – 48,000	1929 – 35,800	1933 – 0
1926 – 42,000	1930 – 42,600	1934 – 31,800
1927 – 33,000	1931 – 46,600	

Amidst the massive rearmament of the second half of the 1930s, naval expenditures increased.[101] In an excellent unpublished article on interwar French naval policy, Philippe Masson, the prominent French naval historian, working inside the Navy, characterized the Washington Conference as resulting in, beyond damaged 'pride', few 'servitudes'. He lauded, and from the Navy's perspective rehabilitated, interwar French governments and parliaments, which, in coordination with the Navy General Staff, had constructed a major 'light fleet' in a very difficult financial 'climate'. Masson suggested that navies might best be made in periods of 'detente' after wars.[102]

When the Second World War came in 1939, the French Navy remained competitive with the German and Italian fleets, although the latter contained greater combined tonnage.[103] Chalmers Hood III writes, 'By any measure of comparison, Admiral Darlan's fleet of 1939 was far better prepared for war than either the army or the air force'.[104] Ironically and tragically, perhaps the French interwar construction programmes succeeded too well. During the dreadful summer of 1940, after the French defeat, and as the survival of the United Kingdom hung on a thread, in trepidation about the consequences if the French fleet should fall into German hands, in July 1940 Winston Churchill and the British attacked a part of it at Mers-el-Kébir, with heavy loss of French sailors' lives. When the Germans occupied all of France in November 1942, the French themselves scuttled approximately half of the remainder at Toulon.[105] Thus, tragedy and destruction ended the two-decade saga of France and the Washington Conference.

In conclusion, let me add some observations about the French role at the Washington Conference in the contexts of interwar France, twentieth-century France, and twentieth-century arms limitation. The 1919 report of Admiral Ronarc'H, the 1920 'Normal' and 'Minimum' Programmes, the 1922 Naval Statute, and the interwar naval building programme all focused on the Mediterranean and light ships (cruisers, destroyers, submarines, others, but not capital ships).

France's weakened finances, the widely accepted priority of ferrying colonial troops to distant European battlefields, and the supporters of France's colonial empire all contributed to the consistent implementation of French policy. During the Washington Conference, Briand discovered with difficulty this wide French naval consensus. The political viability of Briand's Washington policy was proven when Poincaré shepherded the Treaty, with reservations, through the shoals of Parliament, and when the makers of the interwar Navy comfortably reconciled Washington and the Naval Statute. In reality, the Washington Treaty made it easier for France to concentrate on its primary naval objectives. The French lost prestige, little else, at Washington. National prestige matters, though, particularly in domestic politics, and Briand's Government fell because of Washington and other reasons.

Given the French lead in battleships over Italy, French acquiescence at Washington in equality with Italy in capital ships that the French Navy did not intend to build soon was what I have called elsewhere 'a parity that wasn't' or 'The Parity that Meant Superiority'.[106] Indeed, the French designed their interwar policy and their participation at Washington to achieve superiority over Italy. French policy at Washington embodied the opposite of parity. The word 'parity' was not used in the Washington treaty.[107] Briand's and the French handling of the parity issue at Washington created a long-time parity morass. On the one hand, planning prior to Washington and policy there grudgingly granted Italy equality, and on 17 December Sarraut accepted the principle of parity. On the other hand, and consistently without exception, the French affirmed naval levels high enough that Italy could not meet them. The French accepted the idea of Franco-Italian parity at Washington only because they emphatically rejected its *de facto* realization. The Franco-Italian parity issue became one of the long-playing conundrums of the interwar years.[108]

Naval policy reflected some of the dilemmas of interwar French foreign policy. With a large empire and extensive European role, France attempted to remain one of the world's major powers with diminished resources. Soon after the First World War, French naval planning envisaged opposing alliances of Germany–Italy–Soviet Union. It is startling, even somewhat eerie, to come across these post-Great War Cassandra-like forecasts of the summer of 1939, although at least, with reference to the decade 1919–1929, one might ask whether French policies helped create self-fulfilling prophecies. French relations with Germany and the Soviet Union, for different reasons, became the great interwar puzzles that French policy-makers never solved. With regard to Italy, although it was a significant component of the European power balance, French vulnerabilities led French leaders and political opinion to construct an extraordinary mirage of its southern neighbour between the wars, exaggerating, in our story, its danger as a potential enemy, and later its strength as a potential ally. The Washington Conference also highlighted France's chronic problems with Great Britain and the United States. If the British and Americans had really wanted the wholehearted participation of the French in the Washington Conference, they might have offered an exchange of the security guarantee their leaders had promised their First World War ally two years before for French acceptance of limits on lighter ships and submarines. Such a proposal, if jointly offered by the British and Americans, and if open-ended chronologically, would have posed a difficult choice for the French. In December 1921 in London, and in January 1922 at Cannes, Lloyd George and Briand discussed such a trade-off, as did the British Prime Minister and Poincaré after Briand's resignation, but Lloyd George offered relatively little in return for French concessions: too little and perhaps too late.[109] The British and Americans pursued their own self-interest (as did the French), and largely left France to wander its own path.

In the broader context of twentieth-century history, French policies at the Washington Conference and French interwar naval policy reflect attempts to grapple with diminished power, and with reduced human, material, and financial resources. In this regard, reflexive desires to compete as equals against the largest naval powers need to be contrasted with proposals to create a *flotte d'appoint* (fleet of balance). Aspects of French interwar naval policy reveal a France in difficult transition from a major power to a significant intermediary power striving to maintain its independence and to preserve the necessity for other powers to take it into account.[110]

Was the Washington Conference on the limitation of armaments a success? The French pursued their own interests more than arms limitation. The French role emphasizes a need for future arms limitation negotiators (and for historians) to take into account the perspectives and policies of other powers in addition to the strongest, and to concentrate more on other categories of ships or weapons systems beneath the largest. If the French followed something less than a policy of enlightened self-interest, so, too, did the British and Americans in their failure to offer a joint, open-ended guarantee of French security against Germany.[111]

Salvador de Madariaga presented a friend's 'parable' of the Washington Conference. In Renaissance Italy there lived five wealthy bankers, 'loving their good wives and enjoying their still better mistresses'. The two wealthiest had mistresses beyond count, while the other three had a 'comfortable number'. Then bad economic times forced retrenchment. The bankers met in conference and solemnly agreed that the wealthiest two would limit themselves to five, the next to three, and the last two would retain only one mistress each, with occasional visits to another. The conferees publicized 'that their sacrifices were made in deference to the sanctity of marriage'.[112] Even though the French story at Washington is one of a certain Machiavellianism, self-interest, and parity lost, I am reluctant to conclude with a totally negative assessment of the Washington treaty. The period from 1921 to 1935 (or until 1933), at least with regard to Europe, and the period from 1935 to 1940, were very different.[113] In relation to armaments, a measure of order and limits is better than none. Even if flawed, a limitation of the largest and most costly weapons still offers a beneficial 'precedent'.[114]

University of Connecticut

NOTES

The research on which this article is based was begun 20 years ago (1972–73). Additional research was done about 1980, with a brief visit to several archives in January 1992. Monsieur Joel Audoüy, former head of the archives of the French Navy, greatly facilitated my research. He and his successors have reclassified the documents; thus some of the sources cited in this article may be classified differently now. I have written previously an article that developed many of these themes: 'The Parity that Meant Superiority: French Naval Policy towards Italy at the Washington Conference, 1921–22, and Interwar French Foreign Policy', *French Historical Studies*, XII, 2 (Fall 1981), pp. 223–48. That article focused on France and Italy while this one concentrates on France.

1. Salvador de Madariaga, *Disarmament* (New York, 1929), pp. 104–8, particularly 108.
2. Joel Blatt, 'The Parity that Meant Superiority', op. cit., n. 4, p. 225. For the prewar background, see Paul Halpern, *The Mediterranean Naval Situation 1908–1914* (Cambridge, Mass., 1971). Also see Donald S. Birn, 'Britain and France at the Washington Conference 1921–1922', (PhD dissertation, Columbia University, 1964), p. 66. Birn's dissertation provides relevant information on a number of the issues discussed in this article, as does his paper 'The Washington Naval Conference of 1921–22 in Anglo-French Relations', in Donald M. Masterson (ed.), *Naval History: The Sixth Symposium of the United States Naval Academy* (Wilmington, Delaware, 1987, although the symposium was held in 1983), pp. 167–77. See also Paul Halpern, 'Navy', and Joel Blatt, 'Navy: Governmental Policy on Naval Warfare', in Patrick H. Hutton (ed.), *Historical Dictionary of the Third French Republic 1870–1940* (New York and Westport, 1986), pp. 681–9.
3. Donald Birn, 'Open Diplomacy at the Washington Conference of 1921–22: The British and French Experience', *Comparative Studies in Society and History*, XII, 3 (July 1970), pp. 301–2.
4. Note 1512, Navy (Etat Major General – EMG-1), 13 Oct. 1921, AM (Archives de la Marine – Navy Archives at Vincennes), no box, Dossier EMG-1-1921, Programme naval; Birn, op. cit., pp. 301–2.
5. Philippe Masson, 'La politique navale française de 1919 à 1939', *La Revue Maritime*, CCLII (March 1968), pp. 289–90. Also see Philippe Masson, *Histoire de la Marine*, Vol. II, *De la vapeur à l'atome* (Paris-Limoges, 1983), Ch. VIII, 'La marine et l'entre-deux guerres', pp. 321–66; and idem, *La marine française et la guerre 1939–1945* (France, 1991), Ch. 1, 'Une belle marine', pp. 9–34.
6. See Christopher M. Andrew and A.S. Kanya-Forstner, *The Climax of French Imperial Expansion 1914–1924* (Stanford, 1981).
7. Leygues was Deputy from Lot-et-Garonne 1885–1933 and was Navy Minister in the Clemenceau Government from November 1917 to January 1920, premier from September 1920 to January 1921, President of the Foreign Affairs Committee of the Chamber of Deputies 1921–24, and Navy Minister from November 1925 almost continuously until his death in September 1933. See *Dictionnaire des parlementaires français (1889–1940)*, VI (Paris, 1970), pp. 2275–8. Also see Christopher Andrew and A.S. Kanya-Forstner, 'La France à la recherche de la Syrie intégrale 1914–1920', *Relations internationales*, XIX (Autumn 1979), pp. 265, 267, 270 and 273, and 'The French Colonial Party and French Colonial War Aims 1914–1918', *The Historical Journal*, XVII (March 1974), pp. 80 and 83; Ronald Chalmers Hood III, *Royal Republicans: The French Naval Dynasties between the World Wars* (Baton Rouge and London, 1985), pp. 129–31.
8. 'Georges Leygues', in the *Dictionnaire des parlementaires français*.
9. CFD (Commission des Finances, Chambre des Députés), 20 Nov. 1920, Box 22 bis Audition 5.
10. CAED (Commission des Affaires Etrangères, Chambres des Députés), 8 Dec. 1920. (When I consulted the procès-verbaux of parliamentary committees, those for the Chambre des Députés were consulted at the Archives of the Assemblée Nationale and those for the Senate at the Palais du Luxembourg.)
11. CFD, 12 Oct. 1921, Box 22 bis, audition 10.
12. 'Note secrète sur le pétrole', Henry Bérenger to Clemenceau, 10 Dec. 1919, and 'Note résumé sur les pétroles de Mésopotamie et les accords franco-britanniques,' Henry Bérenger, 10 May 1920, both in MAE (Archives Ministère des Affaires Etrangères), Tardieu Papers, carton 56; also see Bérenger, *Le pétrole de la France* (Paris, 1920). In general, see Richard F. Kuisel, *Ernest Mercier: French Technocrat* (Berkeley and Los Angeles, 1967), Chapter 3, pp. 21–44.

13. Letter, Leygues to Briand, 28 Oct. 1921, MAE, I (Série-Conférences Internationales), p. 503.
14. Navy Minister Raiberti, CSDN (Conseil Supérieur de la Défense Nationale), 3 Dec. 1923, SHA (Service Historique de l'Armée-Vincennes).
15. Philippe Masson, 'Le programme naval et la marine de 1939', unpublished article in the Library of the Service Historique de la Marine, 1, and H. Salaun, *La marine française* (Paris, 1934), p. 367.
16. Note, Ronarc'H, undated (but Ronarc'H was chief of the Naval General Staff from May 1919 until he retired in 1920), AM, Cabinet 33.
17. Report, Salaun, 11 March 1920, AM, Box CSM (Conseil Supérieur de la Marine) 1; see also Note, Anon., 4 March 1920, AM, Ca (Cabinet) 32.
18. Report, Salaun, 30 Sept. 1920, AM, Ca 27; Extrait-Procès-verbal, CSM and Salaun (Rapporteur), 15 Oct. 1920, AM, box CSM.
19. CMMD (Commission de la Marine Militaire, Chambre des Députés), 8 March 1921.
20. CMMD, 19 Nov. 1920.
21. CMMD, 8 March 1921.
22. CFD, 29 Nov. 1920.
23. De Kerguézec was a Deputy (1906–20) and a Senator (1921–29) from Côtes-du-Nord, reporter of the Navy budget in 1916 and subsequently, and President of the Senate Navy Committee in 1926 (*Dictionnaire des parlementaires français*, VI (Paris, 1970), p. 2050. See CMMD, 8 March 1921; CFD, 29 Nov. 1920; AM, Carton IX, Conférence de Londres 1930, IBB2/SE; *Journal Officiel*, Sénat, 27 Dec. 1921, p. 2319.
24. CFD, 29 Nov. 1920.
25. Ibid.
26. Ibid.
27. Ibid.
28. CMMD, 8 March 1921; former Naval Attaché in Rome Lacaze – see Comte Rendu, CSM, 13 March 1920, AM, Box CSM.
29. CFD, 29 Nov. 1920.
30. I have written a doctoral dissertation and a number of articles on Franco-Italian relations and French responses to Italian Fascism. See 'French Reaction to Italy, Italian Fascism and Mussolini, 1919–1925: The Views from Paris and the Palazzo Farnese', Ph.D. Dissertation, University of Rochester, 1977 (Dissertation Supervisor: A. William Salomone); 'France and the Franco-Italian Entente, 1918–1923', *Storia Delle Relazioni Internazionali*, Anno, VI–1990/2, 173–97: 'France and the Corfu-Fiume Crisis of 1923', *The Historian*, L, 2 (Feb. 1988), 234–59; 'Franco-Italian Relations, 1880–1940', *Studies in Modern Italian History from the Risorgimento to the Republic* (in honour of A. William Salomone), edited by Frank J. Coppa (New York, 1986), pp. 171–96; 'France and Italy at the Paris Peace Conference', *The International History Review*, VIII, 1(Feb. 1986), pp. 27–40.
31. 'Etude sur la politique navale de la France', 20 Sept. 1921, part of a letter of instructions, Guist'hau to de Bon, 26 Oct. 1921, AM, Ca 50.
32. Letter, Guist'hau to de Bon, 26 Oct. 1921, AM, Cabinet 50; Letter 132, Guist'hau to Briand, 12 Oct. 1921, MAE, B (Série Amérique), Etats-Unis, 82.
33. Letter 132, Guit'hau to Briand, 12 Oct. 1921, MAE, B, Etats-Unis, 82.
34. 'Note sur la limitation des armements', AM, IBB8 II568; 'Résumé de la note sur la limitation des armements du 12 octobre 1921', AM, Ca 53. The preliminary version was 'Note', Navy Ministry, 6 Oct. 1921, AM, Ca 50.
35. Note-Italie, attached to Letter, Guist'hau to de Bon, 26 Oct. 1921, AM, Ca 50; also see Notes, EMG to President of the Council, 19 Oct. 1921, MAE, B, Etats-Unis, 82.
36. René Viviani, the Prime Minister at the outbreak of the First World War, led the delegation after Briand departed. Albert Sarraut, Minister of Colonies, influential

politician and Minister between the wars, Governor General of Indochina during the First World War, took over from Viviani on 14 December (For Sarraut, see David Heisser, *The Impact of the Great War on French Imperialism, 1914–1924*, Ph.D. Dissertation, University of North Carolina, 1972, Chapter 5). Philippe Berthelot accompanied Briand. Berthelot's protégé, Alexis Saint-Léger Léger, was brought back after years in China to join other Foreign Ministry experts at Washington. Vice Admiral de Bon (Navy), General Buat (army), and others completed the Delegation. See Léon Archimbaud, *La Conférence de Washington (12 novembre 1921–6 février 1922)* (Paris, 1923), pp. 79–80. Ambassador Jules Jusserand does not seem to have played a major role.

37. Maurice de Waleffe, *Quand Paris était un paradis*, excerpt in Daniel Langlois Berthelot Collection, Berthelot – Briand folder.

38. For an overall portrait of Briand, see Georges Suarez, *Briand*, 6 vols. (Paris, 1938–1952). For biographical details, see Joel Blatt, 'Aristide Briand', in *Historical Dictionary of the Third French Republic 1870–1940*, edited by Patrick H. Hutton (New York and Westport, 1986), pp. 130–33.

39. For criticisms of Briand's participation, see Georges Suarez, *Briand*, V (Paris, 1941), 231, and Raymond Poincaré, 'Chronique de la quinzaine', *La Revue des Deux Mondes*, 15 Dec. 1921, pp. 947–58.

40. CAED, 26 Dec. 1921; *Journal Officiel*, Sénat, 27 Oct. 1921, 1811; Note, F. Aubert, 14 July 1921, MAE, B, Etats-Unis, 80; Suarez; *Briand*, ibid., pp. 224–6, 236; Thomas H. Buckley, *The United States and the Washington Naval Conference 1921–1922* (Knoxville, 1970), pp. 104–6.

41. *Documents on British Foreign Policy*, I, XIV, No. 437; CAED, 17 March 1922; Telegram 251, Washington to Paris, received 10 Feb. 1922, MAE, B, Etats-Unis, 90. For background, see Donald Birn, 'The Washington Naval Conference of 1921–22 in Anglo-French Relations', in *Naval History*, op. cit., pp. 169–70; Birn, doctoral dissertation, op. cit., pp. 61–3; Sally Marks, *The Illusion of Peace: International Relations in Europe 1918–1933* (New York, 1976), pp. 40–44, and Denise Artaud, *La question des dettes interalliées et la reconstruction de l'Europe (1917–1929)* (Paris, 1978), particularly pp. 351–4 and 366–89.

42. For Briand's speech, see Department of State, *Conference on the Limitation of Armament* (Washington DC. 1922), Third Session, pp. 115–45.

43. Buckly, op. cit., Chapter V, pp. 63–74. For American background, in addition to Buckley, see Roger Dingman, *Power in the Pacific: The Origins of Naval Arms Limitation, 1914–1922* (Chicago, 1976), Chapter 9 and pp. 197–8. Also see *Foreign Relations of the United States*, 1922, 1, pp. 130–33, 135–6.

44. Archimbaud, op. cit., p. 88; Buckley, op. cit., pp. 69–70; Suarez, *Briand*, op. cit., pp. 256–7; Dispatch 672 and 672 bis, Jusserand to Bonnevay, 14 Nov. 1921, MAE, B, Etats-Unis, 83; Donald Birn, doctoral dissertation, op. cit., p. 86.

45. Note. 'Période de discussion secrète entre les representants de la Grande Bretagne, des Etats-Unis, et du Japon, 15 novembre-15 décembre', Cabinet du Ministre, AM, IBB8 I567, Dossier – Conférence de Washington.

46. For extended discussion of these developments, see Joel Blatt, op. cit. (note 30 above), Vol II. pp. 447–8, note 46; see also Blatt, 'The Parity That Meant Superiority', op. cit., p. 235, note 29.

47. 'Note de discussion secrète entre les représentants de la Grande Bretagne, des Etats-Unis, et du Japon-15 novembre-15 décembre', Cabinet du Ministre, no date given, AM, IBB8 I567. Dossier-Conférence de Washington. Also see Memorandum, Hughes, undated but concerning a meeting of 5 Dec. 1921, Department of State, *Papers Relating to the Foreign Relations of the United States*, 1922, Vol I, pp. 86–8.

48. Telegram 1.009, Washington to Paris (MAE), received 13 Nov. 1921, AM, IBB8 I567, Dossier-Télégrammes de l'Amiral de Bon à l'arrivée.
49. Telegram 4, Washington (de Bon) to Paris (Marine), 16 Nov. 1921, AM, Ca 51, Dossier-Correspondance expédiée-reçue, 1919–1921.
50. Telegrams 8272–73, Paris (Marine) to Washington (de Bon), 17 Nov. 1921, AM, Ca 51, Dossier-Correspondance expediée-reçue, 1919–1921. Briand agreed to defend their position on submarines, but asked Guist'hau to avoid a polemic with the British (Telegram 1.006, Washington (Briand) to Paris (Guist'hau), received 23 Nov. 1921, AM, IBB8 I567, Dossier-Télégrammes de Bon à l'arrivée).
51. Report 3M, de Bon to Minister of the Navy, 2 Dec. 1921, AM, Ca 50, Dossier-Rapports de l'Amiral de Bon. Also see Letter 2M, de Bon to Minister of the Navy, Nov. 23, 1921, in the historical outline of C.F. Laurens (Chef de la Section Historique). April 1925, AM, IBB8 I567, Dossier-Historique de la Conférence de Washington; see the same document in AM, Ca 50, Dossier-Rapports de l'Amiral de Bon.
52. Buckley, op. cit., pp. 107–9.
53. Ibid., pp. 133–34; Birn, doctoral dissertation, op. cit., pp. 101–02. Philip Grant Jr. says that Hughes considered France cooperating with the United States if Great Britain and Japan came together ('Naval Disarmament, Reparations, War Debts, and Franco-American Relations, 1921–1928', Mid-America, LX, April, 1978-Special issue, 39).
54. Telegram 1192–97, Washington to Paris, 16 Dec. 1921, MAE, Y, 504 – also see Telegram 1214–26, received 18 Dec.; Department of State, Conference on the Limitation of Armament, Subcommittees, 4–63.
55. Note 11, apparently de Bon, 17 Dec. 1921, AM, Ca 50.
56. Buckley, op. cit., p. 108; Letter 21M, de Bon to Navy Minister, 18 Feb. 1922, MAE, B, Etats-Unis, p. 90; Letter 3M, de Bon to Navy Minister, 2 Dec. 1921, MAE, B, Etats-Unis, p. 85, containing Note 8, de Bon, 19 Nov.; Letter 2M, de Bon to Navy Minister, 23 Nov. 1921, in the historical outline of C.F. Laurens, April 1925, AM, IBB8 I567; FRUS, 1922, 1, 62–3.
57. Telegram 1192–1197, Washington (Sarraut) to Paris (MAE), 16 Dec. 1921, AM, IBB8 I568, Telegrams from Washington received by the Foreign Ministry. Statements of Sarraut and de Bon are in Meetings of 15, 16, 17 Dec, Committee of Fifteen on Naval Limitation, Department of State, Conference on the Limitation of Armament, Subcommittees, pp. 4–63.
58. Note pour le Ministre in response to the Letter of Klotz to Guist'hau of 29 Dec. 1921, Cabinet Militaire, apparently 30 Jan. 1922, AM, Ca 53, Conférence de Washington – Etudes diverses.
59. CAED, 17 March 1922; Journal Officiel, Chambre des Députés, 24 March 1922, p. 1095; Journal Officiel, Chambre des Députés, 7 July 1923, pp. 3231–50; Birn, 'Open Diplomacy . . .', op. cit., note 3, p. 313. These sources give a number of explanations.
60. For Italian decision – making, see Matteo Pizzigallo, 'L' Italia alla Conferenza di Washington (1921–1922)', Storia e Politica, XIV, III (July–Sept. 1975), pp. 408–48, and XIV, IV (Oct.–Dec. 1975), pp. 550–89; Admiral Bernardi, Il disarmo navale fra le due guerre mondiali (1919–1939) (Rome, 1975). Also see Blatt, 'The Parity That Meant Superiority', op. cit., note 34, pp. 236–7.
61. Telegram 15, Washington (de Bon to Paris Navy), 16 Dec. 1921, AM, Ca 51; First Meeting of the Subcommittee of Fifteen on Naval Limitation, Department of State, Conference on the Limitation of Armament, pp. 18–20.
62. CAED, 22 Dec. 1922; Telegram 8931, Paris (Marine) to Washington (de Bon), 16 Dec. 1921, AM, Ca 51, Corres. exp. et récue 1919–1921.

63. Department of State, *Conference on the Limitation of Armament*, Subcommittees, pp. 56–7; Pizzigallo, 'L' Italia . . .', op. cit. pp. 444–45.
64. Pizzigallo, 'L' Italia . . .', pp. 444–8.
65. Telegram 2236–38. Paris to Washington, 17 Dec. 1921, AM, IBB8 I561.
66. Telegram 800. 30/8b, Washington (Secretary of State) to France (Ambassador Herrick) for delivery to Briand, 16 Dec. 1921, *FRUS*, 1922, I, pp. 130–33.
67. Ibid., pp. 135–6. Fourth Meeting, Committee on the Limitation of Armament, pp. 454–60, has Hughes' letter and Briand's reply.
68. Letters 16M and 21M, de Bon to Navy Minister, 16 Jan. and 18 Feb. 1922, MAE, B. Etats-Unis, 89 and 90.
69. With Briand away, President Millerand advised Peretti de la Rocca at the Foreign Ministry to tell Sarraut to stay with the 330,000/90,000 figures, and to publicize that France had accepted 175,000 tons of battleships. See Telegram 2242, Paris (Peretti de la Rocca) to Washington (Sarraut), 19 Dec. 1921, AM, Ca 51, Corres. exp. et réçue 1919–1921; Telegram 3944–45, Paris (Peretti de la Rocca) to London (Briand), 19 Dec. 1921, AM, IBB8 I567, Washington, Affaires Etrangères. Télégrammes au départ; Telegram 3941–42, Paris to London, 19 Dec. 1921, MAE, B, Etats-Unis, 86; Telegram 2246, Paris to Washington, 21 Dec. 1921, MAE, Y, 504.
70. Telegram 3941–42, Paris to London. 19 Dec. 1921, MAE, B, Etats-Unis, 86.
71. Telegram 2246, Paris to Washington, 21 Dec. 1921, MAE, Y, 504.
72. Telegram 2242, Paris (Peretti de la Rocca) to Washington (Sarraut), 19 Dec. 1921, AM, Ca 51, Corres. exp. et réçue 1919–21.
73. Telegram 1129, London (Briand, Saint-Aulaire) to Paris and Washington, 20 Dec. 1921, AM, IBB8 I567, Washington, Affaires Etrangères. Télégrammes au départ.
74. Telegram, no number, Paris (Briand) to Washington (Sarraut), 23 Dec. 1921, AM, IBB8 I567, Washington, Télégrammes de Bon-arrivée et départ.
75. Buckley, pp. 113–14; Salaun, p. 381; Pizzigallo, 'L' Italia . . .', pp. 550–59; Dingman, pp. 207–9; all op. cit.
76. Telegram 1232–37, Washington to Paris, received 21 Dec, MAE, B, Etats-Unis, 86.
77. Telegram 3585, Paris to Rome, 24 Dec, and T 2023, Rome (Barrère) to Paris, 26 Dec 1921, MAE, B, Etats-Unis, p. 86.
78. Telegram (never sent), Paris to Washington, 21 Dec. 1921, MAE, B, Etats-Unis, p. 86. From London, Briand and other officials turned down the proposal over the telephone. In addition, see Telegram 2242, Paris to Washington, and Telegram 3944–45, Paris to London, 19 Dec. 1921, MAE, B, Etats-Unis, p. 86.
79. Telegrams 36–37, Washington (de Bon) to Paris (Navy), 24 Dec. 1921, and T9, 136, Paris (Navy) to Washington (de Bon), 24 Dec. 1921, in History, C.F. Laurens, April 1925, AM, IBB8 I567. In MAE, B, Etats-Unis, 86, Telegrams 36–37 are dated 25 Dec. 1921.
80. CSDN, 26 Dec. 1921; Note de présentation au CSDN, EMG-M, 26 Dec. 1921, AM, Cabinet 53.
81. Telegram 9173–74, Paris (Navy) to Washington (de Bon), 27 Dec. 1921, AM, IBB8 I567.
82. For example, see Birn, 'Open Diplomacy . . .', pp. 308–16, and Birn, doctoral dissertation, op. cit., Chapter VI.
83. *DBFP*, I, XIV, Nos. 421, 452, 456 and 463; Birn, op. cit., pp. 315–16; Dingman, op. cit., pp. 199, 208; Buckley, op. cit., pp. 118, 125–6; Telegram 2178–81, Washington to Paris, 27 Dec. 1921; T 2274–78, Paris to Washington, 30 Dec. 1921; and Telegram 1307–14, Washington to Paris, received 1 Jan 1922; MAE, Y, 505.
84. Telegram 1302–04, Washington to Paris, received 1 Jan 1922, and Telegram 60,

Washington to Paris, 7 Jan 1922, MAE, Y, 505. Also see Blatt, 'The Parity That Meant Superiority', op. cit., p. 241, note 53, and Birn, op. cit., pp. 312–13.

85. The aircraft carrier ratios were 135,000, 135,000, 81,000, 60,000, and 60,000 tons. Cruisers were limited to 10,000 tons. For provisions of the Treaty, see *Treaties and Other International Agreements of the United States of America 1776–1949*. Also see Telegram 1307–14, Washington to Paris, received 1 Jan 1922, MAE, Y, 505.

86. Salaun, *La marine française*, op. cit., pp. 383–4, and Buckley, op. cit., pp. 180–81.

87. CSDN, 22 April 1926, and 13 July 1928.

88. Charles Maurras, *L'Action Française*, 21 Sept. 1923, 1. For 'Trafalgar 11', see *L'Action Française*, 21 Dec. 1921, p. 1.

89. Raymond Poincaré, 'Chronique de la Quinzaine', *La Revue des Deux Mondes*, 15 Dec. 1921, p. 947.

90. Note – Observations sur le Traité de Washington, EMG-M, March 1922, AM, Ca 53, Conference de Washington – Etudes diverses; Note – Treaty of Washington, Chaumie, 3 May 1923, AM, Ca 52, Washington, Corres. exp. et reçue, 1923–1924; Note, Chaumie, 20 Nov. 1922, AM, Ca 53, Washington, Etudes diverses; Letter, Minister of the Navy to President of the Council, drafted in July 1922, but not clear when and if sent, AM, Ca 51, Washington, Corres. exp. et reçue, avril-octobre 1923; Note, EMG-M 3rd. Bureau, 29 June 1922, AM, IBB8 II568, Droit maritime international; Note-Intervenu de M. Jusserand . . . avec M. Raiberti au sujet du Traité de Washington, 25 Aug. 1922, AM, IBB8 II568, Limitation des armements; Note 478, EMG-3, 29 June 1922, MAE, B, Etats-Unis, 92: Letter, Laboulaye to Jusserand, 29 Dec. 1922, MAE, Jusserand Papers, carton 31. There was some opposition in the navy to the Treaty (Birn, op. cit., p. 318).

91. Note 478, EMG-3, 29 June 1922, MAE, B, Etats-Unis, 92; Letter, Laboulaye to Jusserand, 29 Dec. 1922, MAE, Jusserand Papers, carton 31.

92. Letter, Poincaré to Guernier (Rapporteur in the Chamber of Deputies for the law embodying ratification of the Treaty), 16 June 1923, cited in Note, Minister of National Defence (navy), 9 May 1932, Tardieu Papers, MAE, Box 41 bis, Dossier-Marine. Sustained correspondence between Poincaré and Guernier may be found in AM, Ca 52, Dossier-Conférence de Washington, Corres. exp. et reçue, 1923–24.

93. Note de Renseignements 178, EMG-M, 2nd Bureau, 21 March 1925, AM, IBB8 II568, Droit maritime international.

94. *Journal officiel*, Chambre des Députés, 7 July 1923, pp. 3228–50; Sénat, 11 July 1923, pp. 570–80. Also see AM, carton VIII, IBB2/SE, Conférence de Londres 1930, Annex II.

95. Report, presented by Rear-Admiral Marguerye for the EMG-M, 1 July 1922, AM, CSM-Box I, Dossier-CSM 1921–22. The CSM, with Millerand and Poincaré in attendance, approved the Report (Extract of Procès-Verbal, CSM, 7 July 1922, AM, Ca 27, CSM-1920–22).

96. Ibid.

97. Letter 686, Finance to Navy Minister, 20 Oct. 1922, AM, Ca 33; CFD, 29 Nov. 1920; Salaun, *La marine française*, op. cit., pp. 370–75, 422–26; Masson, 'Le programme naval', op. cit., pp. 10–12; Rear-Admiral R. de Belot and André Reussner, *La puissance navale dans l'histoire*, III (Paris, 1961), pp. 200–203, 207–11; Papers of Jacques-Louis Dumesnil, Archives Nationales, 130AP, carton 18.

98. For the left, see Chalmers Hood III, op. cit., p. 128. For the right and for this question in the context of French responses to Italy and Italian Fascism, see Joel Blatt, *French Reaction to Italy, Italian Fascism and Mussolini, 1919–1925* . . ., op. cit., Chapter VIII, particularly pp. 469–75, and the dissertation as a whole.

99. Letter 626, Leygues to General Serrigny, 10 Nov. 1929, SHA (Service Historique de l'Armée (Vincennes)), 2N 11; Letter 574, Navy Minister to President of the Council,

15 Oct. 1929, SHA, 2N 11; De Belot and Reussner, op. cit., p. 209; Blatt, 'The Parity That Meant Superiority', op. cit., p. 245, and note 67, pp. 245–6.

100. Salaun, *La marine française*, pp. 426–41; the figures come from Masson, 'Le programme naval', op. cit., pp. 13–14.
101. Chalmers Hood III, op. cit., pp. 128, 141–2.
102. Philippe Masson, 'Le programme navale et la Marine de 1939', op. cit.; Masson, *Histoire de la Marine*, Vol. II, op. cit., Chapter VIII; Masson, *La marine française et la guerre 1939–1945*, op. cit., Ch. I, 'Une belle marine'.
103. Ibid., p. 19. For comparison of the French and other fleets in 1937, 1938 and 1939, see AM, IBB2 218. Also see Philippe Masson, 'La marine française en 1939–1940', *Revue historique des armées*, IV (1979), pp. 57–77.
104. Hood, op. cit., p. 142; also see Philippe Masson, Michèle Battesti, Jacques C. Favier, *Marine et constructions navales 1789–1989* (Paris, 1989), p. 97. For bibliographical suggestions on the French navy during the 1930s, see Hervé Coutau-Bégarie and Claude Huan, *Darlan* (Paris, 1989), p. 843.
105. Philippe Masson, 'La politique navale française de 1919 à 1939', *La Revue Maritime*, p. 295; Masson, *Histoire de la marine*, vol. II, p. 484; Masson, *La marine française et la guerre 1939–1945*, Chapters III, IV, V, XI.
106. Joel Blatt, Dissertation, op. cit., Chapter 8, 'The Parity That Wasn't'; 'The Parity That Meant Superiority', *French Historical Studies*, op. cit.
107. Note, no author cited, 22 Dec. 1922, MAE, B, Etats-Unis, 92; Letter, Leygues to Poincaré, 12 Dec. 1922, MAE, B, Etats-Unis, 92.
108. In the papers of Jacques-Louis Dumesnil, several times Navy Minister between the wars, one finds a 'Dossier of Naval Parity between France and Italy'. See the papers of J.-L. Dumesnil, Archives Nationales, 130AP, carton 26.
109. Donald Birn, doctoral dissertation, op. cit., Chapter VII and p. 302; Birn, 'The Washington Naval Conference of 1921–22 in Anglo-French Relations', op. cit., pp. 175–6; Carole Fink, *The Genoa Conference: European Diplomacy 1921–1922* (Chapel Hill and London, 1984), pp. 37–45.
110. Blatt, 'The Parity That Meant Superiority', op. cit., 247–8; Birn, doctoral dissertation, op. cit., p. 303.
111. Jonathan Dull, a naval historian and friend, suggested once in conversation that the best one can expect of countries is enlightened self-interest. Professor Dull made the remark in an assessment of the eighteenth century. For the Washington Treaty's influence on interwar cruiser construction, see Ernest Andrade Jr, 'Arms Limitation Agreements and the Evolution of Weaponry: The Case of the "Treaty Cruiser" ' in *Naval History: The Sixth Symposium of the US Naval Academy*, Daniel M. Masterson, (Wilmington, Delaware, 1987). For a doctoral dissertation that is apparently deeply sceptical of the Washington Conference's agreements (I have only seen the abstract), see Rodrigo Garcia y Robertson, 'The Green Table: The Technological Link between Armament and Disarmament in the Beginning of the Twentieth Century', Ph.D. dissertation, University of California, Los Angeles, 1981.
112. Salvador de Madariaga, *Disarmament* (New York, 1929), pp. 99–101.
113. For the French navy of the 1930s, see notes 102, 103, and 104, supra.
114. I am indebted to Sandi Cooper for this observation. When I asked Professor Cooper, one of the leading historians of peace movements, for her thoughts about the Washington Conference, she replied that such agreements make good 'precedents'.

Italian Naval Power and the Washington Disarmament Conference of 1921–22

BRIAN R. SULLIVAN

The Italians played a relatively minor part in the negotiations for the Treaty on Limitation of Naval Armament signed in Washington on 6 February 1922, but Italy acquired major advantages from the treaty. Indeed, judged by their positions before and after, of the countries which took part in the conference Italy made the greatest gains. The Italians entered the negotiations as the weakest by far of the five leading naval powers. They left the conference with signed guarantees of parity in capital ships with the French by the following decade. Even more impressive, the Italians had acquired the right to build a fleet of battleships one-third the size of the Royal Navy's. These concessions and the freedom to build as many cruisers, destroyers and submarines as Italy could afford would allow the Italians to mount a creditable challenge to French and British domination of the Mediterranean by the late 1930s. Considering the situation confronting the Italian Navy at the outbreak of the First World War, just seven years before, this represented an extraordinary diplomatic achievement.

In the period preceding the First World War, the *Regia Marina* had benefited greatly from the unprecedented expansion of the Italian economy that had begun in the late 1890s. Enhanced government revenues had allowed the Italian Navy to outspend its ally-yet-rival, the Austro-Hungarian Navy, by better than two to one in the years 1900–1913. During the period from 1898 to 1915, Italian shipyards had laid down six pre-dreadnoughts, six dreadnoughts and four super dreadnoughts. In comparison, the Austro-Hungarians had laid down six pre-dreadnoughts and four dreadnoughts during that time. While the Italians had feared the possibility of war with the Hapsburg Monarchy, as members of the Triple Alliance they had prepared for war with France.[1]

When measured against the French Navy of the time, the *Regia Marina* was far less impressive. The French had laid down 12 pre-dreadnoughts, seven dreadnoughts and five super dreadnoughts between 1898 and 1914. They planned to start construction on four more super dreadnoughts in January–April 1915. By 1922, the French Parliament had decreed the creation of a battle fleet of 28 modern battleships. The Italians could not hope to match such a construction programme. In the decade before the First World War, the Italian GNP hovered at a level about half that of France. In the period 1900–1914, the Italians had spent the equivalent of about $483 million on their navy, while the French had spent $1 billion. More to the point, naval construction by the Italians had totalled about $140 million during those years, while the French had laid out more than three times as much for new warships – $440 million.[2]

Nonetheless, prior to the First World War, the *Regia Marina* had developed highly aggressive plans in case of conflict with the French. The Italian naval staff planned attacks on the French bases at Bizerte and Mers-el-Kebir, intended to interdict convoys carrying Algerian troops to France, and hoped to destroy the French battle fleet in a great naval encounter. The Italians knew that they could not match the French in numbers of warships, but they believed that by concentrating on the construction of the highest quality battleships and seizing the opportunities for engagements on favourable terms, they could defeat the French battle fleet. The Italian naval leadership also counted on its foreign ministry to prevent a British–French alliance against Italy.

By early 1913, however, the growth in the numbers of French battleships alone had forced the Italians to conclude that such plans had become completely unrealistic. Furthermore, the Italians had become worried that their warships might be distinctly inferior in quality. If the French Navy combined with the Royal Navy's Mediterranean squadron, which recent international developments suggested would occur, the Italians decided that the French would crush them. The Italians feared that the French Navy would be able to sweep the *Regia Marina* from the Mediterranean, seize Italy's African colonies, and then land amphibious forces to capture Genoa, Sardinia and Sicily. Even without undertaking a major land offensive against Italy, it seemed that the French could place Italy in a hopeless strategic situation.

These concerns prompted the Italians to conclude the naval convention of June 1913 with the Austro-Hungarians and Germans. The convention stipulated the formation of a combined Triple Alliance battle fleet in the Mediterranean for operations against the French. But without reinforcement from the Austro-Hungarian fleet and the German Mediterranean squadron the Italians no longer believed that they could engage the French Navy successfully. By the summer of 1914, the French Navy had warships totalling 689,000 tons in service, compared to 286,000 for the Italians.[3]

These worries became temporarily irrelevant after Italy entered the First World War on the Allied side in May 1915, but despite their wartime alliance the *Regia Marina* leadership continued to plan for future conflict with the French. In particular, Admiral Paolo Thaon di Revel, who became Navy Chief of Staff for the second time in February 1917, maintained the strong anti-French attitudes he had held when in the same post from April 1913 to October 1915. Thaon di Revel gained notable successes over the Austro-Hungarian Navy in the Adriatic through the use of naval aviation, torpedo boats, destroyers and submarines, but he husbanded his dreadnoughts for possible future use against the French.[4]

In November 1918, the *Regia Marina* emerged from its naval war as the master of the Adriatic. In the last weeks of the war, the Hapsburg Monarchy fragmented, and, even before the armistice of 4 November, its navy ceased to be an effective fighting force. Immediately following the Austro-Hungarian collapse, Thaon di Revel landed forces along the eastern shore of the Adriatic to occupy most of Dalmatia, but in the three years between the armistice and the opening of the Washington Disarmament Conference, the Italians lost the absolute domination they had gained over the Adriatic. Despite the provisions of the Treaty of London, by which they had entered the war, the Italians failed to secure annexation of the Dalmatian coast at the Paris Peace Conference. Although the Allies did agree to an Italian mandate over central Albania, guerrilla warfare and malaria forced the Italians to withdraw totally from that country in August 1920.

Thaon di Revel and his successor as Navy Chief of Staff from December 1919, Vice-Admiral Alfredo Acton, argued vehemently for Italian retention of Dalmatia as necessary for Italian security in the Adriatic, but they were overruled by their civilian superiors. Vice-Admiral Giovanni Sechi, Navy Minister from June 1919 to July 1921, concurred. The disintegration of Austria–Hungary had left the Kingdom of the Serbs, Croats and Slovenes as Italy's only possible rival in the Adriatic, but with a navy of only 12 small warships in 1920–21, the Yugoslavs could offer no significant naval opposition to the *Regia Marina*. The South Slav kingdom planned to purchase a small force of destroyers and submarines, but even with these naval reinforcements the Yugoslavs could do no more than try to protect their ports and coastal railroads from Italian bombardment. Under these circumstances, Italy's postwar prime ministers, Francesco Saverio Nitti (June 1919–June 1920) and Giovanni Giolitti (June 1920–June 1921), preferred a policy of cooperation, rather than confrontation, with Yugoslavia.

Despite their Albanian debacle, the Italians retained control of Saseno Island, which gave them a precarious control over the Bay of Valona. At the other end of the Adriatic, they secured possession of Istria, four major islands in northern Dalmatia and the city of Zara with its immediate hinterland, through the Treaty of Rapallo with Yugoslavia in November 1920. From their annexation of Trieste and Pola (and effective control over Fiume), the Italians acquired the only three dockyards in the Adriatic capable of large warship construction. As a result, the Italians could consider their eastern sea frontiers reasonably secure, and they concentrated their battle fleet against the French in the western Mediterranean. Thaon di Revel and Acton both considered a future Italian–French war likely. Their attitudes were reciprocated by similar opinion within the French Navy and sections of the French Government.[5]

While Italy's maritime security had improved dramatically between 1914 and 1918, the *Regia Marina* was still no match for the French Navy in the immediate postwar period. In fact, the superiority of the French Navy over the Italian was likely to have grown if a new naval building race had begun. This was particularly true with regard to capital ships. In 1919, the Italian Navy possessed five dreadnoughts, one more capsized but capable of salvage (*Leonardo da Vinci*), and one super dreadnought (*Francesco Caracciolo*) at least officially under construction. In comparison, the French had seven dreadnoughts in commission and five super dreadnoughts in a state of suspended construction. Both the Italians and the French had suspended the building of their super dreadnoughts during the war. Given the overwhelming preponderance of Allied battleships over those of the central powers in the Mediterranean, the Italians had devoted the materials saved to land armaments or the construction of destroyers and submarines. As a result, by 1919, the *Regia Marina* had grown since 1914, while the French Navy had shrunk.

The two countries experienced severe economic difficulties following the war, although their navies were able to construct a small number of new vessels in the 1918–21 period (the French completed seven submarines; the Italians seven torpedo boats, five submarines and a number of motor torpedo boats), but the Italian economic crisis proved far worse than the French, and it also coincided with a major political upheaval. Italian political troubles had led to major labour problems in naval shipyards. On the other hand, while painfully aware of the weakness of national finances, the French Navy had serious plans to resume construction of the five battleships of the *Normandie* class, and along lines greatly improved over the original design. The French Navy was also considering the abandonment of the five super dreadnoughts and the construction instead of an entirely new class of giant battleships armed with 457-mm guns.

Had a battleship building contest between the Italians and French begun in 1920–21, it seems certain that the Italians would have lost badly. By the mid-1920s the French would have possessed 11 or 12 battleships while, given the slowness of their construction methods and the grave weakness of their economy, the Italians would have been lucky even to have had six. Furthermore, four or five of the French warships would have been of postwar design. At best, the

Italians would have been able either to rebuild the *da Vinci* to a somewhat improved design (for 50 million lire) or to complete the *Caracciolo* (for no less than 150 million lire). It would have been highly unlikely that they could have afforded both. Probably the *Caracciolo* could not have been completed. Thus, from a position of near parity with the French in dreadnoughts in mid-1916, the Italian Navy would probably have been outnumbered two-to-one by 1924.[6]

Meanwhile, a serious debate had begun within the *Regia Marina* over the future nature of naval warfare. One group of officers, heavily influenced by the theories of Giulio Douhet, argued that the submarine, torpedo boat and airplane had rendered the battleship obsolete. They called for a navy based on light surface and subsurface torpedo craft, and aircraft carriers designed as floating bases for attacks on the land. At the other extreme, Thaon di Revel and his supporters (both in the Navy and in the steel and shipbuilding industries) countered that recent events in the restricted Adriatic did not offer useful lessons for a future struggle in the open waters of the Mediterranean. There, they contended, the battleship would still reign supreme and the theories of Mahan would still apply.

A third group of naval officers chose positions somewhere between these two schools of thought. They remained sceptical about the efficacy of the submarine in the Mediterranean and dubious about the use of carrier-based aircraft for strikes against shore targets. While they considered existing battleships vulnerable to attack by submarines and aircraft, they believed that more modern designs could solve these problems and create super dreadnoughts fit to form the backbone of a balanced fleet. They advocated a navy of capital ships, escort vessels, aircraft carriers equipped with light aviation for naval battles, heavier land-based naval aviation and submarines.

Admiral Sechi aligned himself most closely with the third group of thinkers. He had no resources for a battleship building race with the French, but Sechi believed that even if the Italian Navy could afford to do so, it was too soon to construct new battleships. Time and study were needed to absorb the lessons of the war and to understand the new developments in naval weapons. After that, Italy should build only a few battleships, but Sechi wanted them equal to those super dreadnoughts being planned by the United States and Britain. Sechi was also impressed by the victories that Thaon di Revel had won in the Adriatic with light craft, submarines and naval aviation, and believed that these methods were applicable elsewhere. He envisioned the eventual creation of a fleet based on modern battleships, a large number of light cruisers, destroyers, torpedo boats and small submarines, and supported by land-based naval aviation. Within the restricted waters of the central Mediterranean, Sechi did not consider aircraft carriers particularly useful.

In order to pave the way for the high costs of future battleship construction and for the more immediate task of building light craft, Sechi ordered a drastic reduction of the older warships of the *Regia Marina*. He also obtained the definitive cession of the construction of the *Caracciolo*, selling off its hull in October 1920, and attempted to scrap the salvaged hulk of the *da Vinci*. These measures prompted howls of outrage from the Italian right. Even moderates in the Chamber of Deputies forced Sechi to proceed with the reconstruction of the *da Vinci*, but by the time Sechi was replaced by the civilian Eugenio Bergamasco as Navy Minister in July 1921, the Admiral had done much to prepare the Navy to begin a construction programme of light craft in the near future. These warships, Sechi believed, would provide adequate protection for the Italian coastline, and would defend the nation from the threat of French naval interdiction that had so concerned the prewar leadership of the *Regia Marina*.[7]

The overt Italian–French hostility in 1919–21 helped mask the growing Italian–British rivalry during the same period. The clash of Italian aspirations with British interests in the Mediterranean, the Middle East and northeast Africa did not capture public attention, but informed diplomats, colonial officials, soldiers and sailors were aware that Italian quests for resources, markets, living space and strategic bases in the region could only be achieved by the ejection of the British. Anti-British attitudes were far stronger within the Italian Army, Colonial Ministry and Foreign Service than in the Navy, however. The Italian Navy felt a distinct inferiority to the British, which it had taken as its model. The idea of a clash between the *Regia Marina* and the Royal Navy was out of the question in the immediate postwar years. After all, in mid-1921, when the Italians possessed only five dreadnoughts, with the possibility of acquiring a sixth, the British had 37 modern battleships and battle cruisers (eight in reserve or training status), with eight more projected. Nonetheless, Italian geopolitical goals pointed toward an eventual confrontation with the British on the seas. Any reduction in the huge superiority that the British Navy enjoyed over the Italian would obviously benefit the *Regia Marina*.[8]

These factors help explain why the new Prime Minister, Ivanoe Bonomi, enthusiastically welcomed the American invitation of July 1921 to participate in a disarmament conference in Washington. The negotiating stance that the Navy Ministry and the Naval General Staff worked out over the following three-and-a-half months reflected the weakness of the Italian position. From the first, the naval staff accepted the idea of both limitations and reductions for the *Regia Marina*, with only one condition about its eventual size or composition. The Italian admirals insisted on absolute equality with the French Navy.

This demand struck the head of the Italian delegation, Senator Carlo Schanzer, as well as Navy Minister Bergamasco, as completely unrealistic. In the autumn of 1921, the displacement of the warships of the French Navy, in service or under construction, totalled 449,000 tons; that of the Italian Navy, just 351,000 tons. After considering the arguments of the navy staff, Bergamasco and Schanzer decided that the best the Italians could hope for was a navy 90 per cent the size of the French. However, they agreed that, if necessary to reach agreement, the Italian delegation could accept limiting the *Regia Marina* to a size 80 per cent that of the French Navy. Instructions incorporating these upper and lower levels were issued to the senior naval counsellor to the Italian delegation, Admiral Acton, who had stepped down as Navy Chief of Staff the previous February.[9]

The Italian Cabinet's choice of its four principal delegates to the Washington Conference indicated that the Bonomi Government sought more than disarmament from the negotiations. Schanzer was a former Minister both of the Treasury and of Finance. Vittorio Rolandi Ricci, Schanzer's deputy on the delegation, as well as Italian Ambassador to the United States, was not a career diplomat but a businessman. Filippo Meda was a prominent lawyer, journalist and bank president, and also a former Minister of Finance and of the Treasury. Luigi Albertini, publisher of the *Corriere della Sera*, had emerged from a banking career to rescue the nation's most influential

newspaper from insolvency, and had impressed the Italian establishment with his financial acumen.

In fact, Schanzer, Rolandi Ricci and Albertini made their intentions
clear, both in interviews with the American press and in discussions
with State Department officials. Their goal in the negotiations was
not so much buttressing Italian national security as seeking relief
from their country's overwhelming economic problems. Prime
Minister Bonomi controlled a fragile coalition government that was
attempting to lessen the appeal of the lawless Fascist movement.
Bonomi relied on the police to hold the Fascist violence in check while
he worked to restore the weak Italian economy. In essence, that
meant securing financial assistance from the United States. If it would
help gain American sympathy, the civilian members of the Italian
delegation were willing to accept considerable sacrifice of their
nation's armament levels.

Of course, in the minds of the civilian Italian delegates, economic
and military strength were closely linked. The Italians promised full
cooperation with American aims at the conference. In return, the
Italians hoped that the United States would reward Italy. This could
take the form of forgiving some of the huge Italian war debt to the
United States, clearing the way for private American financial insti-
tutions to make loans to the Italian Government. Most Americans
believed that the Italians would never repay their war debts. The
Italian Government knew this, and intended to surprise the
Americans by eventually offering a settlement, in return for a reduction in the total debt. In the short run, however, the Italians would
remain silent on the issue and cultivate American gratitude by their
willingness to accept disarmament. Eventually Italian economic
strength, restored with American assistance, could be translated into
more powerful Italian armed forces.

Nonetheless, Schanzer believed that there might be a realistic
alternative to eventual Italian and European rearmament and another
general conflict. He placed a degree of confidence in the ability of the
League of Nations to prevent such a war, particularly if the United
States Government could be persuaded to join the world organization. Schanzer hoped that the disarmament conference might provide an occasion for members of the other delegations to raise the
issue with the Americans.

However, the naval members of the Italian delegation continued to be influenced by less idealistic and more immediate concerns. Unlike the Italian Cabinet and the civilians on the delegation, who considered a future war with France only a possibility, the naval members of the Italian delegation, like their uniformed superiors in Rome, believed such a conflict to be probable. Thus, despite their Government's instructions prior to the conference and the attitude of the civilian delegates, Acton and his staff still wanted the *Regia Marina* to gain parity with the French Navy. Of course, the Italian naval officers were well aware of the advantages to be gained by cultivating the goodwill of the United States Government. They did not intend to alienate the Americans by a blind pursuit of equality with the French. Indeed, this recognition of the advantages of maintaining American–Italian friendship permeated the entire leadership of the Italian armed forces. During the summer and autumn of 1921, Generals Armando Diaz and Pietro Badoglio, respectively the Italian Army Chief of Staff and Vice-Chief of Staff in 1917–18, also visited the United States. Both generals continually stressed their gratitude for American aid during the Great War and their firm belief in the necessity for continued American–Italian cooperation.[10]

As a result of these perspectives, the Italians displayed a mixed reaction to Secretary of State Charles Evans Hughes' surprise revelation of the American negotiating position on 12 November 1921, the first day of the conference, as well as to the responses that followed over the next ten days. The Italians had expected the conference to deal with air and land armaments, as well as with warships. While the Italians believed that they had already reduced their army to the lowest level compatible with national defence, they had hoped that the conference would result in other European powers, notably France, cutting their land forces. American concentration on naval disarmament, and the refusal of the head of the French delegation, premier Aristide Briand, to consider reducing the French Army, disappointed them. Such exclusions reduced the opportunities for further reductions in Italian armaments spending.

However, the Italians said nothing to annoy their American hosts, and showed enthusiasm for the naval disarmament proposals themselves. After all, given the weakness of their navy, their inability to match the French in a naval arms race and their previously low expectations, Hughes' ideas seemed to offer the Italians great advantages. In his opening remarks to the conference, the Secretary of State had hinted that he intended to approach the limitation of the Italian and French navies on the basis of equality. Furthermore, the American revealed that he did not expect the Italians (or the French) to reduce their navies to the degree required under his proposals for the three great naval powers. Hughes' proposals had the added attraction of closely paralleling those made by King Vittorio Emanuele III for naval disarmament, based on tonnage and armament, 11 years earlier. This approach favoured the Italians, given the difficulties they would face in producing large calibre naval guns and battleships of the size then being built or considered by the other powers.[11]

Realizing the implications of Hughes' proposals, Admiral Acton wired the naval staff in Rome to urge the Government to seize this opportunity for obtaining naval parity with the French. He suggested that Italy and France each seek the right to construct 200,000 tons of future battleships and a proportionate tonnage of lesser warships, but after Acton had raised the issue with Schanzer, the head of the Italian delegation argued against the feasibility of the project. Schanzer pointed out to Prime Minister Bonomi that such a large increase in the total displacement of the Italian battle fleet was hardly compatible with the spirit of the American-sponsored disarmament conference. Furthermore, he and Albertini argued, even if such a figure were agreed to, the French could afford to build up to it while the Italians could not. The practical result would be even greater Italian naval inferiority. Schanzer and Albertini also warned Bonomi that even raising the issue of parity could enrage the French and create a crisis in Italian–French relations.

However, responding favourably to Acton's initiative, the naval staff in Rome encouraged him to pursue the goal of parity. Acton received their permission to carry out his suggestion. He would approach the Americans and British to persuade them that Italy should have a navy equal to that of the French. To the Americans, Acton stressed Italian willingness to limit the size of their navy and accept a naval building holiday. Italian–French parity would mean a small French Navy, fulfilling the American desire for European disarmament. Acton pointed out to the British that Italian–French parity served their interests because it would keep the French relatively weak in the Mediterranean. Acton knew that the British considered a future war with the French to be a possibility and that they envisioned the Italians as possible allies in such a conflict.

Meanwhile, Schanzer had come to see naval parity with the French as a realistic goal after all. Acting according to an entirely different negotiating strategy approved by the Bonomi cabinet, Schanzer dealt directly with the French. He attempted to gain their consent to parity as part of a quid pro quo understanding. Briand had already sought out Schanzer on 14 November, and had surprised the Italian by the friendliness of his approach. However, this conversation inspired a highly erroneous news story. On 15 November, the *New York Herald* reported that Schanzer had agreed to accept a markedly lower tonnage of capital ships for the *Regia Marina* than for the French Navy. The news article stated that the Italians might settle for a figure as low as 130,000 tons, while agreeing to 175,000 tons, possibly as much as 200,000, for the French. After Rolandi Ricci had read the newspaper article, he assumed that it was true, sent an angry telegram of protest to Rome, and confronted Schanzer over the supposed surrender of Italian rights. To both his Foreign Ministry and Rolandi Ricci, Schanzer vehemently denied the truth of the *New York Herald* story, but he insisted on his right to continue his private talks with Briand. Rome cabled permission.

Schanzer spoke with Briand again on 21 November, following the French premier's refusal at the third plenary session of the conference to consider reducing the French Army. Schanzer offered to drop Italian demands for military disarmament and cooperate with the French in that regard at the conference, in return for French acceptance of naval parity with Italy, but Schanzer warned that if the French did not agree, he would do his utmost to embarrass France over the issue with American public opinion. Since the French also sought relief from their huge war debt to the Americans, Schanzer's threat carried weight. The Italians could stress the inconsistency of the French pleading poverty while pursuing ruinous rearmament projects.

Briand indicated interest in Schanzer's offer. After considering the matter for several days, Briand accepted the Schanzer proposal on 23 November, and issued instructions to his delegation to settle the details of the question. The premier then left Washington to prepare for conferences in London with the British Prime Minister, David Lloyd George. To help lock in this agreement, the Italians leaked the essence of the conversations to the American press.

Acton had hoped to gain American and British agreement to a future limit of 200,000 tons for new Italian and French capital ships. That would have allowed the Italians to build six battleships and form two divisions of three each. Such warships could displace 32,500 tons each, the maximum displacement being suggested by the Americans, or, with a bit of cheating, 35,000 tons, the maximum tonnage preferred by the British. Instead, Theodore Roosevelt Jr, the American Assistant Secretary of the Navy, and British Admiral David Beatty agreed on a limit of 175,000 tons – with proportionate tonnage for other warships – although they expected violent French objections to such a figure. Still, Acton had gained a major victory. On 15 November, a member of the Italian delegation had foolishly revealed to the Associated Press that his government would accept a ratio of eight to ten with the French Navy. Furthermore, the British feared that the Italians might join the French and Japanese in a future war against them. Despite all this, American and British dislike of French haughtiness, their low opinion of the Italian Navy, and Acton's arguments had persuaded them to propose Italian–French naval parity.[12]

Meanwhile, in early December, the Italian delegates had learned of the four-power negotiations for a Pacific treaty. Schanzer informed Rome, and asked for instructions. After a week's delay, the Italian Foreign Minister, the Marchese Pietro Della Torretta, ordered Schanzer to seek admission to the negotiations for reasons of prestige. Schanzer and Albertini considered this foolish. It was clear to them that Italy would not be admitted to the talks, no matter how hard they tried, and that it would be better to avoid alienating the Americans and British over such an inconsequential issue. It would be wiser to preserve their sympathies for the time when Italian–French naval parity was discussed. Shortly afterwards, the four-power negotiations concluded and the matter became moot. The Italian delegates were able to concentrate their attention on naval matters again.

As a result, in mid-December, after Hughes' formally proposed Italian–French naval parity had suggested a limit of future battleship construction for each of 175,000 tons and a proportionate amount of lesser warship displacement, the Italians found themselves in happy circumstances. The French indignantly rejected the American proposal and instead insisted on 350,000 tons for their future battleship tonnage allotment. Acton attempted to persuade both Schanzer and the Italian Cabinet to hold out for 200,000 tons of battleships, but Schanzer and Albertini argued successfully for accepting the 175,000 ton limit, as a way to win favour with the Americans and British. The Italian delegation then accepted Hughes' offer, appearing to be the epitome of reasonableness, in contrast to the French. Schanzer drove home the point by repeating his Government's desire for a drastic reduction of land, sea and air armaments, so long as Italy retained parity with France.

Despite agreement among participants to keep such discussions confidential, the British leaked the French outburst to the newspapers. This cast the French in the role of villains who threatened to wreck the conference by their refusal to accept a reasonable limit on their naval power. Within a few days, realizing that the French delegation had made a serious misstep, Briand telegraphed Hughes from London to indicate acceptance of a 175,000-ton limit on future French battleship displacement. However, the French Government firmly refused to extend the ratio they had accepted for their battleships to other categories of warships. Furthermore, the French won the right to lay down new battleships in 1927 and 1929, whereas the Americans, British and Japanese could not do so until 1931. Of course, as had been agreed, the Italians gained the same rights that the French had won for themselves. Considering that in late 1921 the Italians had in service five dreadnoughts displacing 112,900 tons, while the French had seven dreadnoughts displacing 164,500 tons, the Italians had won a very considerable concession.

Each of the five navies gained the right to improve the horizontal armour and anti-torpedo protection of their existing battleships by adding up to 3,000 tons of displacement to each vessel, but in recognition of the greater obsolescence of the Italian and French dreadnoughts the navies of those two countries were given the additional right to improve the vertical armour and to increase the calibre of the main guns of their capital ships. Furthermore, within the tonnage limits set, the Italians and French alone were permitted to build as many battleships as they preferred.

These concessions were particularly valuable for the *Regia Marina*. It could improve its five newer prewar dreadnoughts, increasing their displacement from their original 23,000 tons to as much as 26,000 tons. The Italians could also choose not to rebuild the heavily damaged *da Vinci* and to scrap their original dreadnought, *Dante Alighieri*. In that case, the reconstruction of its four other dreadnoughts would still leave the Italian Navy with an additional 70,000 tons from which to construct two, three or even four entirely new capital ships. In theory, by the early 1930s, the Italians could have confronted the French in the Mediterranean with as many as eight rehabilitated or new battleships and battle cruisers.

In fact, the Italians decided against rebuilding the *da Vinci*, deleting it from the naval rolls in March 1922, and scrapped the *Dante* in 1928. While the *Regia Marina* leadership considered building 18,000- and 23,000-ton battle cruisers in 1928–32, they concluded that such ships would lack sufficient fighting power. However, the special concessions given to the Italians and French provided the *Regia Marina* with the legal basis for the radical reconstruction of the four dreadnoughts of the *Cavour* and *Duilio* classes.

The Italians had entered the conference with the advantage of considerable American benevolence in their regard. In its official assessment of Italian foreign policy prior to the conference, the General Board of the US Navy concluded that the Italians were no more than 'uneasy' with regard to the Yugoslavs, and that there was 'very little danger of a serious break' between Italy and France. 'Neither Italy's policies nor her power conflict with nor disturb American policies', the board concluded. The Italians had also benefited from what seem in retrospect to have been absurd British fears of a possible future war with France and even an anti-British alliance between the French and the Japanese. The idea that the Italians and the Japanese might some day ally in an assault on their empire never seems to have occurred to the British (or to the French), but French intransigence on the question of the limitation of submarines and the fears that this raised in British minds helped deflect any consideration of an Italian threat. Rather than recognizing the Italian Navy as a future threat to them both, the French and British each began to view it as a possible ally against the other.[13]

Rigid French insistence on the right to build a future submarine fleet far larger than the British could accept doomed any possibility of the conference limiting that type of warship. Given the thinking within the *Regia Marina* about submarines, the Italians were, if anything, even more devoted to constructing a large fleet of submarines than were the French. The instructions given to the Italian delegation and Admiral Acton's own convictions reflected such thinking, but the Italians escaped any onus for their attitudes, thanks to French behaviour. If the French had gained acceptance of their demands for 90,000 tons of future submarine construction, the principle of parity would have given the same right to the Italians. As it was, French refusal to compromise left submarines completely unlimited by the treaty and the Italians free to build as many as they could afford. The Italians did raise British suspicions to some degree by insisting that submarines were a defensive weapon, while clearly indicating that they viewed them as excellent commerce raiders, but the British did not seem to grasp the danger of the Italians using submarines against them as well as against the French.

For once, when questions regarding the use of submarines were raised, the Italian delegates found themselves in a difficult situation. Schanzer knew that American public opinion, as well as both the American and British delegations, was strongly in favour of outlawing the type of unrestricted submarine warfare practised by the Germans in the Great War. Three resolutions introduced at the conference were aimed at prohibiting attacks on sight by submarines on merchant ships. Backed by Albertini and Rolandi Ricci, Schanzer urged his government to allow him to vote to adopt these resolutions. Not only was it essential to maintain American goodwill, he argued, it was in Italy's interest to ensure the safety of its merchant fleet in wartime. After all, since the Italian economy depended heavily on maritime commerce, it might be crippled by an onslaught by the French submarine fleet.

However, the *Regia Marina* staff was adamant that, in case of war, its submarines must be free to attack French commerce in both the Mediterranean and the Atlantic. The Cabinet adopted the Navy's viewpoint. Schanzer was instructed by Foreign Minister Torretta to insist on the right to conduct unrestricted submarine warfare. Acton received separate orders from the navy that he must not yield on the matter, but Schanzer found himself isolated when he attempted to modify the submarine resolutions in conference. Even the French and the Japanese supported the Americans and British. Albertini and Rolandi Ricci agreed with Schanzer that the Italian position was untenable, but Acton insisted that the delegation was bound by its original instructions.

After ten days of fruitless telegraphic argument with Torretta, Schanzer, Albertini and Rolandi Ricci appealed directly to the Prime Minister. At the same time, Albertini's brother, Alberto, warned Bonomi in person that the three civilian delegates would resign if their orders were not modified. This threat worked. Schanzer gained Bonomi's permission to vote for the resolutions, if the Italians continued to find themselves alone on the issue. This, in fact, remained the case. The three resolutions restricting submarine warfare were adopted unanimously.[14]

The French victory in the submarine question led the British to refuse to limit lighter surface ships, the necessary antidote to enemy submarines. The one exception on which the conferees could agree was a 10,000 ton and eight-inch gun limit on cruisers. In fact, such cruisers were quite large by the standards of the early 1920s (although not really large enough to provide sufficient armour and speed for the eight or nine eight-inch guns most countries would mount on such ships). These dimensions were suggested by the needs of the British, Americans and Japanese for cruisers with sufficient range for operations in the Pacific. Nonetheless, such 'Treaty Cruisers' offered the Italians other possibilities. The wartime experiences of the *Regia Marina* in the Adriatic reinforced the old Italian tendency to stress speed over armour and armament in warships. Ten-thousand-ton warship designs offered the Italian Navy the chance to build both heavy and light cruisers with considerable speed and heavy armament. Such ships could trade off range for such features, since that capability was far less important in the narrow Mediterranean than in the vast Pacific.[15]

Agreement on the limitation of aircraft carriers, reached in the midst of discussions on the employment of submarines, proved much easier for the Italian delegation. The *Regia Marina* possessed no carriers, and the naval staff remained dubious about their usefulness in the Mediterranean. Those few design proposals that circulated among Italian naval thinkers in the early 1920s were for relatively small vessels of 12–15,000 tons, carrying only fighters and reconnaissance aircraft. As previously noted, Italian thinking envisioned that air attacks on enemy warships would be conducted by land-based bombers, a method exemplified by the sinking of the ex-German dreadnought *Ostfriesland* off the Virginia Capes the previous summer.

Secretary of State Hughes originally proposed that each of the five powers receive the right to construct aircraft carriers equal in displacement to 16 per cent of their future capital ship tonnage, with no carrier larger than 27,000 tons. For the Italians this would have meant a maximum of 28,000 tons of carriers. Acton objected to the first part of the proposal, on the grounds that Italy would only be able to build one large carrier. If such a ship were to undergo repairs or be sunk, Italy would be deprived of any carrier for a lengthy period. Instead, Acton asked that Italy be given a tonnage limit of 54,000 tons for aircraft carriers, to allow it to construct two large ones. He also insisted on parity with France.

Given Italian thinking about the optimum size of carriers for the *Regia Marina*, it appears that Acton's argument was actually designed to acquire the right for Italy to build four or five light carriers. In any case, since the British, Japanese and French all insisted on a larger total displacement of carriers than they had been given under Hughes' proposal, the Italians had no difficulty in gaining an increase in their allotment. After a fairly brief discussion, it was agreed that Italy and France would both be allowed to build 60,000 tons of aircraft carriers.[16]

With the end of discussions on submarine warfare, the conference briefly moved on to non-naval matters. Italian efforts to obtain some limitation of war planes failed, but the Italians heartily supported the decision of the conference to reconfirm the prohibition of the use of poison gas, already outlawed by the Hague Convention of 1907 and the Versailles Treaty. Despite attempts to revise the laws of war, the matter was judged too complicated and abandoned. At 6 pm on 3 February 1922, the Italian part in the Washington conference negotiations came to an end. Beset by economic and political problems, the Bonomi Cabinet had resigned the previous day. On 6 February, the representatives of the United States, the British Empire, France, Italy and Japan signed the treaty limiting naval armament.

Considering the few accomplishments of the seven-month Bonomi Government, what its delegates obtained for Italy at the Washington Conference was its only real success. The Washington naval treaty did represent a considerable Italian victory. This was recognized by politicians across the Italian political spectrum, although many refused to acknowledge the fact publicly. By February 1922, the struggle among the Fascists, their allies and their opponents for control of Italy had left no room for objectivity in Italian politics.

Nonetheless, Schanzer was rewarded by appointment as Foreign Minister in the short-lived Government of Luigi Facta, who became Prime Minister in late February 1922. The next month, King Vittorio Emanuele decorated Rolandi Ricci and Albertini for their services at the Washington Conference. Even after the ultra nationalistic Fascists seized power in October 1922, their leader and the new Italian Prime Minister, Benito Mussolini, advocated parliamentary ratification of the Washington treaties. At first, Mussolini's new Navy Minister, Thaon di Revel, criticized the treaty restrictions on submarine warfare, but at Mussolini's urging the Admiral publicly recognized the advantages for Italy of the Washington treaties as a whole, and granted his assent. The Italian Parliament approved the treaties in February 1923.[17]

It has been argued that Italy gained only a hollow success at the Washington Conference. Technically, the Italians had gained only paper parity with the French for the future construction of battleships and aircraft carriers, and the French Navy placed little value on either class of warship. As early as 1920 the French Government had decided to place a very low priority on the construction of new battleships. The French Navy outnumbered the *Regia Marina* in that vessel category, and the Italians could not easily afford to build new ones for years to come. Nor did the French consider aircraft carriers particularly useful. They constructed only one ship of that type between the world wars, and relegated it to a marginal role within their navy.

What the French did consider essential for controlling Mediterranean sea lanes and maintaining communications with their colonial empire were cruisers, destroyers and submarines. The Washington naval treaty allowed them to build as many of these types of warships as they could afford, restricting only the size and armament of cruisers. Furthermore, considering the far greater size of the French national income compared to the Italian, there was every reason for the French Government to expect permanent naval superiority over the Italians. Indeed, between the eve of the First World War and the late 1930s, French national income actually grew substantially in comparison to Italian national income. In 1914, Italian national income stood at about 67 per cent of that of the French. By 1929 it had fallen to about 63 per cent, and by 1937 to about 60 per cent.[18]

Nonetheless, French expectations about maintaining naval superiority over the Italians proved much too optimistic. Between February 1922 and June 1940, the French laid down or reconstructed 775,000 tons of warships, while the Italians rebuilt or laid down 672,000 tons of naval vessels for the *Regia Marina*. Given the French stress on lighter ships, the corresponding figures are even more significant: 464,000 tons laid down by the French, 402,000 tons laid down by the Italians. According to categories, the French began two battle cruisers (both completed) and three battleships (none completed), while the Italians laid down four battleships (two completed); the French built seven heavy cruisers against seven for the Italians; 15 French light cruisers were built to the Italians' 12 (and the Italians also began the 12 unarmoured cruisers of the *Capitani Romani* class); 74 French destroyers were constructed against 54 for the Italians; 35 French destroyer escorts, torpedo boats and sloops were completed compared to 35 of the same types for the Italians; 114 French submarines went into service, in contrast to 115 Italian (plus two more which the Italians donated to the Spanish Nationalists). During the same period, the French built one aircraft carrier (using the hull of the uncompleted battleship *Bearn*) and rebuilt five dreadnoughts; the Italians reconstructed four dreadnoughts into what can be considered almost totally modern battleships.[19]

What the French had not anticipated was the iron determination of Benito Mussolini that Italy would rule the Mediterranean. After the establishment of his Fascist dictatorship in January 1925, he proved both willing and able to place the Italian people under a crushing burden of taxation to achieve that goal. Furthermore, it was Mussolini who benefited from the work begun by Schanzer and Albertini at the Washington Conference to gain American financial assistance. In November 1925, Italy and the United States signed a settlement of the Italian war debt at only four-tenths of one per cent interest, stretched out over 62 years. Within four days, the Morgan Bank lent the Italian Government $100 million. Two months later, the British agreed to a 57 per cent reduction in the Italian war debt, also payable over 62 years, but with no interest. Over the next two years, encouraged by these arrangements, foreign banks lent the Fascist regime the equivalent of another $195 million. These debt settlements and loans help explain the surge in Italian warship construction starting in 1925.[20]

Between the beginning of 1923 and the end of 1939, the French spent the equivalent of $1.575 billion on their navy, while from mid-1922 to mid-1939, the Italians spent the equivalent of $1.752 billion on the *Regia Marina*. Admittedly, in the period 1935–39 the Italian Navy engaged in fairly extensive operations in support of the Italian conquest of Ethiopia and of Italian intervention in the Spanish Civil War. The cost of such activities detracted from the funds available to the Navy for construction. Furthermore, to a far greater degree than the French, the Italians had to import costly raw materials and fuel for the construction and operation of their vessels. The inefficiency of the heavily protected Italian steel mills and shipyards, and the corruption that riddled those industries under the Fascist regime, added still more to the cost of Italian warships. Depending on circumstances, Italian-made steel cost two-and-a-half to four times more than that produced abroad. All this inhibited the ability of the Italian Navy Ministry to compete with its French counterpart in building warships. These factors help explain why the Italian Navy outspent the French Navy by about 11 per cent, but constructed or modernized only about 87 per cent of French naval tonnage in roughly the same period, 1922–39. However, given Italian national poverty, the Italian effort still remains impressive.[21]

The Washington naval treaty had granted the Italians future parity with the French in capital ships, but left both their navies free to engage in a naval building race in other warship categories. Considering their distinctly inferior position in 1922, the Italians made better use of the opportunities the treaty offered than did the French. By the time the two countries went to war in June 1940, the Italians had built a superior group of battleships and had pulled nearly even with the French with regard to lighter vessels. Admittedly, considering the ships both nations had under construction at the time, particularly the nearly complete French battleships *Richelieu* and *Jean Bart*, and the two French fleet aircraft carriers, the French Navy would have regained superiority over the *Regia Marina* by 1941. One of the reasons why Mussolini chose to enter the Second World War when he did was to take advantage of Italy's fleeting opportunities, especially those at sea.

Of course, except for some minor skirmishing between 10 and 22 June 1940, the Italian and French navies never engaged each other. In that sense, their diplomatic contest in Washington in 1921–22, their design of their warships to engage each others', and all their planning for an Italian–French naval war in the Mediterranean, stretching back to the late nineteenth century, proved superfluous. Instead, the *Regia Marina* found itself at war with the Royal Navy from 1940 to 1943, a contest for which it had not prepared, and not one for which it had much enthusiasm. Nonetheless, even in terms of its struggle with the Royal Navy in the Second World War, the Washington naval treaty had brought the *Regia Marina* a number of major benefits.[22]

The treaty required Britain to scrap 20 battleships of 408,500 tons, cancel the construction of four more displacing 180,000 tons, and eventually to limit itself to no more then 15 battleships and 135,000 tons of aircraft carriers. Italy was not required to scrap or cancel any warships, and was allowed to build battleships up to 33 per cent of the displacement, and aircraft carriers up to 44 per cent of the displacement, of those of Britain. Put simply, this created the preconditions for Mussolini's triumph in the Mediterranean crisis of 1935–36, and for the Axis domination of the central Mediterranean in 1941–42. In 1921, the Royal Navy possessed daunting numerical superiority over the *Regia Marina*. Even in late 1923, after the scrapping of its great battle fleet had begun, the Royal Navy was still able to overawe Mussolini's admirals in the Corfu crisis. By 1935, however, the Royal Navy had descended to the level where Mussolini could bluff the British Government into declining the risk of a naval confrontation. By late 1941, the Royal Navy found itself facing the real possibility of defeat by the Italian Navy, the Italian Air Force and the *Luftwaffe*.

Admittedly, the *Regia Marina* hardly took full advantage of the Washington naval treaty to prepare for a maritime struggle with the British Empire. Despite the clear warnings in 1923, 1935–36 and the Czech crisis of 1938 that Mussolini's policies made war with Britain a likelihood, the Italian naval leadership planned almost exclusively for battle fleet engagements with the French Navy. In particular, Mussolini and the naval leaders he favoured remained fascinated with battleships, heavy cruisers and submarines, rather than recognizing the great utility of aircraft carriers and the need for more escort vessels in case of a war of convoy battles with the Royal Navy.

Considering the ultimately disappointing results, the ingenuity and resources poured into the modernization of the four dreadnoughts of the *Cavour* and *Duilio* classes would have been far better spent on the construction of another modern battleship of the *Vittorio Veneto* class, and on hastening the completion of *Roma* and *Impero*, laid down in 1938. In that way, Italy could have entered the Second World War with three modern battleships, reinforced with two more in 1941. Better yet, the funds lavished on the reconstruction of Italy's old dreadnoughts could have been devoted to the building of three or four fleet aircraft carriers. However, it seems that, for reasons of prestige, numbers impressed Mussolini more than quality, and battleships struck him as more imposing threats than aircraft carriers. In fact, in the entire course of the war in the Mediterranean, Italian battleships employed their main batteries on only five occasions. Never once did an Italian battleship score a single hit with a main gun.

Italian concentration on the construction of submarines, rather than that of destroyers and destroyer escorts, indicated *Regia Marina* intentions to emulate the German Navy in the First World War. But flaws in Italian submarine designs and, more seriously, in the tactical and operational doctrine of the Italian underwater arm, severely limited its effectiveness until mid-1941. Thereafter, following the reconstruction of many boats and the rethinking of their employment, Italian submarines did score some notable successes, but whether in the Atlantic or in the Mediterranean, few Italian submarines matched the performance of the average German U-boat. More

Italian escorts, on the other hand, would have proved invaluable on the convoy runs to North Africa.[23]

However, these questions lead far away from the negotiations in Washington in 1921–22. The failure of Mussolini and his admirals to take full advantage of the treaty, and the use to which they put the Italian Navy in the Second World War, provide no justifiable criticisms of the work of Schanzer and Albertini. Acton deserves some blame, not only for his belligerent intentions at the conference, but for his second service period as Navy Chief of Staff, this time under Mussolini, from May 1925 to December 1927. Still, there is no denying that the Italian delegates to the Washington Conference gained a notable diplomatic triumph for their country. Unfortunately, despite the purposes for which the conference was convoked, the Italian victory ultimately served the cause of war, rather than that of peace and disarmament.

Institute for National Strategic Studies

NOTES

1. Giorgio Rochat and Giulio Massobrio, *Breve storia dell 'esercito italiano dal 1861 al 1943* (Turin, 1978), p. 68; Walter Wagner, 'Die K. (U.) K. Armee – Gliederung und Aufgabenstellung', in Adam Wandruszka and Peter Urbanitsch (eds.), *Die Hapsburgermonarchie 1848–1918*, Vol. 5, *Die bewaffnete Macht* (Vienna, 1987), p. 591; Fred T. Jane (ed.), *Fighting Ships* (2nd edn, London, 1914), pp. 292–9, 319–21; Siegfried Breyer, *Battleships and Battle Cruisers, 1905–1970* (Garden City, NY, 1973), pp. 411–12.
   The Austro-Hungarians had planned to lay down four super dreadnoughts in late 1914–early 1915, but cancelled these ships following their entry into the First World War.
2. *Fighting Ships*, pp. 255–61; Breyer, *Battleships and Battle Cruisers*, pp. 429–31; Paul Bairoch, 'Europe's Gross National Product: 1800–1975', *Journal of European Economic History*, 5 (1976), pp. 281, 283; T.A. Brassey (ed.), *The Naval Annual 1909* (London, 1909), p. 63; Viscount Hythe and John Leyland (eds.), *The Naval Annual 1914* (London, 1914), p. 83.
3. David Stevenson (ed.), *British Documents on Foreign Affairs: Reports and Papers from the Foreign Office Confidential Print. Part I: From the Mid-Nineteenth Century to the First World War*, Series F, *Europe, 1848–1914* (Bethesda, MD: 1987) [hereafter, BDFA, followed by volume and page numbers], Vol. 24, *Italy, 1875–1903*, p. 323; ibid., Vol. 25, *Italy, 1904–1914*, pp. 382, 475–7; Giorgio Giorgerini, 'The Cavour & Duilio Class Battleships', in John Roberts (ed.), *Warship*, vol. IV (Annapolis, 1980), pp. 269–70, 278; Antony Preston, *Battleships of World War I* (Harrisburg, 1972), p. 168; Mariano Gabriele, 'Origini della convenzione navale italo-austro-germanica del

1913', *Rassegna storica del Risorgimento*, July–Sept. and Oct–Dec. 1965; Giovanni Bernardi, *Il disarmo navale fra le due guerre mondiali (1919–1939)* (Rome, 1975), p. 44, n. 37.

Italian worries about the quality of their dreadnoughts in comparison to French battleships were largely groundless. But such perceptions proved important in shaping Italian naval policy, nonetheless.

4. Paul Halpern, *The Naval War in the Mediterranean, 1914–1918* (London, 1987), pp. 307–411, 426–567; Ezio Ferrante, *La grande guerra in Adriatico nel LXX anniversario della vittoria* (Rome, 1987), pp. 70–121; idem., *Il Grande Ammiraglio Paolo Thaon di Revel* (Rome, 1989), pp. 69–76; Harald Fock, *Fast Fighting Boats, 1870–1945. Their Design, Construction and Use* (Annapolis, 1978), pp. 47–8; Vittorio Tur, *Plancia ammiraglio*, vol. II (Rome, 1960), p. 343; Frank Freidel, *Franklin D. Roosevelt. The Apprenticeship* (Boston, 1952), pp. 362–4.

5. Christopher Seton-Watson, *Italy from Liberalism to Fascism 1870–1925* (London, 1967), pp. 506, 528–33, 553, 556, 578–80; Ferrante, *Il Grande Ammiraglio*, pp. 77–82; Walter Polastro, 'La marina militare italiana nel primo dopoguerra (1918–1925)', *Il Risorgimento*, No. 3, 1977, pp. 134–5, 141–6; Oscar Parkes and Maurice Prendergast (eds.), *Jane's Fighting Ships 1920* (London, 1920), p. 475; Preston, *Battleships of World War I*, p. 12; *Documents on British Foreign Policy* [hereafter DBFP, followed by series, volume and document number], First Series, Vol. I, No. 4; ibid., series 1, Vol. XXII, No. 698; Joel Blatt, 'The Parity that Meant Superiority: French Naval Policy towards Italy at the Washington Naval Conference, 1921–22, and Interwar French Foreign Policy', *French Historical Studies* (Fall 1981), pp. 224, 226–31; idem., 'France and Italy at the Paris Peace Conference', *The International History Review*, Feb. 1986, p. 30; idem., 'France and the Franco-Italian Entente, 1918–1923', *Storia delle relazioni internazionali*, 1990, No. 2, pp. 178–9.

6. Giovanni Engely, *The Politics of Naval Disarmament* (London, 1932), p. 4; Breyer, *Battleships and Battle Cruisers*, pp. 381, 428–29; National Archives, Record Group 38 (Chief of Naval Operations), Intelligence Division, Naval Attache Reports 1886–1939, O-11-b, box No. 1253, Register No. 4752, report of 11 Dec. 1915; ibid, Register No. 2794, report of 31 May 1920; Tur, *Plancia ammiraglio*, pp. 536–7; Polastro, 'La marina militare italiana', pp. 137–41; Giorgio Giorgerini and Augusto Nani, *Almanacco storico delle navi militari italiane* (Rome, 1978), p. 101; Oscar Parkes (ed.), *Jane's Fighting Ships 1922* (London, 1922), p. 212; Oscar Parkes and Francis E. McMurtrie (eds.), *Jane's Fighting Ships 1924* (London, 1924), pp. 184–6, 226, 228, 239; Fock, *Fast Fighting Boats*, pp. 43–6; William H. Garzke Jr and Robert O. Dulin Jr, *Battleships. Allied Battleships in World War II* (Annapolis, 1980), p. 33; Bernardi, *Il disarmo navale*, p. 32.

7. Polastro, 'La marina militare italiana', pp. 129–41; Lucio Ceva, *Le forze armate* (Turin, 1981), pp. 200–201; Ezio Ferrante, *Il pensiero strategico navale in Italia* (Rome, 1988), pp. 37–48; Ferruccio Botti and Virgilio Ilari, *Il pensiero militare italiano dal primo al secondo dopoguerra (1919–1949)* (Rome, 1985), pp. 139–41.

8. DBFP, First Series, Vol. IV, Nos. 4, 5, 6, 17, 127; ibid., Vol. V, No. 325; ibid., Vol. XIII, Nos. 66, 98, 313, 360; ibid., Vol. XVII, Nos. 69, 249, 532; ibid., Vol. XXII, No. 147; Breyer, *Battleships and Battle Cruisers*, pp. 116–74; Stephen Roskill, *Naval Policy Between the Wars. I: The Period of Anglo-American Antagonism 1919–1929* (London, 1968), pp. 215–27.

9. Giorgerini and Nani, *Almanacco storico*, p. 101; Bernardini, *Il disarmo navale*, pp. 38–49; idem., 'La dibattuta questione della parita navale tra Italia e Francia nel periodo tra le due guerre mondiali', *Revue Internationale d'Histoire Militaire*, No. 39 (1978), pp. 66–70.

10. Seton-Watson, *Italy from Liberalism to Fascism*, pp. 591–601; 'Wants Air Warfare

Taken Up at Parley', 12 Oct. 1921; 'Schanzer Quoted as Hinting at Modification of Article X', 24 Oct. 1921; 'Italy Ready to Back Cut in Armaments', 3 Nov. 1921; 'Who Sit at the Table', 6 Nov. 1921, sect. VIII; 'Italians Urgent for Action on Navy', 26 Nov. 1921; 'Armament Conferees Here', 28 Dec. 1921 (all *The New York Times*); *Papers Relating to the Foreign Relations of the United States* [hereafter, FRUS], 1921, Vol. I, pp. 81–2; FRUS, 1922, Vol. I, pp. 65–6; Matteo Pizzigallo, 'L'Italia alla conferanza di Washington (1921–1922)', part I, *Storia e politica*, July–Sept. 1975, p. 415; Ottavio Barié (ed.), Luigi Albertini, *Epistolario 1911–1926*, Vol. III, *Il dopoguerra* (Milan, 1968), pp. 1516–19; Carlo Schanzer, *Sulla Società delle Nazioni. Discorsi, studi e note* (Rome, 1925); National Archives, Record Group 59, Department of State 1910–29, box 5263, 500A4002/96; Piero Pieri and Giorgio Rochat, *Badoglio* (Turin, 1974), pp. 503–4; National Archives, RG (Record Group) 165 Military Intelligence Division, 2257-E-21/9, 'The Proposed Visit of General G [sic] Badoglio, Italian Chief of Staff'; 'Badoglio Stirs Hearers', 18 July 1921; 'Badoglio and His Mission', 31 July 1921, sect. VII; 'Badoglio for Disarming', 8 Aug 1921; 'War Chiefs Receive Capital's Homage', 24 Oct. 1921; 'Legion Pays Homage to Allied Leaders', 1 Nov. 1921; 'World Must Disarm Declares Gen. Diaz', 9 Dec. 1921; 'Diaz Ship Is Held for His Farewell', 11 Dec. 1921 (all *The New York Times*).

11. 'Italians Here for Arms Conference', 11 Nov. 1921; 'Italy Disappointed Over Army Decision', 24 Nov. 1921; 'Assails Briand's View', 24 Nov. 1921 (all *The New York Times*); Pizzigallo, 'L'Italia alla conferanza di Washington', I, pp. 410–11; Albertini, *Epistolario*, pp. 1519–20; Mark Sullivan, *The Great Adventure at Washington. The Story of the Conference* (Garden City, NY, 1922), pp. 29, 67–9; 67th Congress, 2nd Session, Senate, Document No. 126, *Conference on the Limitation of Armament* (Washington, 1922) [hereafter, *Conference*], pp. 46, 71–3; BDFA, Vol. 25, pp. 321–2; Gino Jori, 'I perchè e i limiti della nostra inferiorità nella seconda guerra mondiale', *Rivista marittima*, Feb. 1988, p. 111.

Despite the disappointment of the other Italian delegates, Albertini considered the French refusal to consider reducing their army an advantage for Italy. Albertini believed that the stronger the French were on the Rhine, the less the Italians would have to worry about their Brenner frontier.

12. Bernardi, *Il disarmo navale*, pp. 58–62, 69–73; idem., 'La dibattuta questione', pp. 72–73; 'Italy and France End Navy Dispute', 14 Nov. 1921, *New York Herald*; 'France and Italy Want Larger Fleets', 16 Nov. 1921; 'Turn Now to Fleets in Mediterranean', 21 Nov. 1921; 'Italians Urgent for Action on Navy', 26 Nov. 1921; 'Italy Agreeing', 30 Nov. 1921; 'Denies Urging Cut of Lesser Armies', 1 Dec. 1921 (all *The New York Times*); *Conference*, pp. 77–91; DBFP, First Series, Vol. XIV, Nos. 424, 442, 443, 448, 452, 517 ,p. 571; ibid., Vol. XV, No. 106, p. 764; A. Ernle M. Chatfield, *It Might Happen Again* (London, 1947), pp. 4–5; Mark Sullivan, *The Great Adventure at Washington*, p. 143; Pizzigallo, 'L'Italia alla conferanza di Washington', I, pp. 412–13, 417–27; Carlo Schanzer, *Il mondo fra la pace e la guerra* (Milan, 1932), pp. 258–9; Albertini, *Epistolario*, pp. 1535–6; Blatt, 'The Parity that Meant Superiority', pp. 236–7; Library of Congress, Theodore Roosevelt Jr papers, container 1, diary for 20 Oct. 1921 – 8 Dec. 1923 [hereafter, TRJP], pp. 5, 12, 37, 40, 44–5.

13. 'Italy Is Willing to Disarm Entirely', 15 Dec. 1921; 'French Ask Navy Ratio Above Japan's', 17 Dec. 1921; 'French Want 300,000 Tons of Light Ships', 22 Dec. 1921 (all *The New York Times*); TRJP, pp. 85, 87–8, 92, 96–7; Bernardi, *Il disarmo navale*, pp. 62–5, 73–9, 122–3; Pizzigallo, 'L'Italia alla conferanza di Washington', pp. 430–48; ibid., part II, *Storia e politica*, Oct. – Dec. 1975, pp. 576–81; Franco Bargoni and Franco Gay, *Orizzonte mare. Navi italiane nella 2a guerra mondiale. Corazzate*, Vol. 1, *Classe Conte di Cavour* (Rome, 1972), pp. 19, 41–2; William H. Garzke Jr and Robert O. Dulin Jr, *Battleships. Axis and Neutral Battleships in World War II*

(Annapolis, 1985), pp. 373–9; DBFP First Series, Vol. XIV, Nos. 474, 483; FRUS 1922, Vol. I, pp. 121–2, 126–7; National Archives, Record Group 80, General Board, Disarmament Conferences, Series I, box 6, 'Action of the General Board of the Navy in Connection with Conference on Limitation of Armament, 1921–1922', Vol. I, G.B. No. 438, p. 12 (quotes); Yamato Ichihashi, *The Washington Conference and After* (Stanford University, CA; 1928), pp. 60–72, 94; Harold and Margaret Sprout, *Toward a New Order of Sea Power. American Naval Policy and the World Scene, 1918–1922* (Princeton, 1943), pp. 181–9; Arnold J. Toynbee, *Survey of International Affairs 1920–1923* (London, 1925), p. 495 n. 2; Donald S. Birn, 'The Washington Naval Conference of 1921–22 in Anglo-French Relations', in Daniel M. Masterson, (ed.), *Naval History, the Sixth Symposium of the US Naval Academy* (Wilmington, DEL; 1987), pp. 173–5; Ronald Chalmers Hood III, *Royal Republicans. The French Naval Dynasties Between the World Wars* (Baton Rouge, 1985), pp. 120–21; Schanzer, *Il mondo fra la pace e la guerra*, p. 262; Albertini, *Epistolario*, p. 1534–6.

14. 'French Want 300,000 Tons of Light Ships', 22 Dec. 1921; 'Doubt Agreement in This Conference on Submarine Cut', 26 Dec. 1921 (both *The New York Times*); DBFP, First Series, Vol. XIV, Nos. 443, 546; TRJP, p. 101, 125; Pizzigallo, 'L'Italia alla conferanza di Washington', II, pp. 550–74; Bernardi, *Il disarmo navale*, pp. 82–92, 94–111; Raymond Leslie Buell, *The Washington Conference* (New York, 1922), pp. 225–6; Ichihashi, *The Washington Conference and After*, pp. 72–82; Sprout and Sprout, *Toward a New Order of Sea Power*, pp. 190–208; Mark Sullivan, *The Great Adventure in Washington*, p. 171; Engely, *The Politics of Naval Disarmament*, p. 7; Albertini, *Epistolario*, pp. 1540–41.

15. Sprout and Sprout, *Toward a New Order of Sea Power*, pp. 208–16; Roskill, *Naval Policy Between the Wars*, pp. 325–6; Giorgerini and Nani, *Almanacco storico*, pp. 255–6, 264; Franco Gay, *Orizzonte mare. Navi italiane nella 2a guerra mondiale*, Vol. 4, *Incrociatori pesanti. Classe Trento*, part 1 (Rome, 1975), pp. 7–9.

16. James J. Sadkovich, 'Aircraft Carriers and the Mediterranean, 1940–1943: Rethinking the Obvious', *Aerospace Historian*, Dec. 1987, p. 265; Bernardi, *Il disarmo navale*, pp. 79–82; *Conference*, pp. 356–60; Sprout and Sprout, *Toward a New Order of Sea Power*, pp. 219–23, 231–5; Ichihashi, *The Washington Conference and After*, pp. 96–9.

17. Seton Watson, *Italy from Liberalism to Fascism*, pp. 601–4; Schanzer, *Il mondo fra la pace e la guerra*, p. 263; 'Ambassador Ricci Receives Cross', 12 March 1922; 'Schanzer Gives Treaty Data', 17 March 1922; 'Arms Treaties Win in Italian Chamber', 7 Feb. 1923; 'Mussolini Speeds Treaty Acceptance', 17 Feb. 1923 (all *New York Times*); Bernardi, *Il disarmo navale*, pp. 130–34; Pizzigallo, 'L'Italia alla conferanza di Washington', part II, pp. 583–9.

18. Blatt, 'The Parity that Meant Superiority', pp. 228–31, 237–42; Quincy Wright, *A Study of War*, second edition (Chicago, 1965), pp. 670–71.

19. Jean Labayle Couhat, *French Warships of World War II* (London, 1971); Aldo Fraccaroli, *Italian Warships of World War II* (London, 1968).

20. *Combined Annual Reports of the World War Foreign Debt Commission* (Washington, 1927), pp. 222–8; Shepard B. Clough, *The Economic History of Italy* (New York, 1964), pp. 227–8.

21. Istituto Centrale di Statistico del Regno d'Italia, *Annuario statistico italiano* (Rome, 1926–42), passim.; Robert Frankenstein, 'A propos des aspects financiers du réarmement français (1935–1939)', *Revue d'histoire de la deuxième guerre mondiale*, April 1976, tables 1, 2; Alfred Sauvy, *Histoire économique de la France entre les deux guerres*, Vol. I (Paris, 1965), p. 516; Herbert Hoover Presidential Library, William R. Castle papers, 'Belgium 1923–25' [*sic*], box 1, Dominian to Castle, 15 Jan. 1924; Lucio Ceva and Andrea Curami, *Industria bellica anni trenta. Commesse militari,*

L'Ansaldo ed altri (Milan, 1992); Lucio Ceva, 'Grande industria e guerra', in Romain H. Rainero and A. Biagini (eds.), *L'Italia in guerra: Il primo anno – 1940* (Rome, 1991), pp. 48–50.

The conversions of lira and franc amounts into dollar equivalents are based on yearly averages of noon buying rates for cable transfers in New York City, provided by the Federal Reserve Board, as contained in *The World Almanac and Book of Facts for 1930* (New York, 1930), p. 300; ibid., *1942*, p. 515.

22. Blatt, 'The Parity that Meant Superiority', pp. 244–7; Paul Auphan and Jacques Mordal, *The French Navy in World War II* (Annapolis, 1959), pp. 14–15, 96–103; Breyer, *Battleships and Battle Cruisers*, pp. 369, 376–80, 415, 419, 422–3, 435; Brian R. Sullivan, 'A Fleet in Being: The Rise and Fall of Italian Sea Power, 1861–1943', *The International History Review*, Feb. 1988, pp. 116–21; idem., 'The Impatient Cat. Assessments of Military Power in Fascist Italy, 1936–1940', in Williamson Murray and Allan R. Millett (eds.), *Calculations. Net Assessment and the Coming of World War II* (New York, 1992), pp. 120–35.

In June 1940, the French Navy possessed two new battle cruisers of the *Dunkerque* class, two partially modernized dreadnoughts of the *Courbet* class and three partially modernized dreadnoughts of the *Provence* class. The Italian Navy had the two recently completed battleships of the *Vittorio Veneto* class and the two completely rebuilt dreadnoughts of the *Cavour* class. Two more rebuilt dreadnoughts of the *Duilio* class were about to rejoin the fleet.

The two modern Italian battleships outclassed any French capital ships in service in the spring of 1940. Considering their armament, protection and speed, the rebuilt *Cavours* and *Duilios* were slightly inferior to the French battle cruisers, slightly superior to the three *Provence* class battleships, and clearly superior to the two *Courbets*.

23. Roskill, *Naval Policy Between the Wars*, p. 331; Ezio Ferrante, 'Un rischio calcolato? Mussolini e gli ammiragli nella gestione della crisi di Corfu', *Storia delle relazioni internazionali*, no. 2, 1989; Emilia Chiavarelli, *L'opera della marina nella guerra italo-etiopica* (Milan, 1969), pp. 76–97, 144–53; Brian R. Sullivan, 'A Fleet in Being', pp. 123–4; Franco and Valerio Gay, *The Cruiser Bartolomeo Colleoni* (Annapolis, 1987), p. 6; Giorgerini and Nani, *Almanacco storico*, pp. 106, 108, 110, 213, 216–18, 399, 484–5; Franco Bargoni and Franco Gay, *Orizzonte mare. Navi italiane nella 2a guerra mondiale. Corazzate*, vol. 2, *Classe Caio Duilio* (Rome, 1972), pp. 52–3; Erminio Bagnasco and Mark Grossman, *Italian Battleships of World War Two* (Missoula, Mont.; 1986), pp. 22–3; Lucio Ceva, 'L'evoluzione dei materiale bellici in Italia', in Ennio Di Nolfo, Romain H. Rainero and Brunello Vigezzi (eds.), *L'Italia e la politica di potenza in Europa (1938–1940)* (Milan, 1985), p. 389–90; Romeo Bernotti, 'Italian Naval Policy Under Fascism', *United States Naval Institute Proceedings*, July 1956; Erminio Bagnasco, *Submarines of World War Two* (London, 1977), pp. 130–36.

In fairness to the Italian submarine arm in the Second World War, it should be pointed out that the two top-scoring Italian submarines matched or surpassed the records of the two best American submarines in sinking enemy ship tonnage. Operating in the Atlantic and Indian Oceans, *Leonardo da Vinci* sank at least 110,231 tons, possibly 116,686 tons; *Enrico Tazzoli* sank 96,650 tons in the Atlantic. USS *Flasher* sank 110,231 tons; USS *Rasher* sank 99,901 tons. Yet, under admittedly difficult conditions, Italian submarines destroyed only 123,263 tons of enemy shipping in the Mediterranean between June 1940 and September 1943. From when they began operating in the Mediterranean in October 1941 until the armistice of September 1943, German U-boats sank 469,474 tons. Even after the armistice, when they operated under far more difficult circumstances, until the end of their cruises in May 1944, German submarines sank an additional 130,784 tons in the Mediterranean. In the

Mediterranean alone, five German U-boats managed to destroy 40,000 tons or more of enemy shipping; one, U-371, under Waldemar Mehl, sank an extraordinary 62,213 tons between January 1943 and March 1944.

Jürgen Rohwer, *Axis Submarine Successes 1939–1945* (Annapolis, 1983), passim.; Theodore Roscoe, *United States Submarine Operations in World War II* (Annapolis, 1949), p. 525; Paolo M. Pollina and Aldo Cocchia, *I sommergibili italiani, 1895–1962* (Rome, 1963), pp. 232, 256–7.

China's Place in the New Pacific Order

DAVID ARMSTRONG

Like any major international conference of its kind, the Washington Conference was required to satisfy the numerous special interests of the powers attending it, and at the same time to devise an overall set of arrangements that would provide for some measure of international order in the longer term. It came remarkably close to realizing both of these major objectives. Its ultimate failure has been attributed to many factors, but of fundamental importance was its failure to deal adequately with the problem of China. In the 1920s and 1930s, this problem had two principal and interrelated aspects: the dynamics of internal developments in China and China's continuing ability to arouse contention and rivalry among the major powers. The Washington Conference attempted to tackle both aspects, but with only limited and temporary success at best. Its failure in this respect helped to ensure that what appeared to be solid and far-reaching achievements elsewhere would come under strain when China's underlying vulnerability helped to weaken the entire structure of order that the Washington Conference had tried to build.

The emphasis given here to China requires some preliminary explanation, since the China issue is sometimes seen as peripheral to the main business of the Conference, being added to the agenda as an afterthought and to appease American public opinion. In fact the Conference records devote 353 pages to the proceedings of the Committee on Pacific and Far Eastern Questions, which dealt with China, as against only 215 pages for the Committee on Limitation of Armaments.[1] However, this fact, while suggestive, is not in itself sufficient to demonstrate the centrality of the China question to the prospects for success of the Washington Conference system as a whole. For this it is necessary to assess the place of the decisions relating to China in the overall Washington settlement.

The purpose of the Four-Power and Five-Power Treaties agreed in Washington was to construct a balance of power in the Pacific such that all signatories could feel reasonably satisfied that their interests had been safeguarded. These interests were complex, especially in the case of Britain. Britain was not so much a satisfied power as a satiated one. Her world-wide territorial, financial and commercial interests remained far greater than those of any of her competitors, while her navy was still greater than that of her nearest rival, the United States, by a significant margin. However, her capacity to defend those interests had been severely overstretched during the first two decades of the twentieth century, while her ability to maintain her margin of naval superiority for more than a few more years was very much open to question. Negotiating the Anglo-Japanese Alliance in 1902 had been an implicit acknowledgement of Britain's inability to rely purely upon her own resources to defend her world-wide interests but by 1921 Britain faced strong pressure from the United States, Canada and China to abandon the Alliance. Equally strong pressure to retain it came from two other Dominions, Australia and New Zealand and from some members of the Foreign Office.[2] Lord Curzon argued at the Imperial Conference of 1921 that the Alliance had enabled Britain to 'exercise a very powerful controlling influence on the sometimes dangerous ambitions of Japan'.[3] While this was certainly a far too flattering estimate of British influence over Japan, it did draw attention to the fact that the Alliance was not intended simply to establish a stable balance of power in the Far East but to provide some underpinning for the open-door principles of Chinese territorial and administrative integrity. In this regard, a more realistic appraisal than Curzon's came a year earlier from Victor Wellesley, an Assistant Secretary in the Foreign Office:

> The Alliance has notoriously failed, as far as the activities of Japan herself are concerned to 'preserve the common interests of all the Powers in China' . . . The policy of Japan has shown itself to be one of peaceful penetration not less thorough and certainly more ruthless, more brutal and more insidious than that employed by Germany all the world over before the war, having for its ultimate aim a complete Japanese hegemony over China.[4]

More sympathetic observers were aware of the economic and population pressures inside Japan which, denied outlets in North America and Australasia, focused inevitably upon China for their relief. However, the central point was that, whatever strategic arrangements might be agreed at Washington, unless the underlying political sources of instability were addressed there could be little prospect of long-term peace in the region.

Recognition of this ran through British discussions prior to the Conference. The essential problem was that for more than ten years all internal order had disappeared in China and there was no central authority with whom any meaningful negotiations could take place. Amongst other consequences, this meant that all of the powers, not just Japan, were obliged to rely upon their own resources to defend their interests in China, while China's impotence made it all the more likely that Japan would at some point be tempted to take decisive action to seize by force the dominant position in China that she had earlier set out in the infamous Twenty One Demands. As the Foreign Office acknowledged in a general survey of Far Eastern affairs just before the Conference opened,

> It is the weakness of China as much as the aggressive policy of Japan which is the constant source of danger in the Far East. The jealousies and rivalries to which it gives rise constitute the really disturbing element in the situation, for they make China a cockpit of international strife.[5]

There was, however, a bleak assessment from the General Staff of the ability of British forces in the Far East to defend Britain's interests in China in the event of an anti-foreign uprising there: 'Our military strength in China bears no relation to the possible strain which might be put on it by an outbreak against foreign action in that country'.[6]

This meant that Britain would only be able to act alongside the military forces of other major powers 'even though our prestige may be temporarily lessened thereby'.[7]

The logical conclusion towards which such an analysis of the Chinese situation was inexorably leading was clear enough, and was spelled out in a report by the Foreign Office Committee on the Anglo-Japanese Alliance early in 1921:

> In the last analysis the independence and integrity of China, which is among our foremost aims, depends upon the reality or otherwise of the open door policy. That is the crux of the whole situation. All forms of economic penetration are opposed to that principle, for they ultimately lead to the closing of the door and the usurpation of political control. Experience has shown us that neither military nor naval force, nor any treaty formula can, in themselves, be regarded as a sufficient safeguard against that insidious method of political encroachment. Salvation must, therefore, be sought elsewhere. In our opinion the best safeguard against a danger which lies as much in the weakness of China as in the aggressive tendencies of Japan, is to be found in a constructive policy for the rehabilitation of China . . . We would, however, repeat that in our opinion it would be hopeless to embark upon such a policy singlehanded, or without adequate naval support. Japan could thwart us at every turn. The war has left us too exhausted to cope with so great a problem. To succeed in such an effort we believe the cooperation of the United States to be indispensable.[8]

So, the key to long-term stability in the Far East was the rehabilitation of China; Britain was too weak to promote this on her own; the Anglo-Japanese Alliance would not serve as the basis for a collaborative approach to this end; therefore the support of the United States was essential. Not all agreed with this assessment of the situation – indeed a lengthy and sometimes acrimonious debate was to take place before ending the Alliance became official British policy – but with hindsight the termination of the Alliance seemed inevitable. The problem was that the new policy rested heavily on two imponderables. First, it was far from clear that the United States would be willing to play the part envisaged by Britain. Secondly, and even more difficult, to agree to the principle of the administrative integrity of China was one thing; to implement the same principle was quite another matter. Even assuming that a single Chinese government with authority to speak for the whole country could be discovered, the question of the administrative integrity (or full sovereignty) of China embraced a vast range of complex sub-issues, as outlined in a somewhat acerbic memorandum from Curzon:

> How can Chinese authority be re-established without disbanding the 800,000 armed men who batten upon the country, and who is to undertake this task? How can privileges be accorded or restored unless there be a stable Chinese Government to exercise them? Will administrative independence be held to be consistent with foreign post offices and foreign garrisons? When we come to Shantung, we embark upon a whole field of embittered controversy, involving questions of ports, railways, customs, gendarmerie, economic rights and privileges and so on. When we deal with leased or ceded territories we are brought up against the thorny problems of Kwantung Peninsula (Dairen), Kiaochow (Tsingtao), Wei-hai-wei, Kwangchow Wan and Kowloon. When we deal with 'spheres of interest or influence' we have to enquire into the still undefined meaning of the Lansing-Ishii Agreement of November 1917 . . .
>
> Further, while these subjects are under examination, is it to be believed that the Powers in Conference assembled will be able to shut out all discussion upon the points that will inevitably arise out of them, viz. fiscal autonomy for China, the extra-territorial system, foreign settlements, financial reform, railway unification? It will not be easy to rebuild China in sections or compartments or to leave her partially free and partially in chains.[9]

The task of devising specific proposals to give substance to the broad principles of British policy fell to Arthur Balfour, leader of the British negotiating team at the Washington Conference. His declared aim was to substitute a 'system of international cooperation for the international rivalry in China which has in the past produced such unhappy results in that country'.[10] To this end he drew up a draft treaty which, after acknowledging the open-door principles, committed the major powers and China to consult with each other whenever these principles were endangered and before taking independent military action or entering into arrangements involving financial liability with the Chinese authorities. This draft treaty embodied ideas that had been under discussion in the Foreign Office since 1919.[11] It was somewhat more specific in its stipulations than the eventual Nine-Power Treaty on China, but in any case it was preempted by Chinese and American statements of principle (considered shortly) which formed the basis of the discussions on the China question.

If Britain's policy towards China was complicated by her declining power, the conflicting interests of the Dominions and the impossibility of reconciling American and Japanese wishes on the issue of the renewal of the Anglo-Japanese Alliance, the objectives of the United States and Japan on the eve of the Conference were clearer and less troubled by contradictory pressures. They were, however, still ultimately dependent for their realization upon a satisfactory resolution of the China question. In the case of the United States, there were a number of specific issues causing friction with Japan, including immigration and a dispute over cable rights on the island of Yap. The American delegation also had to keep one eye on the Senate's reaction to anything that it might interpret as an 'entangling alliance', given the recent debacle over the Versailles Treaty.[12] The central American aims were clear enough though: to prevent a costly arms race and to promote a more favourable overall balance of power in the Pacific by encouraging the ending of the Anglo-Japanese Alliance. Other aims were secondary to these. The Four-Power Treaty, by which the United States, Britain, Japan and France agreed to respect each other's 'insular possessions and insular dominions' in the Pacific and to consult in the event of a threat from another power or a crisis amongst themselves was, in essence, the necessary price that had to be paid to Japan for the ending of the Anglo-Japanese Alliance. In the case of the Nine-Power Treaty, although in one sense this represented a triumph for long-standing American principles relating to China, since it was the first time that these principles were enshrined in treaty form, the triumph was a strictly limited one as the treaty lacked any kind of enforcement mechanism and its provisions fell considerably short of Chinese requests. A major reason for this was that the United States – the loudest devotee of China's interests – was in practice unwilling to entertain any commitment that would jeopardize the more important American objective of avoiding foreign entanglements. In any case, the American economic stake in China was less than it was in Japan and the United States, like all the powers, was well aware that the term 'China', while having a certain sentimental resonance with American public opinion, could not translate into a clearly defined sovereign authority exercising unambiguous control over a determinate territory. The American delegation was also aware of the power struggle in Japan between those advocating a more liberal and conciliatory foreign policy and the right-wing advocates of expansionism. If Japan were pushed too hard over its position in China, this might only serve to tilt the balance in favour of the militarists. Since the United States was not prepared to support its open-door principles by force, there was little point in pressing for a less anodyne Nine-Power Treaty.

Japan, needless to say, would have preferred the China question not to be discussed at all at the Conference. Given Anglo-American determination that China should be on the Conference agenda, Japan only had two realistic choices: to stand firm and make no concessions whatsoever or to yield some ground while defending the most important Japanese interests. That the latter option was selected was due, essentially, to four factors. First, the Chinese people had demonstrated through their boycott of Japanese goods following the Versailles grant of Shantung to Japan that they were not entirely powerless: indeed they possessed the means to inflict significant economic damage upon Japan at a time when the Japanese economy was feeling the pinch of the collapse of the wartime boom. Secondly, the leader of the Japanese delegation, Shidehara, was the most prominent representative of the school of thought in Japan that believed that traditional imperialism was no longer the most productive means for Japan to achieve her objectives. In Shidehara's view, Japan stood to gain more from trade and overseas investment than from territorial acquisition and this entailed a more liberal and conciliatory international posture, particularly towards the United States, with whom Japanese trade was growing faster than the trade of either country with China. Thirdly, although Japan did make several genuine concessions relating to China at the Conference, there is considerable evidence that the Japanese believed that what they had agreed to in respect of their most important Chinese interests amounted to little

more than a change in the form of words used to define the position
of the major powers in China.[13] Expressions such as 'spheres of
influence' might be abandoned but the underlying reality had not
altered. Finally, Japan, like the United States, was primarily interested
in the issue of the strategic balance in the Pacific. Intransigence over
China might jeopardize what were seen as more important strategic
gains, such as the Pacific fortifications agreement, which gave Japan
effective hegemony over a significant area of the Pacific.

The reluctance of the major powers to confront the China question
in anything more than a superficial way was apparent at an early
stage of the deliberations of the Committee on Pacific and Far Eastern
questions. At its first meeting on 16 November, Mr Sze, the leader of
the Chinese delegation, set out ten principles which he believed
should guide the discussion. He acknowledged the difficult political
situation in China but argued that this could be eased if China could
be freed from the threat of foreign aggression and relieved of externally imposed constraints on her administrative autonomy and ability
to collect revenue. While some of Sze's ten principles were of sufficient generality not to trouble any of the major powers – such as
agreements to respect China's independence and territorial integrity
and to provide for the peaceful settlement of international disputes in
the Far East – others were clearly more problematical. This was
particularly the case of the third, fifth and sixth principles, which read
in part:

> 3 . . . the Powers agree not to conclude between themselves any
> treaty or agreement directly affecting China or the general peace
> in these regions without previously notifying China and giving
> her an opportunity to participate.
> 5. Immediately, or as soon as circumstances will permit, existing
> limitations upon China's political, jurisdictional and adminis-
> trative freedom of action are to be removed.
> 6. Reasonable, definite terms of duration are to be attached to
> China's present commitments which are without time limits.[14]

The third principle was, from the Chinese perspective, merely an
attempt to assert China's dignity as a sovereign state but for the
powers it went to the heart of their reluctance to deal with China on
terms of equality, which derived from the fact that China's internal

anarchy made it difficult to accept any government as the true sovereign authority in China. The Japanese, French and American responses to the ten principles all hinted at this problem, albeit in different ways. Admiral Kato, while asserting that Japan was 'entirely uninfluenced' by considerations of territorial aggrandizement, offered the caustic suggestion that China's chaotic domestic situation was as much the cause of her difficulties as her foreign relations.[15] M. Briand was the only one to ask openly, if somewhat mischievously, what exactly was meant by the expression 'China' – what, in particular, were its territorial boundaries.[16] This produced an immediate impasse since the American delegate, Mr Root, accepted that not all of the territory claimed by the Chinese Government should necessarily be considered part of 'China proper', to which Mr Koo objected on behalf of the Chinese delegation that China's territory was defined by its constitution and the Chinese delegation could not even discuss any question which might give the impression of attempting to modify China's territorial boundaries.[17]

The American response was to seek to base discussions on a far more anodyne set of four principles enunciated by Mr Root. These stated the 'firm intention' of the powers:

> 1. To respect the sovereignty, the independence, and the territorial and administrative integrity of China.
> 2. To provide the fullest and most unembarrassed opportunity to China to develop and maintain for herself an effective and stable government . . .
> 3. To safeguard for the world so far as it is within our power, the principle of equal opportunity for the commerce and industry of all nations throughout the territory of China.
> 4. To refrain from taking advantage of the present conditions in order to seek special rights or privileges which would abridge the rights of the subjects or citizens of friendly states, and from countenancing action inimical to the security of such states.[18]

It should be noted that the fourth of these principles repeated verbatim part of the wording of the Lansing–Ishii agreement of 1917, which Japan had always interpreted as giving American recognition to its special interests in China. Although the careful ambiguity of this phrase meant that it was also open to an American interpretation that saw it as constraining Japan, its repetition by Root was inevitably liable to be taken by the Japanese as a tacit signal of reassurance from the United States.[19] Such an interpretation was confirmed, to Japanese satisfaction at least, when their delegation asked Root if the reference to China's 'administrative integrity' was intended to affect the existing privileges of the powers and was informed that it did not.[20]

On 22 November Mr Sze was asked to elaborate upon the specific issues that lay behind his ten points. More than ten months of detailed negotiation followed, including a separate discussion over Shantung between Japan and China. Long-standing Chinese complaints over tariffs, extraterritoriality, the presence of foreign troops, foreign control over post offices, railways and radio stations, territories leased or otherwise occupied by foreigners, and the consequences of Japan's infamous Twenty One Demands took up the remaining discussion in the main committee. Much of this debate was concerned with the minutiae of the major powers' interests in China and, for the most part, does not merit detailed consideration here. However, it is worthwhile briefly to outline some of the main points of contention since they illustrate the complexity of the issues confronting the nine delegations.

One of the most vital questions for China where realistic prospects of progress existed (as opposed to issues like the Japanese presence in Manchuria) concerned China's demand for greater tariff autonomy. Prior to 1842, China had enjoyed the normal sovereign right of fixing whatever tariffs she felt appropriate on foreign imports. After the Opium War, however, 'unequal treaties' with Britain, France and the United States had restricted China to a maximum tariff of five per cent. By the beginning of the twentieth century, the effective rate had fallen to 3.5 per cent, much of which had to go towards the repayment of numerous foreign loans and the Boxer indemnity, thus reducing still further the amount available to the Government. As Wellington Koo, who presented the Chinese case on this issue, pointed out, China had to pay the full rate – which could be as high as 300 per cent on its exports to the Western powers.[21] An additional disadvantage was that a uniform rate did not permit China to discriminate against products it regarded as undesirable, such as cigarettes or alcohol, or in favour of needed goods, such as machinery. Koo did not propose complete autonomy, merely that the maximum rate should be raised to 12.5 per cent. In the event, a separate treaty was negotiated on tariffs, but one that fell far short of Chinese hopes, as Koo pointed out, arguing that, although the tariff question was 'intimately connected with the well-being of the Chinese State, the interests of the Treaty Powers appear to be placed at times before the legitimate interests of China'.[22] In fact, this was not entirely correct. The United States had been prepared to consider tariff autonomy but was reluctant to agree to measures that would give the Chinese Government additional revenue which, at a time of civil war, might be spent mainly on more armaments.[23] The inescapable linkage between China's internal chaos and the prospects for ending the international constraints upon China was amply demonstrated in 1926, when the conference held in that year to work out a final resolution of the tariff issue had to be abandoned because of a change of government in China.[24]

Essentially the same pattern recurred throughout the discussion of the questions raised by the Chinese delegation. For instance, when the Chinese issued the opening statement in the debate on extraterritoriality – the freedom of foreigners from the jurisdiction of Chinese courts – they did so from a perspective that closely resembled their arguments over tariffs. Extraterritoriality, they declared, reasonably enough, was a derogation of China's sovereign rights and was regarded by the Chinese people as a national humiliation. It also created numerous practical difficulties: foreigners were able to claim immunity from local taxes, the same locality might contain several distinct courts, and the status of the law was uncertain.[25] However Balfour's response clearly implied that while the powers were still unable to trust the law in China – or at least its administration – little progress could be expected on this matter.[26] In the event the delegates agreed to set up a commission to investigate the current practice of extraterritoriality. This did not meet until 1926. Although it recommended the eventual abolition of extraterritoriality, the main thrust of its report was to call for extensive reform of the Chinese legal system.[27] In particular, it recommended that extensive measures should be taken to uphold the principle of the independence of the judiciary, especially from the armed forces.

The same issue of the powers' mistrust of China's ability to perform the duties that accompanied the sovereign rights she so desired ran though the discussions of even the most detailed aspects of the Chinese proposals. For example, the major powers all operated their own postal services in China, which deprived the Government of much needed revenue, as Mr Sze pointed out in calling for the foreign post offices to be closed down.[28] In this instance the powers accepted the Chinese case but agreed to close down their post offices only on condition that China could demonstrate its capacity for efficient administration in this regard and that the French Director General of the Chinese postal service was retained. On more sensitive matters, the Chinese made little progress, especially where Japanese interests were concerned. On several occasions between 28 November and 3 December the Chinese raised the two most fundamental issues involving violations of Chinese sovereignty: the maintenance of foreign troops and police in various parts of China, especially in Manchuria, and the retention by the powers of numerous territories leased under various 'unequal treaties' of the nineteenth century. The Japanese responded to the raising of the former question at first by delaying tactics, arguing that prior notice should be given for such 'complicated proposals' as the Chinese were advancing.[29] After the Chinese delegation had circulated documents detailing its case in relation to Manchuria and other parts of China, the Japanese expressed their strong opposition to the Chinese arguments, while simultaneously claiming to be willing to withdraw from North China 'as soon as the actual conditions warrant it'.[30] For the present, however, they stood by their fundamental contention that the state of affairs in China justified the retention of foreign troops, offering in support of this assertion detailed accounts of lawlessness in Manchuria and elsewhere, including numerous attacks on Japanese citizens.[31]

Wellington Koo's raising of the question of the leased territories on 3 December provoked a more general irritation, particularly from the British, who had even less intention of relinquishing their Hong Kong territory than the Japanese had of withdrawing from Manchuria. However, Balfour urged London to consider the possibility of conceding another British leased territory, Weihaiwei, in order to defuse Chinese criticisms and encourage Japan to be equally conciliatory over Shantung.[32] Weihaiwei, he argued, was, in any case, virtually useless, a view that was strongly disputed by Winston Churchill at the Colonial Office and other diehard British imperialists.[33] Once again the issue of China's internal chaos intruded. As Curzon cabled Balfour on 24 November, giving the Cabinet response to his proposals,

> To hand back any territory to a government that is devoid of any authority and is all but bankrupt would appear to be an act of pointless generosity. It would be much better to wait till China has put her house in order before conferring such favours, and to be certain that we obtain something that will contribute to general solution in return.[34]

Balfour had by this point had time to acquire some sympathy for the Chinese position and also to perceive that, unless significant progress were made in the direction of a stable and sovereign China, the prospects for constructing an enduring Far Eastern order were limited, if not nonexistent. He made his feelings clear in a remarkable cable to Curzon on 27 November. He began by deriding the notion that Weihaiwei possessed any value for Britain. 'To cling to our treaty rights in a narrow spirit', he asserted, would be a 'profound mistake even from the point of view of our material interests'.[35] Conceding Weihaiwei would cost Britain nothing but would help to soften the blow for Japan in giving up her rights in Shantung, where Japan had already spent millions. The heart of his argument is worth quoting in full:

> To hand back territory to bankrupt China may, as you say, appear to be an act of pointless generosity, but it is in reality an act which will be warmly appreciated by the Chinese people and it is to them and not to the government which can no longer claim their allegiance that we have, in the interests of our trade and general relations, to look for recognition.
>
> Feeling here is that there can be no permanent peace in the Far East as long as China remains in her present disintegrated condition. State into which she has fallen is not thought to be entirely her own fault but to be due, in part at least, to the unfair treatment she has received at the hands of the powers in the past, and there seems to be a consensus of opinion which, I am glad to note, is shared by the Japanese, that we should all do our best at the cost of mutual sacrifices to help her to put her house in order by dropping, as far as possible, spheres of influence and

other restrictions upon her territorial and administrative integrity which have hampered her freedom of action and retarded
her development in the past. The only return we can expect from
China is the goodwill of the Chinese people, which, as Japan has
realised, is far more valuable to a trading nation than territorial
expansion producing resentment and commercial boycotts.[36]

In the event Weihaiwei was not returned until 1930.

If the powers were unwilling to grant China full sovereign rights,
they were somewhat readier to cite international law and sovereignty
in support of their own interests in China. When Wellington Koo
called for the rescinding of the 1915 treaties that had been forced
upon China in the aftermath of the Twenty One Demands, Shidehara
countered with the argument that if rights 'solemnly granted by
treaty' could be revoked on the grounds put forward by the Chinese,
this would establish 'an exceedingly dangerous precedent'.[37] The
Chinese response to this, to the effect that an even more dangerous
precedent would be established if it were accepted that a power could
obtain concessions from a weaker state in the way that Japan had in
1915 won little support, although Japan did retreat from the more
extreme of its Twenty One Demands.

Similarly the third of China's ten principles, urging the powers not
to sign agreements that concerned her without consulting Peking,
provoked a robust defence from several powers of their sovereign
right to reach any agreement they wished.[38] In the end the powers
would only accept a weak resolution proposed by the American
delegation in which all agreed not to enter into any treaty, agreement,
arrangement or understanding that would infringe or impair the four
Root principles.

It is clear from this brief outline that the constant spectre at the
Washington feast was the internal situation of China. This deteriorated even during the three months of the conference, causing serious
dissension to come to the surface among the Chinese delegation, the
consequences of which were noted in a cable dated 7 December from
the American Secretary of State, Hughes, to the American Minister in
China:

> Internal differences which have arisen within the Chinese dele-
> gation cause grave concern to the friends of China. During the

earlier part of the Conference their reasonable attitude had aroused the admiration of the public and of other delegations but a regrettable change has become manifest. Partly doubtless as a result of pressure from home and possibly through bad advice based on lack of knowledge of the full facts, certain members of the delegation have taken the attitude that no accommodation or compromise can be considered even in unimportant matters.[39]

The British view was even bleaker since the Chinese delegation as a whole was seen as representative of a government in Peking that was itself little more than a charade, 'a group of persons who call themselves a government but who have long ceased to function as such in the Western sense of the term', in the words of the British ambassador to China.[40] His opinion, just before the Conference began, was that the likely emphasis on such matters as China's sovereign rights and prestige that would dominate the arguments of Wellington Koo and others was not just misleading but positively harmful to China's true interests. What China really needed, in his view, was a delegation that would tell the truth about China's situation in the hope of persuading the Western powers to involve themselves even more fully in China's internal affairs, not to concentrate on urging a reduction of the foreign presence there. In his words

> A delegation representative of China's interests as a whole could be relied on to present such a picture of China in a light which would be almost certain to appeal to Anglo-Saxon sympathies and to elicit support and protection in no small measure. A delegation which represented Peking as a political unit would not and could not, however, tell the truth about China. It would on the other hand present a distorted picture of China and pretend to represent a working and workable and perfectly solvent administration, and would obscure, out of a mistaken sense of loyalty to Peking and an undue regard for 'face', China's real condition and needs.[41]

Whether this kind of 'enlightened imperialism' was any longer appropriate to the situation is beside the point. What is important is that it accurately reflected an influential Western view – shared by many – of the realistic prospects for the emergence of a stable, modernizing government in China. Without a sincere Western belief in the possibility of such a government, Chinese pleas for dignity, still less for full sovereignty, were certain to fall on stony ground. The most China could hope for in 1922 was a few limited gestures. In the event, the Washington Conference's two treaties and nine resolutions on China, together with the separate agreement on Shantung, could be seen as a relative success for the Chinese negotiators, and have been so regarded by many historians. What they really offered was the possibility of a fresh start – a framework for a new China – but in the absence of a government with an authentic claim to legitimacy and authority throughout the country, very little could be constructed on the foundations laid at Washington.

Ironically, when a government did begin to emerge under Chiang Kai-shek's Kuomintang with a better claim to be a truly national government than any regime since the fall of the Manchu dynasty, the international situation had radically altered. The liberal diplomacy of Shidehara was under increasing strain as the economic benefits it had promised failed to materialize, while Japan still faced racially inspired bans on immigration to the large, underpopulated Anglo-Saxon nations.[42] What many Japanese had seen as excessive conciliation of China at the Washington Conference had failed to improve Japanese popularity in China. The success of Chiang Kai-shek's Northern Expedition brought for the first time the possibility of effective Chinese forces in the north, who might turn their attention to Manchuria. The Soviets, who had been seen as a multifaceted threat by Japan ever since the Bolshevik revolution, had cleverly exploited China's internal situation to their advantage and had close links with both the Kuomintang and the rising force of the Chinese Communist Party – a further cause for Japanese alarm. Finally, the collapse of world trade from 1929 onwards dealt a final blow to Shidehara's case for a liberal and conciliatory foreign policy and strengthened the hands of those in the army who had maintained all along that only force would enable Japan to achieve her place in the sun. The seizure of Manchuria in 1931 set Japan upon a course that decisively uncoupled it from the Western powers and led eventually to Pearl Harbor; but from the perspective of the Japanese militarists in

Manchuria, who were increasingly taking matters into their own hands, they had been left with very little choice.

It was suggested at the beginning of this essay that the failure of the Washington Conference to deal adequately with the China question was a significant factor in the failure of the Washington Conference system as a whole. The full dimension of the China factor can best be appreciated if one imagines an alternative history in which a stronger and more unified and stable China had emerged in the early 1920s at a time when Japan was committed to liberal policies and able to benefit through trade and investment from a fast growing Chinese economy. It is still impossible to say with certainty that the two countries would not have gone to war eventually with the onset of the Depression. However, what with hindsight seems an inevitable slide to war in the Pacific during the 1930s might have taken a radically different course if the China of 1922 had been in a fit state to take full advantage of what was on offer at Washington, or to win even more because it had gained the trust of the powers. That, in essence, is why the considerable achievements of the Washington Conference in arms control and the construction of a regional balance of power depended, in the final analysis, on the success of the Conference in what many saw as a secondary matter: the rehabilitation of China.

University of Birmingham

NOTES

1. *Conference on the Limitation of Armaments*, Washington, 1922.
2. See, in particular, the Eighth Meeting of the Imperial Conference of 1921, CAB 32/2, Cabinet Office Paper, Public Record Office, London.
3. Ibid., 4th Meeting, p. 3
4. *Documents On British Foreign Policy 1919–1939 (DBFP)*, First Series, Volume XIV, (London, 1966) p. 32.
5. Ibid., p. 437.
6. Ibid., p. 90.
7. Ibid., p. 91.
8. Ibid., p. 226.
9. Ibid., p. 349.
10. Ibid., p. 468.
11. See Ira Klein, 'Whitehall, Washington and the Anglo-Japanese Alliance, 1919–1921', *Pacific Historical Review*, Vol. XLI (November 1972), No. 4, pp. 460–83.

12. J.C. Vinson, *The Parchment Peace. The United States Senate and the Washington Conference 1921–1922* (Athens, Georgia, 1955), passim.
13. Akira Iriye, *After Imperialism. The Search for a New Order in the Far East 1921–1931* (New York, 1973), p. 19.
14. *Conference on the Limitation of Armament*, op.cit., pp. 866–8.
15. Ibid., pp. 874–6.
16. Ibid., p. 876
17. Ibid., pp. 882–4.
18. Ibid., p. 890.
19. See Sadao Asada, 'Japan's Special Interests and the Washington Conference, 1921–22', *American Historical Review*, LXVII, (Oct. 1961), pp. 62–70, and also the discussion of Asada's article in T.H. Buckley, *The United States and the Washington Conference, 1921–22* (Knoxville 1970), pp. 152–4.
20. *Washington Conference*, op,cit., pp. 890–92.
21. *Washington Cònference*, op.cit., pp. 920–24.
22. Wunz King (ed.), *V.K. Wellington Koo's Foreign Policy* (Shanghai), p. 41.
23. T.H. Buckley, op.cit., p. 169.
24. William L. Tung, *China and the Foreign Powers* (Dobbs Ferry, NY, 1970), p. 204.
25. *Washington Conference*, op.cit., p. 932.
26. Ibid., p. 936.
27. H.B. Morse and H.F. MacNair, *Far Eastern International Relations* (Cambridge, Mass., 1931), p. 713.
28. *Washington Conference*, op.cit., p. 940.
29. Ibid., p. 982.
30. Ibid., p. 1006.
31. Ibid., pp. 1090–98.
32. *DBFP*, op.cit., pp. 479–80.
33. Ibid., p. 501n.
34. Ibid., p. 502.
35. Ibid., p. 516.
36. Ibid., p. 517.
37. *Washington Conference*, op.cit., p. 1098.
38. Ibid., pp. 1104–24.
39. *Foreign Relations of the United States 1922*, Vol. 1 (Washington 1938), pp. 274–5.
40. *DBFP*, op.cit., p. 463.
41. Ibid., p. 463.
42. W.G. Beasley, *The Rise of Modern Japan* (London, 1990), pp. 163–4.

Arms Control and the Washington Conference

JOHN H. MAURER

I

More than 70 years have passed since representatives of the major powers met in Washington in an attempt to curtail the naval rivalries threatening to embroil them in a cold war. At the time, the results of the Washington Conference exceeded the expectations of its participants. An arms control agreement was reached that cancelled the battleship-building programmes scheduled for completion during the 1920s by Great Britain, Japan, and the United States. In addition, the conference yielded agreements that promised to provide for great-power cooperation and political stability throughout East Asia. These accomplishments were considerable and attest to the importance that was assigned to the Washington Conference by statesmen and policy commentators.

Although the battle fleet made up of heavily armoured, big-gunned capital ships is no longer the queen on the strategic chessboard, the Washington Conference nonetheless continues to fascinate and arouse controversy among historians and international relations analysts. This scholarly interest in the Washington Conference is driven in part by the emotionally charged policy debates of the 1970s and 1980s about the prominent role played by arms control in relations between the United States and the Soviet Union. Since the naval limitation treaty agreed to at the Washington Conference has come to epitomize a successful arms control system, modern-day arms controllers and their critics have examined it in an attempt to validate current-day policy prescriptions. After all, if the naval limits agreed to at Washington promoted great-power cooperation during the 1920s, why did Soviet–American arms control efforts prove so barren in bringing an end to the superpowers' cold war? The Washington Conference has thus provided an important historical case for the study of generic political and strategic issues that surround arms control negotiations. The result of this scholarly inquiry has been to enrich both current policy debates about arms control and the historical investigation of great-power relations in the earlier part of this century.

The purpose of this essay is to evaluate the results of the Washington Conference by drawing upon the insights of recent analyses done on the topic of arms control. Why were the great powers competing with each other in the building of battleships? What were the expectations of decision makers when they entered into negotiations to limit their naval rivalries? Was the outcome of the Washington Conference foreordained by political forces at work in each of the major powers? What impact did arms control have on the overall strategic relationship of the participants? These questions form the framework for my evaluation and illustrate why the Washington Conference remains such a fascinating topic for historians, political scientists, and policy analysts.

II

Although Great Britain, Japan, and the United States had fought a common enemy in imperial Germany during the First World War, at the end of fighting a naval competition emerged between them. To a generation that had been brought up on the geopolitical theories of Alfred Thayer Mahan and witnessed the slaughter of the First World War, this naval competition was a manifestation of underlying shifts in power balances within the international system.[1] Japan and the United States were rising great powers, and they challenged Britain's position of leadership in international trade, finance, and naval power. This competition, left unchecked, portended an eventual conflict on the magnitude of the one that had just ended. At the Paris

Peace Conference, Colonel Edward House, President Woodrow Wilson's unofficial national security adviser, certainly thought so. He pointedly told Britain's Prime Minister David Lloyd George that, if a naval rivalry occurred between the two countries, 'England and the United States would be in the same attitude toward one another in the future as England and Germany had been in the past'. Lloyd George agreed with House's gloomy assessment of the likely international consequences of a naval competition between Britain and the United States.[2]

The United States was, of course, already an industrial giant and possessed the world's largest economy before the First World War. The war further strengthened the position of the United States in the international economy by making it into the world's leading trading state and financial centre. The United States' share of world exports increased from 12.4 per cent in 1913 to 16 per cent in 1929. The surge in exports was led by the sale of manufactured goods, such as cars and automobile parts, oil and petroleum products, and machinery. American exports and imports in 1929 reached $10.2 billion, more than double the value of its total foreign trade for 1913. This growth in American foreign trade stood in marked contrast to the sluggish performance of Britain's economy during the same period. Between 1913 and 1929 Britain's share of world exports dropped from 15.4 to 11.8 per cent. The growth in American trade was paralleled by the rise in its foreign investments, which supplanted British holdings in the Western Hemisphere and challenged Britain's position in other regions around the globe. By 1922 American investments in Canada surpassed British holdings, and United States investments in Latin America equalled those of Britain in 1929.[3] In foreign trade and international finance, Britain and the United States were trading places during the 1920s.[4]

However, the growing importance of United States economic power does not tell the full story. The rise of the United States during the twentieth century as a superpower was accompanied by its growth as a naval power. The First World War had awakened a security consciousness among American decision makers about the political and strategic importance of naval power. Germany and Britain had showed disregard for American interests on the high seas. Consequently, the Wilson Administration sponsored and the

Congress passed in August 1916 legislation authorizing a naval build-ing programme designed to give the United States a navy as strong as that possessed by any other great power. If Germany had won the First World War, the 1916 programme would have created a navy capable of providing for the security of the Western Hemisphere from any expansionist German colonial ambitions. If Britain and its allies won, the Navy would help shape the peace settlement along the lines wanted by Woodrow Wilson. In the new world order envisioned by Wilson, Britain's traditional standing as the world's dominant naval power would come to an end. The diplomatic disagreement with Britain during the war over the rights of neutral shipping contributed to the naval build-up by the United States. A battle fleet at least equal to that of Britain meant that American decision makers would have a powerful bargaining lever in negotiations between the two countries. In particular, Wilson wanted to compel Britain into accepting the League of Nations and sharing leadership within the new inter-national system with the United States. The United States would be an equal of Britain in the world political arena if it also possessed equality in naval strength.

Although Wilson's vision of the United States playing a leading role in the League of Nations failed to materialize, the change of adminis-trations in the United States, with the election of Warren Gamaliel Harding as President, did not result in a reduction in the 1916 naval building programme. Indeed, as a candidate, President-elect, and during his first 100 days in office, Harding appeared bent on com-pleting the 1916 programme. In December 1920, upon returning from a Caribbean vacation, the sun-tanned President-elect called for 'a big navy and a big merchant marine'. In Harding's view, the United States 'must be a maritime people, since no nation has ever written a complete page in history that has not taken a prominent place in maritime affairs. . . . No nation can hope to be eminent in commerce in these times without a naval institution adequate to protect those rights'.[5] The future of the United States as a trading state, then, appeared intertwined with its rise as a naval power.

The United States was also building a strong battle fleet to streng-then its strategic position in the Pacific. Japan's expansion on the Asian mainland and in the Pacific threatened the United States throughout East Asia. To defeat Japan in any future war, American naval planners had devised the so-called Orange Plan, which called for a trans-Pacific advance by the battle fleet and required a considerable superiority over Japan in naval strength.[6] In addition to its wartime role, a strong navy would provide American decision-makers with a useful stick in negotiations with the Japanese.

Japanese statesmen and admirals looked with alarm at the naval stick being fashioned by the United States. Since 1907, Japanese naval leaders had looked on the United States as a potential adversary. In their view, Japan's dominant position in East Asia depended on the ability of the navy to defeat any naval thrust across the Pacific by the United States. To defeat the United States at sea, Japanese naval planners devised and won governmental approval for a major programme of shipbuilding, the so-called eight–eight program, which called for a first-line strength of eight battleships and eight battle cruisers.[7] With this level of naval strength, the United States was unlikely to push a confrontation with Tokyo to the point of war, and Japan's sphere of influence in East Asia would be secure.

The growth of the United States and Japan as naval powers seriously eroded the hegemony exercised by Britain on the high seas. To be sure, immediately after the First World War, Britain's naval position in European waters was much more secure than it had been in 1914: imperial Germany's naval challenge was completely defeated, and Britain's nineteenth-century naval rivals France and Russia were seriously weakened by the war. Outside of European waters, however, Britain's naval position had deteriorated. This naval weakness threatened to undercut Britain's diplomatic standing as a great power and its leadership position within the Empire. Moreover, the decline of Britain's naval power made the Empire more vulnerable to attack.

Nor could British decision makers derive much comfort from the fact that Japan and the United States were principally building up their naval forces for use against each other in the Pacific. The enormous naval building programmes projected by Japan and the United States would soon place them ahead of Britain in modern capital ships. Lloyd George worried: 'If Japan and the United States build against each other, one of the fleets eventually might be used against Britain'.[8]

This fear was shared by Admiralty planners. Britain would be reduced to third in the standings of the naval powers if it did not keep pace with American and Japanese naval construction. Of course, Britain's naval leadership was determined to prevent this from happening at all costs. Admiral Sir John Jellicoe, Britain's naval commander at the famous battle of Jutland and a former First Sea Lord, recommended in 1919 a minimum naval building programme of 12 capital ships to keep abreast of the United States.[9] Successive British First Sea Lords, Admiral Sir Rosslyn Wester Wemyss and Admiral Sir David Beatty, saw no realistic option other than a naval building programme to keep the Royal Navy at least as strong as that of the United States. The Admiralty certainly wanted to maintain Britain's premier standing among the world's naval powers. Vice-Admiral Sir Osmond de Beauvoir Brock, the Deputy Chief of Naval Staff, provided the Admiralty's assessment of the importance of not falling behind the United States in capital-ship strength. In drawing the strategic contours of a war between Britain and the United States, Brock argued that the conflict's outcome would be determined by the relative strength of the two countries' battle fleets. As Brock succinctly put it: 'give the Americans capital ships and give us none, America will defeat Great Britain.'[10] The Royal Navy's leadership were determined to fight for the construction of battleships and battle cruisers to keep abreast of the United States. Beatty intended 'to resign rather than go down to posterity as the First Sea Lord in office at the time such a shameful decision' – that is, surrender 'supremacy of the sea to America' – was made.[11]

Lloyd George's Government resisted the idea of a major shipbuilding programme and naval competition with the United States. While committed to maintaining Britain's naval primacy, Lloyd George wanted to avoid a naval rivalry with the United States. First, it was by no means clear to Britain's leaders that their country could defeat a naval challenge by the United States in the same way that they had defeated imperial Germany. Even the Admiralty's projections showed that, in an all-out competition, the United States could stay ahead of Britain in a battleship competition. Second, heavy naval spending would act as a drag on Britain's economy by dramatically increasing government spending. Economic expansion would be choked off by higher government spending requiring increased taxes or heavier borrowing. Britain's financial picture was further complicated by the huge war debt it owed to American lenders. Lloyd George's

Government wanted to put Britain's economic house in order by curtailing government spending, and it did not relish increased expenditure on new naval construction. High government spending, so it was argued within the British Government, would endanger Britain's economic recovery. Lloyd George worried that a costly naval rivalry with the United States would endanger Britain's competitive position within the international economy.

The cost of providing for the naval defence of the British Empire against Japan or the United States was indeed staggering. Some notion of the potential costs of competing with either of them can be gleaned from the reports provided by Admiral Jellicoe, who had been sent in 1919 on an around-the-world tour to survey the naval needs of the Empire. His recommendations painted a serious picture of Britain's naval requirements. For the Pacific, Jellicoe recommended the stationing of a battle fleet of 16 capital ships, that is battleships and battle cruisers. This force level was derived from Jellicoe's calculation that Britain required in the Pacific a fleet approximately equal to the front-line naval strength of Japan. Jellicoe estimated that the annual operating expenses for maintaining a fleet in the Pacific would amount to £14 million. A strong British battle fleet stationed in the Pacific would be able to contain Japan during the initial stages of an Anglo-Japanese war, providing time for Britain to send substantial reinforcements to the Far East from European waters. In addition to naval forces more than double that of Japan, Jellicoe called for the development of the logistical infrastructure – bases, fuel supplies and storage – to support the world-wide naval movements of Britain's Navy.[12] The expense of building up the navies of Britain and the Commonwealth states to the point where they could single-handedly defend the British Empire against Japan was immense. Given the high cost involved in any programme for naval rearmament, Lloyd George's fears that a renewed naval competition would hinder Britain's economic recovery were not unfounded.

Instead of naval building, the British Government pinned its faith on arms control as a way of heading off a naval rivalry with the United States. Arms control potentially offered a neat solution to the defence dilemma facing the British Government, namely to retain naval superiority while at the same time hold down naval spending. The British Government was eager to enter into either a formal or tacit arms control agreement. To that end, Britain halted capital-ship construction at the end of the First World War, cancelling three ships of the so-called Hood class that were then being built. By taking unilateral steps to reduce their own naval building and spending, Britain's leaders hoped that the United States naval building programme would slow down as well. British moderation, it was thought, would moderate American shipbuilding. Lord Grey of Fallodon, Britain's Ambassador in Washington during the second half of 1919, was 'convinced that the best course for us is to produce moderate navy estimates . . . in the expectation that example set by us will be followed here [by the United States]'.[13] Lloyd George expected the United States to reciprocate for the restraint in shipbuilding shown by Britain.[14]

Yet repeated British efforts to reach an arms control agreement with the United States failed to halt the 1916 naval building programme. By the end of 1920, confronted by the ongoing naval building programmes of Japan and the United States, Lloyd George's Government could not temporize for much longer: if Britain was not to fall seriously behind in relative naval strength, it needed to make a decision about renewed capital ship construction.[15] Lloyd George still held out hope that an arms control agreement might be reached in the near future. If another arms control initiative failed, however, Britain would respond by staying abreast of American and Japanese naval construction. Far from accepting the relegation to second or third place among the world's naval powers, the British Government reluctantly concluded during the winter of 1920–21 to compete in the building of battleships with Japan and the United States.

III

The success of the Washington Conference in curtailing the naval arms competition between the great powers, it has been argued, was foreordained because it simply codified existing strategic and political realities. Bruce Berkowitz, for example, in his study of arms control *Calculated Risks*, maintains that limitations would have occurred on naval building even without a formal agreement. The great powers, in Berkowitz's view, were not likely to compete in battleships because domestic political constraints ruled out heavy spending on armaments. Berkowitz contends that 'the Washington Treaty, perhaps the most celebrated arms control agreement of all, may have been, in reality, irrelevant'.[16] But the Washington Conference was far from irrelevant. By projecting back onto the 1920s a view about arms control that is largely derived from the Soviet–American experience in negotiating limits on their nuclear forces during the 1970s and 1980s, Berkowitz understates the political and strategic problems that might have frustrated an agreement at the Washington Conference. The result is an overly deterministic view of the naval arms control negotiations that took place during the 1920s. An examination of the Washington Conference underscores the contingent nature of history and reveals that an agreement between Britain, Japan, and the United States to cut their battleship construction programmes was far from inevitable.

The arms control agreement reached at Washington had eluded statesmen at other negotiations undertaken in the immediate aftermath of the First World War. At the Paris Peace Conference, for example, Britain's Prime Minister, David Lloyd George, had pressed the United States for a naval limitation agreement during the spring of 1919. He even threatened to withhold British support for the League of Nations as a way of inducing Woodrow Wilson to accept a naval arms control agreement that maintained Britain's dominant position on the high seas. This heavy-handed arms control initiative failed, however, as Britain and the United States could not agree about the relative size of their navies. Lloyd George renewed his search for naval arms control during the second half of 1919 by promoting a high-level diplomatic mission by Lord Grey. One of Grey's principal objectives during his short-lived tenure as Ambassador to the United States was to reach an agreement to prevent Anglo-American naval rivalry. Despite the determination of Grey and Lloyd George to obtain a settlement, this special diplomatic mission also failed.[17]

The immediate background to the Washington Conference, then, did not provide much grounds for optimism that an arms control agreement could be reached to limit the number of battleships being built by Britain, Japan, and the United States. To many observers of world politics, the three countries appeared poised at the beginning of 1921 on the verge of a major naval building programme that would poison relations between them, much as Germany's naval challenge had caused a deterioration in Anglo-German relations before the First World War. Lloyd George had this ominous historical parallel in mind when he told the Committee of Imperial Defence that, if Britain entered into a naval shipbuilding competition with the United States, 'it would be the biggest decision they had taken since 1914, and conceivably greater than that taken in 1914. . . . There would follow precisely the same tension as had resulted from our naval competition with Germany'.[18] Meanwhile, Sir William Tyrrell, then serving as Assistant Under-Secretary at the British Foreign Office, wrote to his American friend Edward House: 'We are hearing a great deal about the naval agitation in your country, and I cannot help being struck by the similarity of arguments being used in support of that policy with those that were trotted out by the Tirpitz crowd.'[19] Even Winston Churchill, who generally deprecated the likelihood of naval competition between Britain and the United States, was alarmed by the naval situation and began comparing it to the pre-1914 circumstances. 'The naval position vis-à-vis Japan & America', he wrote, 'is rapidly becoming very serious. . . . I think we ought without further delay to declare a programme of approximately four capital ships a year for four or five years on the lines of the programme I declared against Germany in 1912.'[20] It is only in retrospect that the fears of British decision makers appear overblown.

That the meeting at Washington was unlikely to result in success is further attested by the fact that such an astute politician as Lloyd George decided not to lead the British delegation to the conference's opening. To be sure, Lloyd George had other pressing political problems – such as the critical negotiations over Ireland – that demanded his close attention and appeared to rule out an extended trip to the United States. Many of Lloyd George's colleagues and advisers still thought that, despite the political problems his Government faced closer to home, he should lead the British delegation at the opening of the conference. Churchill urged Lloyd George to travel to Washington

> to establish friendly personal relations with Harding and Hughes, that you ought to make them conscious of the loyalty and friendliness of our motives and at the same time of our strong determination not to be ousted from our world position,

and generally to get the Conference started as far as possible on sound lines and to arrive at some informal understandings on its great underlying issues with the statesmen of America and Japan.[21]

Britain's Ambassador in the United States, Sir Auckland Geddes, even argued that the 'presence or absence of Prime Minister for few days at opening of Conference may make all the difference between success and failure.'[22] Had he rated chances for success more highly, surely Lloyd George would have seized the opportunity to stand in the political limelight and take credit for the achievements of a major international conference. However, Lloyd George was not at all sanguine about the chances of a productive negotiation with the United States. Lloyd George confided to Frances Stevenson, his confidential secretary and mistress, that he did not want to go to the conference – she recorded in her diary, he 'loathes the idea' – even though he was expected to attend. 'Personally – and naturally – I think he is the only person who can carry off disarmament', she wrote. 'But so many feuds and prejudices have been roused by this proposal & by the attitude of America that it is difficult to say what will be the outcome of it.'[23] If Lloyd George shared his mistress' opinion that only he could crown the conference with success, then by not attending the British Prime Minister was dooming the talks to failure.[24]

The difficulties standing in the way of the great powers arranging mutual limits on their naval armaments programmes are also shown by follow-up arms control negotiations that tried to build upon the framework established by the Washington Conference. Although Britain and the United States had agreed at Washington to parity in capital-ship strength, they could not reach a settlement about their relative cruiser strengths at the failed Geneva Conference of 1927.[25] For Britain's leaders, parity in battle-fleet strength did not mean overall equality. Instead, they insisted that Britain's special strategic requirements of defending a global empire meant the Royal Navy must be superior in overall strength. In particular, Britain required a superior force of cruisers. The First London Naval Conference, which represented the high point of interwar naval arms control, depended on the resolution of serious disagreements about relative force levels in cruisers. Only the determination of President Herbert Hoover and

Prime Minister Ramsay MacDonald broke the impasse on the cruiser controversy in Anglo-American relations.[26] In addition, the London agreement depended upon the firm stand by Japan's Prime Minister Hamaguchi Osachi in overriding the objections of the Japanese Navy's General Staff.[27] Meanwhile, France and Italy could not compose their differences over naval building programmes. These differences led to the refusal of France and Italy to join in on the London agreement of 1930.[28] Naval arms control agreements during the 1920s, then, were more difficult to achieve than they often appear to modern-day analysts. The agreement on setting mutual limits on naval armaments that occurred at Washington thus appears far from overdetermined.

To be sure, by the summer of 1921 the governments in power in Britain, Japan, and the United States wanted to obtain some relief from the prospect of expensive naval building programmes. However, the actual terms of the agreement reached at the Washington Conference were not predestined, even if some form of arms control was the likely outcome. Most informed commentators and policy-makers assumed that any arms control agreement reached at the conference would codify the 1916 building programme that the United States had under way. The General Board of the US Navy for its part insisted on the completion of the 1916 programme as part of an agreement.[29]

The General Board was not alone in expecting that arms control would enable the United States to complete the 1916 programme. Admiral Beatty, Britain's First Sea Lord, thought 'that the new [Harding] Administration, even if possessed of the best motives in the world, could scarcely be expected to refrain from completing the ships already laid down'.[30] In response to the United States naval programme, the British Government was resigned to building at least eight and perhaps as many as 12 new capital ships.[31] Given Beatty's view that a 'naval holiday' would cripple Britain's shipbuilding industry, the British delegation envisioned an arms control agreement that permitted the construction of new capital ships.

Japan's naval leaders came to the same conclusion. While Admiral Kato Tomosaburo signalled Japan's willingness to forgo the completion of its eight–eight building programme of capital ships, Japanese leaders did not anticipate a drastic cutback in their shipbuilding. In preparation for arms control negotiations, the Japanese Navy's leadership drew up a menu of shipbuilding options, running from completion of the programmed eight–eight plan to a naval holiday that froze the world's battle fleets to their existing size. They also considered scaling back the eight–eight plan to an eight–four or eight–six programme of battleships and battle cruisers. On the eve of the conference, the Japanese Navy's leadership concluded that they could accept any arms control agreement – even if it meant abandoning most of the eight–eight programme – so long as a seven-to-ten ratio in capital ships with regard to the United States was obtained.[32] The Japanese negotiating stance was flexible and depended on what the United States decided to build.

Agreement at Washington, then, might have codified a strategic reality far different from the one that it did. The negotiations in Washington might have resulted in an arms control settlement that permitted a substantial naval build-up, much as the SALT I and SALT II accords reached by the United States and the Soviet Union during the 1970s permitted the superpowers to deploy an extensive array of new nuclear weapons systems. Indeed, a 'managed build-up' was a much more likely outcome, given the expectations of the participants, than the dramatic cuts presented by Charles Evans Hughes in his speech at the conference's opening. That the reality of Washington did not fit the expectations of its participants shows the importance of statesmanship and diplomatic strategy in shaping the outcome of negotiations.

An examination of the Washington Conference also shows that several important sticking points might have broken up the talks. Two major obstacles stood in the way of agreement. First, the 'stop-now' proposal ran counter to the projected building programmes of the major naval powers. Hughes' scheme required that the navies of the major powers forgo new construction and stay content with the battleships already completed. Second, the ratio system devised to balance the naval requirements of the major powers was very controversial, and there was opposition in each country to the ratio that they had been granted. Agreement required compromise and changes in Hughes' original proposal.

One road-block was the Japanese insistence on retaining the battleship *Mutsu*. This battleship was largely completed by the end of

1921, and Japan hastened to finish its construction as a way of presenting the conference with a *fait accompli*. Although the *Mutsu*'s design did not embrace all of the lessons of the combat experience of the First World War, it was nonetheless a powerful warship, mounting 16-inch heavy guns as its main armament, good armour protection, and a faster speed than any battleships in the United States Navy. By insisting on the *Mutsu*'s completion, Japan upset Hughes' 'stop-now' proposal. Since Japan intended to complete the *Mutsu*, Britain and the United States decided to complete two extra battleships as a way of offsetting this gain for the Japanese Navy.

Japan was not alone in rejecting Hughes's 'stop-now' formula: Britain's naval leadership was also unhappy with the American proposal for a battleship holiday. Beatty thought it essential that Britain acquire new battleships that embodied the lessons learned from the combat experience of the First World War. Without the construction of new battleships, Britain's battle fleet would qualitatively lag behind the latest generation of American and Japanese battleships. He was also troubled that the capacity of British shipyards to build large warships would be run down if they were idled, thereby hurting Britain's capability to rearm when the naval holiday ended. Beatty's concern, then, was that, if his Government accepted the holiday proposal, Britain would find itself unable to build modern battleships and outclassed at sea by naval rivals. Lloyd George's Government, in its quest to reduce government spending, was willing to run that risk, and it intended to accept the American limitation scheme even if the Admiralty did not agree. Alarmed by the Government's decision, Beatty hurriedly returned to Britain in an attempt to alter it. Beatty confided to a former mistress that he would be 'more use soothing Lloyd George and keeping him straight' on naval spending than by staying on with the negotiating team in Washington.[33] That Britain eventually built the new battleships *Nelson* and *Rodney*, however, had less to do with Beatty's politicking than with Japan's insistence on retaining the *Mutsu*. Japan's stance played into the Admiralty's hands.[34]

Another stumbling block to an agreement was the French demand for a larger battle fleet. The French delegation wanted a battleship force equal to that accorded Japan and superior to the Italian fleet. The French were especially incensed that their country was accorded parity in battle-fleet strength with Italy. Although the American delegation was willing to go along with the French demand for a higher ratio – after all, a stronger French Navy would undermine Britain's relative strategic position in Europe – this was unacceptable to Britain and Italy.[35] Thus, the French stand threatened Hughes' plan.

However, this threat was hollow, and the French Government eventually gave way on the issue of relative battle-fleet strength. France's retreat on this issue can largely be explained by the exorbitant cost it would have faced in trying to build up the French battle fleet to equal that of Japan. For a country trying to rebuild from the devastation of the First World War, the expense would have been prohibitive. Furthermore, the French bargaining hand was weak because France did not have under way a major building programme of warships. Thus, the French Government had little ground to assert their claim for a higher ratio of strength. Had France walked away from the negotiations, a settlement between Britain, Japan, and the United States would still most likely have been reached, since only a substantial (and improbable) French naval build-up to gain parity with the Japanese fleet would have overturned the ratios established at Washington. In settling this dispute, France did get its way by refusing to accept restrictions on smaller combatants. By building cruisers and submarines, the French Government thought it could stay ahead of Italy as a naval power and obtain political leverage on Britain.

Of course, the inability of the great powers to agree at Washington about limits for cruisers, destroyers, and submarines opened a new arena for great-power naval competition. Indeed, some analysts argue that the naval arms competition was simply rechannelled into these uncontrolled weapons, whose development was spurred by the agreement.[36] There is considerable merit to these arguments. The Washington Conference did underscore the disagreements between the great powers when they attempted to set further limits on cruisers and submarines during the 1920s. While Britain was willing to concede a rough parity with the United States in capital-ship strength, it also wanted to retain overall naval superiority by building a larger force of cruisers.[37] British decision makers argued that their country's strategic position required a superiority in cruisers. Moreover, both

Japan and France tried to compensate for the inferior ratios accorded their battle fleets by building cruisers and submarines. Thus, the Washington agreement provided impetus to the construction of large cruisers.

The Washington agreement also permitted the modernization of capital ships, although it did set limits on what improvements could be undertaken. Both the United States and Japan took advantage of this provision to improve substantially the combat capabilities of their battleships. Britain, on the other hand, did not follow suit, and by the early 1930s many American naval officers concluded that the United States battle fleet was superior to that possessed by Britain.[38] This improvement in the capability of the United States battle fleet was resented by British policy makers, who complained that the United States was violating the provisions of the Washington treaty on permitted modernization.

In an important way, however, the Washington agreement did not follow the dictates of modern-day arms control theory, which contends that countries typically are only willing to scrap old weapons while avoiding limitations on promising new systems.[39] According to this line of reasoning, the major naval powers should have scrapped older battleships and protected their ability to build the most modern capital ships. But the Washington arms control agreement did not conform to this pattern. The great powers agreed to hold on to older systems and largely forego new capital ships, much to the chagrin of many admirals who wanted to build larger battleships that incorporated the lessons of the First World War.

Another major hurdle in the way of an agreement was Japan's claim that its battle fleet be accorded a higher ratio with regard to that of the United States. In an attempt to overcome Japanese opposition, a sophisticated trade-off between bases and ships was required that offset Japan's inferior capital-ship ratio. Britain and the United States agreed to limit the defences protecting forward bases in the western Pacific, thereby undermining their ability to project naval power into the region during the initial stages of a conflict with Japan. Both Britain and the United States made concessions on this issue because neither government wanted to incur the cost of building up the strong defensive positions and logistical infrastructure required for the forward deployment of their naval power in East Asia. Although Britain and the United States undercut their ability to carry out offensive operations in the early stages of a war against Japan, they did reserve the right to build up bases to support a distant defence of their positions in the Pacific. Britain worked throughout the interwar period to strengthen its defensive bastion at Singapore, intended as the linchpin in the defence of the British Empire in the Far East. The United States also wanted to have a free hand in developing Hawaii into a first-class naval base. The net strategic result of this trade-off was to accord Japan naval dominance in the western Pacific. Despite the inferior ratio in battle-fleet strength, Japan thus emerged from the Washington Conference in a relatively strong strategic position.

IV

What if Washington had failed? It was by no means certain that the Washington Conference would result in an agreement. Many obstacles stood in the way of that agreement, and these hurdles tested the ingenuity and patience of the negotiators. That these impediments were overcome does not mean, however, that an agreement was inevitable. Of course, to answer a counterfactual question is to risk the danger of idle speculation, but that danger has not stopped some arms control analysts and historians from grappling with this question. Indeed, much of the controversy surrounding the consequences of the Washington Conference is derived from speculations about alternative outcomes. These alternative outcomes are then typically used to evaluate the actual results of the Washington Conference.

Corelli Barnett, for example, argues that Britain would have been strategically better off if the Washington Conference had failed. Britain could then have renewed the Anglo-Japanese Alliance as a counterweight to the rise of United States naval power. For Barnett, Britain had a fall-back strategy of an alliance with Japan and increased naval building that would have better provided for the security of the British Empire than cooperation with the United States. Indeed, according to Barnett, 'the Washington Conference was one of the major catastrophes of English history'.[40]

However, would Britain's security have been enhanced by building 12 new capital ships and renewing its alliance with Japan? Was a British naval build-up the best response to the challenge that the United

States posed to Britain's standing within the international system? For that matter, would Japan have been better served by the failure of the Washington Conference? How might the United States have benefited from the failure of arms control? These questions bring into sharp focus the security dilemmas facing decision makers at the time of the Washington Conference.

The American negotiating team understood that these talks might fail, and they framed their proposals with this in mind. In preparing for the negotiations in Washington, the Harding Administration was positioning itself to overcome the domestic political opposition arrayed against continuation of the 1916 naval building programme. If Britain or Japan had refused to agree to the American arms control proposals, the arguments of arms controllers would be discredited. That the American proposal was intended to disarm domestic political critics as well as foreign governments is clear. A month before opening the conference, President Harding sketched his basic approach to the negotiations to a friendly journalist: 'We'll talk sweetly and patiently to them [the other major naval powers] at first; but if they don't agree then we'll say "God damn you, if it's a race, then the United States is going to go to it" '.[41] The President's intentions were clear to the team of policy makers drawing up the American negotiating proposal, as can be seen from the diary of Senator Henry Cabot Lodge. On 12 October 1921, as the State Department and the Navy were preparing the American bargaining position, Lodge dined with the President at the White House, where the discussion revolved around the forthcoming arms control conference. Lodge found that President Harding felt 'very strongly about having our six battle cruisers built'. But the President 'also felt the great necessity . . . of making some offer at the very outset as to a general limitation of armaments which would satisfy the desires of the country and put the question straight to the other Powers'. Lodge did 'not for a moment believe that either Japan or England will accept it [the American proposal], but if they do not accept it we shall have made our position clear and will lay the responsibility where it will belong – with them'.[42] Harding insisted, in a high-level meeting with Hughes and Secretary of the Navy Edwin Denby, that the opening American proposal must 'prove the honesty of our intentions to the country and to place us therefore, in a position where, if any refusal came on the part of any European powers, Congress and the Senate would be behind the administration's plans'.[43] During his campaign for the Presidency, Harding was for a big navy, and championed the completion of the 1916 naval programme. Hughes' highly publicized 'stop-now' proposal was intended to regain the initiative for the administration in its domestic political struggle for a larger navy. Thus, Roger Dingman's conclusion is certainly on the mark: 'The United States shaped the kind of limited arms control proposal it did primarily for domestic political reasons.'[44] Much like the zero option on intermediate nuclear forces put forward by President Reagan in November 1981, the Harding Administration presented a negotiating proposal that would establish a domestic political consensus for a continued arms build-up if the talks failed.

The competition could have become more intense if the Harding Administration had responded to the failure of negotiations by moving forward to complete the 1916 naval programme. At the close of the First World War the competition in capital ships was qualitative as well as numerical. Britain had built the battle cruiser *Hood*, a new generation of capital ship displacing over 40,000 tons and carrying heavy guns of 15 inches and larger. The United States was not far behind. Twelve of the battleships and battle cruisers in the American 1916 programme were roughly comparable to the *Hood*, and Britain's battle fleet would be distinctly outclassed if these ships were completed. To prevent this from happening, Britain intended to go one step ahead of the American 1916 programme and build a new generation of capital ships, the so-called super-Hoods. These ships were designed to fight at long ranges, carrying the largest calibre heavy gun and thick deck armour. As the naval analyst Hector Bywater noted: 'Compared with the gigantic programmes . . . in train [by the United States, Britain, and Japan], the Anglo-German competition of 1907–14 was a mere bagatelle.'[45] The Washington and London agreements foreclosed the construction of these battleships for 15 years, until Japan began building the Yamato class of super battleships. When compared to the prospective costs of a major build-up by the great powers of their battleship forces, the cruiser competition that did occur during the 1920s was much less expensive and provocative.

If the Washington Conference had failed and another year passed

without an agreement limiting battleship construction, the shipbuilding programmes of Japan and the United States would have moved
closer to completion and became more difficult to scrap. How much
more work remained to be done on the United States 1916 programme can only be estimated, since the construction rate depended
on the availability of funds.[46] The battleships *Colorado*, *Washington*,
and *West Virginia* were closest to completion, and they might have
been finished within another 18 months. It was also likely that five
battleships of the South Dakota class and two battle cruisers would
reach the stage where they were more than 50 per cent completed.[47]
Meanwhile, the Japanese battleships *Tosa* and *Kaga* were scheduled
for completion in 1922, and the construction of the battle cruisers
Akagi and *Amagi* was under way.[48] With the passage of another year,
the political will to scrap these ships might not exist, as the controversy over the *Mutsu* showed. The Washington Conference thus
occurred at a moment when the cost of giving up the battleship
construction programmes was still politically tolerable.

V

The United States emerged from the First World War as the world's
leading trading state and financial power, and it aspired to building a
battle fleet stronger than that possessed by Britain. These developments were rapidly altering the global balance of power, challenging
Britain's position within the international system. Although Britain's
leaders were alarmed by the challenge posed by the United States,
they did not see the decline of British power as inevitable.
Furthermore, they were determined to uphold Britain's strategic position even if this meant building battleships in competition with the
United States. Despite the misgivings of Lloyd George's Government
about provoking the United States, British decision makers had no
intention of jumping on the American bandwagon. As Lloyd George
told intimates, 'he would pawn his shirt rather than allow America to
dominate the seas'.[49] By the beginning of 1921, Britain's leaders were
prepared to resume the building of capital ships and renew the
Anglo-Japanese Alliance, even though these steps threatened to wor-
sen relations with the United States. Many decision makers on both
sides of the Atlantic genuinely believed that Britain and the United

States were poised to begin a naval, commercial, and financial rivalry that would dwarf the pre-1914 Anglo-German antagonism. Britain and the United States, then, were serious rivals on the international stage, contending over high stakes.

However, Britain and the United States avoided the worst consequences of a full-blown naval competition between them. A precondition for an understanding was Britain's agreement to concede parity in battle-fleet strength with the United States.[50] In addition, Britain ended the Anglo-Japanese Alliance. These important concessions on Britain's part met the most important security demands desired by the United States in an agreement. In return for understanding with Britain on these issues, the United States gave up the 1916 battleship building programme that would have conferred battle-fleet superiority by the mid-1920s. Britain avoided, then, the heavy expense of completing its own programme of capital ship construction to meet the American naval challenge.

Instead of a battleship-building competition, Britain and the United States laid the basis for a dual hegemony at sea at the Washington Conference. Although American and British naval leaders continued to think of each other as potential adversaries throughout the 1920s, the naval rivalry remained limited in scope so that Anglo-American relations did not follow the script of the pre-1914 pattern of increasing naval building programmes and antagonism. Because of the open political systems in both countries, the international rivalry between Britain and the United States was unlikely to have resulted in war.[51] Yet statesmen at the time cannot be faulted for their prudence, which grew out of the fear that war often accompanies major power transitions in the international system. After all, they had just lived through a terrible conflict that had resulted from Germany's bid to gain hegemony in Europe and supplant Britain in the hierarchy of great powers. While it might appear clear to us today that Britain and the United States were not destined to fight each other, it was by no means so apparent to the statesmen alive some 70 years ago.[52] If the Washington Conference had failed, and Britain and the United States had completed their projected battleship building programmes, the naval competition would have loomed much larger in Anglo-American relations during the 1920s. By preventing this competition in capital ships, the Washington Conference forestalled an incipient cold war between Britain and the United States and demonstrated the ability of liberal great powers to reduce the security dilemmas that ordinarily drive arms competitions.

The Washington Conference also established a basis for co-operation between the great powers in the Pacific. Finding a formula for cooperation between Britain, Japan, and the United States required coming to grips with three interrelated security issues. First, Britain and the United States needed to reach an accommodation with Japan about China. Second, a revision of the Anglo-Japanese Alliance was required so that it did not form the basis for a coalition directed against the United States. Third, an agreement was needed to restrain the naval rivalry between Japan and the United States. The linkage of these three security issues was essential for reaching an overall settlement. On all three issues, Japan accepted the necessity for compromise. Tokyo eased the suspicions of other powers about Japanese ambitions on the Asian mainland by agreeing to the Nine-Power Treaty about China.[53] The agreement about China, in conjunction with the replacement of the Anglo-Japanese Alliance by the Four-Power Treaty, showed Japan's willingness to cooperate with Britain and the United States in promoting stability in East Asia. The end of the alliance with Britain had served Japan well during the preceding 20 years, and its demise diminished Japanese security. Finally, the Japanese Navy went along with the 60 per cent ratio in battle-fleet strength. This step was anathema to many Japanese admirals, and a concession that was difficult for the Navy to make. If Kato Tomosaburo had refused to accept the ratio formula – and he was under considerable pressure to do so from within the Navy – an arms control agreement would have fallen through.[54] Of course, on the other side of the ledger, Japan derived important benefits from the Washington settlement that enhanced its security. In particular, Japan's relative strategic position was significantly improved by the agreement of Britain and the United States to eschew the further fortification of bases in the western Pacific. The stark fact remains that Tokyo's decision to cooperate with Britain and the United States permitted the political settlement over East Asia and the successful conclusion of the arms control negotiations at Washington.

This willingness to promote cooperation stands in marked contrast to Japan's truculence during the 1930s, when Japanese actions caused the breakdown of stability in East Asia and doomed naval arms control between the two world wars. The rise of Chinese nationalism, and the fear that this caused in the Japanese military, led to conflict between China and Japan and a widening struggle for mastery in East Asia. The fighting between China and Japan, along with the impact of the Great Depression, radicalized Japanese domestic politics and eroded the basis for Tokyo's further cooperation with Britain and the United States in maintaining stability in the region.[55] By the early 1930s, then, naval arms control had played itself out, since the Washington system could not accommodate the expansionist territorial ambitions and increased naval building programmes demanded by Japan.

In addition, the growth in power of Fascist Italy, Nazi Germany, and the Soviet Union further undermined the Washington arms control framework. These states were no longer willing to accept the leadership of Britain and the United States on the high seas. Indeed, in the changed international circumstances of the 1930s, the most useful role that arms control could play was in rallying public opinion in Britain and the United States behind the necessity for a naval build-up in response to the threat posed by the actions of Japan, Germany, Italy, and the Soviet Union. The Washington system provided a criterion for measuring American and British naval security and, when other states violated these guidelines, Britain and the United States needed to assert their leadership by outbuilding the challengers.[56] By trying to perpetuate the Washington arms control system in the radically changed international political environment of the 1930s, rather than using its demise as a tocsin for greater naval rearmament, statesmen and naval leaders in Britain and the United States committed a serious strategic blunder. This conclusion is unpalatable to those policy analysts and decision makers who want to construct narrowly conceived agreements that focus on weapons and their characteristics. The Washington Conference demonstrates that arms control simply cannot exist in a political vacuum: a country's foreign policy objectives and domestic political make-up matter in determining whether arms control is a useful instrument for promoting international stability or a sham.

Naval War College

NOTES

1. See Mahan's classic study about naval war and imperial rivalries, *The Influence of Sea Power Upon History, 1660–1783* (Boston: Little, Brown and Company, 1890). For two studies that examine the relationship between underlying shifts in power balances and international conflict, see Paul Kennedy, *The Rise and Fall of the Great Powers* (New York: Random House, 1987); and Robert Gilpin, *War and Change in World Politics* (Cambridge: Cambridge University Press, 1981).
2. See the House Diary, 6 March 1919, House Papers, Sterling Memorial Library, Yale University.
3. On the United States economy during the 1920s, see Melvyn P. Leffler, '1921–1932: Expansionist Impulses and Domestic Constraints', in William H. Becker and Samuel F. Wells Jr (ed.), *Economics and World Power* (New York: Columbia University Press, 1984), pp. 225–75; and Frank Costigliola, *Awkward Dominion: American Political, Economic, and Cultural Relations with Europe, 1919–1933* (Ithaca: Cornell University Press, 1984), pp. 140–66.
4. For two astute assessments that highlight Britain's strengths in facing the challenge posed by the United States during the 1920s, see Brian McKercher, 'Wealth, Power, and the New International Order: Britain and the American Challenge in the 1920s', *Diplomatic History*, Vol. 12, No. 4 (Fall 1988), pp. 411–41; and John R. Ferris, ' "The Greatest Power on Earth": Great Britain in the 1920s', *The International History Review*, Vol. 13, No. 4 (November 1991), pp. 726–50.
5. 'Harding Ashore, Asks for Big Navy and Trade Fleets', *New York Times*, 5 Dec. 1920, pp. 1 and 4.
6. On the early evolution of the Orange Plan, see Edward S. Miller's detailed study *War Plan Orange: The U.S. Strategy to Defeat Japan, 1897–1945* (Annapolis: Naval Institute Press, 1991), pp. 9–121.
7. On the eight–eight plan, see Roger Dingman, *Power in the Pacific: The Origins of Naval Arms Limitation, 1914–1922* (Chicago: The University of Chicago Press, 1976), pp. 48–63, 122–35.
8. Committee of Imperial Defence (CID), 134th meeting, 14 Dec. 1920, Cabinet Papers 2/3.
9. A. Temple Patterson (ed.), *The Jellicoe Papers* (London: Navy Records Society, 1968), Vol. 2, pp. 290–95. Jellicoe also recommended that Britain retain for its own use the four most modern German battleships then interned at the British naval anchorage at Scapa Flow.
10. Fifth Meeting of the Sub-Committee to take evidence, 11 Jan. 1921, Cabinet Papers 16/37.
11. Stephen Roskill, *Admiral of the Fleet Earl Beatty, The Last Naval Hero: An Intimate Biography* (New York: Atheneum, 1981), pp. 302–3.
12. See the various reports printed in *Jellicoe Papers*, Vol. 2, pp. 284–398.
13. Grey to Lloyd George, 27 Nov. 1919, Admiralty Papers 167/61.
14. See House Diary, 7 Aug. 1919, House Papers.
15. At a critical meeting of the Committee of Imperial Defence held on 14 Dec. 1920, the issue of building against the United States was discussed by British decision makers. See CID, 134th Meeting, 4 Dec. 1920, Cabinet Papers 2/3.
16. Bruce D. Berkowitz, *Calculated Risks* (New York: Simon and Schuster, 1987), p. 149. Colin Gray in *House of Cards: Why Arms Control Must Fail* (Ithaca: Cornell University Press, 1992), his scathing critique of modern arms control theory, also maintains that the Washington Conference illustrates the maxim that arms control can only be effective when it is not really needed.
17. On the Grey mission, see Leon E. Boothe, 'A Fettered Envoy: Lord Grey's Mission to

the United States, 1919–1920', *The Review of Politics*, Vol. 33, No. 1 (January 1971), pp. 78–94.

18. CID, 134th Meeting, 14 Dec. 1920, Cabinet Papers 2/3.

19. Tyrrell to House, 27 Jan. 1921, Edward M. House Papers. Tyrrell was referring, of course, to Admiral Alfred von Tirpitz, Germany's Navy's Secretary from 1897–1916, who was the architect of the German naval challenge against Britain before the First World War.

20. Churchill to Balfour, 26 Feb. 1921, in Martin Gilbert (ed.), *Winston S. Churchill*, companion vol. IV, part 2 (Boston: Houghton Mifflin, 1978), p. 1379. Only 19 months earlier, in August 1919, Churchill argued that Britain could stop construction of all major warships and drastically curtail the Royal Navy's budget. See his Cabinet memorandum, dated 1 Aug. 1919, in ibid, pp. 780–86.

21. Churchill to Lloyd George, 8 Oct. 1921, in Gilbert, editor, *Churchill*, companion Vol. IV, part 3, pp. 1642–4.

22. Geddes to Curzon, 21 Sept. 1921, in Rohan Butler and J. P. T. Bury, editors, *Documents on British Foreign Policy, 1919–1939* (London: Her Majesty's Stationery Office, 1966), first series, Vol. xiv, No. 379, pp. 399–400. Hereafter referred to as *DBFP*.

23. A.J.P. Taylor (ed.), *Lloyd George: A Diary by Frances Stevenson* (New York: Harper and Row, 1971), pp. 229–30.

24. Sir William Tyrrell bluntly criticized Lloyd George's decision not to attend the conference. In Tyrrell's estimation, Lloyd George actions 'towards the Washington Conference are wrecking tactics'. Quoted in Ian H. Nish, *Alliance in Decline: A Study in Anglo-Japanese Relations, 1908–23* (London: The Athlone Press, 1972), p. 362, n. 25. Also see Erik Goldstein's essay in this collection.

25. See David Carlton, 'Great Britain and the Coolidge Naval Disarmament Conference of 1927', *Political Science Quarterly*, 82 (1968), pp. 573–99; Richard W. Fanning, 'The Coolidge Conference of 1927: Disarmament in Disarray', and Marc Epstein, 'The Historians and the Geneva Naval Conference', in B. J. C. McKercher (ed.), *Arms Limitation and Disarmament: Restraints on War, 1899–1939* (Westport, Connecticut: Praeger, 1992), pp. 105–48.

26. See Raymond G. O'Connor, *Perilous Equilibrium: The United States and the London Naval Conference of 1930* (Lawrence: University of Kansas Press, 1962), passim; Gregory C. Kennedy, 'The 1930 London Naval Conference and Anglo-American Maritime Strength, 1927–1939', in B. J. C. McKercher (ed.), *Arms Limitation and Disarmament: Restraints on War, 1899–1939* (Westport, Connecticut: Praeger, 1992), pp. 149–71.

27. Kobayashi Tatsuo, 'The London Naval Treaty, 1930', in James William Morley (ed.), *Japan Erupts: The London Naval Conference and the Manchurian Incident, 1928–1932* (New York: Columbia University Press, 1984), pp. 11–17.

28. For a first-rate analysis of French naval policy and arms control, see William Gregory Perett, 'French Naval Policy and Foreign Affairs, 1930–1939', Ph.D. dissertation, Stanford University, 1977, pp. 1–172.

29. On the US Navy's role in planning for the negotiation, see William Reynolds Braisted, *The United States Navy in the Pacific, 1909–1922* (Austin: University of Texas Press, 1971), pp. 580–95.

30. CID, 134th Meeting, 14 Dec. 1920, Cabinet Papers 2/3.

31. See the table comparing the post-Jutland capital-ship construction of Britain, Japan, and the United States, in 'Statistics Prepared for the British Delegation', Admiralty Papers 116/3448. The Admiralty projected that Britain would complete 13 post-Jutland capital ships by 1928, while Japan finished its eight–eight programme and the United States possessed 24 modern battleships and battle cruisers.

32. Dingman, *Power in the Pacific*, pp. 183–93.
33. Roskill, *Last Naval Hero*, p. 311.
34. These battleships were scaled down versions of the battle cruisers that the Admiralty intended to build. Britain might have insisted on finishing two of the larger super-battle cruisers. These ships, displacing 48,000 tons, would have been distinctly superior in size, armour, speed, and overall fighting qualities to any battleships finished by Japan or the United States. Their completion might have put considerable pressure on Japan and the United States to build comparable ships. Under pressure from Hughes not to build new battleships over 35,000 tons displacement, Balfour agreed. See Department of State, *Papers Relating to the Foreign Relations of the United States, 1922* (Washington: Government Printing Office, 1938), Vol. 1, pp. 99–126; *DBFP*, first series, Vol. xiv, pp. 556–61; Admiralty Papers 1/8615.
35. Braisted, *Navy in the Pacific*, p. 588.
36. Berkowitz, for example, maintains that the naval arms race continued despite the agreement reached at Washington. Furthermore, he argues that the agreement actually spurred the development of new weapons developments. He uses the analogy to price controls, which attempt to arrest rising prices but do not eliminate the underlying causes for inflation. See his *Calculated Risks*, pp. 25–9.
37. The British Admiralty aimed at more than a two-to-one superiority over the United States in cruisers; see Hankey to Lloyd George, 29 Dec. 1921, Lloyd George Papers, F/62/1/12.
38. Michael Vlahos, *The Blue Sword: The Naval War College and the American Mission, 1919–1941* (Newport: Naval War College Press, 1980), pp. 110–11; Gerald E. Wheeler, *Prelude to Pearl Harbor: The United States Navy and the Far East, 1921–1931* (Columbia, Missouri: University of Missouri Press, 1968), pp. 111–17.
39. Berkowitz, *Calculated Risks*, pp. 93–4.
40. Corelli Barnett, *The Collapse of British Power* (New York: William Morrow, 1972), p. 272.
41. Dingman, *Power in the Pacific*, p. 157.
42. Diary of Henry Cabot Lodge, 12 Oct. 1921, Henry Cabot Lodge Papers, Massachusetts Historical Society, Boston.
43. Roosevelt Diary, 20 Oct. 1921, Theodore Roosevelt Jr Papers, Library of Congress, Washington DC.
44. Dingman, *Power in the Pacific*, p. 158.
45. Hector C. Bywater, *Their Secret Purposes: Dramas and Mysteries of the Naval War* (London: Constable, 1932), p. 276. Also see at the back of this book the graphic presentation of the British, Japanese, and United States 'Post-Jutland Battle Fleets' as they would have appeared by the late 1920s if an arms control agreement had not been reached to limit battleship strength.
46. See the various estimates on the cost of completing the 1916 programme presented by Thomas H. Buckley, *The United States and the Washington Conference, 1921–1922* (Knoxville: The University of Tennessee Press, 1970), pp. 24, 52, 56.
47. See Table 23 in *Navy Yearbook 1920–1921* (Washington: Government Printing Office, 1922), p. 884. My assessment is based on the figures provided by this table, to which I have estimated that another year's work would have advanced the building of these ships by an additional 20 or 25 per cent.
48. Anthony J. Watts and Brian G. Gordon, *The Imperial Japanese Navy* (Garden City, New York: Doubleday and Company, 1971), pp. 62–5.
49. *Lord Riddell's Intimate Diary of the Peace Conference and After, 1918–1923* (New York: Reynal and Hitchcock, 1934), p. 259.
50. On Britain's decision to agree to parity in battle-fleet strength with the United States, see the excellent studies done by J. Kenneth McDonald, 'Lloyd George and the Search

for a Postwar Naval Policy, 1919', in A.J.P. Taylor (ed.), *Lloyd George: Twelve Essays* (New York: Atheneum, 1971), pp. 191–222; John R. Ferris, 'The Symbol and Substance of Seapower: Great Britain, the United States, and the One-Power Standard, 1919–1921', in B.J.C. McKercher (ed.), *Anglo-American Relations in the 1920s: The Struggle for Supremacy* (London: Macmillan, 1991), pp. 55–80.

51. On the inhibitions that stand in the way of liberal democracies going to war with each other, see the three valuable articles by Michael Doyle, 'Kant, Liberal Legacies, and Foreign Affairs', *Philosophy and Public Affairs*, 12, 3 (Summer 1983), pp. 205–235; 'Kant, Liberal Legacies, and Foreign Affairs, Part 2', *Philosophy and Public Affairs*, 12, 4 (Fall 1983), pp. 323–53; and 'Liberalism and World Politics', *American Political Science Review*, 80, 4 (December 1986), pp. 1151–69.

52. War between Japan and the United States in the early 21st century might also be considered highly improbable, yet serious analysts of world affairs nonetheless argue that their economic rivalry is bound to result in a showdown. See, for example, George Friedman and Meredith Lebard, *The Coming War with Japan* (New York: St. Martin's Press, 1991).

53. See Sadao Asada, 'Japan's "Special Interests" and the Washington Conference, 1921–1922', *American Historical Review*, Vol. 66, No. 1 (October 1961), pp. 62–70.

54. Before the First World War, Germany's Navy Secretary Admiral Alfred von Tirpitz spurned repeated British arms control offers, thereby ruining any possibility of compromise on naval shipbuilding and prospect for a serious improvement in Anglo-German relations. See John H. Maurer, 'Arms Control and the Anglo-German Naval Rivalry', *Political Science Quarterly*, forthcoming.

55. Arthur Waldron, *How the Peace was Lost* (Stanford: Hoover Institution Press, 1992), pp. 27–56. In addition, see the insightful analysis on the interrelationship between Japanese domestic politics and foreign policy offered in a memorandum by F.T. Ashton-Gwatkin on the Anglo-Japanese Alliance and constitutional changes in Japan, published in *DBFP*, first series, Vol. vi, No. 789, pp. 1049–50. Ashton-Gwatkin argued that a liberalization of Japanese domestic politics would result in Japan pursuing a more cooperative foreign policy toward Britain, China, and the United States. He urged the British Government to promote 'democratisation' in Japan by delaying renewal of the Anglo-Japanese Alliance.

56. At the Second London Conference, the United States skilfully carried out the negotiations so that Japan was forced into the position of walking away from the talks. However, the Roosevelt Administration threw away the potential domestic political impetus provided by its diplomacy by failing to inaugurate a major shipbuilding programme in 1937. Instead, Japan's naval build-up initially went unanswered. See the perceptive account of Roosevelt's actions offered in Robert Gordon Kaufman, *Arms Control During the Pre-Nuclear Era: The United States and Naval Limitation between the Two World Wars* (New York: Columbia University Press, 1990), pp. 180–91.

Notes on Contributors

David Armstrong is a Senior Lecturer at the University of Birmingham, and former Director of its Graduate School of International Studies. He is editor of the journal *Diplomacy & Statecraft*, the author of *Revolutionary Diplomacy: Chinese Foreign Policy and the United Front Doctrine* (1977), *The Rise of the International Organisation* (1982), and *Revolution and World Order* (1993), and co-editor of *The End of the Cold War* (1990).

Sadao Asada is Professor of International History at Doshisha University. He received his Ph.D. from Yale University and was Executive Secretary of the Center for American Studies, Doshisha University, 1963–71. He is the editor of *Japan and the World, 1853–1952: A Bibliographical Guide to Japanese Scholarship in Foreign Relations* (1989) and the author of *Senkanki no Nichi-Bei kankei – Kaigun to seisaku kettei katei* [Japanese–American Relations Between the Wars: The Navies and the Decision-Making Process] (1993).

Joel Blatt is Associate Professor of European History at the University of Connecticut, Stamford Campus, where he has been awarded the 1992 Outstanding Teacher Award. He is the author of numerous articles on interwar Franco-Italian relations, and is working on two books, 'Non Mollare: The Assassination of Carlo and Nello Rosselli' and 'The Italian Civil War in France: Episodes of Conflict Between Italian Fascists and Italian Antifascists in France, 1922–40'.

William R. Braisted is Professor Emeritus of History at the University of Texas in Austin. He is author of the pathbreaking studies *The United States Navy in the Pacific, 1897–1909* (1958), *The United States Navy in the Pacific, 1897–1909* (1971), and *Meiroku Zasshi: Journal of the Japanese Enlightenment* (1977).

Thomas H. Buckley is Professor of American Diplomatic History at the University of Tulsa. He is the author of *The United States and the Washington Conference, 1921–1922* (1970) and co-author of *American Foreign and National Security Policies, 1914–1945* (1987).

Michael Graham Fry is Professor of International Relations, University of Southern California. He is the author of *Illusions of Security: North Atlantic Diplomacy 1918–1922* (1972), *Lloyd George and Foreign Policy*, Volume One. *The Education of a Statesman, 1890–1916* (1977) and *History, the White House and the Kremlin. Statesmen as Historians* (1991).

Erik Goldstein is Reader in International History at the University of Birmingham. He is co-editor of *Diplomacy & Statecraft* and author of *Winning the Peace: British Diplomatic Strategy, Peace Planning, and the Paris Peace Conference, 1916–1920* (1991), *Wars & Peace Treaties, 1816–1991* (1992), and co-editor of *The End of the Cold War* (1990).

John H. Maurer is an Associate Professor in the Strategy Department of the Naval War College in Newport, Rhode Island. He is also the assistant editor of *Diplomacy & Statecraft*. Before joining the faculty of the Naval War College he served as executive editor of *Orbis: A Journal of World Affairs* and as a research analyst at the Foreign Policy Research Institute. He is co-editor of *Military Intervention in the Third World* (1984) and is at present completing a book on the outbreak of the First World War.

B.J.C. McKercher is an Associate Professor of History at the Royal Military College of Canada. He is the author of *The Second Baldwin Government and the United States, 1924–1929* (1984) and *Esme Howard: A Diplomatic Biography* (1989). He is the editor of *Anglo-American Relations in the 1920s: The Struggle for Supremacy* (1991) and *Arms Limitation and Disarmament: Restraints on War, 1899–1939* (1992).

Brian R. Sullivan is a Senior Fellow at the Institute for National Strategic Studies at the National Defense University. He served in

Vietnam as a Marine infantry platoon commander, winning the Silver Star. After receiving his Ph.D. from Columbia University he taught at Yale University and the Naval War College. He is co-author of *Il Duce's Other Woman* (1993), a biography of Margherita Sarfatti, and has published numerous articles on Italian military, naval and diplomatic history.

Bibliography

I. PRIMARY SOURCES: GOVERNMENT ARCHIVES

Australia: Australian Archives, Canberra.
   Papers of the Department of External Affairs.
Canada: National Archives of Canada, Ottawa
   Department of External Affairs Papers
France: Archives de l'Assemblée Nationale, Paris
   Commission des Affaires Etrangères, Chambre des Députés
   Commission des Finances, Chambre des Députés
   Commission de la Marine Militaire, Chambre des Députés
France: Archives du Sénat, Palais du Luxembourg, Paris
France: Archives de la Marine, Vincennes
France: Archives du Ministère des Affaires Etrangères, Paris
   Series B: Amerique, 1918–40
   Series Y: Internationale, 1918–40
France: Service Historique de l'Armée, Vincennes
Japan: Diplomatic Record Office, Ministry of Foreign Affairs, Tokyo.
Japan: War History Department, National Institute of Defence Studies of the Defence
   Agency, Tokyo.
New Zealand: National Archives of New Zealand, Wellington
   External Affairs Department Papers
   Governors-General Papers
   Navy Department Papers
   Prime Minister's Papers
United Kingdom: Public Record Office, Kew, London
   Admiralty Papers
      ADM 1   Admiralty and Secretariat Papers
      ADM 116   Admiralty: Secretary's Department
      ADM 167   Board Minutes, Memoranda, etc.
   Cabinet Papers
      CAB 2   Committee of Imperial Defence: Committee on Co-Ordination of
      Departmental Action
      CAB 4   Committee of Imperial Defence: Memoranda
      CAB 16   Committee of Imperial Defence Ad-Hoc Sub-Committees of Inquiry:
      Proceedings and Memoranda
      CAB 21   Registered Cabinet Office Files: Miscellaneous Papers
      CAB 23   Cabinet Minutes
      CAB 24   Cabinet Memoranda
      CAB 30   Washington (Disarmament) Conference
      CAB 32   Imperial Conferences

Foreign Office Papers
    FO 371   General Correspondence: Political
    FO 800   Private Collections
United States: National Archives, Washington, DC
    RG 38 Chief of Naval Operations Papers
    RG 59 Department of State, 1910–29 Papers
    RG 80 General Board Papers
    RG 225 Joint Army and Navy Board Papers
United States: Naval Historical Center Archives
Unites States: Naval War College Archives, Newport, RI

II. PRIMARY SOURCES: PRIVATE PAPERS

Baldwin, 1st Earl. University Library, Cambridge.
Balfour, 1st Earl of. British Library, London
Borden, Sir Robert. National Archives of Canada, Ottawa.
Bridgeman, Lord. Churchill College Archive Centre, Cambridge.
Castle, William R. Hoover Presidential Library, West Branch, Iowa.
Cecil of Chelwood. British Library, London.
Christie, Loring. National Archives of Canada, Ottawa.
Churchill, Sir Winston. Churchill College Archive Centre, Cambridge.
Lodge, Henry Cabot. Massachusetts Historical Society, Boston.
Dumesnil, Jacques-Louis. Archives Nationales, Paris.
Enomoto Juji. (Photocopies in possession of Sadao Asada)
Gardiner, William Howard. Houghton Library, Harvard University.
Hardinge of Penshurst, Lord. University Library, Cambridge.
Hori Teikichi. (Photocopies in possession of Sadao Asada)
House, Edward. Sterling Memorial Library, Yale University.
Hughes, William. Australian Archives, Canberra.
Jusserand, Jules. Archives, Ministère des Affaires Etrangères, Paris.
Lloyd George, 1st Earl. House of Lords Record Office, London.
Lodge, Henry Cabot. Massachusetts Historical Society, Boston.
MacDonald, Ramsay. Public Record Office, London.
Makino Nobukai. Kensei Shiryo Shitsu [Depository for Documents on Political and
    Constitutional History], Diet Library, Tokyo.
Piesse, E.L. Australian Archives, Canberra.
Pratt, William. Naval Historical Division, Washington, D.C.
Roosevelt Jr. Theodore, Library of Congress, Washington, D.C.
Saito Makoto. Kensei Shiryo Shitsu [Depository for Documents on Political and Constitu-
    tional History], Diet Library, Tokyo.
Tardieu, André. Archives du Ministère des Affaires Etrangères, Paris.

Government Publications

France. *Journal Officiel*, Chambre des Députés.
—— *Journal Officiel*, Sénat.
Great Britain. *Documents on British Foreign Policy, 1919–1939*, First Series (London,
    1947–67).

—— Command Papers
Command Papers 619, 1581, 1582, 1603, 1818, 2071, 2366, 2595, 2816, 3052, 3283, 3485, 3556
Command Paper 2029. *Treaty Between the British Empire, France, Italy, Japan, and the USA for the Limitation of Naval Armaments (The Washington Treaty).*
—— *Parliamentary Debates, Commons.*
—— *Parliamentary Debates, Lords*
Italy. Istituto Centrale di Statistico del Regno d'Italia. *Annuario statistico italiano* (Rome, 1926–1942).
Japan. Foreign Ministry, ed. *Nihon gaiko bunsho: Washington kaigi* [Documents on Japanese Foreign Policy: Washington Conference], 2 vols. (Tokyo, 1977–78).
—— Foreign Ministry, ed. *Nihon gaiko bunsho: Junevu kaigun gunshuku kaigi* [Documents on Japanese Foreign Policy: Geneva Naval Conference] (Tokyo, 1982).
—— Foreign Ministry, ed. *Nihon gaiko bunsho: 1930 – nen rondon kaigun gunshuku kaigi* [Documents on Japanese Foreign Policy: London Naval Conference of 1930], 2 vols. (Tokyo, 1983–84).
—— Boeicho Senshishitsu [War History Office, Defence Agency], ed. *Senshi sosho, Daihon'ei kaigunbu: Rengo kantai* [War history series: Imperial Headquarters, Navy].
—— *Sensi sosho: Daihon'ei rikugunbu* [War history series: Imperial Headquarters, Army] (Tokyo, 1967).
—— *Sensi sosho: Kaigun gunsenbi* [War history series: Naval armaments and preparations] (Tokyo, 1969).
Japan. Navy Minister's Secretariat, ed. *Kaigun gunbi enkaku* [The development of naval armaments] (Tokyo, 1934, reprinted 1970).
United States, *Congressional Record.*
—— Department of the Navy. *Navy Yearbook, 1920–1921* (Washington, 1922)
—— Department of State. *Conference on the Limitation of Armament. Washington. November 12, 1921 – February 6, 1922* (Washington, 1922).
—— Department of State. *Conference on the Limitation of Armament. Washington. November 12, 1921 – February 6, 1922: Subcommittees* (Washington, 1922)
—— *Papers Relating to the Foreign Relations of the United States, 1921* (Washington, 19).
—— *Papers Relating to the Foreign Relations of the United States, 1922* (Washington, 1938).
—— *Papers Relating to the Foreign Relations of the United States, 1927*, vol. I (Washington, 1942).
—— *Proceedings of the London Naval Conference of 1930* (Washington, 1931).
—— *Treaties and Other International Agreements of the United States of America, 1776–1949* (Washington, 1950).
—— World War Foreign Debt Commission. *Combined Annual Reports of the World War Foreign Debt Commission* (Washington, 1927).

Published Documents

Albertini, Luigi. *Epistolario 1911–1926*, vol III, *Il dopoguerra*, Ottavio Barie, ed. (Milan 1968).
Gilbert, Martin, ed. *Winston S. Churchill*, companion volume IV, part 1 (London, 1977); part 2 (London, 1977 and Boston, 1978); part 3 (London, 1977); companion vol V, part 1 (London, 1979).
Hara Keiichiro, ed. *Hara Kei nikki* [Diary of Hara Kei], Vol. 5 (Tokyo, 1965).

Harada Kumao. *Saionjiko to seikyoku* [Prince Saionji and politics], Vol 8 and supplementary vols. (Tokyo, 1950–56).

Ikei Masaru, Hatano Masuru, Kurosawa Fumitaka, eds. *Hamaguchi Osachi nikki zuikanroku* [Diary and memos of Hamaguchi Osachi] (Tokyo, 1991).

Ito Takashi and Nomura Minoru, ed. *Kaigun Taisho – Kobayashi Seizo oboegaki* [Memos of Admiral Kobayashi Seizo] (Tokyo, 1981).

Kido Nikki Kenkyukai, ed. *Kido Koichi kankei monjo* [Papers relating to Kido Koichi] (Tokyo, 1966).

Kobayashi Tatsuo and Shimada Toshihiko, eds. Gendaishi shiryo [Documents on Contemporary history], vol. 7 (Tokyo, 1964).

Middlemas, K., ed. *Thomas Jones. Whitehall Diary* (London, 1969).

Nihon Kokusai Seiji Gakkai [Japan Association of International relations], ed., *Taiheiyo Senso e no michi: Bekkan shiryohen* [The Road to the Pacific War: Supplementary volume of documents] (Tokyo, 1963)

Patterson, A. Temple, ed. *The Jellicoe Papers*, 2 vols. (London, 1968).

Ramm, A., ed. *The Political Correspondence of Mr. Gladstone and Lord Granville, 1876–86*, vol. I (Oxford, 1962)

Saito Shishaku Kinenkai, ed. *Shishaku Saito Makoto den* [Biography of Viscount Saito Makoto], 4 vols. (Tokyo, 1941–42).

Taylor, A.J.P., ed. *Lloyd George: A Diary by Frances Stevenson* (New York, 1971).

Watt, D.C. and Bourne, K., eds. British Documents on Foreign Affairs: Reports from the Foreign Office Confidential Print. Part I: From the Nineteenth Century to the First World War. Stevenson, David, ed. Series F. *Europe, 1848–1914* (Bethesda, Maryland, 1987).

Newspapers and Periodicals
Jane's Fighting Ships
L'Action Française
Naval Annual
New York Herald
New York Times
Washington Post

Secondary Sources

Ando Yoshio, ed. *Showa keizaishi e no shogen* [Witness account of the economic history of the Showa period] (Tokyo, 1956).

Andrade Jr., Ernest. 'Arms Limitation Agreements and the Evolution of Weaponry: The Case of the "Treaty Cruiser"' in

Daniel M. Masterson, ed. *Naval History. The Sixth Syposium of the US Naval Academy* (Wilmington, 1987).

Andrew, Christopher and A.S. Kanya-Forstner. *The Climax of French Imperial Expansion, 1914–1924* (Stanford, 1981).

—— 'La France à la recherche de la Syrie intégrale, 1914–1920' *Relations internationales* 19 (1979).

—— 'The French Colonial Party and French Colonial War Aims, 1914–1918' *Historical Journal* 17 (1974).

Archimbaud, Léon. *La Conférence de Washington, 12 novembre 1921 – 6 février 1922* (Paris, 1923).

Aritake Shuji. *Saito Makoto* (Tokyo, 1958).

—— *Okada Keisuke* (Tokyo, 1956).

Artaud, Denise. *La question des dettes interalliées et la recontruction de l'Europe, 1917–1929* (Paris, 1978).

Asada, Sadao. 'Japanese Admirals and the Politics of Naval Limitation: Kato Tomosaburo vs Kato Kanji', in Gerald Jordan, ed. *Naval Warfare in the Twentieth Century, 1909–1945: Essays in Honour of Arthur Marder* (London, 1977).

—— 'Japan's "Special Interests" and the Washington Conference, 1921–1922', *American Historical Review* 66:1 (October 1961):62–70.

—— 'Japanese Navy and the United States' in Dorothy Borg and Shumpei Okamoto, *Pearl Harbor as History: Japanese American Relations, 1931–1941* (New York, 1973)

—— *Ryo-taisenkan no Nichi-Bei kankei – Kaigun to seisaku kettei* [Japanese-American relations between the World Wars: Navies and the decision-making process] (Tokyo, 1993).

—— 'Washington kaigi o meguru Nichi-Bei seisaku kettei katei no hikaku: Hito to kiko' [A comparative study of the Japanese and American decision-making process at the time of the Washington Conference: Decision-makers and mechanisms], in Hosoya Chihiro and Watanuku Joji, *Taigai seisaku kettei katei no Nichi-Bei hikaku* [Comparative Studies of the foreign policy decision-making process in Japan and the United States] (Tokyo, 1977).

Auphan, Paul and Jacques Mordal. *The French Navy in World War II* (Annapolis, 1959).

Baioroch, Paul. 'Europe's Gross National Product, 1800–1975' *Journal of European Economic History* 5 (1976):273–340.

Bargoni, Franco and Franco Gay. *Orizzonte mare. Navi italiane nella 2a guerra mondiale. Corazzate*, vol 1, *Classe Conte di Cavour*, vol 2, *Classe Caio Duilio* (Rome, 1972).

Barnett, Corelli. *The Collpase of British Power* (New York, 1972).

Beasley, W.G. *The Rise of Modern Japan* (London, 1990).

Beaverbrook, Lord. *The Decline and Fall of Lloyd George* (London, 1963).

Bell, A.C. *A History of the Blockade of Germany* (London, 1937).

Becker, William H. and Samuel F. Wells, Jr., eds., *Economics and World Power* (New York, 1984).

Bérenger, Henry. *Le pétrole de la France* (Paris, 1920).

Berkowitz, Bruce D. *Calculated Risks* (New York, 1987)

Bernardini, Giovanni. *Il disarmo navale fra le due guerre mondiali, 1919–1939* (Rome, 1975)

—— 'La dibattuta questione della parita navale tra Italia e Francia nel periodo tra le due guerre mondiali' *Revue Internationale d'Histoire Militaire* 39 (1978): 66–70.

Bernotti, Romeo. 'Italian Naval Policy Under Fascism', *United States Naval Institute Proceedings* (1956).

Bertram-Libal, G. *Aspekte der britischen Deutschlandspolitik, 1919–1922* (Göppingen, 1972).

Bickel, W.H. *Die Anglo-Amerikanische Beziehungen 1927–1930 im Licht der Flottenfrage* (Zurich, 1970).

Birn, Donald S. 'Britain and France at the Washington Conference, 1921–1922' Ph.D. dissertation, Columbia University, 1964.

—— 'Open Diplomacy at the Washington Conference of 1921–22: The British and French Experience' *Comparative Studies in Society and History* 12 (1970):297–319.

—— 'The Washington Naval Conference of 1921–22 in Anglo-French Relations' in Daniel M. Masterson, ed. *Naval History. The Sixth Syposium of the US Naval Academy* (Wilmington, 1987).

Blatt, Joel. 'Aristide Briand' in Patrick H. Hutton, ed., *Historical Dictionary of the Third French Republic, 1870–1940* (New York and Westport, 1986).

—— 'France and the Corfu-Fiume Crisis of 1923' *The Historian* 50 (1988):234–59.

——'France and Italy at the Paris Peace Conference' *International History Review* 8 (1986): 27–40.

—— France and the Franco-Italian Entente, 1918–1923' *Storia delle relazioni internazionali* 6 (1990/2): 173–97.

—— 'Franco-Italian Relations, 1880–1940', in Frank J. Coppa, ed., *Studies in Modern Italian History from the Risorgimento to the Republic* (in honor of A. William Salomone) (New York, 1986), pp. 171–96.

—— 'French Reaction to Italy, Italian Fascism and Mussolini, 1919–1925: The Views from Paris and the Palazzo Farnese', Ph.D. dissertation, University of Rochester, 1977.

—— 'The Parity that Meant Superiority: French Naval Policy towards Italy at the Washington Naval Conference, 1921–22, and Interwar French Foreign Policy' *French Historical Studies* 12 (1981):223–48.

Boothe, Leon E. 'A Fettered Envoy: Lord Grey's Mission to the United States, 1919–1920' *The Review of Politics* 33:1 (January 1971):78–94.

Borg, Dorothy and Shumpei Okamoto, *Pearl Harbor as History: Japanese American Relations, 1931–1941* (New York, 1973).

Botti, Ferruccio, and Virgilio Ilari. *Il pensiero militare italiano dal primo al secondo dopoguerra, 1919–1949* (Rome, 1985).

Brailsford, H.N. *The Origins of the Great War*, Union for Democratic Control Pamphlet No. 4 (London, undated).

Braistead, William Reynolds. 'On the American Red and Red-Orange Plans, 1919–1939' in Gerald Jordan, *Naval Warfare in the Twentieth Century, 1900–1945: Essays in Honor of Arthur Marder* (London, 1977).

—— 'On the 1925 Australian Cruise of the American Fleet' *Pull Together: Newsletter of the Naval Historical Center* 29 (1990):1–4.

—— *The United States Navy in the Pacific, 1909–1922* (Austin, 1971).

Brandes. J. *Herbert Hoover and Economic Diplomacy: Department of Commerce Policy, 1921–1928* (Pittsburgh, 1962).

Breyer, Siegfried. *Battleships and Battle Cruisers, 1905–1970.* (Garden City, New York, 1973).

Brodie, Bernard. *A Guide to Naval Strategy* (rev. ed. New Yrok, 1963)

Buckley, Thomas H. *The United States and the Washington Conference, 1921–1922* (Knoxville, 1970).

—— 'The Washington Naval Treaties' in Michael Krepon and Dan Caldwell, eds. *The Politics of Arms Control Treaty Ratification* (New York, 1991)

Burk, Kathleen, *Britain, America and the Sinews of War, 1914–1918* (London, 1985).

—— 'The Diplomacy of Finance: British Financial Missions to the United States, 1914–1918' *Historical Journal* 22 (1979): 405–16.

—— 'The Mobilization of Anglo-American Finance During World War I' in N.F. Dreisziger, ed., *Mobilization for Total War* (Waterloo, Ontario, 1981).

—, ed. *War and State: the Transformation of the British Government, 1914–1919* (London, 1982).

Buell, Raymond Leslie. *The Washington Conference* (New York, 1922).

Burns, Richard Dean and David Urquidi. *Disarmament in Perspective: An Analysis of Selected Arms Control and Disarmament. Agreements between the World Wars, 1919–1939* (Washington, 1968).

Butler, D. and A. Sloman. *British Political Facts 1900–1975* (London, 1975).

Bywater, Hector C. *The Great Pacific War* (Boston, 1925).

—— *Their Secret Purposes: Dramas and Mysteries of the Naval War* (London, 1932).

Campbell, J. *Lloyd George: The Goat in the Wilderness, 1922–31* (London, 1977).
Carlton, David. 'Great Britain and the Coolidge Naval Disarmament Conference of 1927' *Political Science Quarterly* 82 (1967):573–99.
—— *MacDonald versus Henderson. The Foreign Policy of the Second Labour Government* (London, 1970).
Cassels, A. 'Repairing the *Entente Cordiale* and the New Diplomacy' *Historical Journal* 23 (1980): 133–53.
Ceadl, M. *Pacifism in Britain 1914–1945: The Defining of a Faith* (Oxford, 1980).
Cecil of Chelwood, Lord. *A Great Experiment* (London, 1941).
Ceva, Lucio. 'L'evoluzione dei materiale bellici in Italia' in Ennio Di Nolfo, Romain H. Rainero and Brunello Vigezzi, eds. *L'Italia e la politica di potenza in Europa, 1938–1940* (Milan, 1985).
—— *Le forze armate* (Turin, 1981).
—— 'Grande industria e guerra' in Romain H. Rainero and A. Biagini, eds., *L'Italia in guerra: Il primo anno – 1940* (Rome, 1991).
Ceva, Lucio and Andrea Curami. *Industria bellica anni trenta. Commesse militari, l'Ansaldo ed altri* (Milan, 1992).
Chamberlain, A. *Peace in Our Time: Addresses on Europe and the Empire* (London, 1928).
Chatfield, A. Ernle M. *It Might Happen Again* (London, 1947).
Chiavarelli, Emilia. *L'Opera della marina nella guerra italo-etiopica* (Milan, 1969).
Cline, C.A. *E.D. Morel, 1873–1924: The Strategies of Protest* (Belfast, 1980).
Clough, Shepheard B. *The Economic History of Italy* (New York, 1964).
Coppa, Frank J., *Studies in Modern Italian History from the Risorgimento to the Republic* (in honor of A. William Salomone) (New York, 1986).
Costigliola, Frank. 'Anglo-American Financial Rivalry in the 1920's' *Journal of Economic History* 37 (1977):911–34.
—— *Awkward Dominion: American Political, Economic, and Cultural realtions with Europe, 1919–1933* (Ithaca, 1984).
Couhat, Jean Labayle. *French Warships of World War II* (London, 1971).
Coutau-Bégarie, Hervé and Claud Huan. *Darlan* (Paris, 1989).
Dayer, Roberta Allbert, 'The British War Debts to the United States and the Anglo-Japanese Alliance, 1920–1923' *Pacific Historical Review* 45:4 (1976):569–95.
Dictionnaire des parlementaires français, 1889–1940, vol. VI (Paris, 1970)
Dingman, Roger. *Power in the Pacific: The Origins of Naval Arms Limitation, 1914–1922* (Chicago, 1976).
Doyle, Michael. 'Kant, Liberal Legacies, and Foreign Affairs' *Philosophy and Public Affairs* 12:3 (Summer 1983):205–35 and 12:4 (Fall 1983):323–53.
—— 'Liberalism and World Poltics' *American Political Science Review* 80:4 (December, 1986):1151–1169.
Dreisziger, N.F., ed., *Mobilization for Total War* (Waterloo, Ontario, 1981).
Egerton, G.W. *Great Britain and the Creation of the League of Nations: Strategy, Politics, and International Organization, 1914–1919* (London, 1979).
Egremont, Max. *Balfour: A Life of Arthur James Balfour* (London, 1980).
Ehrman, J. 'Lloyd George and Churchill as War Ministers' *Transactions of the Royal Historical Society*, 5th Series, 11 (1961):101–15.
Engely, Giovanni. *The Politics of Naval Disarmament* (London, 1932).
Epstein, Marc. 'The Historians and the Geneva Naval Conference' in B.J.C. McKercher, ed., *Arms Limitation and Disaramament: Restraints on War, 1899–1939* (Westport, Connecticut, 1992)
Fanning, Richard W. 'The Collidge Conference of 1927: Disarmament in Disarray' in

B.J.C. McKercher, ed., *Arms Limitation and Disaramament: Restraints on War, 1899–1939* (Westport, Connecticut, 1992).

Ferrante, Ezio. *La grande guerra in Adriatico nel LXX anniversario della vittoria* (Rome, 1987).

—— *Il Grande Ammiraglio Paolo Thaon di Revel* (Rome, 1989).

—— *Il pensiero strategico navale in Italia* (Rome, 1988).

—— 'Un rischio calcolato? Mussolini e gli ammiragli nella gestione della crisi di Corfu' *Storia della relazioni internazionali* 2 (1989): 221–44.

Ferris, John R. 'The Greatest Power on Earth: Great Britain in the 1920's' *International History Review* 13:4 (November 1991): 726–50.

—— *Men, Money, and Diplomacy: The Evolution of British Strategic Policy, 1919–26* (Ithaca, 1989).

—— 'The Symbol and the Substance of Seapower: Great Britain, the United States, and the One-Power Standard, 1919–1921' in B.J.C. McKercher, ed., *Anglo-French Relations in the 1920's: The Struggle for Supremacy* (London, 1991).

Fink, Carole. *The Genoa Conference: European Diplomacy, 1921–1922* (Chapel Hill and London, 1984).

Fock, Harald. *Fast Fighting Boats, 1870–1945. Their Design, Construction and Use* (Annapolis, 1978).

Fraccaroli, Aldo. *Italian Warships of World War II* (London, 1968).

Frankenstein, Robert. 'A propos des aspects financiers du réarmement français, 1935–1939' *Revue d'histoire de la deuxième guerre mondiale'* 26 (1976): 1–20.

Freidel, Frank. *Franklin D. Roosevelt: The Apprenticeshop* (Boston, 1952).

Friedman, George and Meredith Lebard. *The Coming War with Japan* (New York, 1991)

Fritz, S.E. 'La Politque de la Ruhr and Lloyd Georgian Conference Diplomacy: The Tragedy of Anglo-French Relations, 1919–1923' *Proceedings of the Annual Meeting of the Western Society for French History* 3 (1975):566–82.

Fry, Michael. 'Anglo-American-Canadian Realations, with special reference to Naval and far Eastern Issues, 1918–1922', Ph.D. dissertation, University of London, 1963.

—— *Illusions of Security: North Atlantic Diplomacy, 1918–1922* (Toronto, 1972)

Gabriele, Mariano. 'Origini della convenzione naval italo-austro-germanica del 1913' *Rassegna storica del Risorgimento* 52(1965):325–44, 489–509.

Garcia y Robertson, Rodrigo. 'The Green Table: The Technological Link between Armament and Disarmament in the Beginning of the Twentieth Century' Ph.D. dissertation, University of California, Los Angeles, 1981.

Garzke, William H. Jr., and Robert O. Dulin, Jr. *Battleships: Allied Battleships in World War II* (Annapolis, 1980).

—— *Battleships: Axis and Neutral Battleships of World War II* (Annapolis, 1985).

Gay, Franco. *Orizzonte mare. Navi italiane nella 2a guerra mondiale*, vol. 4, *Incrociatori pesanti. Classe Trento*, part 1 (Rome, 1975).

Gay, Franco and Valerio. *The Cruiser Bartolomeo Colleoni.* (Annapolis, 1987).

Gilpin, Robert. *War and Change in World Politics* (Cambridge, 1981)

Giorgerini, Giorgio. 'The Cavour & Duilio Class Battleships' *Warship* 4 (1980).

Giorgerini, Giorgio and Augusto Nani. *Almanacco storico delle navi militari italiane* (Rome, 1978).

Goldman, Emily O. 'The Washington Treaty System: Arms Racing and Arms Control in the Interwar Period' Ph.D. dissertation, Stanford University, 1989.

Goldstein, Erik. *Winning the Peace: British Diplomatic Strategy, Peace Planning, and the Paris Peace Conference, 1916–1920* (Oxford, 1991).

Gray, Colin. *House of Cards: Why Arms Control Must Fail* (Ithaca, 1992).

Grossman, Mark. *Italian Battleships of World War Two* (Missoula, Montana, 1986).

Hall, C. *Britain, America, and Arms Control, 1921–37* (London, 1987).

Halpern, Paul. *The Mediterranean Naval Situation, 1908–1914* (Cambridge, Massachusetts, 1971).

—— *The Naval War in the Mediterranean, 1914–1918* (London, 1987).

Hamill, Ian. *The Strategic Illusion: The Singapore Strategy and the Defense of Australia and New Zealand* (Singapore, 1981).

Hanmachi Eiichi. *Ningen Yamamoto Isoroku* [Yamamoto Isoroku as a human being] (Tokyo, 1964).

Hattendorf, John B. and Robert S. Jordan, eds. *Maritime Strategy and the Balance of Power: Britain and America in the Twentieth Century* (New York, 19).

Hawley, E.W. 'Herbert Hoover, the Commerce Department Secreteriat, and the Vision of an Associated State, 1921–1928' *Journal of American History* 61 (1974–75):116–40.

Heisser, David. 'The Impact of the Great War on French Imperialism, 1914–1924.' Ph.D. dissertation, University of North Carolina, 1972.

Henderson, A. *Labour and Foreign Affairs* (London, 1922)

Hoag, Charles L. *Preface to Preparedness: the Washington Conference and Public Opinion* (Washington, 1941).

Hogan, M.J. *Informal Entente: the private structure of cooperation in Anglo-American economic diplomacy, 1918–1928.* (Columbia, Missouri, 1977).

Honan, William H. *Visions of Infamy: The Untold Story of How Journalist Hector C. Bywater Devised the Plans that Led to Pearl Harbor* (New York, 1991)

Hood, Ronald Chalmers. *Royal Republicans. The French Naval Dynasties Between the World Wars* (Baton Rouge and London, 1985).

Hosoya Chihiro and Watanuku Joji, *Taigai seisaku kettei katei no Nichi-Bei hikaku* [Comparative Studies of the foreign policy decision-making process in Japan and the United States] (Tokyo, 1977).

Hudson, W.J. *Australia and the League of Nations* (Sydney, 1980).

Ichihashi, Yamoto. *The Washington Conference and After* (Stanford, 1928).

Ikeda Kiyoshi. *Nihon no kaigun* [A history of the Japanese navy] 2 vols. (Tokyo, 1967; revised ed. 1987).

—— 'Rondon gunshuku joyaku to tosuiken mondai' [The London Naval Treaty and the problem of the right of the supreme command] *Hogaku zasshi* 15 (1968):1–35.

Iriye, Akira. *After Imperialism: The Search for a New World Order in the Far East, 1921–1931* (New York, 1973).

Ishii Kikujiro. *Gaiko yoroku* [Diplomatic commentaries] (Tokyo, 1930).

Ito Takashi. *Showa shoki seijishi kenkyu: Rondon kaigun gunshuku mondai o meguru sho seiji shudan no taiko to teikei* [A study of the political history of the early Showa period: conflicts and alignments of political groups over the issue of naval limitation] (Tokyo, 1969).

Joll, James. *The Origins of the First World War* (London, 1984).

Johnson, P.B. *Land Fit for Heroes: The Planning of British Reconstruction, 1916–1919* (London, 1968).

Jordan, Gerald, *Naval Warfare in the Twentieth Century, 1900–1945: Essays in Honor of Arthur Marder* (London, 1977).

Jori, Gino. 'I perchè e i limiti della nostra inferiorità nella seconda guerra mondiale' *Revista marittima* (1988).

Kato Kanji Taisho Denki Kankokai, comp. *Kato Kanji taisho den* [Biography of Admiral Kato Kanji] (Tokyo, 1941).

Kaufman, Robert Gordon. *Arms Control During the Pre-Nuclear Era: The United States and Naval Limitation between the Two World Wars* (New York, 1990).

Kennedy, Gregory C. 'The 1930 London Naval Conference and Anglo-American Maritime Strength, 1927–1930' in *Arms Limitation and Disaramament: Restraints on War, 1899–1939* (Westport, Connecticut, 1992).

Kennedy, Paul. *The Rise and Fall of the Great Power* (New York, 1987).

Kiba Kosuke. *Nomura Kichisaburo* (Tokyo, 1961).

King, Wunsz, ed. *V.K. Wellington Koo's Foreign Policy* (Shanghai).

Klein, Ira. 'Whitehall, Washington and the Anglo-Japanese Alliance, 1919–1921' *Pacific Historical Review* 41 (1972): 460–83.

Ko Matsudaira Tsuisokai, comp. *Matsudaira Tsuneo tsuisoroku* [Reminiscences of Matsudaira Tsuneo] (Tokyo, 1961).

Kobayashi Tatsuo. 'The London Treaty, 1930' in James William Morley, ed. *Japan Erupts: The London Naval Conference and the Manchurian Incident, 1928–1932* (New York, 1984).

Krepon, Michael and Dan Caldwell, eds. *The Politics of Arms Control Treaty Ratification* (New York, 1991)

Kuisel, Richard F. *Ernest Mercier: French Technocrat* (Berkley and Los Angeles, 1967).

Kurihara Hirota, ed. *Gensui Kato Tomosaburo den* [Biography of Fleet Admiral Kato Tomosaburo] (Tokyo, 1928).

Lefler, Melyvn P. '1921–1932: Expansionist Impulses and Domestic Constraints' in William H Becker and Samuel F. Wells, Jr., eds., *Economics and World Power* (New York, 1984).

Lowe, P. 'The Rise to Premiership, 1914–1916', in A.J.P. Taylor, *Lloyd George: Twelve Essays* (London, 1971).

MacDonald, J.R. *The Foreign Policy of the Labour Party* (London, 1923).

MacGibbon, I.C. *Blue Water Rationale: the Naval Defense of New Zealand, 1914–1942* (Wellington, 1981).

—— 'The Consitutional Implications of Lord Jellicoe's Influence on New Zealand Naval Policy, 1919–1930' *New Zealand Journal of History* 6:1 (1972):57–80.

Mackay, Ruddock. *Balfour: Intellectual Statesman* (Oxford, 1985).

Madriaga, Salvador de. *Disarmament* (New York, 1929).

Marks, Sally. *The Illusion of Peace: International Relations in Europe, 1918–1933* (New York, 1976).

—— 'Ménage à Trois: The Negotiations for an Anglo-French-Belgian Alliance in 1922' *International History Review* 4 (1982):524–52.

Masson, Philippe, Michèle Battesti and Jacques C. Favier. *Marine et constructions navales, 1789–1989* (Paris, 1989).

Masson, Philippe. *Histoire de la Marine*, vol. 2, *De la vapeur à l'atome* (Paris-Limoges, 1983).

—— 'La marine française en 1939–1940' *Revue historique des armées* 4 (1979): 57–77.

—— *La marine française et la guerre 1939–1945* (Paris, 1991).

—— 'La politique navale française de 1919 à 1939' *La Revue Maritime* 252 (1968).

Masterson, Daniel M., ed. *Naval History. The Sixth Syposium of the US Naval Academy* (Wilmington, 1987).

Maurer, John H. 'Arms Control and Anglo-German Naval Rivalry' *Political Science Quarterly*.

Mahan, Alfred Thayer. *The Influence of Sea Power Upon History, 1660–1783* (Boston, 1890).

—— *The Interest of America in Sea Power, Present and Future* (Boston, 1897).

Marquand, D. *Ramsay MacDonald* (London, 1977).

McCarthy, J.M. *Australia and Imperial Defense, 1918–1939: A Study in Air and Sea Power* (St. Lucia, Queensland, 1976).

McIntyre, D.W. *New Zealand Prepares for War: Defense Policy, 1919–1939* (Christchurch, 1986),

The Rise and Fall of the Singapore Naval Base, 1919–1942 (London, 1979).

McDonald, J. Kenneth. 'Lloyd George and the Search for a Postwar Naval Policy, 1919' in A.J.P. Taylor, ed. *Lloyd George: Twelve Essays* (New York, 1971).

—— 'The Washington Conference and the Naval Balance of Power, 1921–22' in John B. Hattendorf and Robert S. Jordan, eds. *Maritime Strategy and the Balance of Power: Britain and America in the Twentieth Century* (New York, 19).

McKercher, B.J.C., ed., *Anglo-French Relations in the 1920's: The Struggle for Supremacy* (London, 1991).

—— , ed., *Arms Limitation and Disaramament: Restraints on War, 1899–1939* (Westport, Connecticut, 1992).

—— 'Austen Chamberlain's Control of British Foreign Policy, 1924–1929' *International History Review* 6 (1984): 507–680.

—— 'Belligerent Rights in 1927–1929: Freign Policy versus Naval Policy in the Second Baldwin Government' *Historical Journal* 29 (1986): 963–74.

—— *Esme Howard. A Diplomatic Biography* (Cambridge, 1989).

—— *The Second Baldwin Government and the United States, 1924–1929: attitudes and diplomacy* (Cambridge, 1984)

—— 'Wealth, Power, and the New International Order: Britain and the American Challenge in the 1920's' *Diplomatic History* 12:4 (Fall 1988):411–41.

Middlemas, Keith and J. Barnes. *Baldwin: A Biography* (London, 1967).

Miller, Edward S. *War Plan Orange: The U.S. Strategy to Defeat Japan, 1897–1945* (Annapolis, 1991).

Morel, E.D. *The Morrow of the War*, Union for Democratic Control Pamphlet No. 1 (London, 1914).

Morgan, K.O. *Consensus and Disunity: The Lloyd George Coalition Government, 1918–1922* (London, 1979).

—— 'Lloyd George's Premiership: A Study in Prime Minsiterial Government' *Historical Journal* 13 (1970): 130–57.

Mori Shozo. *Sempu nijunen* [Twenty tumultuous years] (Tokyo, 1968).

Morley, James William, ed. *Japan Erupts: The London Naval Conference and the Manchurian Incident, 1928–1932* (New York, 1984).

Morse, H.B. and McNair, H.F. *Far Eastern International Relations* (Cambridge, Mass., 1931)

Murray, Gilbert. *The Ordeal of this Generation. The War, the League, and the Future* (London, 1929).

Murray, Williamson and Allan R. Millet, eds., *Calculations: Net Assessment and the Coming of World War II* (New York, 1992).

Nakamura Kikuo, ed. *Showa kaigun hishi* [Secret history of the navy during the Showa era] (Tokyo, 1969).

Nakamura Takafusa, et al., eds. *Gendai o tsukuru hitobito* [Men who shaped contemporary Japan] (Tokyo, 1971).

Neilson, K.E. *Strategy and Supply: The Anglo-Russian Alliance, 1914–1917* (London, 1984).

Nish, Ian. *Alliance in Decline: A Study in Anglo-Japanese Relations, 1908–23* (London, 1972).

—— *Japanese Foreign Policy* (London, 1977).

Noel Baker, P.J. *Disarmament and the Coolidge Conference* (London, 1927).

Nolfo, Ennio Di, Romain H. Rainero and Brunello Vigezzi, eds. *L'Italia e la politica di potenza in Europa, 1938–1940* (Milan, 1985).

Nomura Minoru. 'Tai-Bei-Ei kaisen to kaigun no tai-Bei shichi-wari shiso' [The outbreak of war with the United States and Great Britain, and the idea of a 70 percent ratio] *Gunji shigaku* 9 (1973): 23–34.

—— *Tenno, Fushiminomiya to Nihon kaigun* [The Emperor, Prince Fushimi, and the Japanese Navy] (Tokyo, 1988).

O'Connor, Raymond G. *Perilous Equilbrium: The United States and the London Naval Conference on 1930* (Lawrence, 1962).

Okada Sadanori, ed. *Okada Keisuke kaikoroku [Memoirs of Okada Keisuke]* (Tokyo, 1977).

Okada Taisho Kiroku Hensaikai, ed. *Okada Keisuke* (Tokyo, 1956).

Orde, A. *Great Britain and International Security, 1920–1926* (London, 1977)

Parrini, C.P. *Heir to Empire: United States Economic Diplomacy, 1916–1923* (Pittsburgh, 1969).

Pelz, Stephen E. *Race to Pearl Harbor: The Failure of the second London Naval Conference and the Onset of World War II* (Cambridge, Massachusetts, 1974)

Perett, William Gregory. 'French Naval Policy and Foreign Affairs, 1930–1939' Ph.D. dissertation, Stanford University, 1977.

Pieri, Piero and Giorgio Rochat. *Badoglio* (Turin, 1974).

Pizzigallo, Matteo. 'L'Italia alla conferenza di Washington, 1921–1922' *Storia e politica* 14 (1975): 408–48, 550–89.

Poincaré, Raymond. 'Chronique de la quinzaine' *La Revue des Deux Mondes* (15 Dec. 1921): 947–58.

Polastro, Walter. 'La marina miliitaire italiana nel primo dopoguerra, 1918–1925' *Il Risorgimento* 3 (1977).

Pollina, Paolo M. and Aldo Cocchia. *I sommergibili italiani* (Rome, 1963).

Ponsonby, A. *Now is the Time: An Appeal for Peace* (London, 1925).

Preston, Antony. Battleships of World War I (Harrisburg, 1972).

Rainero, Romain H. and A. Biagini, eds., *L'Italia in guerra: Il primo anno – 1940* (Rome, 1991).

Reussner, André. *La puissance navale dans l'histoire* (Paris, 1961).

Richardson, D. *The Evolution of British Disarmament Policy in the 1920's* (London and New York, 1989).

Riddell, Lord. *Lord Riddell's Intimate Diary of the the Peace Conference and After, 1918–1923* (London, 1933 and New York, 1934).

Rochat, Giorgio and Giulio Massobrio. *Breve storia dell'esercito italiano dal 1861 al 1943* (Turin, 1948).

Rohwer, Jürgen. *Axis Submarine Successes, 1939–1945* (Annapolis, 1983).

Roscoe, Theodore. *United States Submarine Operations in World War II* (Annapolis, 1949).

Roskill, Stephen. *Admiral of the Fleet Earl Beatty, The Last Naval Hero: An Intimate Biography* (New York, 1981).

—— *Naval Policy Between the Wars*, vol I., *The Period of Anglo-American Antagonism, 1919–1929* (London, 1968).

Rowland, P. *Lloyd George* (London, 1975).

Russell, Bertrand. War – *The Offspring of Fear*, Union for Democratic Control Pamphlet No. 3. (London, undated).

Sadkovich, James J. 'Aircraft Carriers and the Meditteranean, 1940–1943: Rethinking the Obvious' *Aerospace Historian* (1987).

Salaun, H. *La marine française* (Paris, 1934).

Sato Naotake. *Kaiko hachijunen* [Eighty years in reminiscences] (Tokyo, 1964).

Sato Tetsutaro. *Teikoku kokubo shiron* [A historical treatise on the national defence of the Japanese Empire] (Tokyo, 1908).

Sauvy, Alfred. *Histoire économique de la France entre les deux guerres*, vol I. (Paris, 1965).

Schanzer, Carlo. *Il mondo fra la pace e la guerra* (Milan, 1932).

Sulla Società delle Nazioni. Discorsi, studi e note (Rome, 1925)

Seton-Watson, Christopher. *Italy from Liberalism to Facism, 1870–1925* (London, 1967).

Shimanuki Takeharu. 'Nichi-Ro senso iko ni okeru kokubo hoshin, shoyo heiryoku, yohei koryo no hensen' [The development of the Imperial National Defence Policy, the Estimate of Requisite Armament, and the Outline of Strategy since the Russo-Japanese War] *Gunji shigaku* 8 (1973).

Shuker, R. 'New Zealand Naval Defense Policy and the Washington Conference, 1921–1922' Victoria University Honors Research Paper 1909.

Sinney, M.C. *The Allied Blockade of Germany* (Ann Arbor, 1955)

Sprout, Harold and Margaret. *Toward a New Order of Sea Power: American Naval Policy and the World Scene, 1918–1922* (Princeton, 1943).

Suarez, Georges. *Briand: sa vie – son œuvre* (6 vols., Paris, 1938–52).

Sullivan, Brian R. 'A Fleet in Being: The Rise and Fall of Italian Sea Power, 1861–1943' *International History Review* 10 (1988):106–24.

—— 'The Impatient Cat. Assessments of Miliitary Power in Fascist Italy, 1936–1940' in Williamson Murray and Allan R. Millet, eds., *Calculations: Net Assessment and the Coming of World War II* (New York, 1992).

Sullivan, Mark. *The Great Adventure at Washington. The Story of the Conference* (Graden City, New York, 1922).

Summerton, N.W. 'Dissenting Attitudes to Foreign Relations, Peace, and War, 1840–1890' *Journal of Ecclesiastical History* 28 (1977):151–78.

Swanick, H. *Builders of Peace* (London, 1924).

Swartz, M. *The Union for Democratic Control in British Politics During the First World War* (Oxford, 1971).

Takagi Sokichi. *Shikan Taiheiyo senso* [A personal interpretation of the Pacific War] (Tokyo, 1969).

Taylor, A.J.P., ed. *Lloyd George: Twelve Essays* (London and New York, 1971).

Taylor, Charles C. *The Life of Mahan* (New York, 1920).

Terashima Ken Denki Kankokai, ed. *Terashima Ken den* [Biography of Terashima Ken] (Tokyo, 1973).

Thorne, C. *The Limits of Foreign Policy: The West, the League, and the Far Eastern Crisis of 1931–1933* (London, 1972).

Thornton, Robert. 'The Semblance of Security: Australia and the Washington Conference, 1921–22' *The Australian Outlook* 32:1 (1977):65–83.

Tur, Vittorio. *Planica ammiraglio*, vol II (Rome, 1960).

Turner, J. 'Cabinets, Committees, and Secreteriats: the Higher Direction in War' in K.M. Burk, ed. *War and State: the Transformation of the British Government, 1914–1919* (London, 1982).

Tung , William L. *China and the Foreign Powers* (Dobbs Ferry, NY, 1970)

Twomey, Paul. 'Small Power Security through Great Power Arms Control Australian Perceptions of Disarmament, 1919–1933' *War and Society* 8:1 (1990): 71–99.

Unno Yoshiro. *Nihon gaikoshi*, vol 16, *Kaigun gunshuku kosho, fusen joyaku* [Japanese diplomatic history, vol. 16, Naval limitation negotiations / the Kellogg-Briand Pact] (Tokyo, 1973).

Vinson, John Chalmers. *The Parchment Peace, the United States Senate and the Washington Conference, 1921–1922* (Athens, Georgia, 1955).

—— 'The Problem of Australian Representation at the Washington Conference for the Limitation of Naval Armament' *Australian Journal of Politics and History* 3–4 (1957–1958):155–64.

Vlahos, Michael. *The Blue Sword: The Naval War College and the American Mission, 1919–1941* (Newport, 1980).

Wagner, Walter. 'Die K. (U.) K. Armee – Gliederung und Aufgabenstellung' in Adam Wandruszka and Peter Urbanitsch, eds,., *Die Hapsburgermonarchie, 1848–1918* vol. 5, *Die bewaffenete Macht* (Vienna, 1987).

Wakatsuki Reijiro. *Kofuan kaikoroku* [Memoirs] (Tokyo, 1950).

Waldron, Arthur. *How the Peace was Lost* (Stanford, 1992)

Watanabe Yukio. *Gunshuku: Rondon joyaku to Nihon kaigun* [Naval limitation: The London Treaty and the Japanese navy] (Tokyo, 1988).

Watts, Anthony J. and Brian G. Gordon. *The Imperial Japanese Navy* (Garden City, New York, 1971)

Wheeler, Gerald E. *Admiral William Veazie Pratt* (Washington, DC, 1974).

—— *Prelude to Pearl Harbor: The United States Navy and the Far East, 1921–1931* (Columbia, Missouri, 1968).

Williamson, P. 'Safety First: Baldwin, the Conservative Party and the 1929 General Election' *Historical Journal* 25 (1982):385–409.

Wilson, D. *Gilbert Murray, O.M., 1866–1957* (Oxford, 1987).

Wilson, K.M. *The Policy of the Entente: Essays in the Determinants of British Foreign Policy, 1904–1914* (Cambridge, 1985).

Wright, Quincy. *A Study of War* (Chicago, 1965).

Yamaji Kazuyoshi. *Nihon kaigun no kobo to sekininsha tachi* [The rise and fall of the Japanese navy and its leaders] (Tokyo, 1959).

Yamamoto Eisuke, comp. *Danshaku Osumi Mineo* [Biography of Baron Osumi Mineo] (Tokyo, 1943).

Yamanashi Katsunoshin Sensei Kinen Shuppan Iinkai, ed. *Yamanashi Katsunoshin sensei ihoroku* [Memoirs of Admiral Yamanashi Katsunoshin] (Tokyo, 1968).

Zwehl, K. von. *Die Deutschlandspolitik Englands von 1922 bis 1924 unter besonderer Berücksichtigung der Reparationen and Sanktionen* (Augsburg, 1974).

Abbreviations

AM	Archives de la Marine
BDFA	*British Documents on Foreign Affairs*
BED	British Empire Delegation
Ca	Cabinet (France)
CAB	Cabinet (Britain)
CAED	Commission des Affaires Etrangères, Chambre de Députés
CFD	Commission des Finances, Chambre de Députés
CMMD	Commission de la Marine Militaire, Chambre de Députés
CSDN	Conseil Supérieur de la Défense Nationale
CSM	Conseil Supérieur de la Marine

DBFP	Great Britain. *Documents on British Foreign Policy, 1919–1939*, First Series (London, 1947–67).
DEA	Department of External Afairs
EMG	Etat Major Général
FRUS	*Foreign Relations of the United States*
IJN	Imperial Japanese Navy
JMFA	Japanese Ministry of Foreign Affairs
MAE	Ministère des Affaires Etrangères
NA	United States National Archives
NAC	National Archives of Canada
PRO	Public Record Office, London
SHA	Service Historique de l'Armée
TSM	Nihon Kokusai Seiji Gakkai [Japan Association of International relations], ed., *Taiheiyo Senso e no michi: Bekkan shiryohen* [The Road to the Pacific War: Supplementary Volume of Documents].

Index

Key to abbreviations BE: British Empire; F: France, GB: Great Britain; J: Japan; USA: United States of America